Fuzzy Logic

Other Books by Darby Conley

The Dog Is Not a Toy (House Rule #4)

GET FUZZY 2
Fuzzy Logic

by

Darby Conley

Andrews McMeel
Publishing

Kansas City

Get Fuzzy is distributed internationally by United Feature Syndicate.

Fuzzy Logic copyright © 2002 by Darby Conley. All rights reserved. Printed in the United States of America. No part of this book may be used or reproduced in any manner whatsoever without written permission except in the case of reprints in the context of reviews. For information, write Andrews McMeel Publishing, LLC, an Andrews McMeel Universal company, 4520 Main Street, Kansas City, Missouri 64111.

06 07 08 09 BAH 14 13 11 10

ISBN-13: 978-0-7407-2198-4
ISBN-10: 0-7407-2198-4

Library of Congress Control Number: 2001095890

Get Fuzzy can be viewed on the internet at:
www.comics.com/comics/getfuzzy

To my dog Patch, the reason I love animals so much,
and whom I miss like crazy

INTRODUCTION

The story of how *Get Fuzzy* became a comic strip is something like the story of how Marie Curie discovered radium—it's long, sort of technical, and only interesting to about twelve people, most of whom are either related to me or have me confused with Berke Breathed.

So instead, I thought I'd write a little about my dog Patch.

Patch showed up on our doorstep as a muddy, little lost puppy one rainy night in Knoxville, Tennessee, when I was in elementary school. Because of her unique markings (see photo, please) and my still developing sense of humor, I actually wanted to name her "Spot"... Fortunately, my brother and sister were old enough to know to vote me down on that one.

We sat on pins and needles for a couple of weeks but, unbelievably, no one claimed her and she became a member of our family for the next fifteen years. She had a litter of puppies on my sister's bed. She figured out that ice cream melts and that you have to eat it right away. She survived her scare with anesthesia. She learned to burp for treats. She chased seagulls—and ran from fiddler crabs—in Florida. She ate chocolate almost every single day of her life*. She would sneeze on you when she wanted you to put her down. And she was the most perfect being I've ever known.

And, if only for the fact that I could never stop wondering what she was thinking, she's probably the reason I'm drawing a comic strip about talking animals today.

I hope you like the rest of the book. Give your little pals a scritch for me,

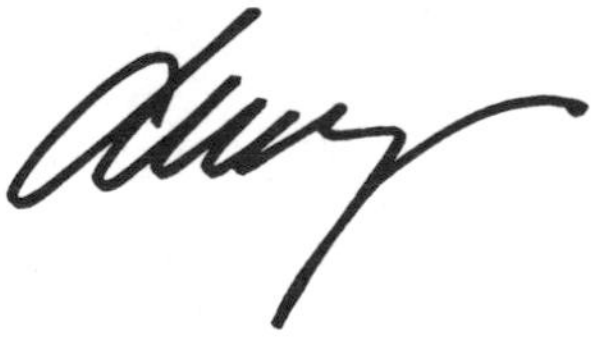

* I'm not recommending that you feed your pet this way, I'm just sayin'.

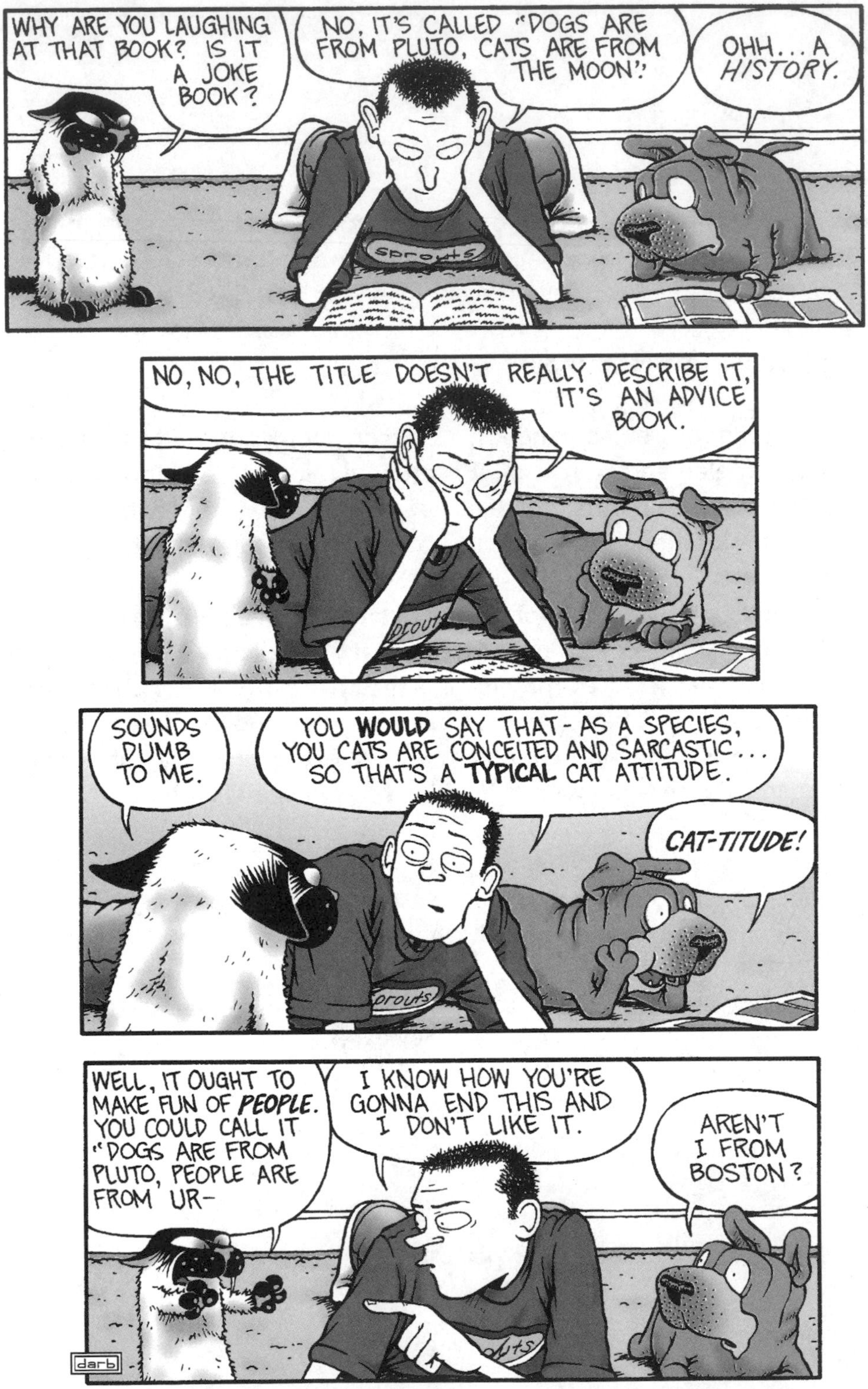
WHY ARE YOU LAUGHING AT THAT BOOK? IS IT A JOKE BOOK?
NO, IT'S CALLED "DOGS ARE FROM PLUTO, CATS ARE FROM THE MOON."
OHH... A *HISTORY*.
sprouts
NO, NO, THE TITLE DOESN'T REALLY DESCRIBE IT, IT'S AN ADVICE BOOK.
SOUNDS DUMB TO ME.
YOU **WOULD** SAY THAT- AS A SPECIES, YOU CATS ARE CONCEITED AND SARCASTIC... SO THAT'S A **TYPICAL** CAT ATTITUDE.
CAT-TITUDE!
WELL, IT OUGHT TO MAKE FUN OF ***PEOPLE***. YOU COULD CALL IT "DOGS ARE FROM PLUTO, PEOPLE ARE FROM UR–
I KNOW HOW YOU'RE GONNA END THIS AND I DON'T LIKE IT.
AREN'T I FROM BOSTON?
darb

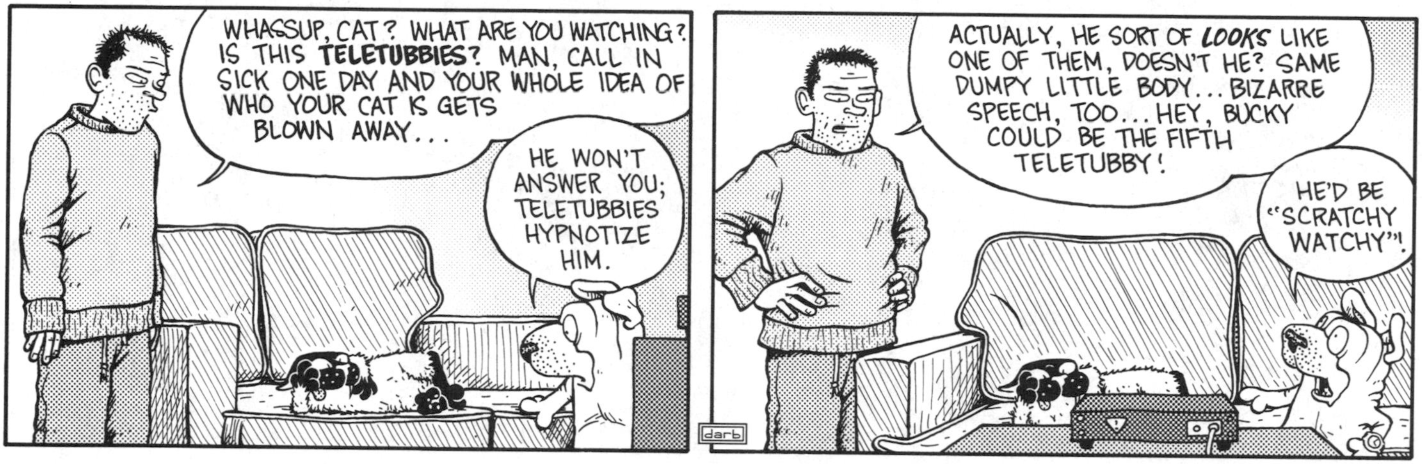
WHASSUP, CAT? WHAT ARE YOU WATCHING? IS THIS **TELETUBBIES**? MAN, CALL IN SICK ONE DAY AND YOUR WHOLE IDEA OF WHO YOUR CAT IS GETS BLOWN AWAY...
HE WON'T ANSWER YOU; TELETUBBIES HYPNOTIZE HIM.
darb
ACTUALLY, HE SORT OF ***LOOKS*** LIKE ONE OF THEM, DOESN'T HE? SAME DUMPY LITTLE BODY... BIZARRE SPEECH, TOO... HEY, BUCKY COULD BE THE FIFTH TELETUBBY!
HE'D BE "SCRATCHY WATCHY"!

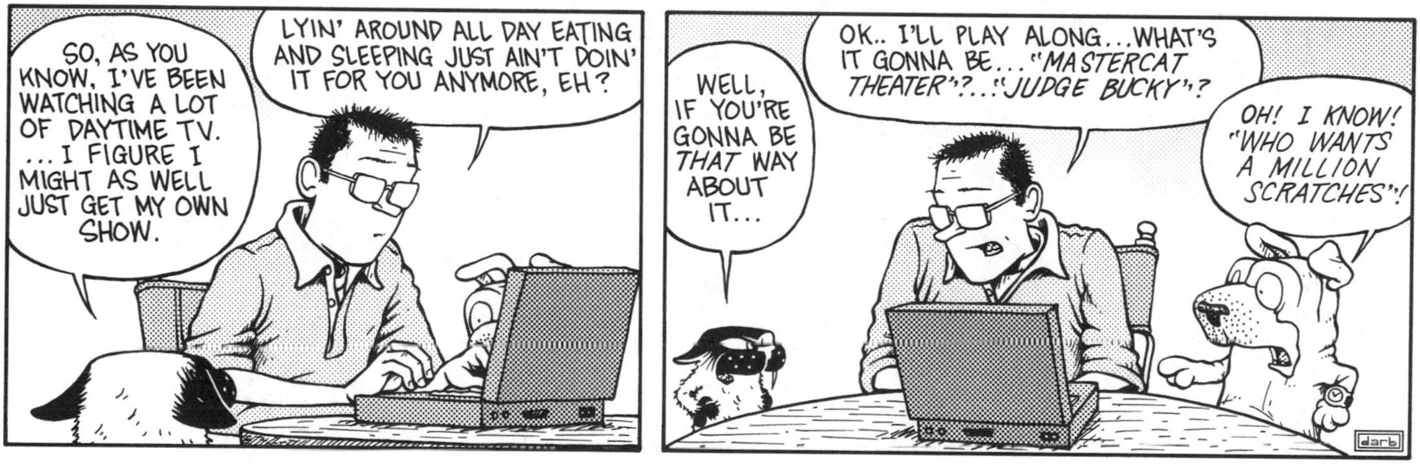
SO, AS YOU KNOW, I'VE BEEN WATCHING A LOT OF DAYTIME TV. ...I FIGURE I MIGHT AS WELL JUST GET MY OWN SHOW.
LYIN' AROUND ALL DAY EATING AND SLEEPING JUST AIN'T DOIN' IT FOR YOU ANYMORE, EH?
WELL, IF YOU'RE GONNA BE *THAT* WAY ABOUT IT...
OK.. I'LL PLAY ALONG...WHAT'S IT GONNA BE..."*MASTERCAT THEATER*"?..."*JUDGE BUCKY*"?
OH! I KNOW! "WHO WANTS A MILLION SCRATCHES"!
darb

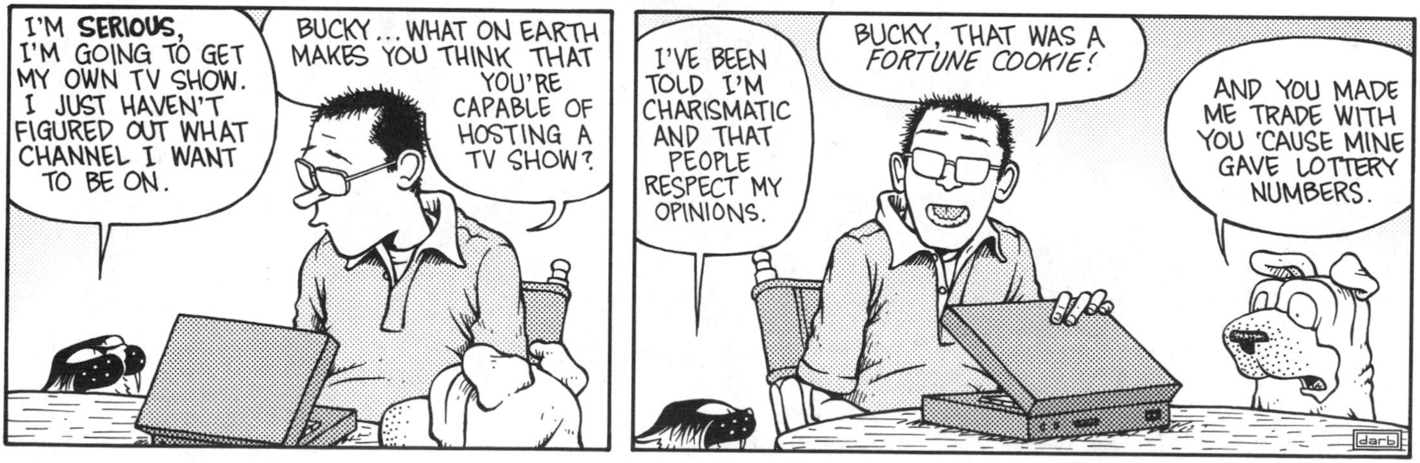
I'M **SERIOUS**, I'M GOING TO GET MY OWN TV SHOW. I JUST HAVEN'T FIGURED OUT WHAT CHANNEL I WANT TO BE ON.
BUCKY... WHAT ON EARTH MAKES YOU THINK THAT YOU'RE CAPABLE OF HOSTING A TV SHOW?
I'VE BEEN TOLD I'M CHARISMATIC AND THAT PEOPLE RESPECT MY OPINIONS.
BUCKY, THAT WAS A *FORTUNE COOKIE!*
AND YOU MADE ME TRADE WITH YOU 'CAUSE MINE GAVE LOTTERY NUMBERS.
darb

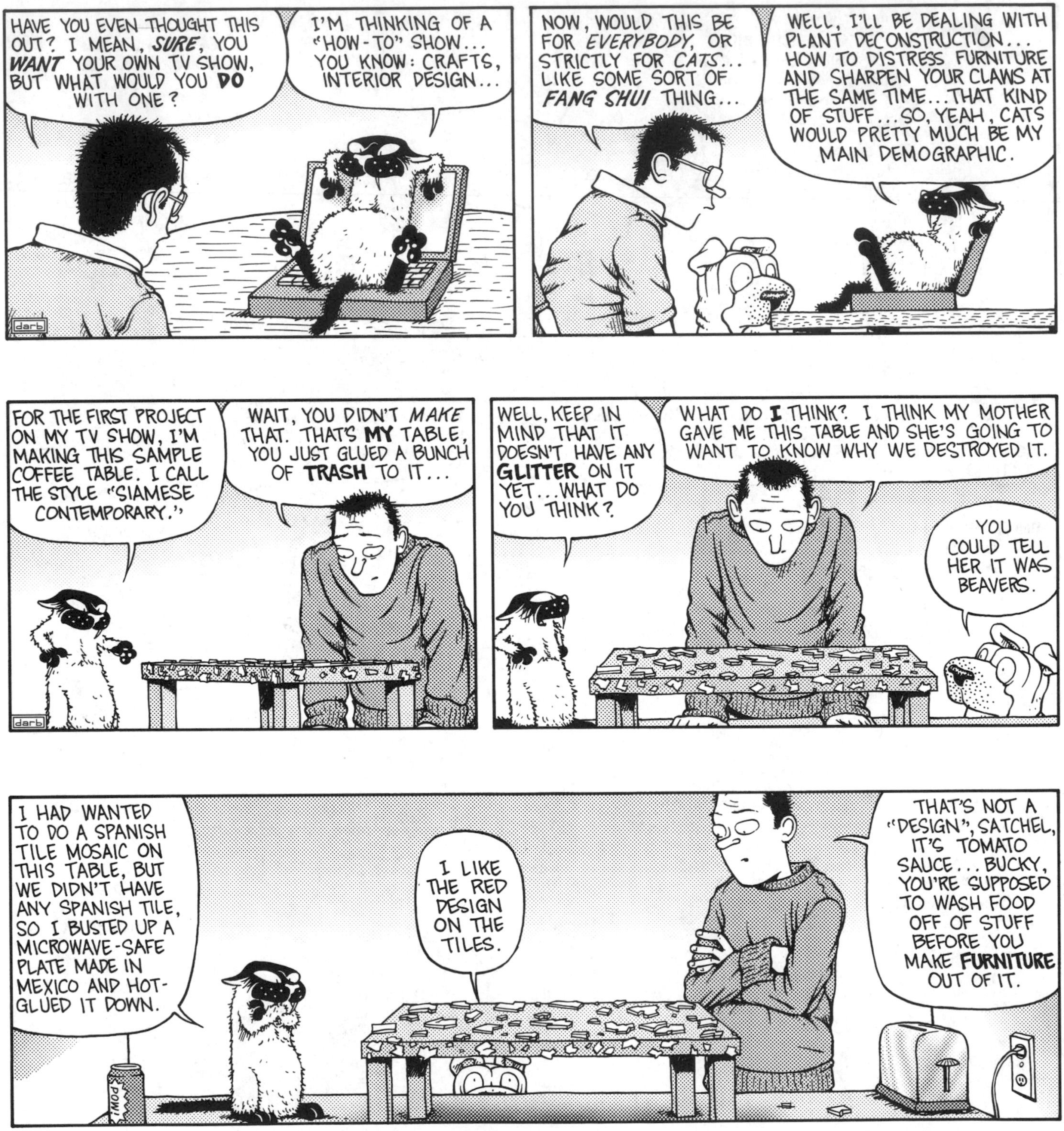
HAVE YOU EVEN THOUGHT THIS OUT? I MEAN, *SURE*, YOU ***WANT*** YOUR OWN TV SHOW, BUT WHAT WOULD YOU **DO** WITH ONE?
I'M THINKING OF A "HOW-TO" SHOW... YOU KNOW: CRAFTS, INTERIOR DESIGN...
darb
NOW, WOULD THIS BE FOR *EVERYBODY*, OR STRICTLY FOR *CATS*... LIKE SOME SORT OF ***FANG SHUI*** THING...
WELL, I'LL BE DEALING WITH PLANT DECONSTRUCTION... HOW TO DISTRESS FURNITURE AND SHARPEN YOUR CLAWS AT THE SAME TIME... THAT KIND OF STUFF... SO, YEAH, CATS WOULD PRETTY MUCH BE MY MAIN DEMOGRAPHIC.
FOR THE FIRST PROJECT ON MY TV SHOW, I'M MAKING THIS SAMPLE COFFEE TABLE. I CALL THE STYLE "SIAMESE CONTEMPORARY."
WAIT, YOU DIDN'T *MAKE* THAT. THAT'S **MY** TABLE, YOU JUST GLUED A BUNCH OF **TRASH** TO IT...
darb
WELL, KEEP IN MIND THAT IT DOESN'T HAVE ANY **GLITTER** ON IT YET... WHAT DO YOU THINK?
WHAT DO **I** THINK? I THINK MY MOTHER GAVE ME THIS TABLE AND SHE'S GOING TO WANT TO KNOW WHY WE DESTROYED IT.
YOU COULD TELL HER IT WAS BEAVERS.
I HAD WANTED TO DO A SPANISH TILE MOSAIC ON THIS TABLE, BUT WE DIDN'T HAVE ANY SPANISH TILE, SO I BUSTED UP A MICROWAVE-SAFE PLATE MADE IN MEXICO AND HOT-GLUED IT DOWN.
I LIKE THE RED DESIGN ON THE TILES.
THAT'S NOT A "DESIGN", SATCHEL, IT'S TOMATO SAUCE... BUCKY, YOU'RE SUPPOSED TO WASH FOOD OFF OF STUFF BEFORE YOU MAKE **FURNITURE** OUT OF IT.
POW!

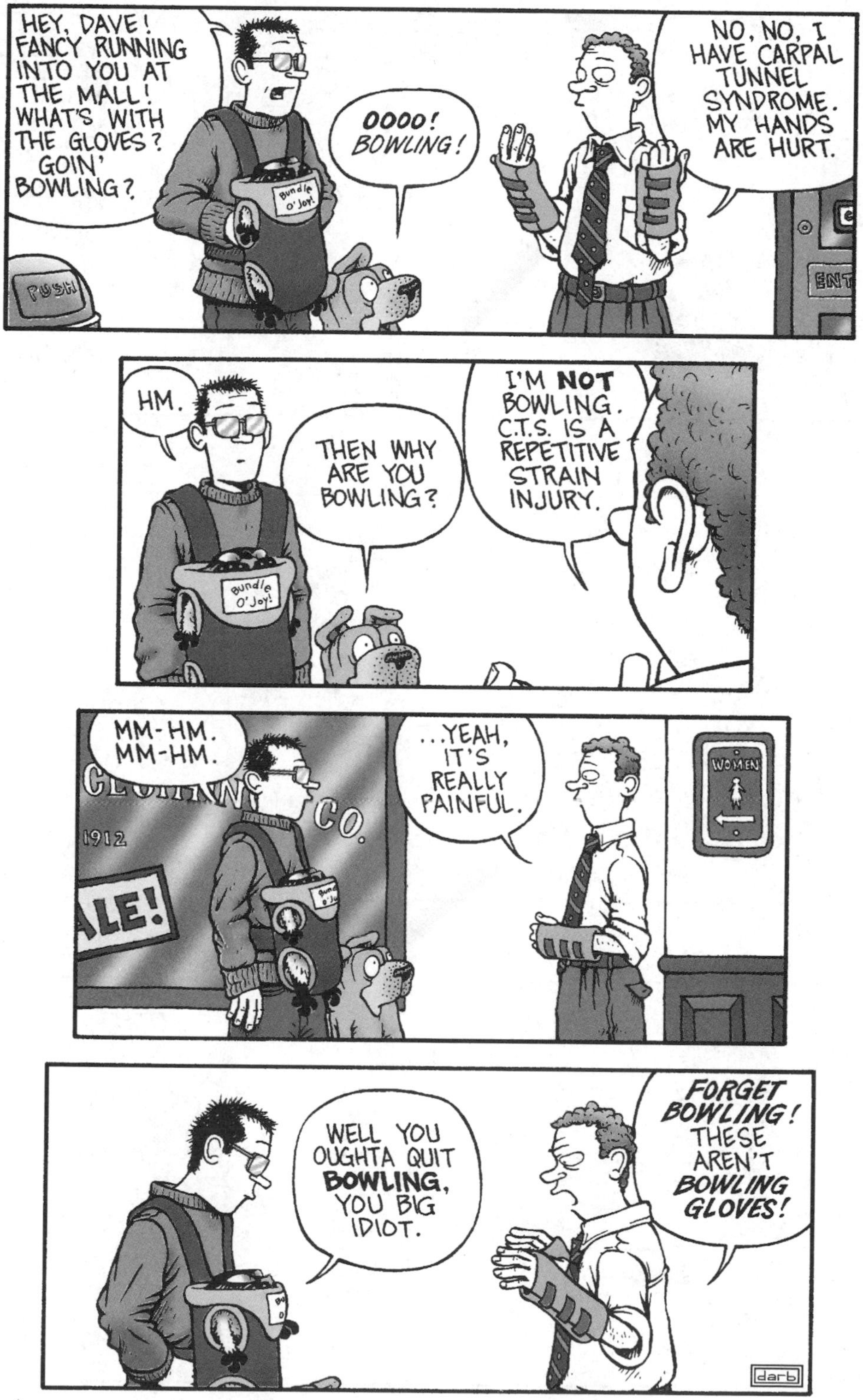
HEY, DAVE! FANCY RUNNING INTO YOU AT THE MALL! WHAT'S WITH THE GLOVES? GOIN' BOWLING?
OOOO! BOWLING!
NO, NO, I HAVE CARPAL TUNNEL SYNDROME. MY HANDS ARE HURT.
Bundle O' Joy!
PUSH
HM.
THEN WHY ARE YOU BOWLING?
I'M NOT BOWLING. C.T.S. IS A REPETITIVE STRAIN INJURY.
Bundle O' Joy!
MM-HM. MM-HM.
...YEAH, IT'S REALLY PAINFUL.
CO.
1912
WOMEN
WELL YOU OUGHTA QUIT BOWLING, YOU BIG IDIOT.
FORGET BOWLING! THESE AREN'T BOWLING GLOVES!
darb

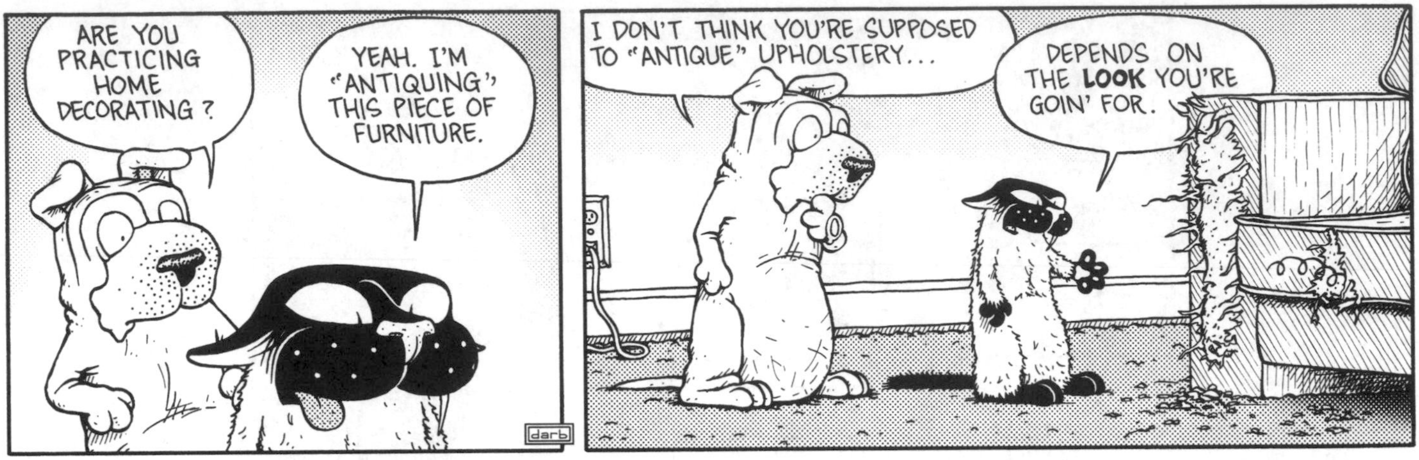
ARE YOU PRACTICING HOME DECORATING ?
YEAH. I'M "ANTIQUING" THIS PIECE OF FURNITURE.
darb
I DON'T THINK YOU'RE SUPPOSED TO "ANTIQUE" UPHOLSTERY...
DEPENDS ON THE **LOOK** YOU'RE GOIN' FOR.

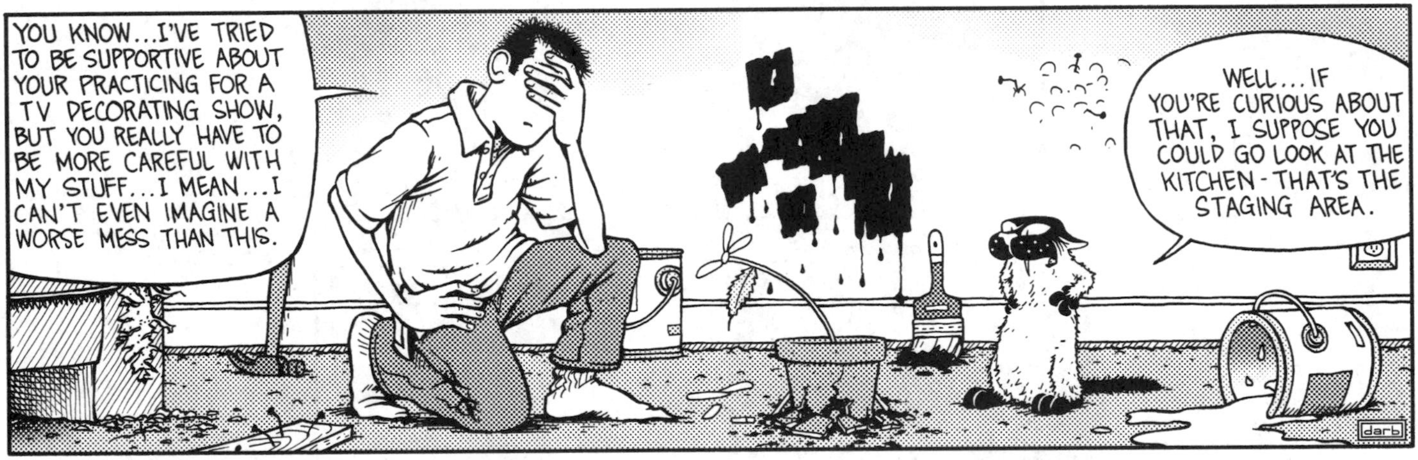
YOU KNOW...I'VE TRIED TO BE SUPPORTIVE ABOUT YOUR PRACTICING FOR A TV DECORATING SHOW, BUT YOU REALLY HAVE TO BE MORE CAREFUL WITH MY STUFF...I MEAN...I CAN'T EVEN IMAGINE A WORSE MESS THAN THIS.
WELL...IF YOU'RE CURIOUS ABOUT THAT, I SUPPOSE YOU COULD GO LOOK AT THE KITCHEN - THAT'S THE STAGING AREA.
darb

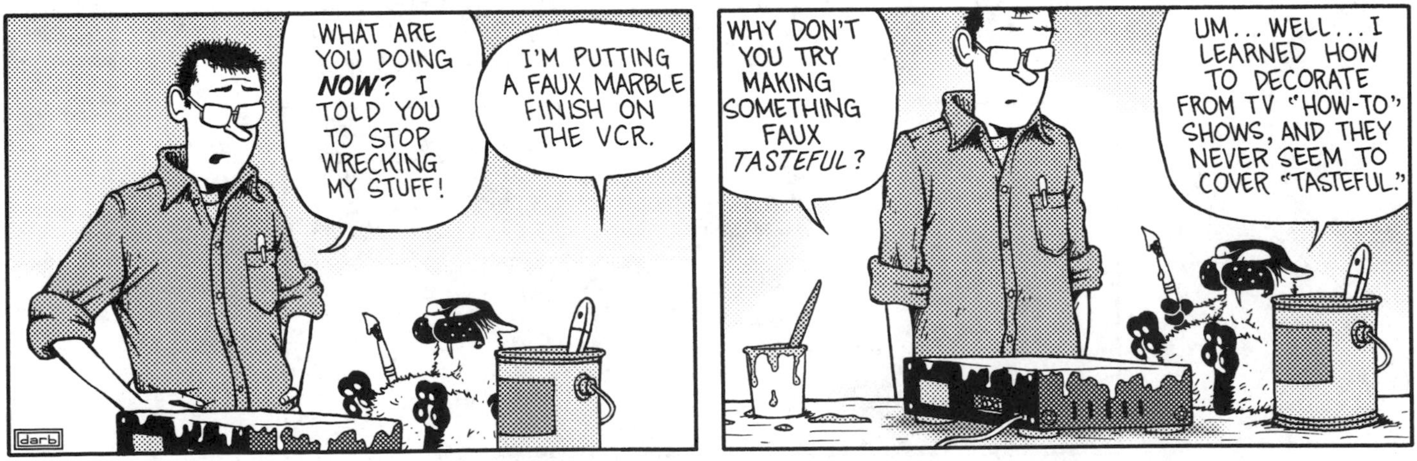
WHAT ARE YOU DOING ***NOW***? I TOLD YOU TO STOP WRECKING MY STUFF!
I'M PUTTING A FAUX MARBLE FINISH ON THE VCR.
darb
WHY DON'T YOU TRY MAKING SOMETHING FAUX *TASTEFUL*?
UM...WELL...I LEARNED HOW TO DECORATE FROM TV "HOW-TO" SHOWS, AND THEY NEVER SEEM TO COVER "TASTEFUL."

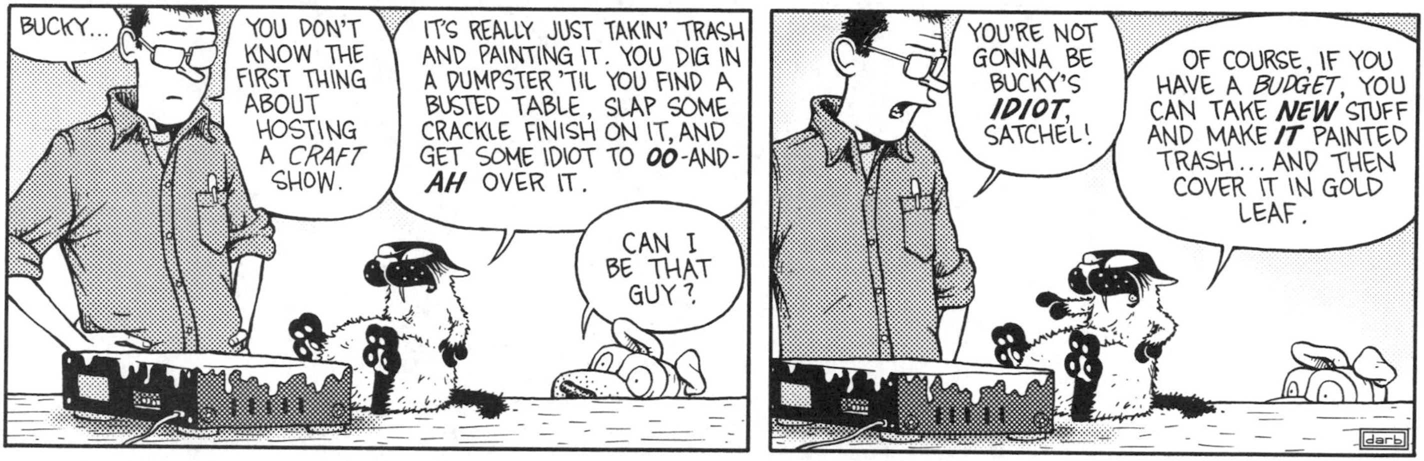
BUCKY...
YOU DON'T KNOW THE FIRST THING ABOUT HOSTING A *CRAFT* SHOW.
IT'S REALLY JUST TAKIN' TRASH AND PAINTING IT. YOU DIG IN A DUMPSTER 'TIL YOU FIND A BUSTED TABLE, SLAP SOME CRACKLE FINISH ON IT, AND GET SOME IDIOT TO ***OO***-AND-***AH*** OVER IT.
CAN I BE THAT GUY?
YOU'RE NOT GONNA BE BUCKY'S ***IDIOT***, SATCHEL!
OF COURSE, IF YOU HAVE A *BUDGET*, YOU CAN TAKE ***NEW*** STUFF AND MAKE ***IT*** PAINTED TRASH... AND THEN COVER IT IN GOLD LEAF.
darb

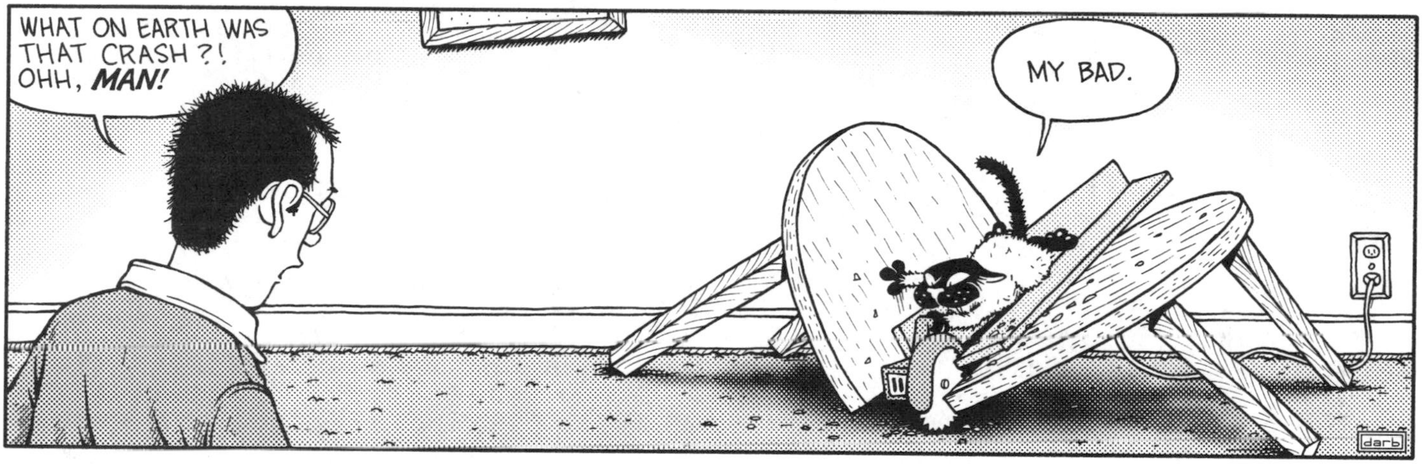
WHAT ON EARTH WAS THAT CRASH?! OHH, ***MAN!***
MY BAD.
darb

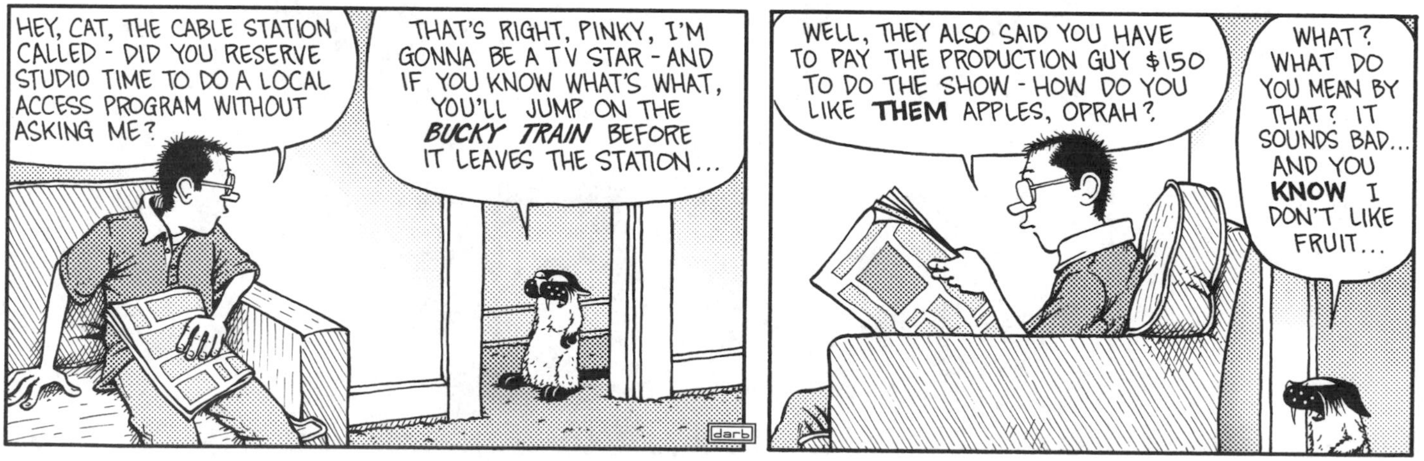
HEY, CAT, THE CABLE STATION CALLED - DID YOU RESERVE STUDIO TIME TO DO A LOCAL ACCESS PROGRAM WITHOUT ASKING ME?
THAT'S RIGHT, PINKY, I'M GONNA BE A TV STAR - AND IF YOU KNOW WHAT'S WHAT, YOU'LL JUMP ON THE ***BUCKY TRAIN*** BEFORE IT LEAVES THE STATION...
darb
WELL, THEY ALSO SAID YOU HAVE TO PAY THE PRODUCTION GUY $150 TO DO THE SHOW - HOW DO YOU LIKE **THEM** APPLES, OPRAH?
WHAT? WHAT DO YOU MEAN BY THAT? IT SOUNDS BAD... AND YOU **KNOW** I DON'T LIKE FRUIT...

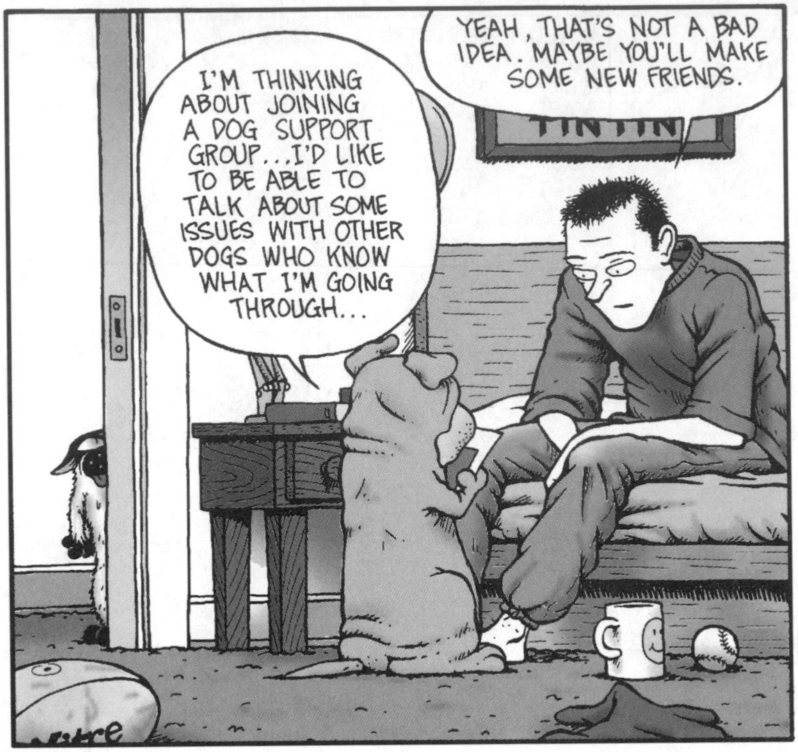
I'M THINKING ABOUT JOINING A DOG SUPPORT GROUP...I'D LIKE TO BE ABLE TO TALK ABOUT SOME ISSUES WITH OTHER DOGS WHO KNOW WHAT I'M GOING THROUGH...
YEAH, THAT'S NOT A BAD IDEA. MAYBE YOU'LL MAKE SOME NEW FRIENDS.
TINTIN

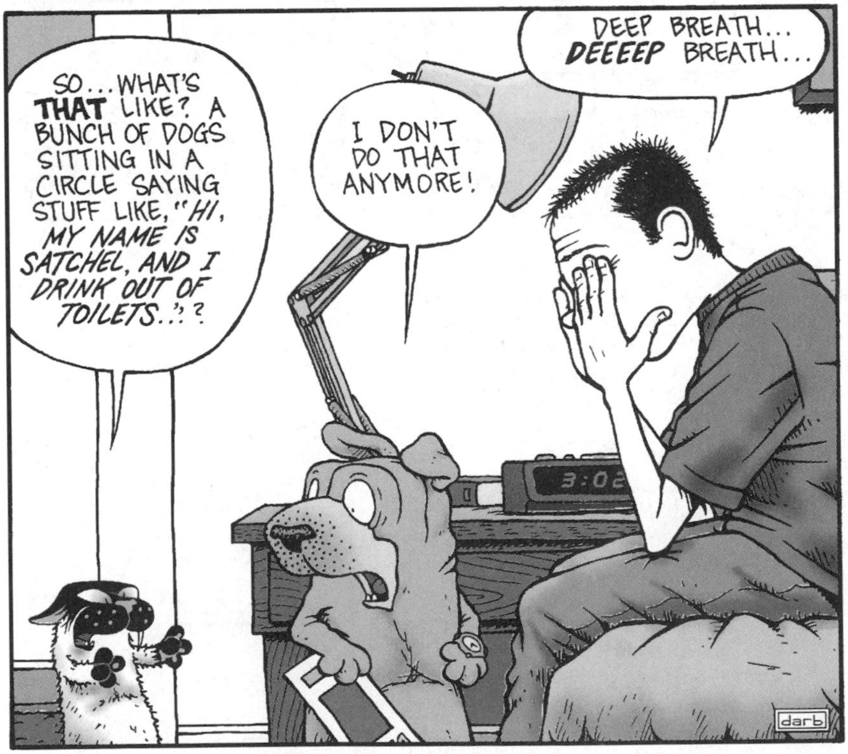
SO...WHAT'S **THAT** LIKE? A BUNCH OF DOGS SITTING IN A CIRCLE SAYING STUFF LIKE, "*HI, MY NAME IS SATCHEL, AND I DRINK OUT OF TOILETS...*"?
I DON'T DO THAT ANYMORE!
DEEP BREATH... ***DEEEEP*** BREATH...
3:02
darb

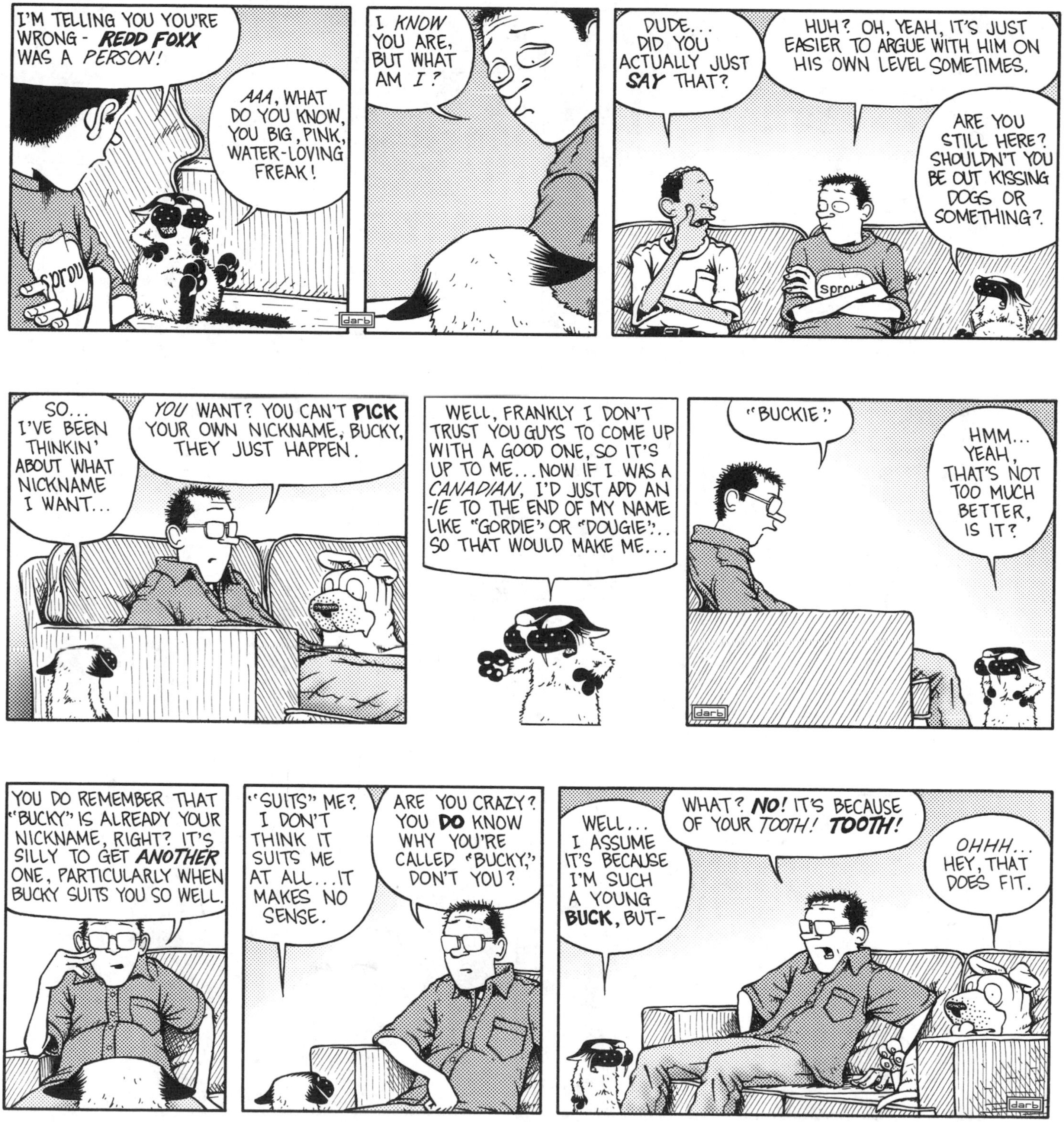
I'M TELLING YOU YOU'RE WRONG - REDD FOXX WAS A PERSON!
AAA, WHAT DO YOU KNOW, YOU BIG, PINK, WATER-LOVING FREAK!
I KNOW YOU ARE, BUT WHAT AM I?
DUDE... DID YOU ACTUALLY JUST SAY THAT?
HUH? OH, YEAH, IT'S JUST EASIER TO ARGUE WITH HIM ON HIS OWN LEVEL SOMETIMES.
ARE YOU STILL HERE? SHOULDN'T YOU BE OUT KISSING DOGS OR SOMETHING?
SO... I'VE BEEN THINKIN' ABOUT WHAT NICKNAME I WANT...
YOU WANT? YOU CAN'T PICK YOUR OWN NICKNAME, BUCKY, THEY JUST HAPPEN.
WELL, FRANKLY I DON'T TRUST YOU GUYS TO COME UP WITH A GOOD ONE, SO IT'S UP TO ME...NOW IF I WAS A CANADIAN, I'D JUST ADD AN -IE TO THE END OF MY NAME LIKE "GORDIE" OR "DOUGIE"... SO THAT WOULD MAKE ME...
"BUCKIE."
HMM... YEAH, THAT'S NOT TOO MUCH BETTER, IS IT?
YOU DO REMEMBER THAT "BUCKY" IS ALREADY YOUR NICKNAME, RIGHT? IT'S SILLY TO GET ANOTHER ONE, PARTICULARLY WHEN BUCKY SUITS YOU SO WELL.
"SUITS" ME? I DON'T THINK IT SUITS ME AT ALL...IT MAKES NO SENSE.
ARE YOU CRAZY? YOU DO KNOW WHY YOU'RE CALLED "BUCKY," DON'T YOU?
WELL... I ASSUME IT'S BECAUSE I'M SUCH A YOUNG BUCK, BUT-
WHAT? NO! IT'S BECAUSE OF YOUR TOOTH! TOOTH!
OHHH... HEY, THAT DOES FIT.

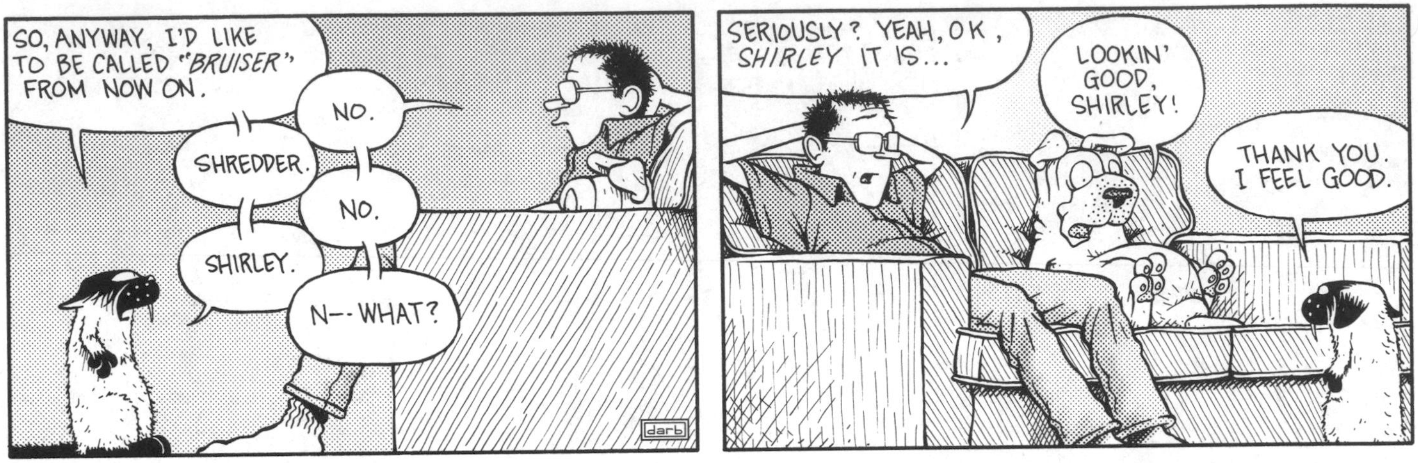
SO, ANYWAY, I'D LIKE TO BE CALLED "BRUISER" FROM NOW ON.
NO.
SHREDDER.
NO.
SHIRLEY.
N-- WHAT?
SERIOUSLY? YEAH, OK, SHIRLEY IT IS...
LOOKIN' GOOD, SHIRLEY!
THANK YOU. I FEEL GOOD.
darb

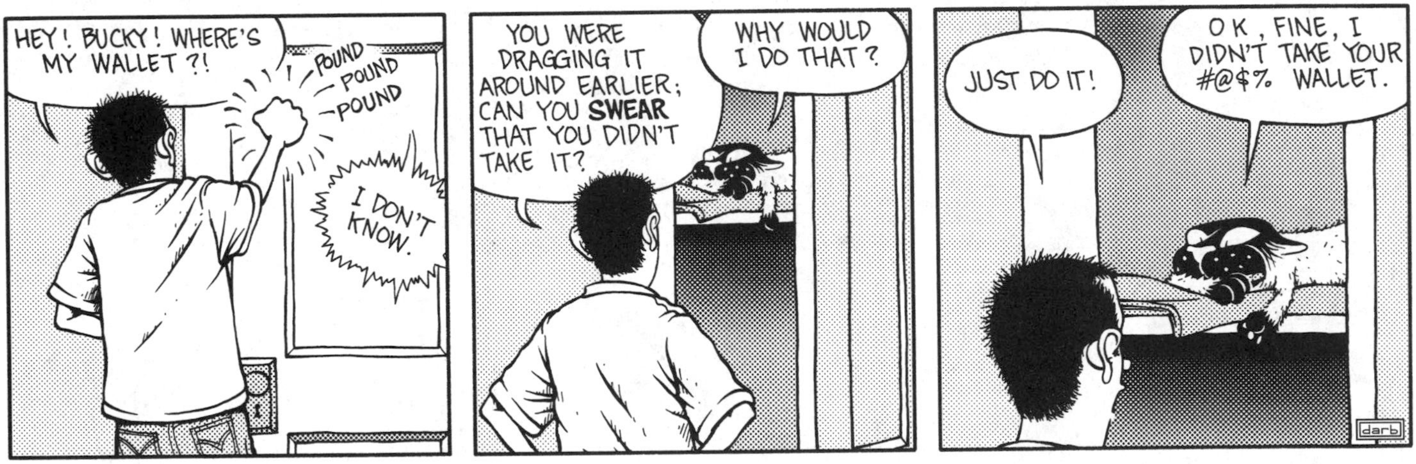
HEY! BUCKY! WHERE'S MY WALLET?!
POUND POUND POUND
I DON'T KNOW.
YOU WERE DRAGGING IT AROUND EARLIER; CAN YOU SWEAR THAT YOU DIDN'T TAKE IT?
WHY WOULD I DO THAT?
JUST DO IT!
OK, FINE, I DIDN'T TAKE YOUR #@$% WALLET.
darb

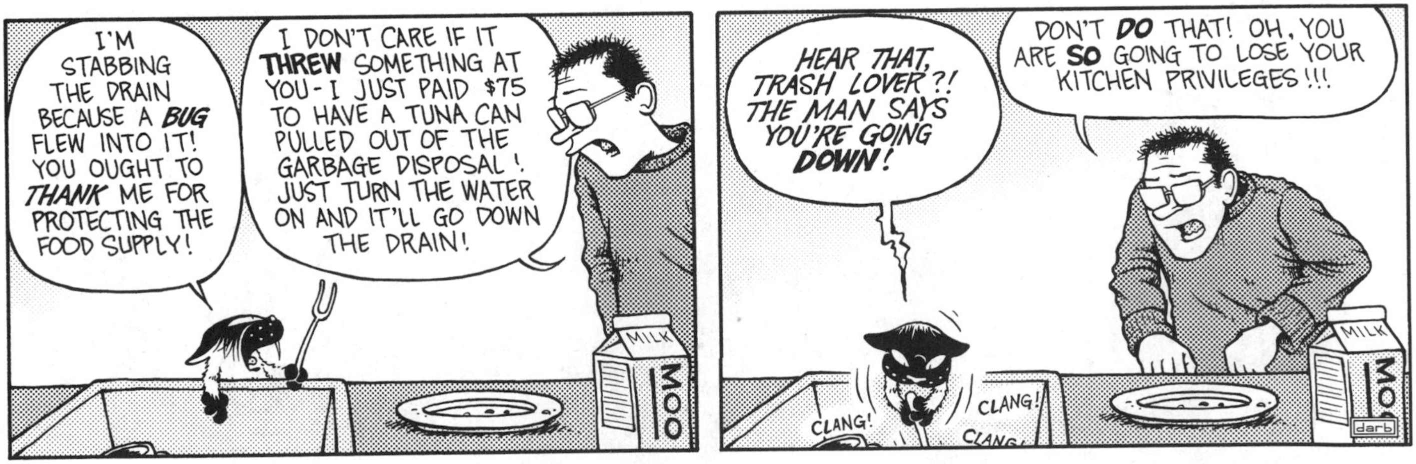
I'M STABBING THE DRAIN BECAUSE A BUG FLEW INTO IT! YOU OUGHT TO THANK ME FOR PROTECTING THE FOOD SUPPLY!
I DON'T CARE IF IT THREW SOMETHING AT YOU - I JUST PAID $75 TO HAVE A TUNA CAN PULLED OUT OF THE GARBAGE DISPOSAL! JUST TURN THE WATER ON AND IT'LL GO DOWN THE DRAIN!
MILK
MOO
HEAR THAT, TRASH LOVER?! THE MAN SAYS YOU'RE GOING DOWN!
DON'T DO THAT! OH, YOU ARE SO GOING TO LOSE YOUR KITCHEN PRIVILEGES!!!
CLANG!
CLANG!
darb

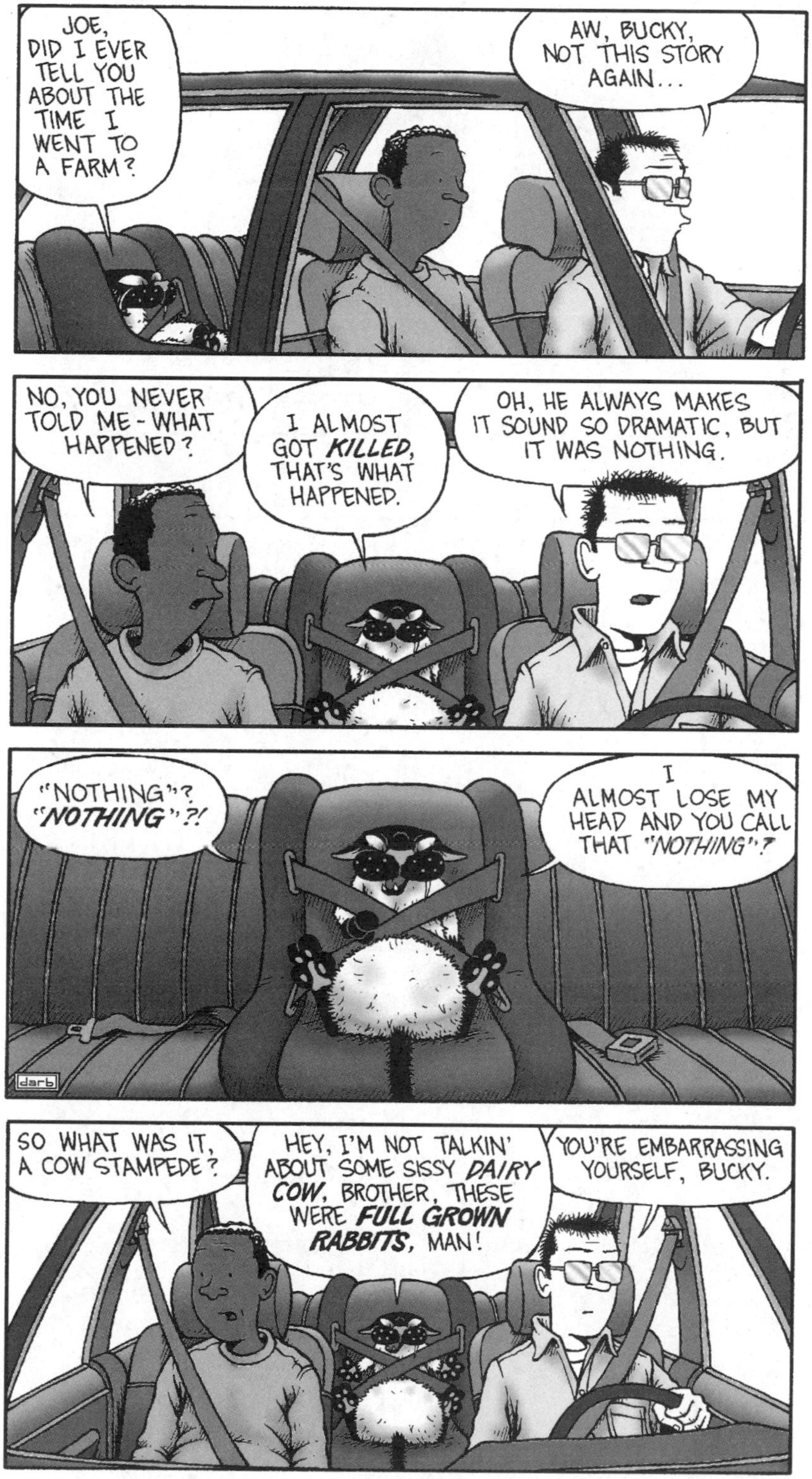
JOE, DID I EVER TELL YOU ABOUT THE TIME I WENT TO A FARM?
AW, BUCKY, NOT THIS STORY AGAIN...
NO, YOU NEVER TOLD ME - WHAT HAPPENED?
I ALMOST GOT *KILLED*, THAT'S WHAT HAPPENED.
OH, HE ALWAYS MAKES IT SOUND SO DRAMATIC, BUT IT WAS NOTHING.
"NOTHING"? "*NOTHING*"?!
I ALMOST LOSE MY HEAD AND YOU CALL THAT "*NOTHING*"?
darb
SO WHAT WAS IT, A COW STAMPEDE?
HEY, I'M NOT TALKIN' ABOUT SOME SISSY *DAIRY COW*, BROTHER, THESE WERE ***FULL GROWN RABBITS***, MAN!
YOU'RE EMBARRASSING YOURSELF, BUCKY.

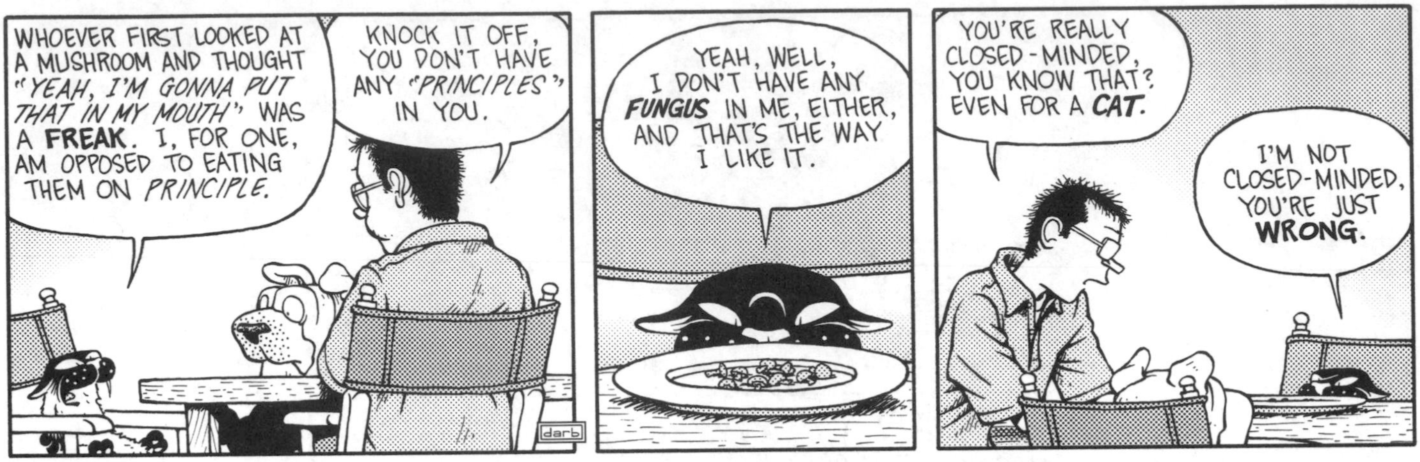
WHOEVER FIRST LOOKED AT A MUSHROOM AND THOUGHT *"YEAH, I'M GONNA PUT THAT IN MY MOUTH"* WAS A **FREAK**. I, FOR ONE, AM OPPOSED TO EATING THEM ON *PRINCIPLE*.
KNOCK IT OFF, YOU DON'T HAVE ANY *"PRINCIPLES"* IN YOU.
darb
YEAH, WELL, I DON'T HAVE ANY ***FUNGUS*** IN ME, EITHER, AND THAT'S THE WAY I LIKE IT.
YOU'RE REALLY CLOSED-MINDED, YOU KNOW THAT? EVEN FOR A ***CAT***.
I'M NOT CLOSED-MINDED, YOU'RE JUST **WRONG**.

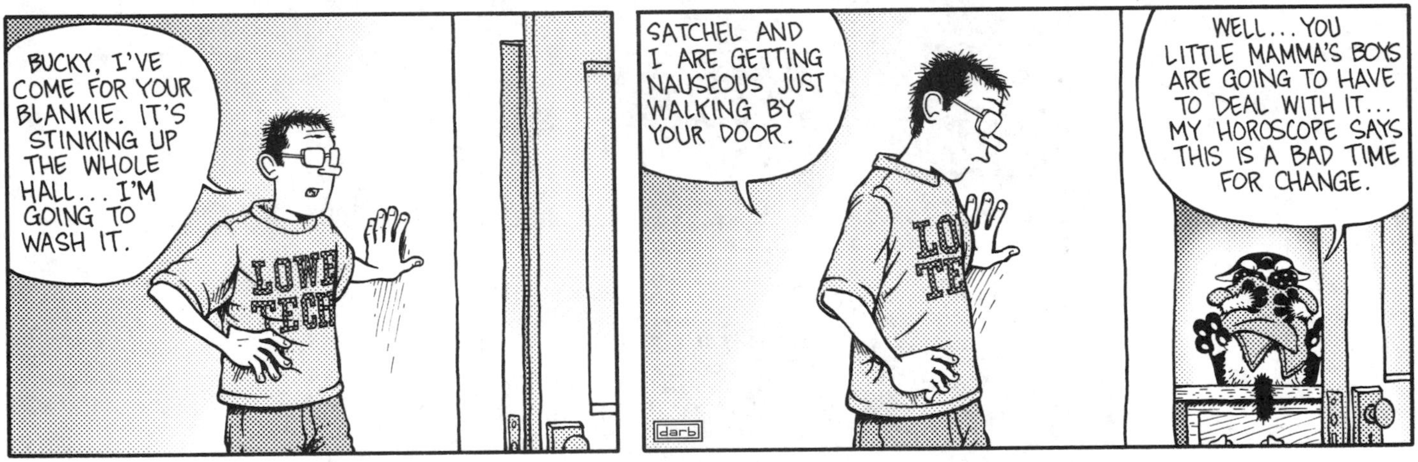
BUCKY, I'VE COME FOR YOUR BLANKIE. IT'S STINKING UP THE WHOLE HALL... I'M GOING TO WASH IT.
SATCHEL AND I ARE GETTING NAUSEOUS JUST WALKING BY YOUR DOOR.
darb
WELL... YOU LITTLE MAMMA'S BOYS ARE GOING TO HAVE TO DEAL WITH IT... MY HOROSCOPE SAYS THIS IS A BAD TIME FOR CHANGE.

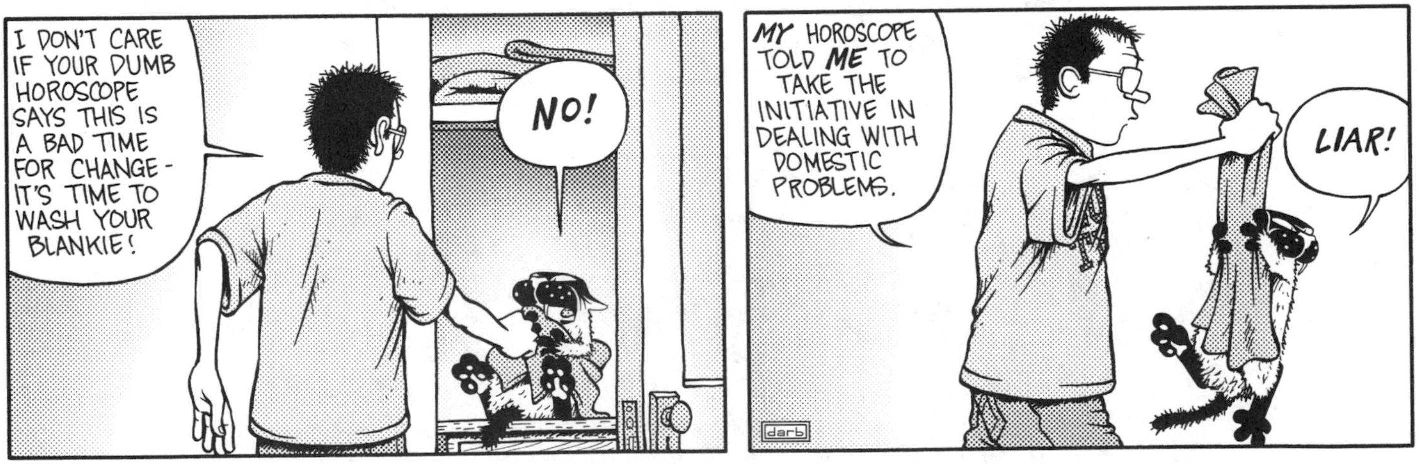
I DON'T CARE IF YOUR DUMB HOROSCOPE SAYS THIS IS A BAD TIME FOR CHANGE - IT'S TIME TO WASH YOUR BLANKIE!
NO!
MY HOROSCOPE TOLD ***ME*** TO TAKE THE INITIATIVE IN DEALING WITH DOMESTIC PROBLEMS.
LIAR!
darb

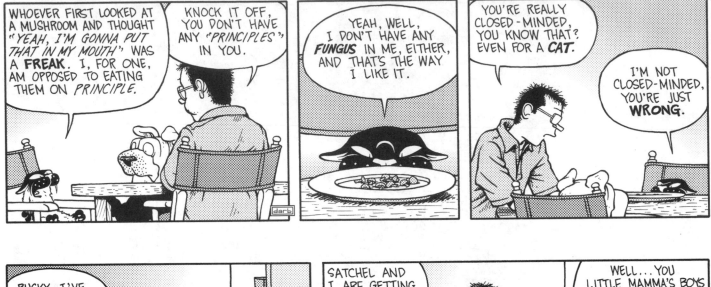

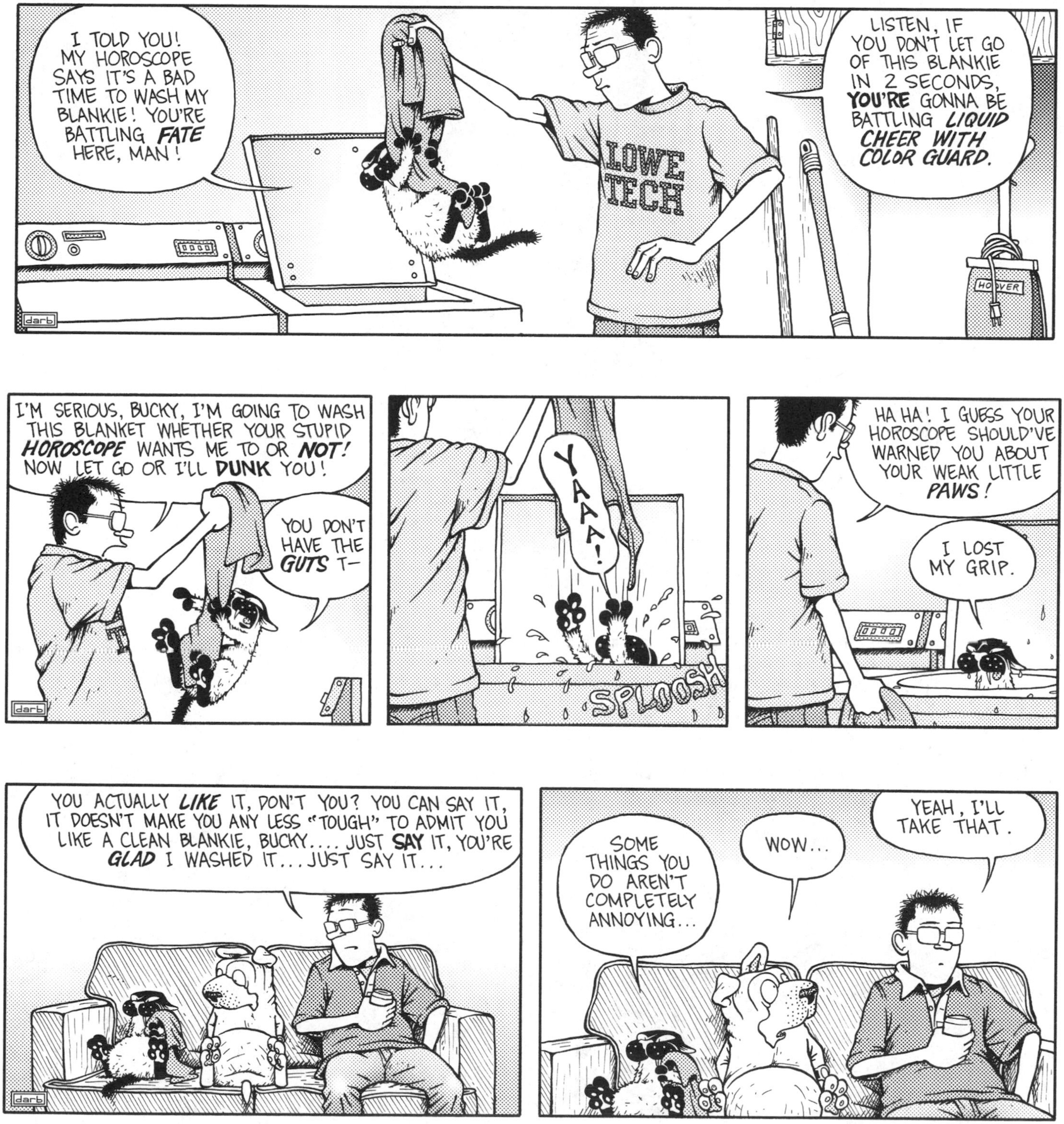
I TOLD YOU! MY HOROSCOPE SAYS IT'S A BAD TIME TO WASH MY BLANKIE! YOU'RE BATTLING FATE HERE, MAN!
LISTEN, IF YOU DON'T LET GO OF THIS BLANKIE IN 2 SECONDS, YOU'RE GONNA BE BATTLING LIQUID CHEER WITH COLOR GUARD.
LOWE TECH
HOOVER
darb
I'M SERIOUS, BUCKY, I'M GOING TO WASH THIS BLANKET WHETHER YOUR STUPID HOROSCOPE WANTS ME TO OR NOT! NOW LET GO OR I'LL DUNK YOU!
YOU DON'T HAVE THE GUTS T—
darb
YAAA!
SPLOOSH
HA HA! I GUESS YOUR HOROSCOPE SHOULD'VE WARNED YOU ABOUT YOUR WEAK LITTLE PAWS!
I LOST MY GRIP.
YOU ACTUALLY LIKE IT, DON'T YOU? YOU CAN SAY IT, IT DOESN'T MAKE YOU ANY LESS "TOUGH" TO ADMIT YOU LIKE A CLEAN BLANKIE, BUCKY.... JUST SAY IT, YOU'RE GLAD I WASHED IT... JUST SAY IT...
darb
SOME THINGS YOU DO AREN'T COMPLETELY ANNOYING...
WOW...
YEAH, I'LL TAKE THAT.

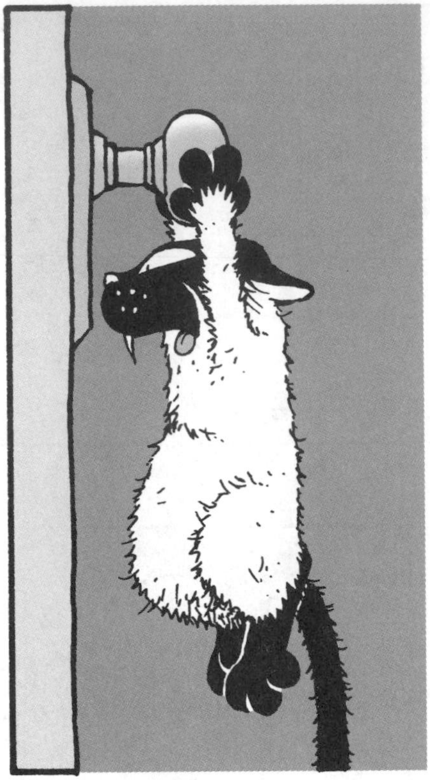

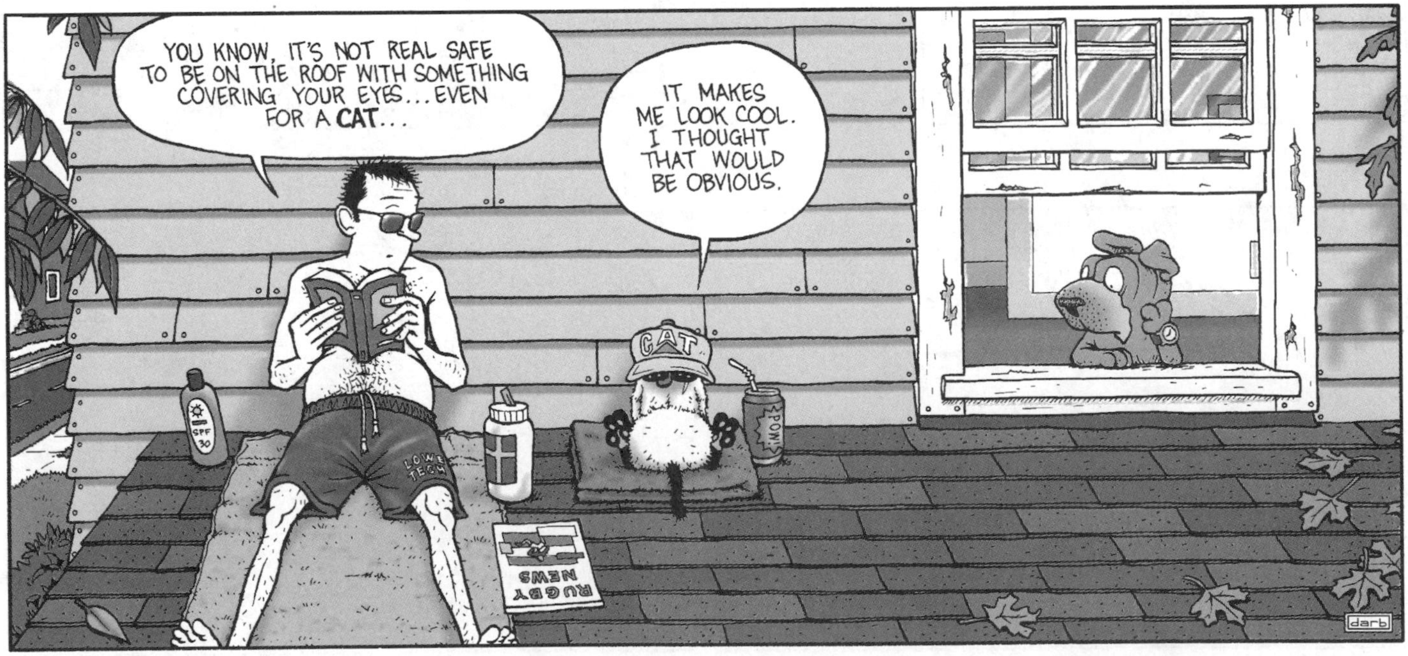
YOU KNOW, IT'S NOT REAL SAFE TO BE ON THE ROOF WITH SOMETHING COVERING YOUR EYES... EVEN FOR A **CAT**...
IT MAKES ME LOOK COOL. I THOUGHT THAT WOULD BE OBVIOUS.
CAT
SPF 30
LOWE TECH
POW!
RUGBY NEWS
darb

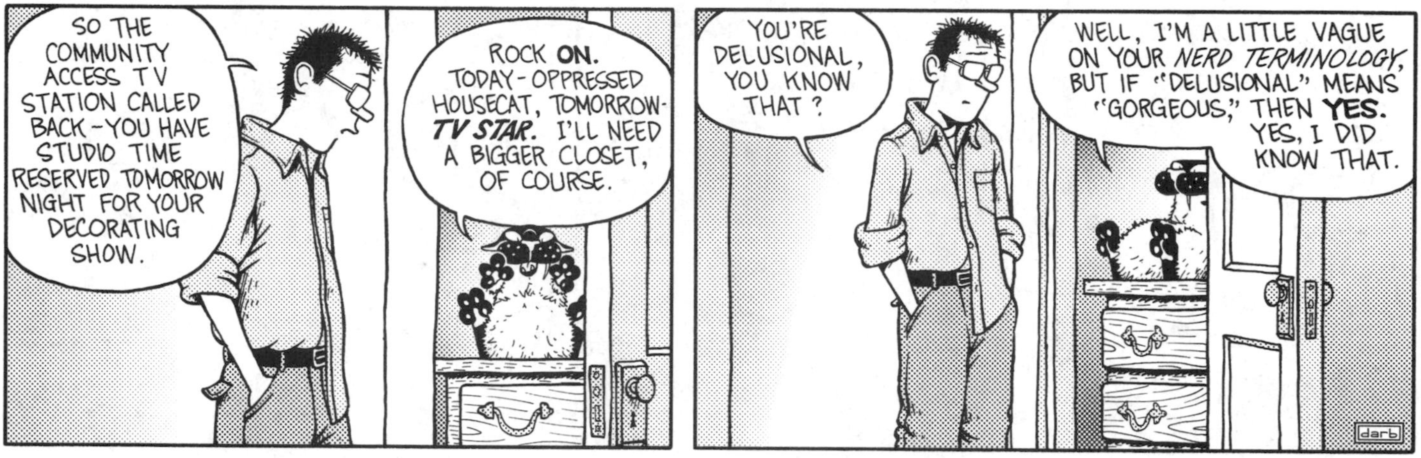
SO THE COMMUNITY ACCESS TV STATION CALLED BACK - YOU HAVE STUDIO TIME RESERVED TOMORROW NIGHT FOR YOUR DECORATING SHOW.
ROCK **ON.** TODAY - OPPRESSED HOUSECAT, TOMORROW - ***TV STAR.*** I'LL NEED A BIGGER CLOSET, OF COURSE.
YOU'RE DELUSIONAL, YOU KNOW THAT?
WELL, I'M A LITTLE VAGUE ON YOUR *NERD TERMINOLOGY,* BUT IF "DELUSIONAL" MEANS "GORGEOUS," THEN **YES.**
YES, I DID KNOW THAT.
darb

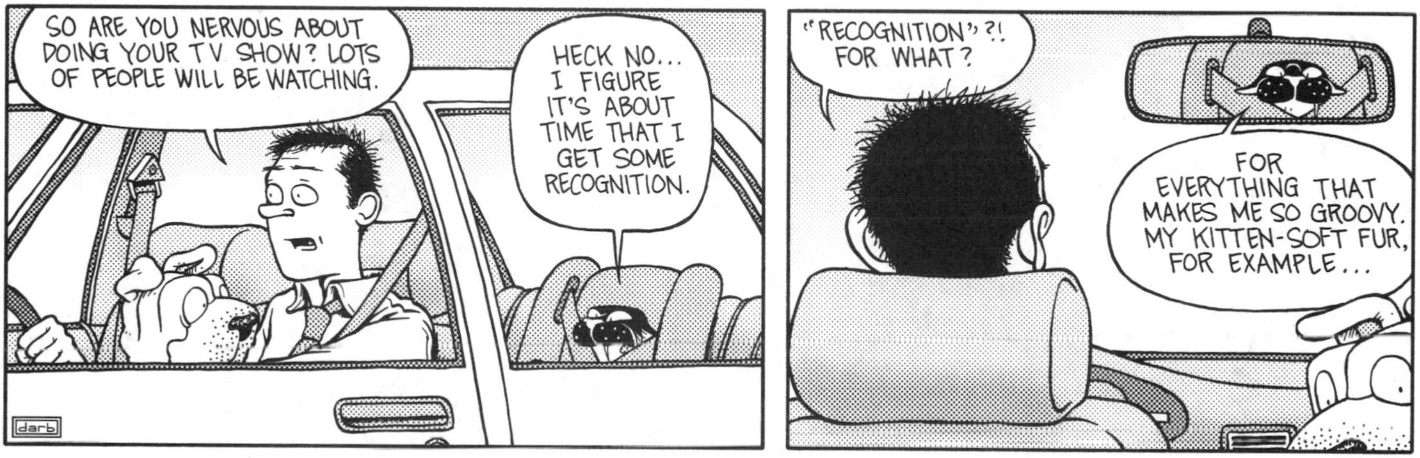
SO ARE YOU NERVOUS ABOUT DOING YOUR TV SHOW? LOTS OF PEOPLE WILL BE WATCHING.
HECK NO... I FIGURE IT'S ABOUT TIME THAT I GET SOME RECOGNITION.
darb
"RECOGNITION"?! FOR WHAT?
FOR EVERYTHING THAT MAKES ME SO GROOVY. MY KITTEN-SOFT FUR, FOR EXAMPLE...

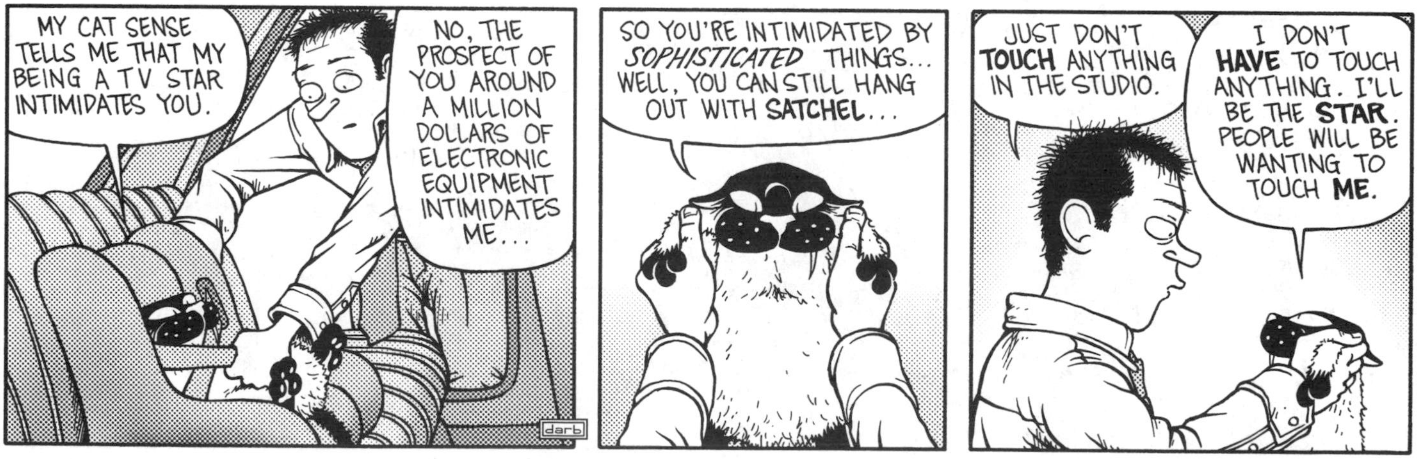
MY CAT SENSE TELLS ME THAT MY BEING A TV STAR INTIMIDATES YOU.
NO, THE PROSPECT OF YOU AROUND A MILLION DOLLARS OF ELECTRONIC EQUIPMENT INTIMIDATES ME...
darb
SO YOU'RE INTIMIDATED BY *SOPHISTICATED* THINGS... WELL, YOU CAN STILL HANG OUT WITH **SATCHEL**...
JUST DON'T **TOUCH** ANYTHING IN THE STUDIO.
I DON'T **HAVE** TO TOUCH ANYTHING. I'LL BE THE **STAR**. PEOPLE WILL BE WANTING TO TOUCH **ME.**

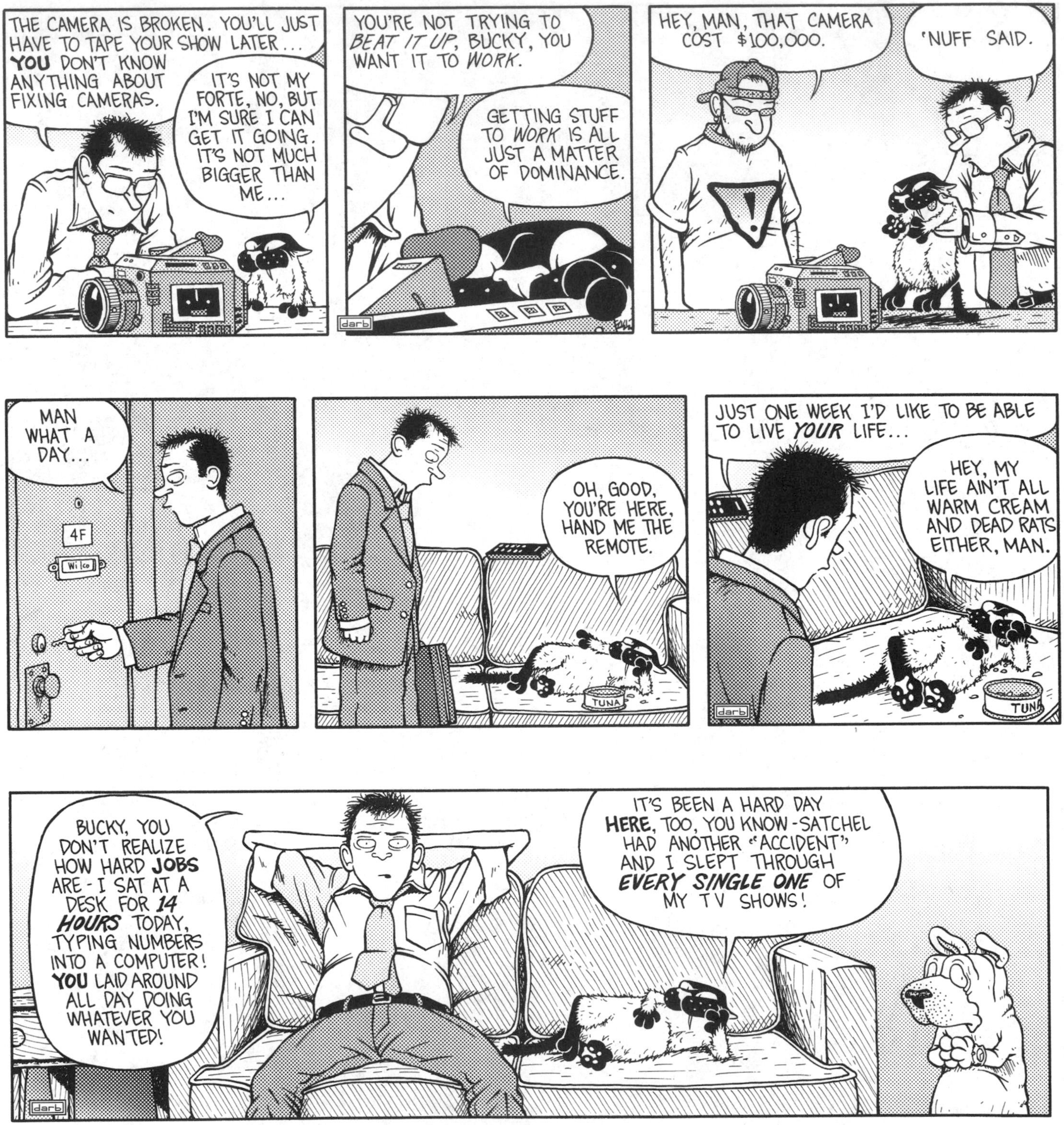
THE CAMERA IS BROKEN. YOU'LL JUST HAVE TO TAPE YOUR SHOW LATER... **YOU** DON'T KNOW ANYTHING ABOUT FIXING CAMERAS.
IT'S NOT MY FORTE, NO, BUT I'M SURE I CAN GET IT GOING. IT'S NOT MUCH BIGGER THAN ME...
YOU'RE NOT TRYING TO *BEAT IT UP*, BUCKY, YOU WANT IT TO *WORK*.
GETTING STUFF TO *WORK* IS ALL JUST A MATTER OF DOMINANCE.
darb
HEY, MAN, THAT CAMERA COST $100,000.
'NUFF SAID.
MAN WHAT A DAY...
4F
Wilco
OH, GOOD, YOU'RE HERE, HAND ME THE REMOTE.
TUNA
JUST ONE WEEK I'D LIKE TO BE ABLE TO LIVE ***YOUR*** LIFE...
HEY, MY LIFE AIN'T ALL WARM CREAM AND DEAD RATS EITHER, MAN.
darb
BUCKY, YOU DON'T REALIZE HOW HARD **JOBS** ARE - I SAT AT A DESK FOR ***14 HOURS*** TODAY, TYPING NUMBERS INTO A COMPUTER! **YOU** LAID AROUND ALL DAY DOING WHATEVER YOU WANTED!
IT'S BEEN A HARD DAY **HERE**, TOO, YOU KNOW - SATCHEL HAD ANOTHER "ACCIDENT" AND I SLEPT THROUGH ***EVERY SINGLE ONE*** OF MY TV SHOWS!
darb

YOU WANNA BUY THAT BOOK, SATCH? YOU SEEM PRETTY INTO IT. WHAT'S IT ABOUT?
UM...I'M NOT REALLY CLEAR ON THAT YET...IT'S SORT OF HARD TO FOLLOW...
CAT WORLD
WHAT'S HAPPENING IN IT?
I'M NOT TOO SURE...
YANKEE
RUGBY NEWS
CAT WORLD
WELL...WHERE'S IT SET? WHO'S IN IT?
THIS GUY NAMED "LES" SEEMS TO COME UP A LOT...
Bird Watching
LEMME SEE THAT...SATCHEL, THIS IS A FRENCH-TO-ITALIAN DICTIONARY...
IS THAT GOOD?
YOWZA.
darb

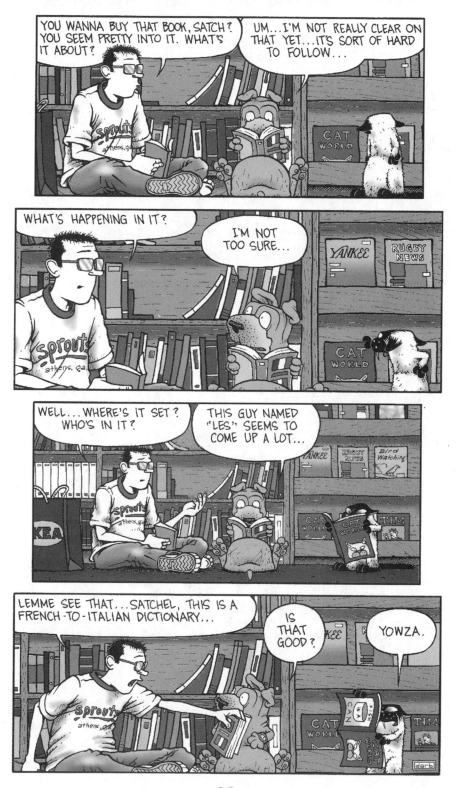

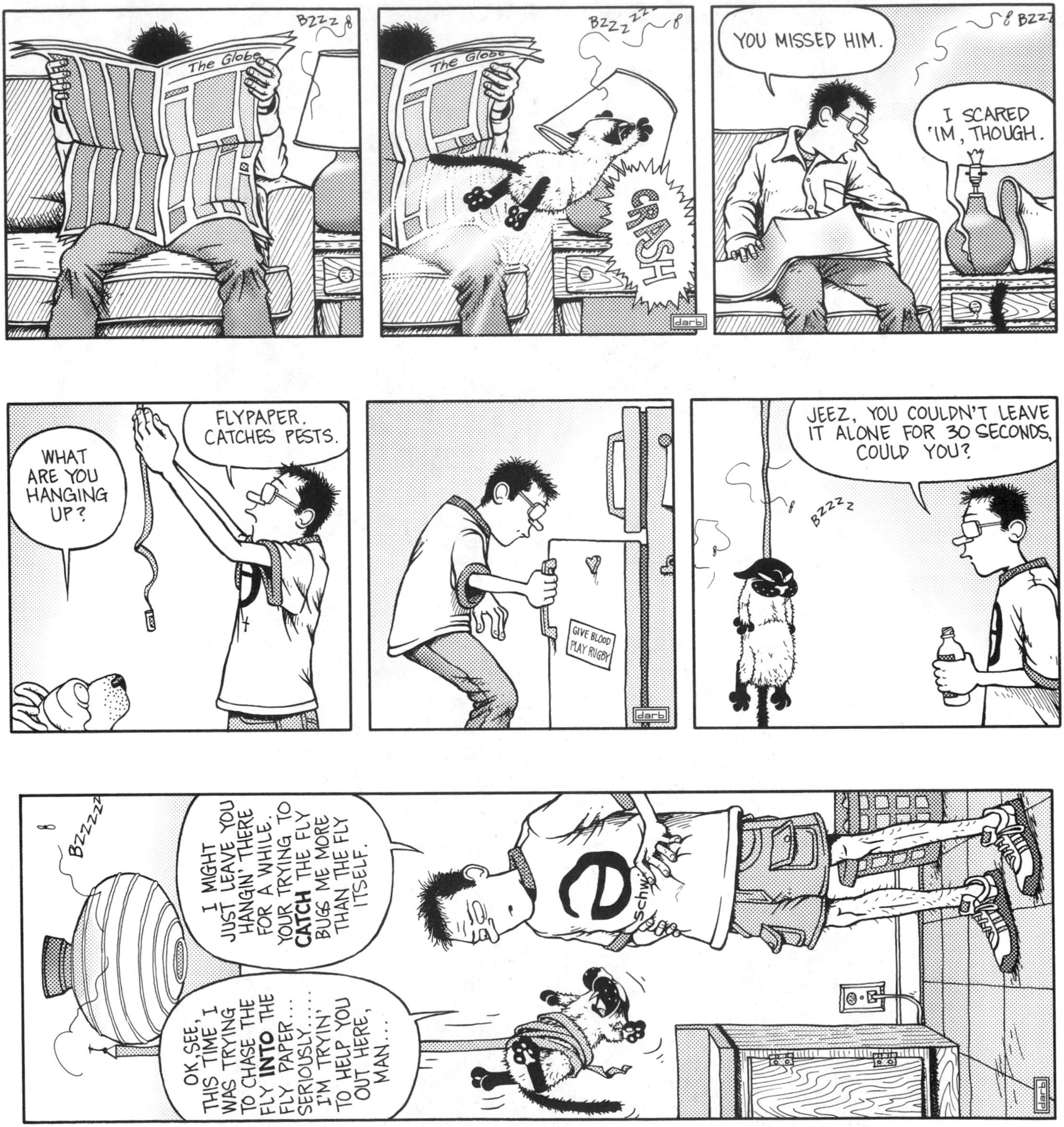
BZZZ
The Globe
BZZZZZZ
The Globe
CRASH
darb
YOU MISSED HIM.
BZZZ
I SCARED 'IM, THOUGH.
WHAT ARE YOU HANGING UP?
FLYPAPER. CATCHES PESTS.
GIVE BLOOD PLAY RUGBY
darb
JEEZ, YOU COULDN'T LEAVE IT ALONE FOR 30 SECONDS, COULD YOU?
BZZZZ
BZZZZZ
OK, SEE, THIS TIME I WAS TRYING TO CHASE THE FLY **INTO** THE FLY PAPER.... SERIOUSLY..... I'M TRYIN' TO HELP YOU OUT HERE, MAN...
I MIGHT JUST LEAVE YOU HANGIN' THERE FOR A WHILE. YOUR TRYING TO **CATCH** THE FLY BUGS ME MORE THAN THE FLY ITSELF.
darb

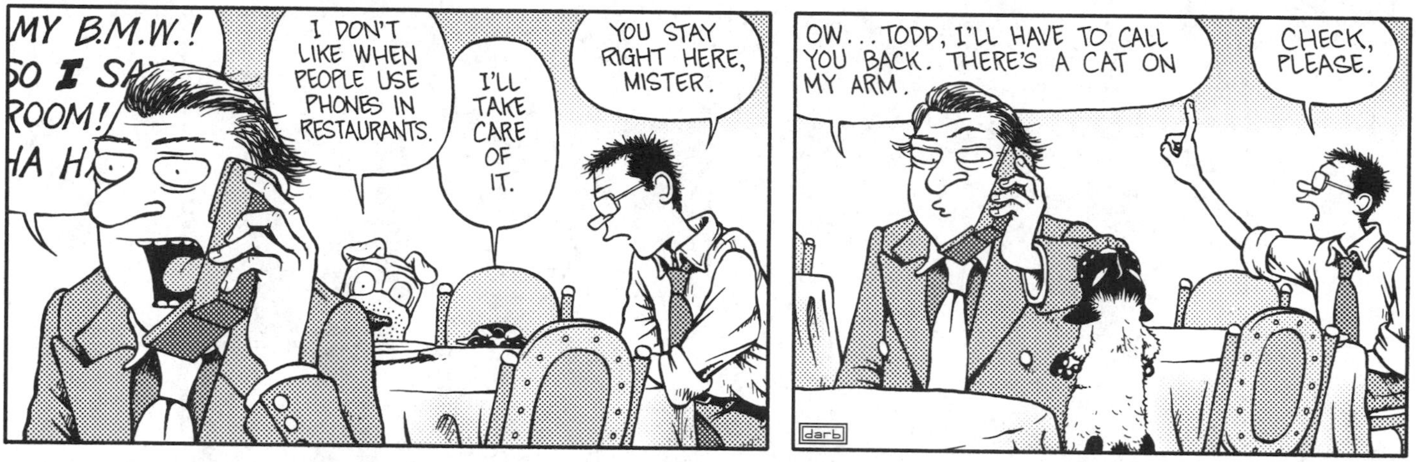
MY B.M.W.!
SO **I** SA
ROOM!
HA H
I DON'T LIKE WHEN PEOPLE USE PHONES IN RESTAURANTS.
I'LL TAKE CARE OF IT.
YOU STAY RIGHT HERE, MISTER.
OW... TODD, I'LL HAVE TO CALL YOU BACK. THERE'S A CAT ON MY ARM.
CHECK, PLEASE.
darb

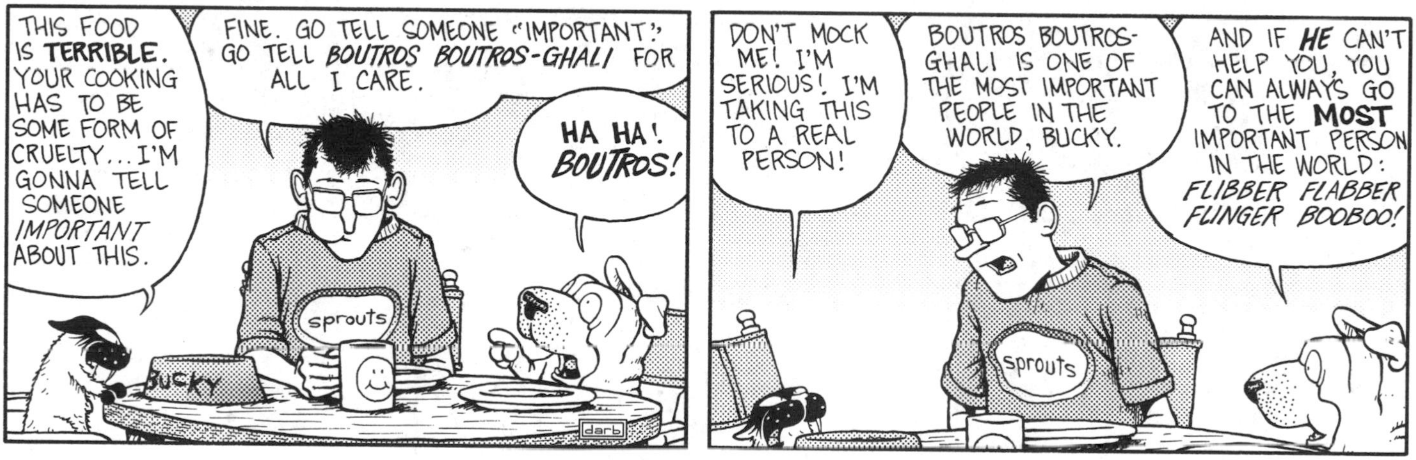
THIS FOOD IS **TERRIBLE**. YOUR COOKING HAS TO BE SOME FORM OF CRUELTY... I'M GONNA TELL SOMEONE *IMPORTANT* ABOUT THIS.
FINE. GO TELL SOMEONE "IMPORTANT." GO TELL *BOUTROS BOUTROS-GHALI* FOR ALL I CARE.
HA HA! *BOUTROS!*
sprouts
BUCKY
darb
DON'T MOCK ME! I'M SERIOUS! I'M TAKING THIS TO A REAL PERSON!
BOUTROS BOUTROS-GHALI IS ONE OF THE MOST IMPORTANT PEOPLE IN THE WORLD, BUCKY.
AND IF ***HE*** CAN'T HELP YOU, YOU CAN ALWAYS GO TO THE **MOST** IMPORTANT PERSON IN THE WORLD: ***FLIBBER FLABBER FLINGER BOOBOO!***
sprouts

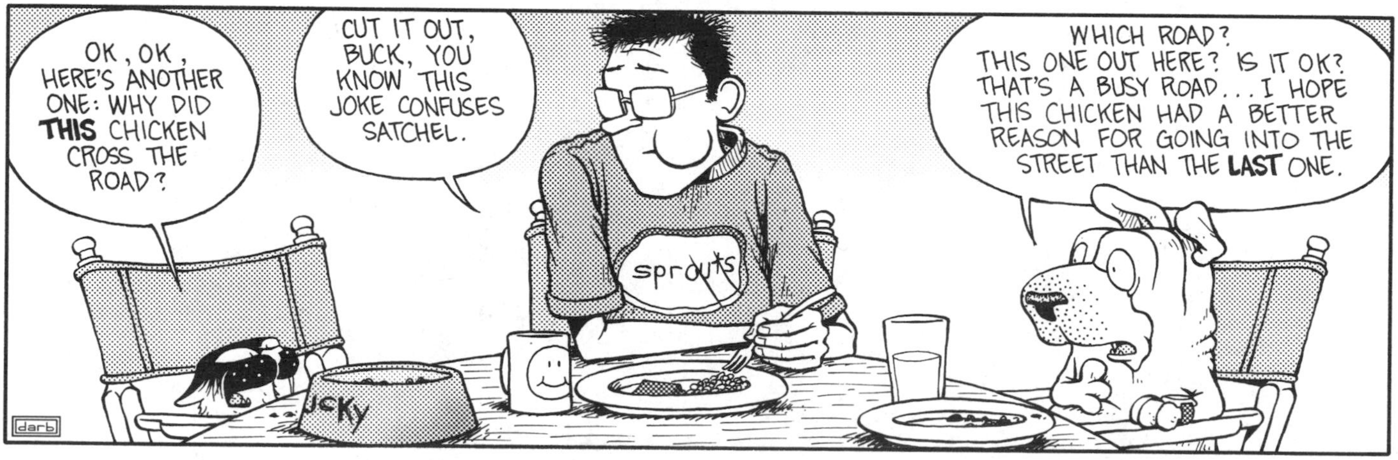
OK, OK, HERE'S ANOTHER ONE: WHY DID **THIS** CHICKEN CROSS THE ROAD?
CUT IT OUT, BUCK, YOU KNOW THIS JOKE CONFUSES SATCHEL.
WHICH ROAD? THIS ONE OUT HERE? IS IT OK? THAT'S A BUSY ROAD... I HOPE THIS CHICKEN HAD A BETTER REASON FOR GOING INTO THE STREET THAN THE **LAST** ONE.
sprouts
UCKY
darb

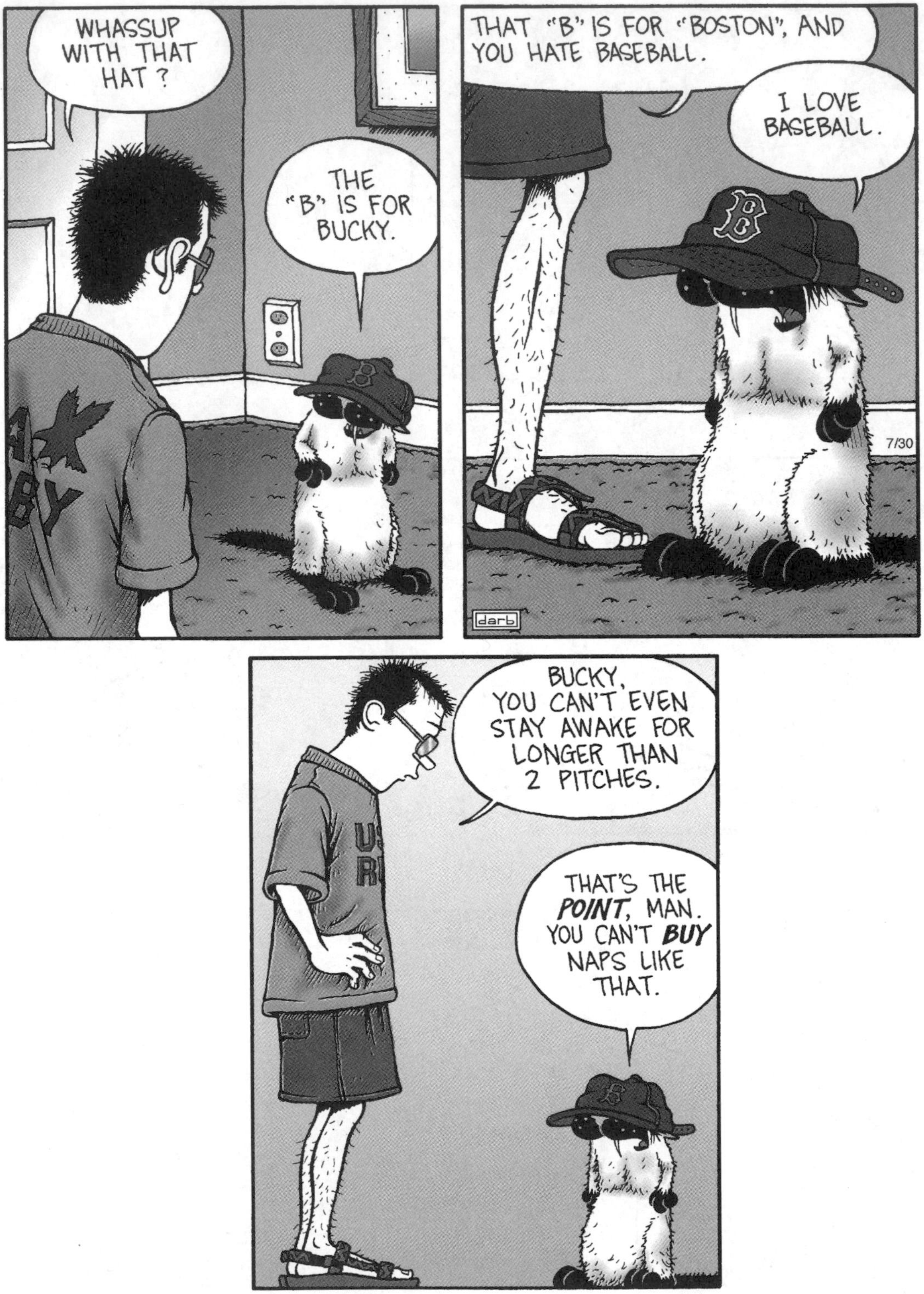
WHASSUP WITH THAT HAT ?
THE "B" IS FOR BUCKY.
THAT "B" IS FOR "BOSTON", AND YOU HATE BASEBALL.
I LOVE BASEBALL.
7/30
darb
BUCKY, YOU CAN'T EVEN STAY AWAKE FOR LONGER THAN 2 PITCHES.
THAT'S THE ***POINT***, MAN. YOU CAN'T ***BUY*** NAPS LIKE THAT.

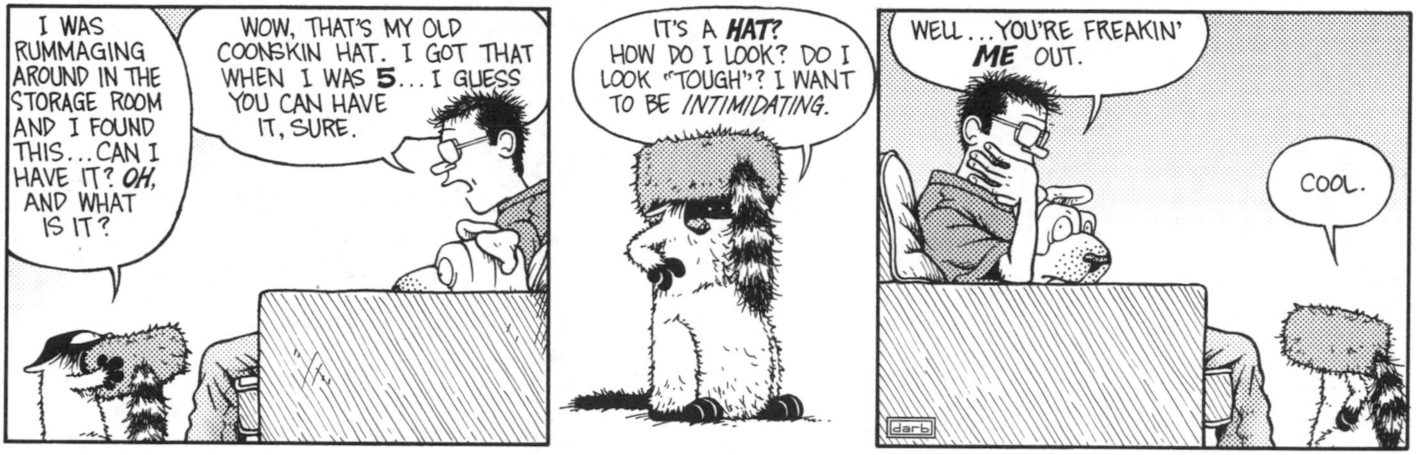
I WAS RUMMAGING AROUND IN THE STORAGE ROOM AND I FOUND THIS...CAN I HAVE IT? OH, AND WHAT IS IT?
WOW, THAT'S MY OLD COONSKIN HAT. I GOT THAT WHEN I WAS 5... I GUESS YOU CAN HAVE IT, SURE.
IT'S A HAT? HOW DO I LOOK? DO I LOOK "TOUGH"? I WANT TO BE INTIMIDATING.
WELL... YOU'RE FREAKIN' ME OUT.
COOL.
darb

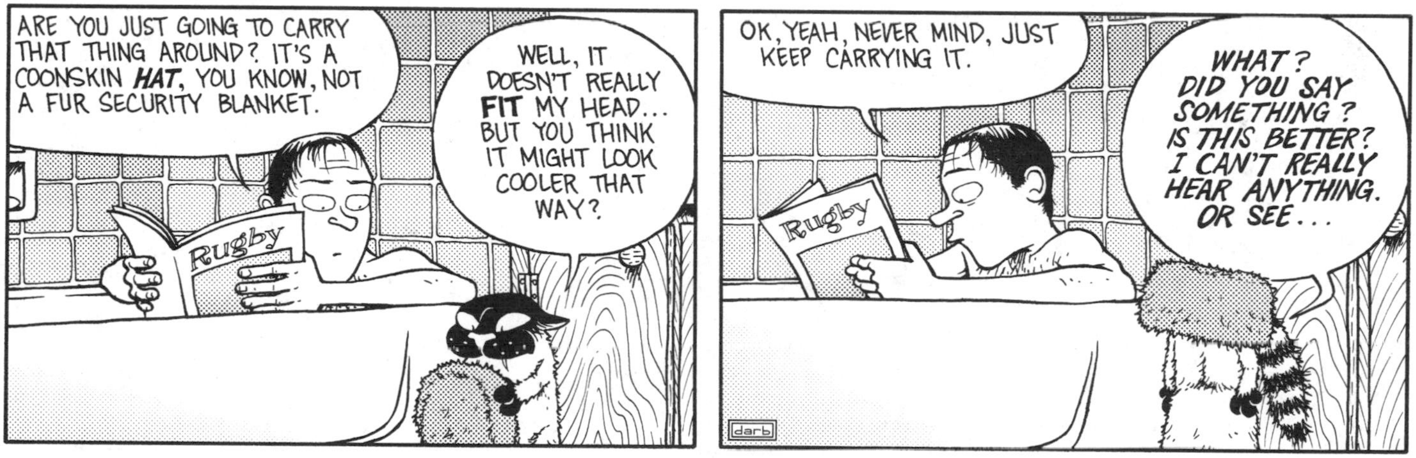
ARE YOU JUST GOING TO CARRY THAT THING AROUND? IT'S A COONSKIN HAT, YOU KNOW, NOT A FUR SECURITY BLANKET.
WELL, IT DOESN'T REALLY FIT MY HEAD... BUT YOU THINK IT MIGHT LOOK COOLER THAT WAY?
Rugby
OK, YEAH, NEVER MIND, JUST KEEP CARRYING IT.
WHAT? DID YOU SAY SOMETHING? IS THIS BETTER? I CAN'T REALLY HEAR ANYTHING. OR SEE...
Rugby
darb

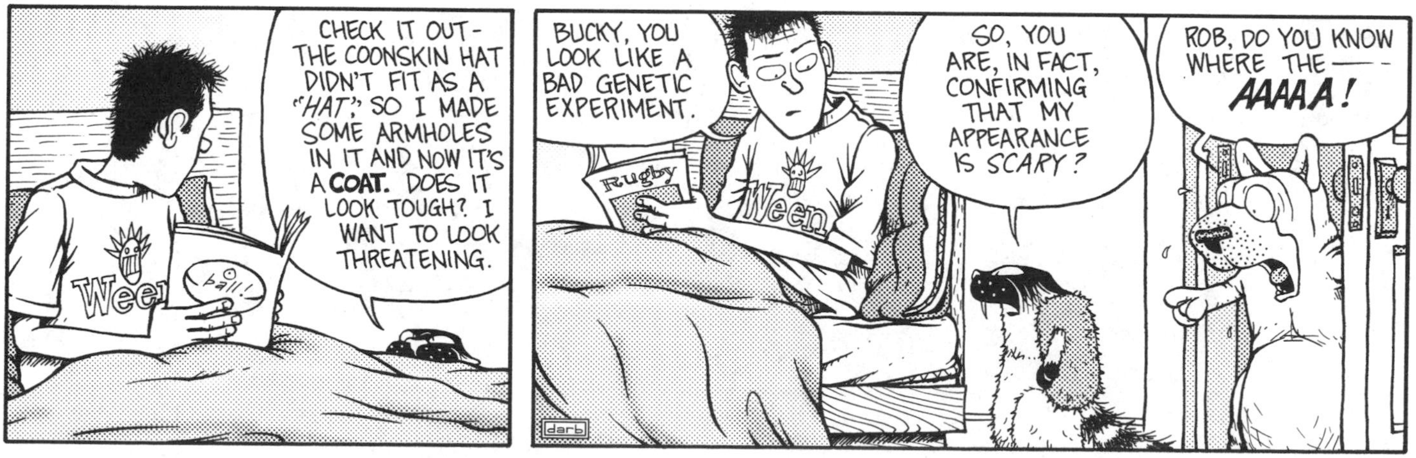
CHECK IT OUT- THE COONSKIN HAT DIDN'T FIT AS A "HAT," SO I MADE SOME ARMHOLES IN IT AND NOW IT'S A COAT. DOES IT LOOK TOUGH? I WANT TO LOOK THREATENING.
BUCKY, YOU LOOK LIKE A BAD GENETIC EXPERIMENT.
SO, YOU ARE, IN FACT, CONFIRMING THAT MY APPEARANCE IS SCARY?
ROB, DO YOU KNOW WHERE THE——
AAAAA!
Ween
Rugby
darb

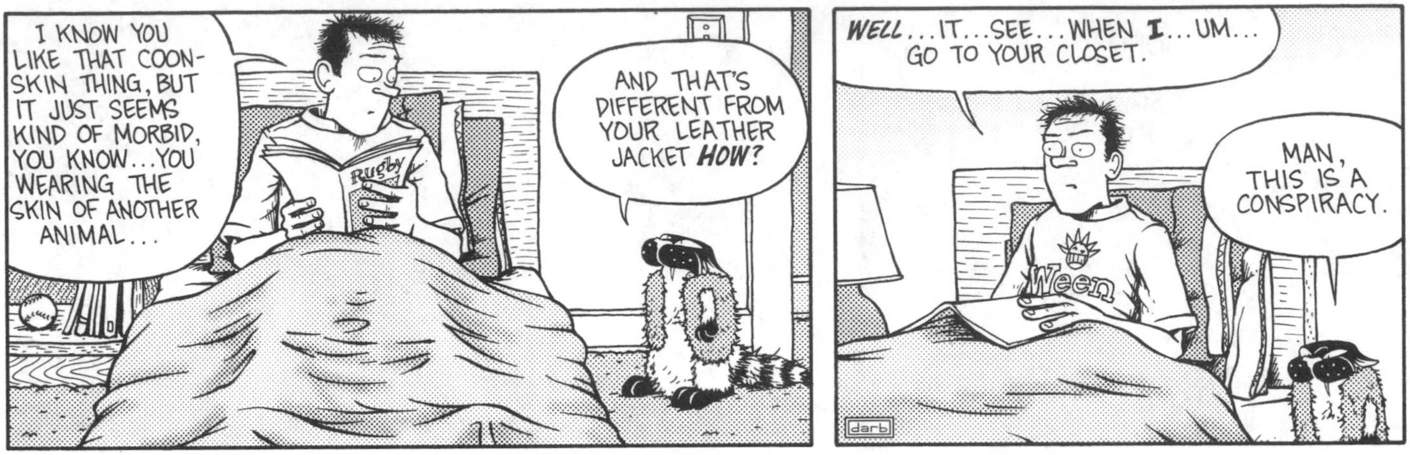
I KNOW YOU LIKE THAT COON-SKIN THING, BUT IT JUST SEEMS KIND OF MORBID, YOU KNOW...YOU WEARING THE SKIN OF ANOTHER ANIMAL...
AND THAT'S DIFFERENT FROM YOUR LEATHER JACKET **HOW**?
WELL...IT...SEE...WHEN **I**...UM... GO TO YOUR CLOSET.
MAN, THIS IS A CONSPIRACY.

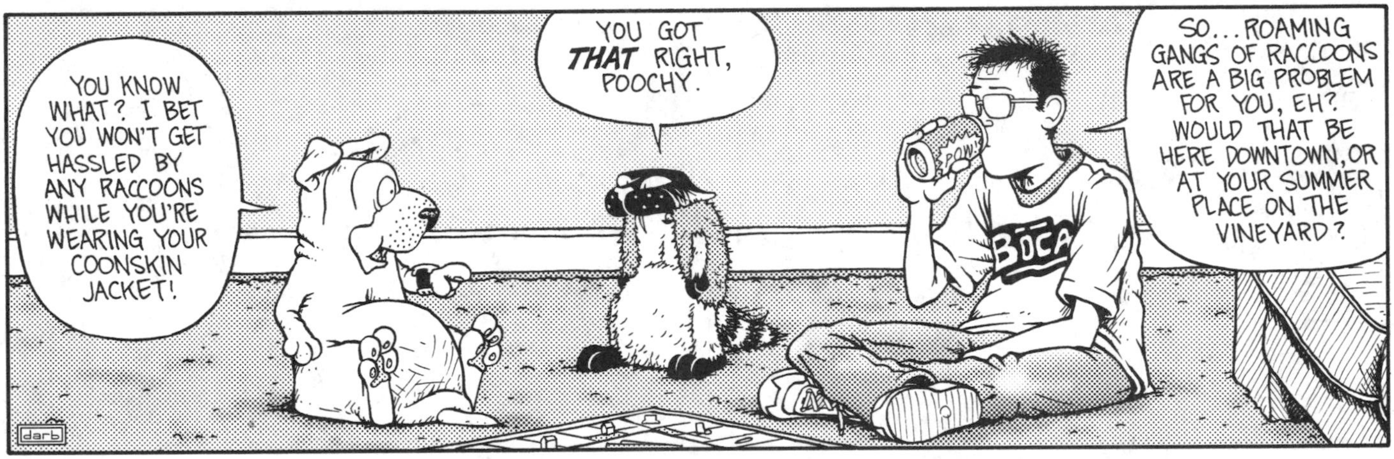
YOU KNOW WHAT? I BET YOU WON'T GET HASSLED BY ANY RACCOONS WHILE YOU'RE WEARING YOUR COONSKIN JACKET!
YOU GOT **THAT** RIGHT, POOCHY.
SO...ROAMING GANGS OF RACCOONS ARE A BIG PROBLEM FOR YOU, EH? WOULD THAT BE HERE DOWNTOWN, OR AT YOUR SUMMER PLACE ON THE VINEYARD?

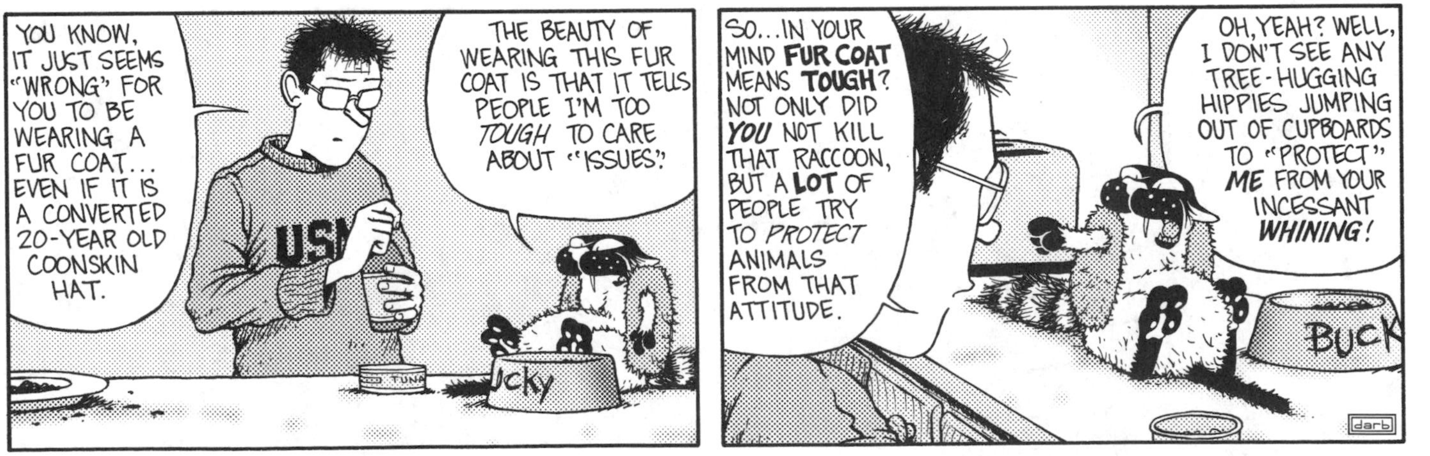
YOU KNOW, IT JUST SEEMS "WRONG" FOR YOU TO BE WEARING A FUR COAT... EVEN IF IT IS A CONVERTED 20-YEAR OLD COONSKIN HAT.
THE BEAUTY OF WEARING THIS FUR COAT IS THAT IT TELLS PEOPLE I'M TOO *TOUGH* TO CARE ABOUT "ISSUES."
SO...IN YOUR MIND **FUR COAT** MEANS **TOUGH**? NOT ONLY DID ***YOU*** NOT KILL THAT RACCOON, BUT A **LOT** OF PEOPLE TRY TO *PROTECT* ANIMALS FROM THAT ATTITUDE.
OH, YEAH? WELL, I DON'T SEE ANY TREE-HUGGING HIPPIES JUMPING OUT OF CUPBOARDS TO "PROTECT" ***ME*** FROM YOUR INCESSANT ***WHINING***!

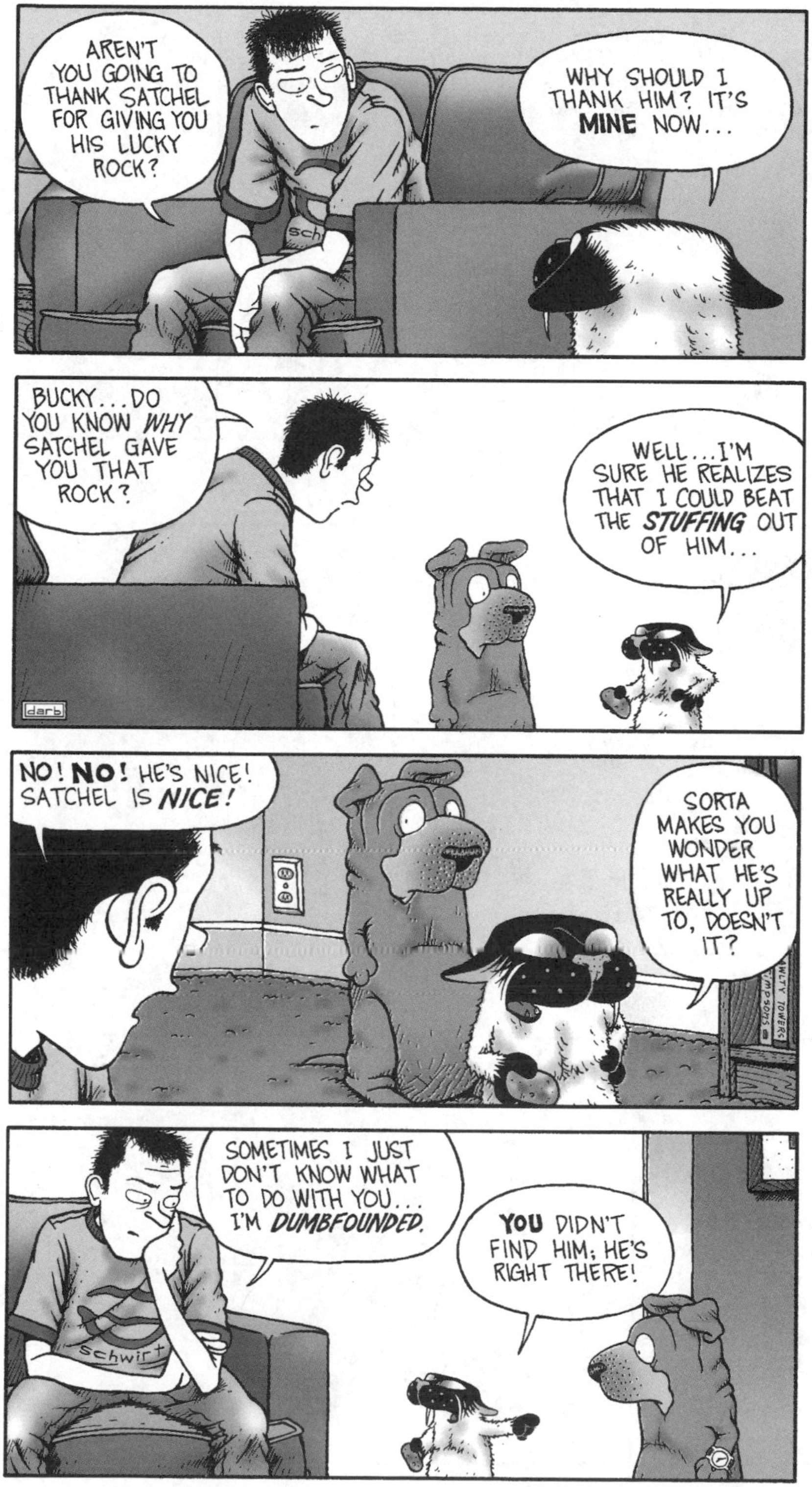
AREN'T YOU GOING TO THANK SATCHEL FOR GIVING YOU HIS LUCKY ROCK?
WHY SHOULD I THANK HIM? IT'S **MINE** NOW...
BUCKY...DO YOU KNOW *WHY* SATCHEL GAVE YOU THAT ROCK?
WELL...I'M SURE HE REALIZES THAT I COULD BEAT THE ***STUFFING*** OUT OF HIM...
darb
NO! **NO!** HE'S NICE! SATCHEL IS ***NICE!***
SORTA MAKES YOU WONDER WHAT HE'S REALLY UP TO, DOESN'T IT?
SOMETIMES I JUST DON'T KNOW WHAT TO DO WITH YOU... I'M ***DUMBFOUNDED.***
YOU DIDN'T FIND HIM; HE'S RIGHT THERE!

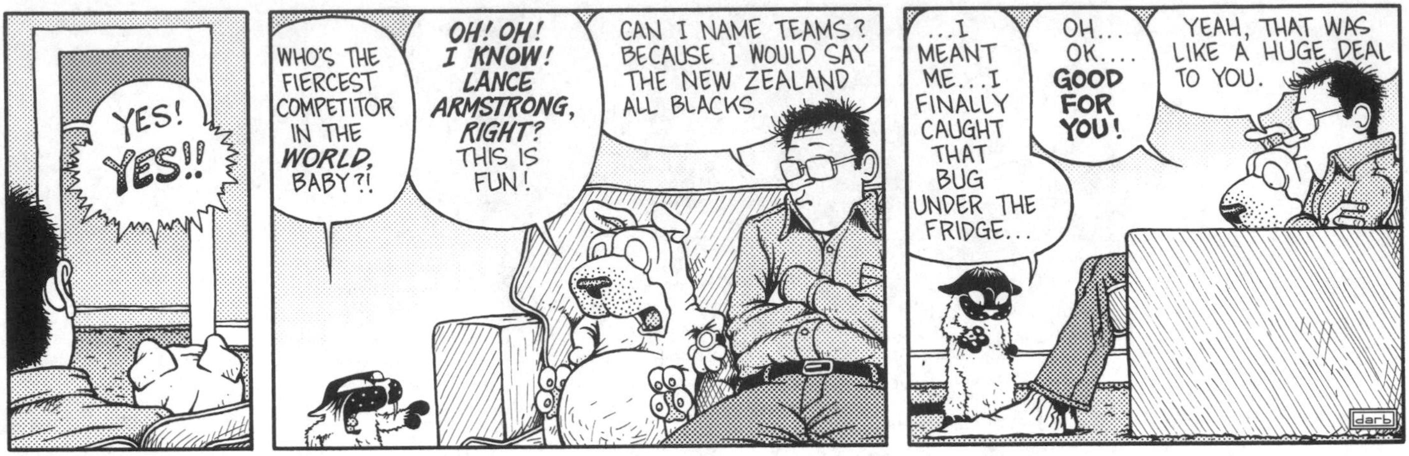
YES! YES!!
WHO'S THE FIERCEST COMPETITOR IN THE WORLD, BABY?!
OH! OH! I KNOW! LANCE ARMSTRONG, RIGHT? THIS IS FUN!
CAN I NAME TEAMS? BECAUSE I WOULD SAY THE NEW ZEALAND ALL BLACKS.
...I MEANT ME...I FINALLY CAUGHT THAT BUG UNDER THE FRIDGE...
OH... OK.... GOOD FOR YOU!
YEAH, THAT WAS LIKE A HUGE DEAL TO YOU.
darb

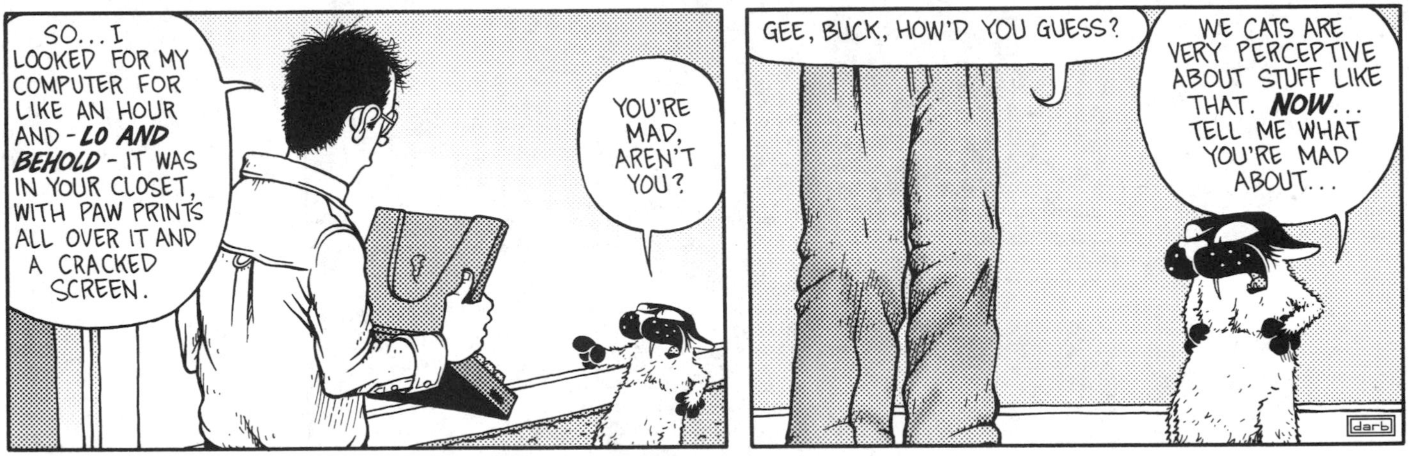
SO...I LOOKED FOR MY COMPUTER FOR LIKE AN HOUR AND - LO AND BEHOLD - IT WAS IN YOUR CLOSET, WITH PAW PRINTS ALL OVER IT AND A CRACKED SCREEN.
YOU'RE MAD, AREN'T YOU?
GEE, BUCK, HOW'D YOU GUESS?
WE CATS ARE VERY PERCEPTIVE ABOUT STUFF LIKE THAT. NOW... TELL ME WHAT YOU'RE MAD ABOUT...
darb

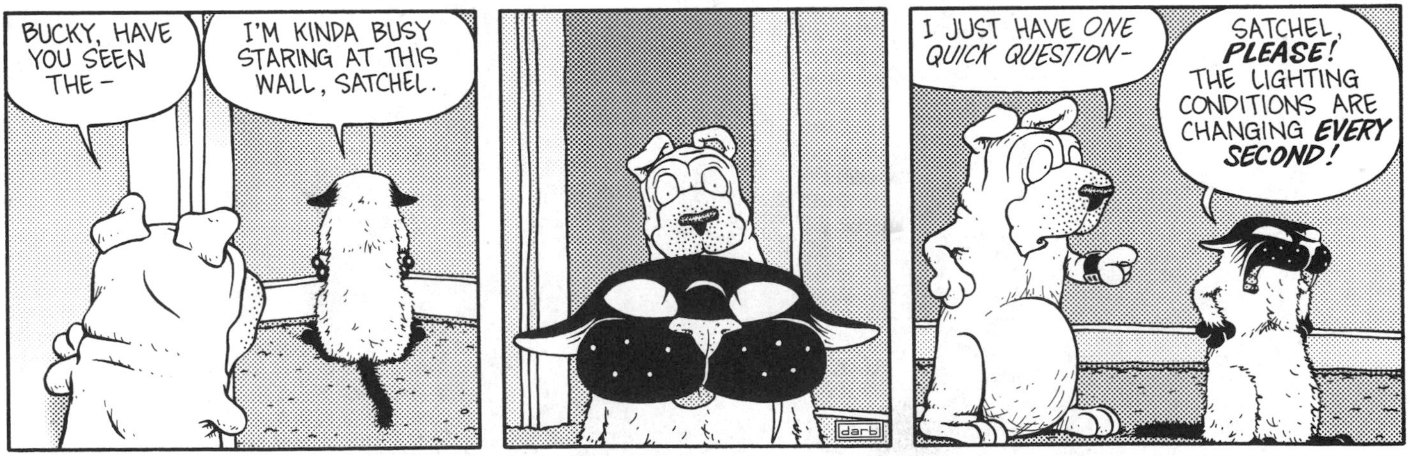
BUCKY, HAVE YOU SEEN THE -
I'M KINDA BUSY STARING AT THIS WALL, SATCHEL.
I JUST HAVE ONE QUICK QUESTION -
SATCHEL, PLEASE! THE LIGHTING CONDITIONS ARE CHANGING EVERY SECOND!
darb

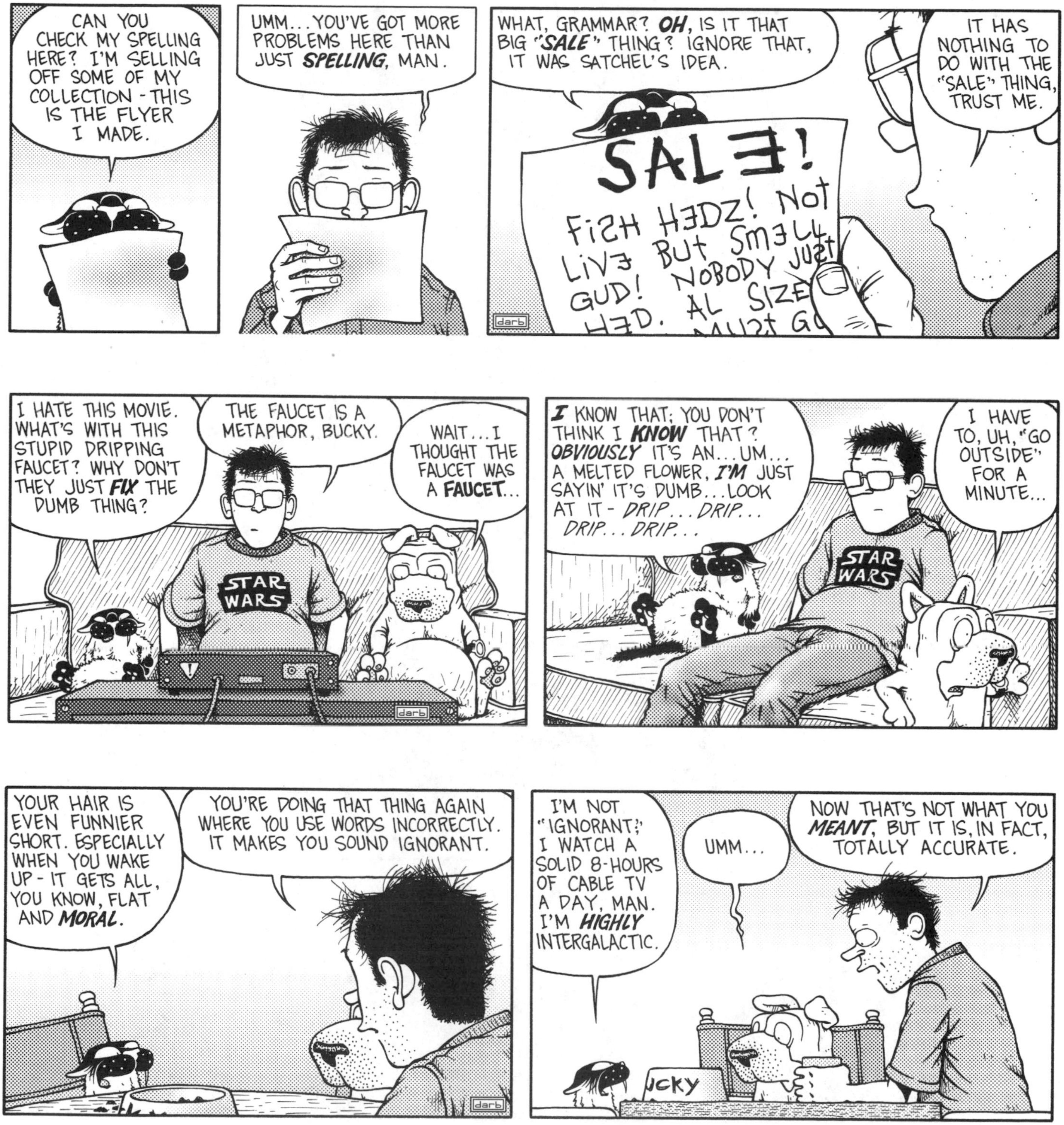
CAN YOU CHECK MY SPELLING HERE? I'M SELLING OFF SOME OF MY COLLECTION - THIS IS THE FLYER I MADE.
UMM... YOU'VE GOT MORE PROBLEMS HERE THAN JUST **SPELLING**, MAN.
WHAT, GRAMMAR? **OH,** IS IT THAT BIG "**SALE**" THING? IGNORE THAT, IT WAS SATCHEL'S IDEA.
SALƎ!
FISH HƎDZ! Not LIVƎ But SMƎLL GUD! NOBODY JUST HƎD. AL SIZE
IT HAS NOTHING TO DO WITH THE "SALE" THING, TRUST ME.
darb
I HATE THIS MOVIE. WHAT'S WITH THIS STUPID DRIPPING FAUCET? WHY DON'T THEY JUST **FIX** THE DUMB THING?
THE FAUCET IS A METAPHOR, BUCKY.
WAIT... I THOUGHT THE FAUCET WAS A **FAUCET**...
STAR WARS
darb
I KNOW THAT; YOU DON'T THINK I **KNOW** THAT? **OBVIOUSLY** IT'S AN... UM... A MELTED FLOWER, **I'M** JUST SAYIN' IT'S DUMB... LOOK AT IT - *DRIP... DRIP... DRIP... DRIP...*
I HAVE TO, UH, "GO OUTSIDE" FOR A MINUTE...
STAR WARS
YOUR HAIR IS EVEN FUNNIER SHORT. ESPECIALLY WHEN YOU WAKE UP - IT GETS ALL, YOU KNOW, FLAT AND **MORAL**.
YOU'RE DOING THAT THING AGAIN WHERE YOU USE WORDS INCORRECTLY. IT MAKES YOU SOUND IGNORANT.
darb
I'M NOT "IGNORANT;" I WATCH A SOLID 8-HOURS OF CABLE TV A DAY, MAN. I'M **HIGHLY** INTERGALACTIC.
UMM...
NOW THAT'S NOT WHAT YOU **MEANT**, BUT IT IS, IN FACT, TOTALLY ACCURATE.
UCKY

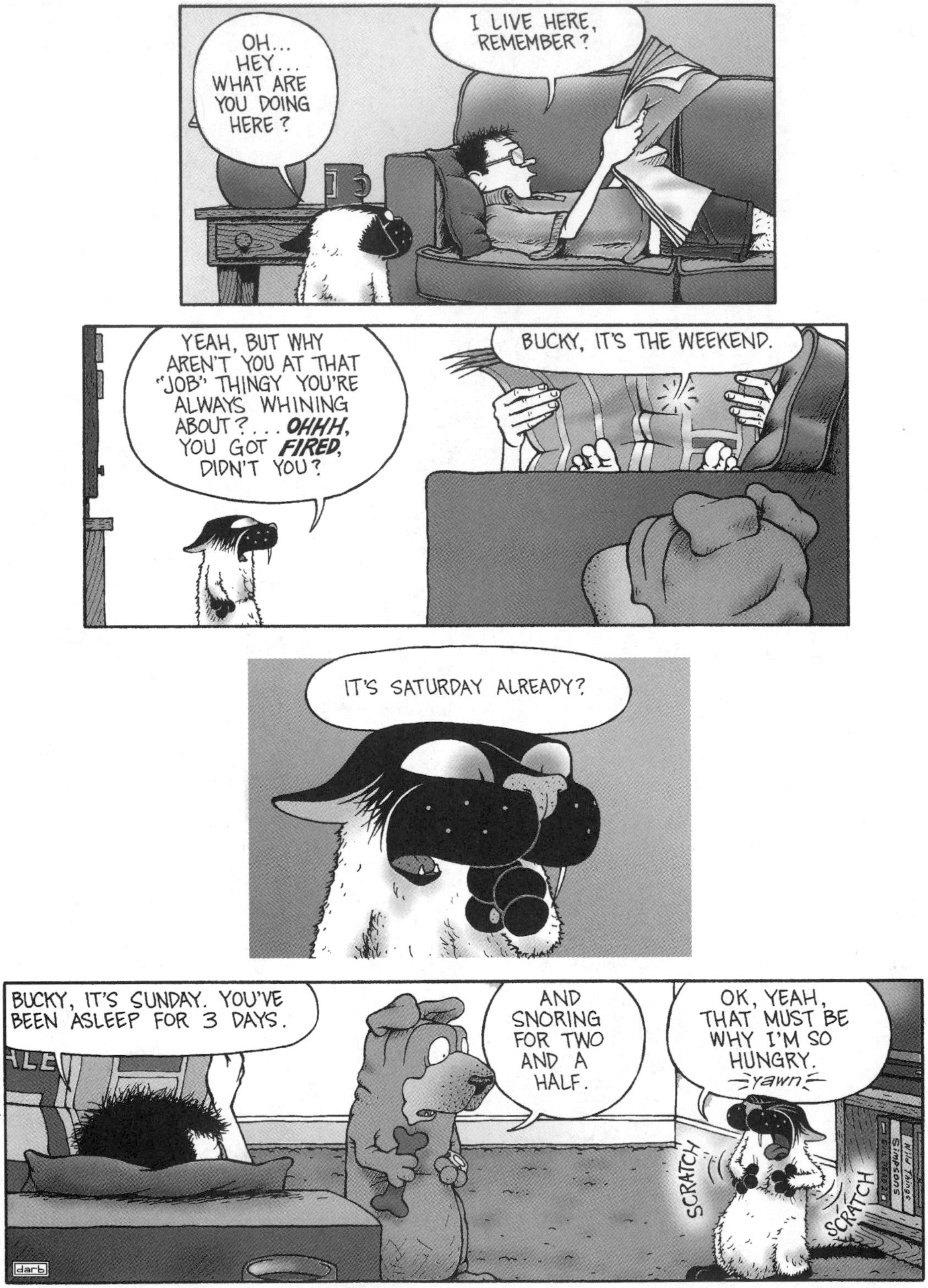
OH... HEY... WHAT ARE YOU DOING HERE?
I LIVE HERE, REMEMBER?
YEAH, BUT WHY AREN'T YOU AT THAT "JOB" THINGY YOU'RE ALWAYS WHINING ABOUT?... OHHH, YOU GOT FIRED, DIDN'T YOU?
BUCKY, IT'S THE WEEKEND.
IT'S SATURDAY ALREADY?
BUCKY, IT'S SUNDAY. YOU'VE BEEN ASLEEP FOR 3 DAYS.
AND SNORING FOR TWO AND A HALF.
OK, YEAH, THAT MUST BE WHY I'M SO HUNGRY.
yawn
SCRATCH
SCRATCH
darb

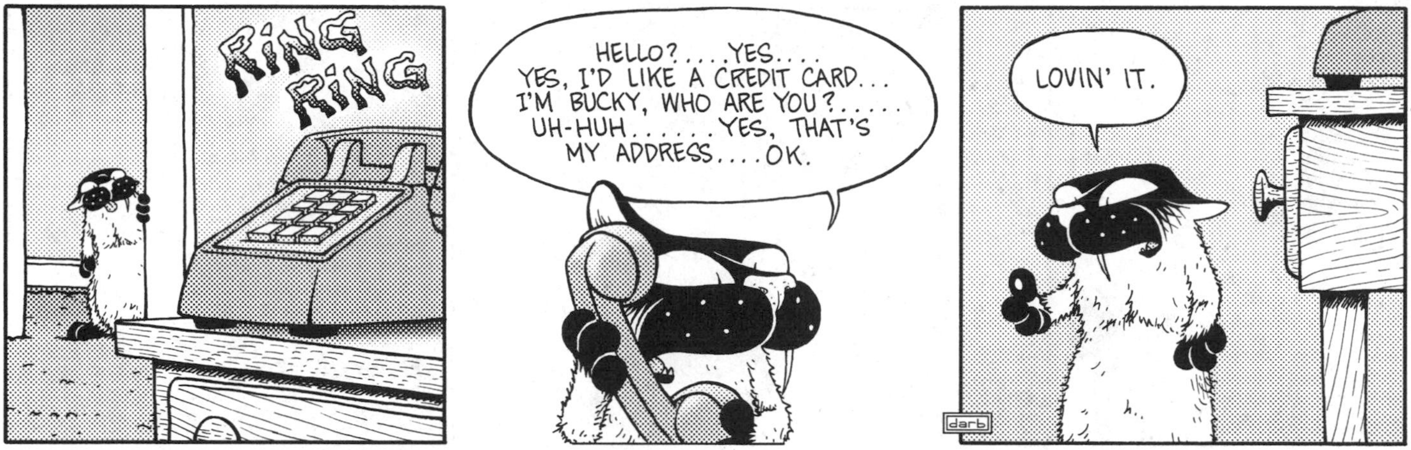
RING RING
HELLO?....YES.... YES, I'D LIKE A CREDIT CARD... I'M BUCKY, WHO ARE YOU?..... UH-HUH......YES, THAT'S MY ADDRESS....OK.
LOVIN' IT.
darb

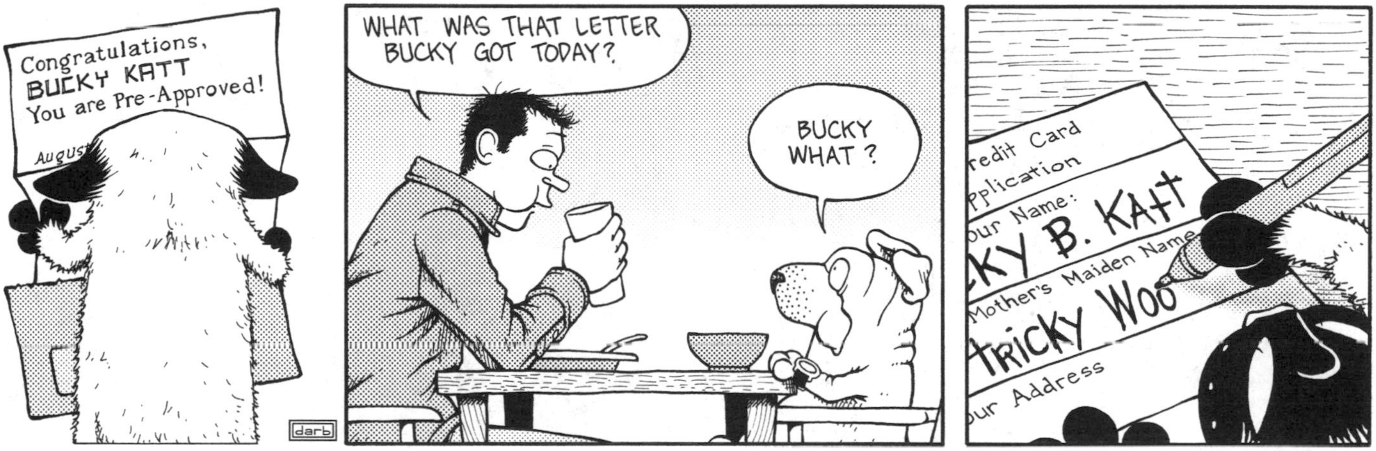
Congratulations, BUCKY KATT You are Pre-Approved!
August
darb
WHAT WAS THAT LETTER BUCKY GOT TODAY?
BUCKY WHAT?
redit Card
pplication
our Name:
cky B. Katt
Mother's Maiden Name
Tricky Woo
our Address

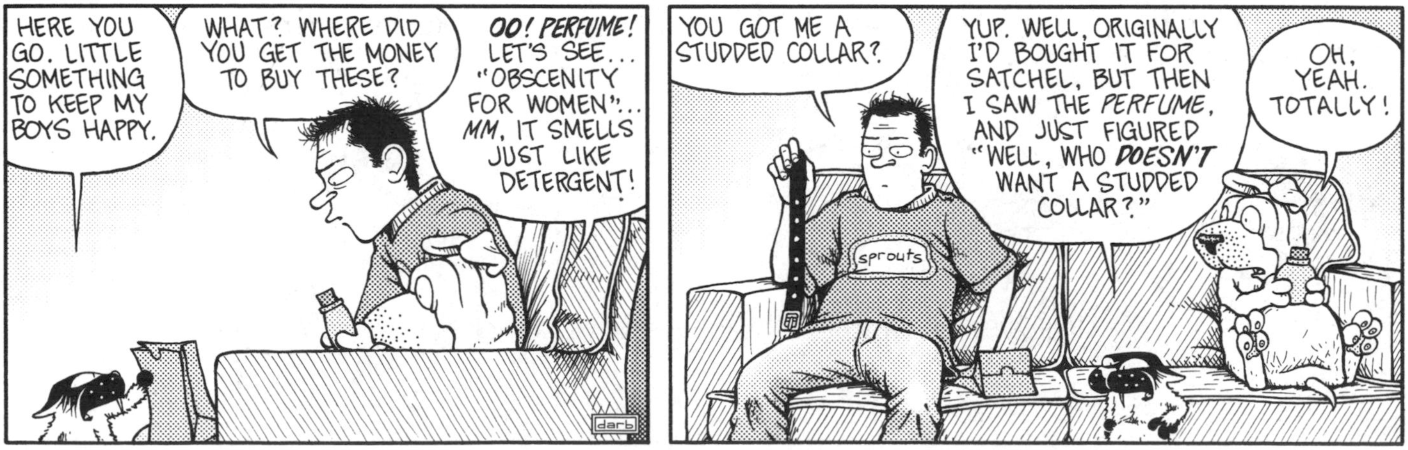
HERE YOU GO. LITTLE SOMETHING TO KEEP MY BOYS HAPPY.
WHAT? WHERE DID YOU GET THE MONEY TO BUY THESE?
OO! PERFUME! LET'S SEE... "OBSCENITY FOR WOMEN"... MM, IT SMELLS JUST LIKE DETERGENT!
darb
YOU GOT ME A STUDDED COLLAR?
YUP. WELL, ORIGINALLY I'D BOUGHT IT FOR SATCHEL, BUT THEN I SAW THE PERFUME, AND JUST FIGURED "WELL, WHO DOESN'T WANT A STUDDED COLLAR?"
OH, YEAH. TOTALLY!
sprouts

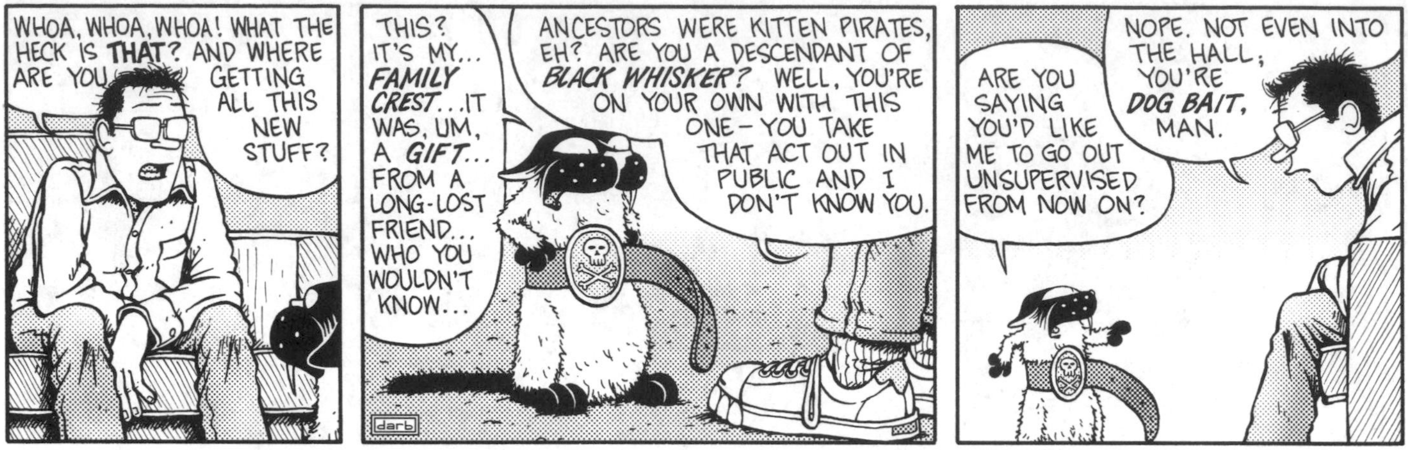
WHOA, WHOA, WHOA! WHAT THE HECK IS **THAT**? AND WHERE ARE YOU GETTING ALL THIS NEW STUFF?
THIS? IT'S MY... ***FAMILY CREST***...IT WAS, UM, A ***GIFT***... FROM A LONG-LOST FRIEND... WHO YOU WOULDN'T KNOW...
ANCESTORS WERE KITTEN PIRATES, EH? ARE YOU A DESCENDANT OF ***BLACK WHISKER?*** WELL, YOU'RE ON YOUR OWN WITH THIS ONE – YOU TAKE THAT ACT OUT IN PUBLIC AND I DON'T KNOW YOU.
ARE YOU SAYING YOU'D LIKE ME TO GO OUT UNSUPERVISED FROM NOW ON?
NOPE. NOT EVEN INTO THE HALL; YOU'RE ***DOG BAIT,*** MAN.

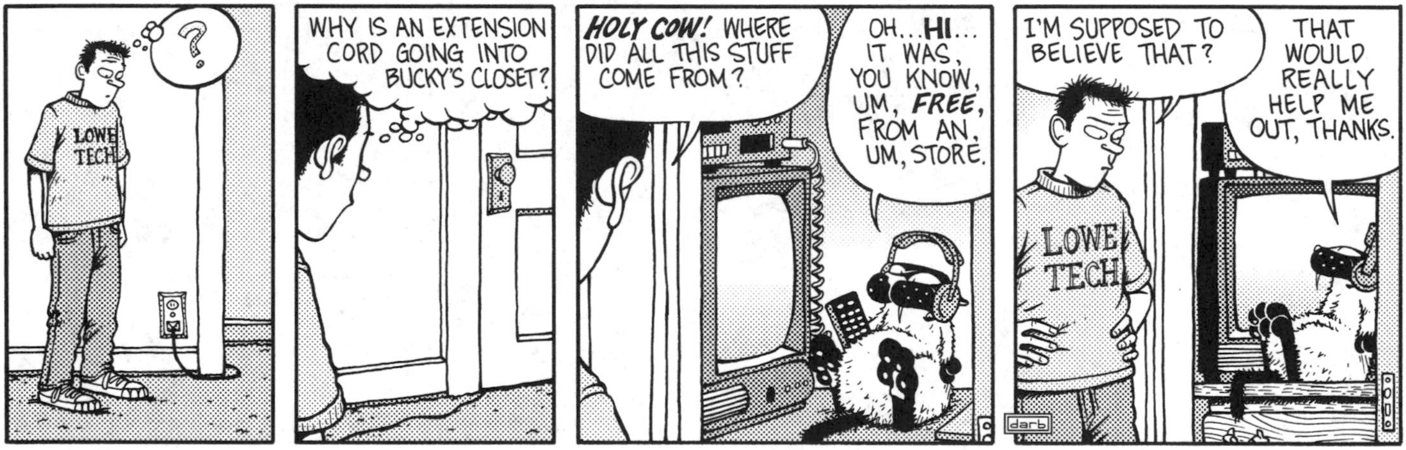
?
WHY IS AN EXTENSION CORD GOING INTO BUCKY'S CLOSET?
HOLY COW! WHERE DID ALL THIS STUFF COME FROM?
OH...**HI**... IT WAS, YOU KNOW, UM, ***FREE***, FROM AN, UM, STORE.
I'M SUPPOSED TO BELIEVE THAT?
THAT WOULD REALLY HELP ME OUT, THANKS.

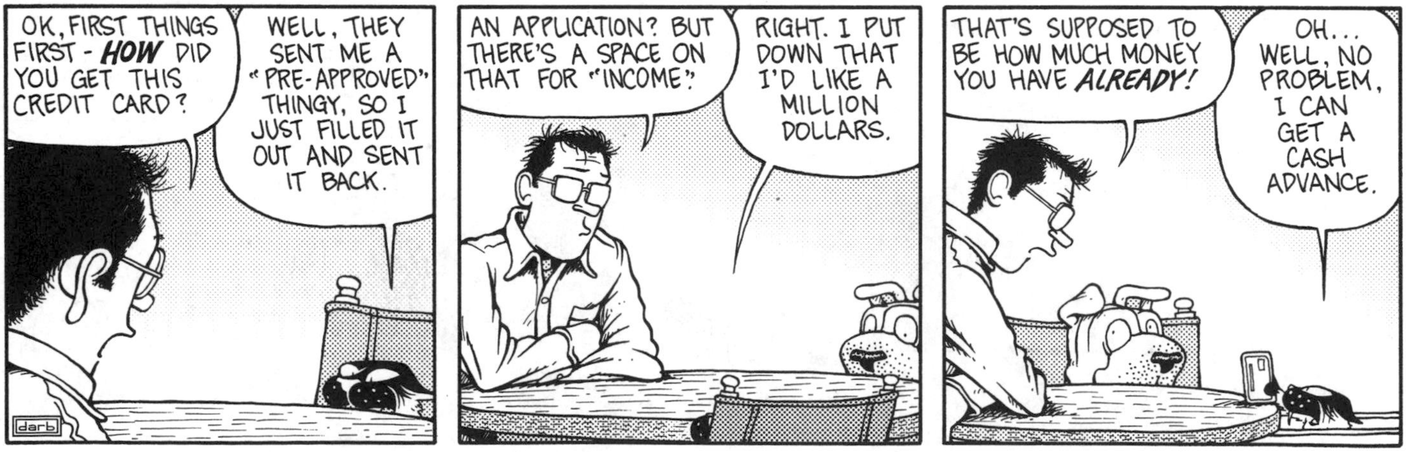
OK, FIRST THINGS FIRST - ***HOW*** DID YOU GET THIS CREDIT CARD?
WELL, THEY SENT ME A "PRE-APPROVED" THINGY, SO I JUST FILLED IT OUT AND SENT IT BACK.
AN APPLICATION? BUT THERE'S A SPACE ON THAT FOR "INCOME"
RIGHT. I PUT DOWN THAT I'D LIKE A MILLION DOLLARS.
THAT'S SUPPOSED TO BE HOW MUCH MONEY YOU HAVE ***ALREADY!***
OH... WELL, NO PROBLEM, I CAN GET A CASH ADVANCE.

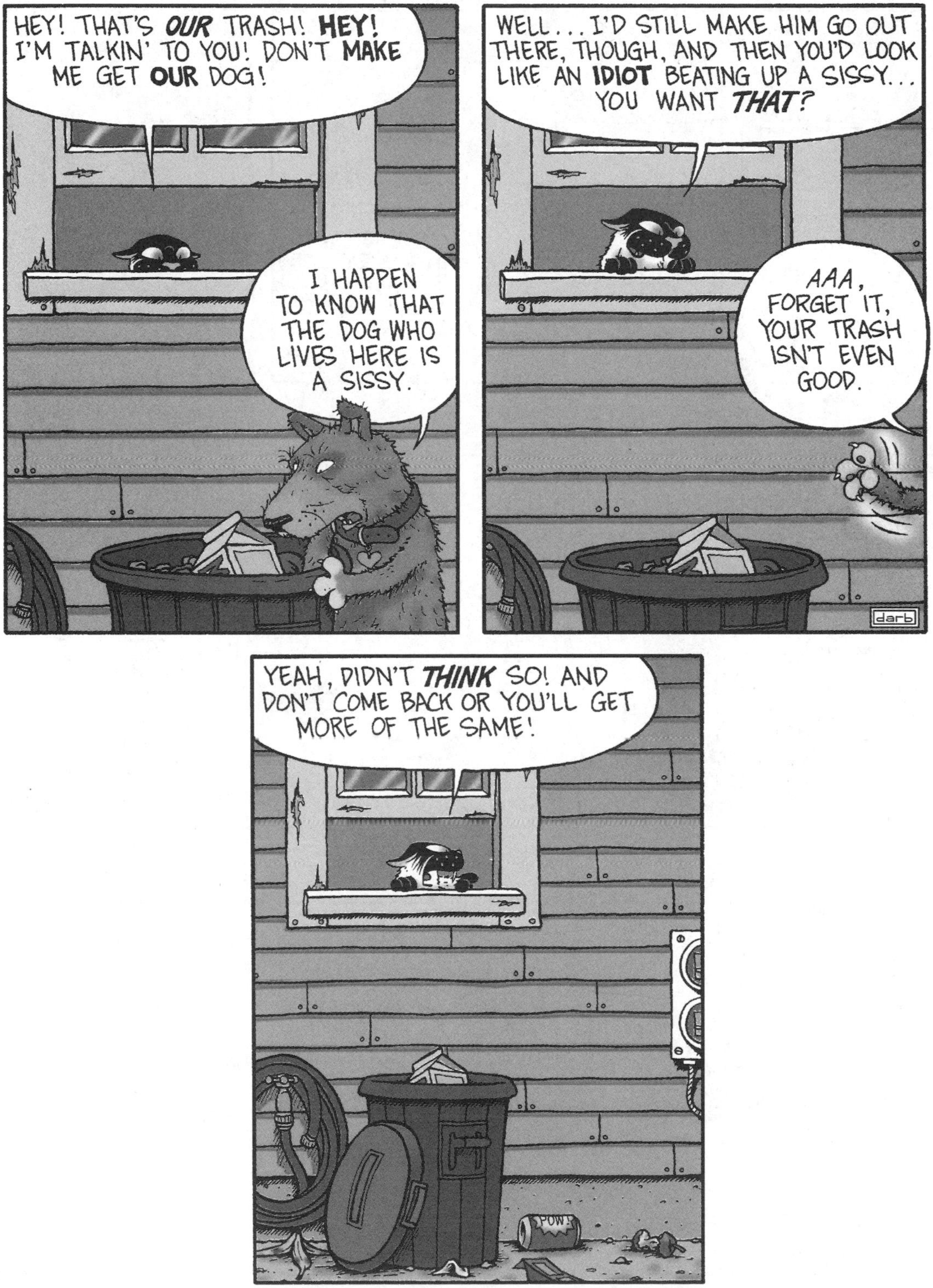

HEY! THAT'S OUR TRASH! HEY! I'M TALKIN' TO YOU! DON'T MAKE ME GET OUR DOG!
I HAPPEN TO KNOW THAT THE DOG WHO LIVES HERE IS A SISSY.
WELL... I'D STILL MAKE HIM GO OUT THERE, THOUGH, AND THEN YOU'D LOOK LIKE AN IDIOT BEATING UP A SISSY... YOU WANT THAT?
AAA, FORGET IT, YOUR TRASH ISN'T EVEN GOOD.
darb
YEAH, DIDN'T THINK SO! AND DON'T COME BACK OR YOU'LL GET MORE OF THE SAME!

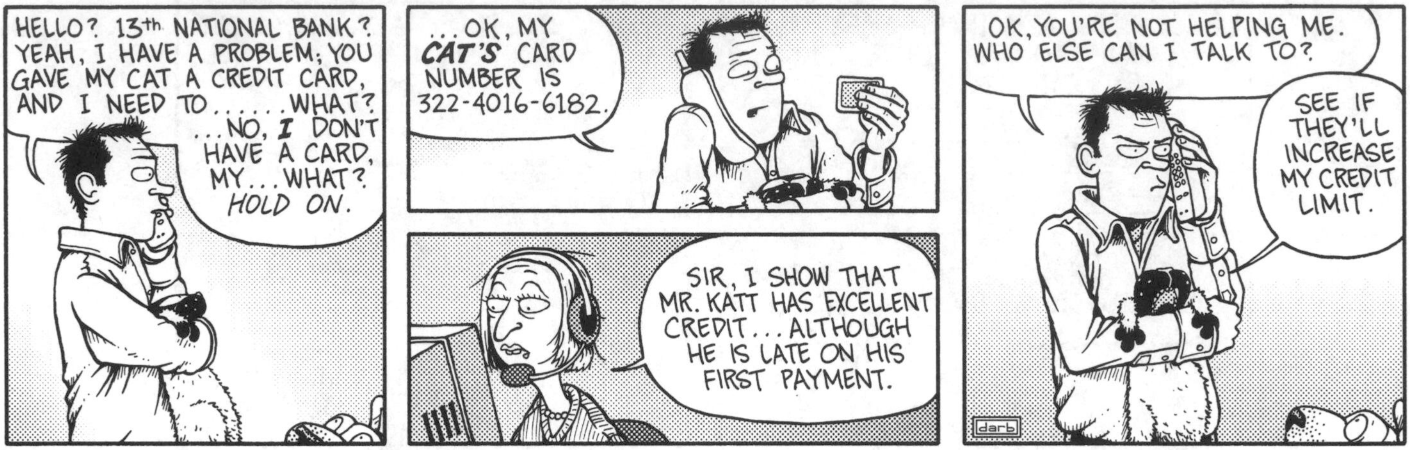
HELLO? 13th NATIONAL BANK? YEAH, I HAVE A PROBLEM; YOU GAVE MY CAT A CREDIT CARD, AND I NEED TO......WHAT? ...NO, I DON'T HAVE A CARD, MY...WHAT? HOLD ON.
...OK, MY CAT'S CARD NUMBER IS 322-4016-6182.
SIR, I SHOW THAT MR. KATT HAS EXCELLENT CREDIT... ALTHOUGH HE IS LATE ON HIS FIRST PAYMENT.
OK, YOU'RE NOT HELPING ME. WHO ELSE CAN I TALK TO?
SEE IF THEY'LL INCREASE MY CREDIT LIMIT.
darb

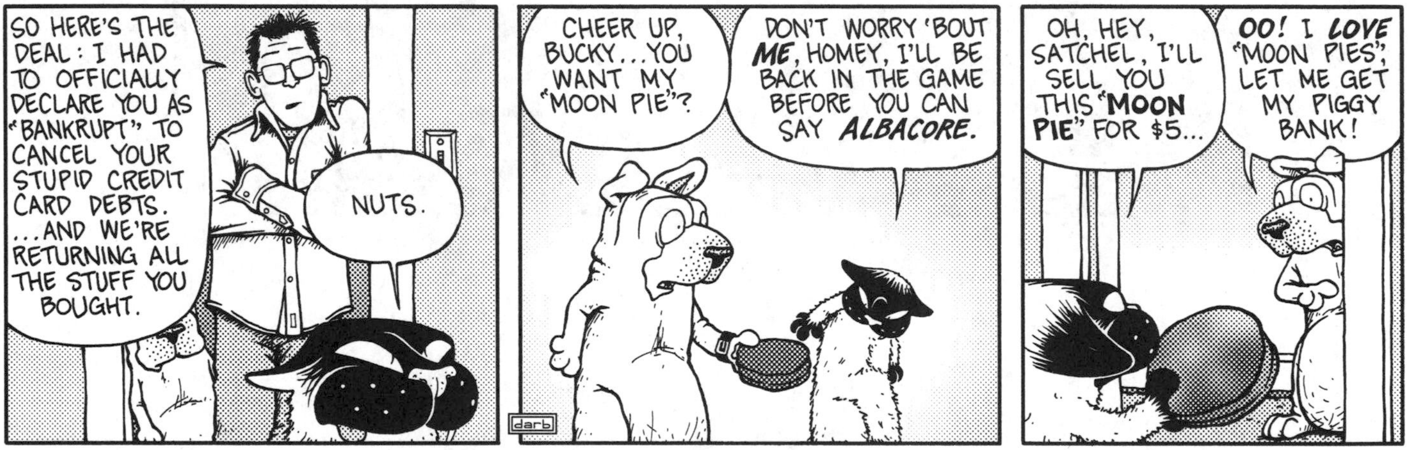
SO HERE'S THE DEAL: I HAD TO OFFICIALLY DECLARE YOU AS "BANKRUPT" TO CANCEL YOUR STUPID CREDIT CARD DEBTS. ...AND WE'RE RETURNING ALL THE STUFF YOU BOUGHT.
NUTS.
CHEER UP, BUCKY...YOU WANT MY "MOON PIE"?
DON'T WORRY 'BOUT ME, HOMEY, I'LL BE BACK IN THE GAME BEFORE YOU CAN SAY ALBACORE.
darb
OH, HEY, SATCHEL, I'LL SELL YOU THIS "MOON PIE" FOR $5...
OO! I LOVE "MOON PIES"; LET ME GET MY PIGGY BANK!

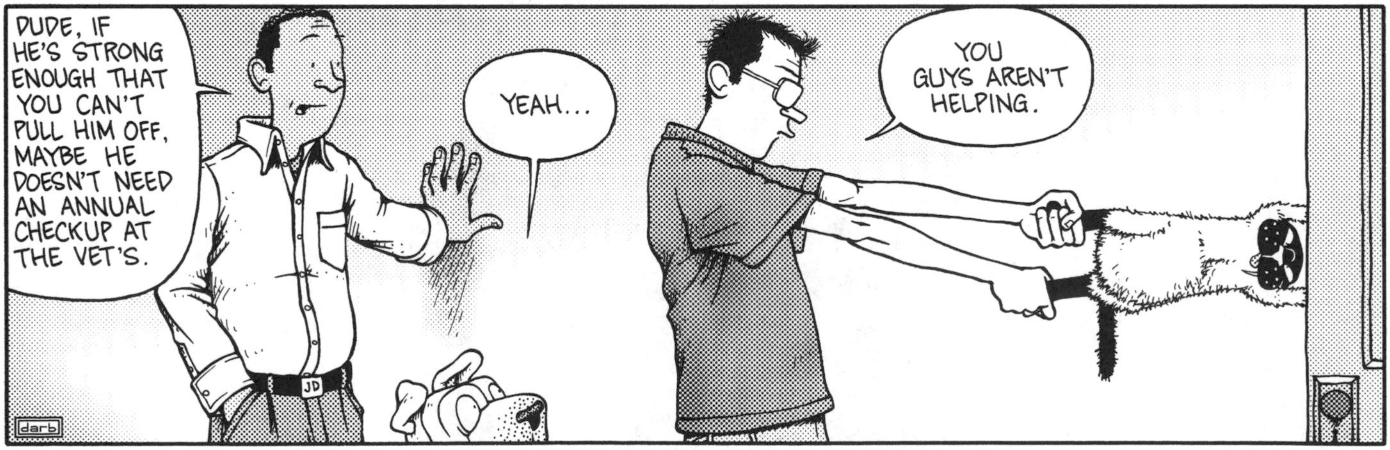
DUDE, IF HE'S STRONG ENOUGH THAT YOU CAN'T PULL HIM OFF, MAYBE HE DOESN'T NEED AN ANNUAL CHECKUP AT THE VET'S.
YEAH...
YOU GUYS AREN'T HELPING.
JD
darb

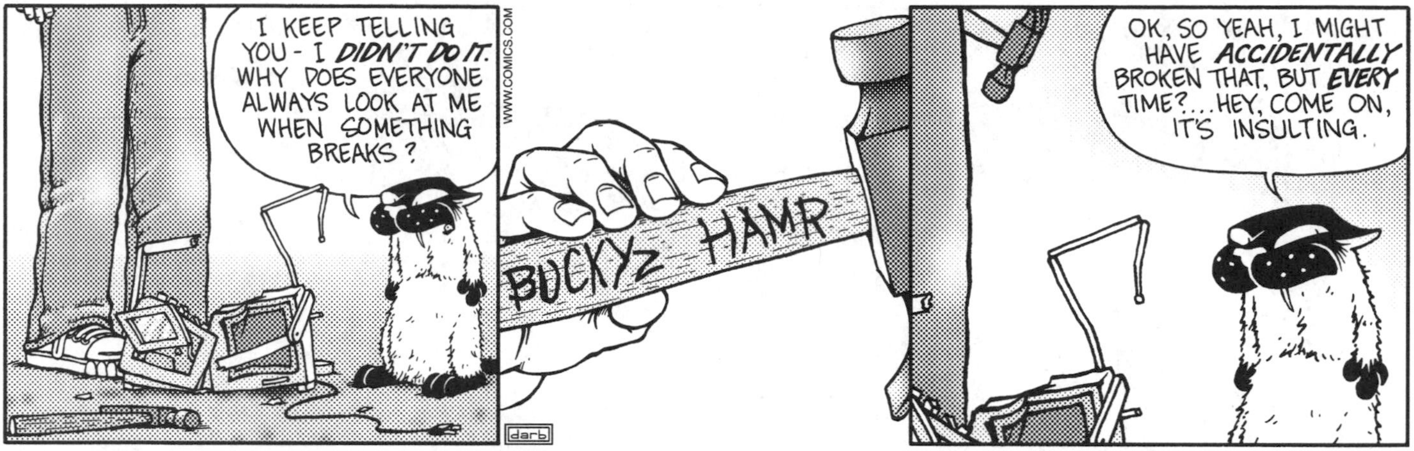
I KEEP TELLING YOU - I *DIDN'T DO IT.* WHY DOES EVERYONE ALWAYS LOOK AT ME WHEN SOMETHING BREAKS?
WWW.COMICS.COM
BUCKYZ HAMR
OK, SO YEAH, I MIGHT HAVE *ACCIDENTALLY* BROKEN THAT, BUT *EVERY* TIME?...HEY, COME ON, IT'S INSULTING.
darb

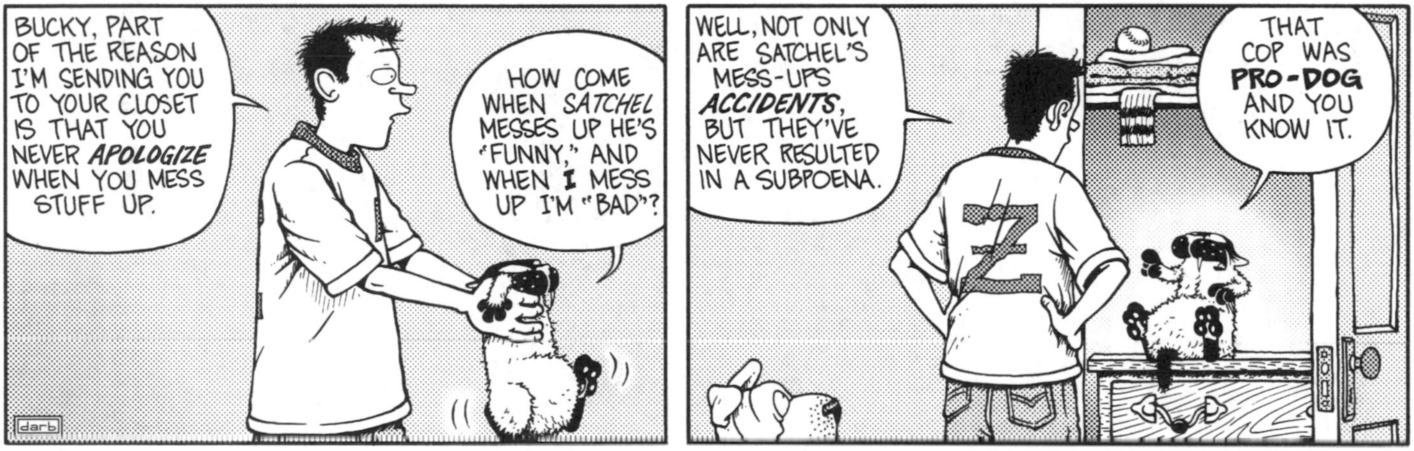
BUCKY, PART OF THE REASON I'M SENDING YOU TO YOUR CLOSET IS THAT YOU NEVER *APOLOGIZE* WHEN YOU MESS STUFF UP.
HOW COME WHEN *SATCHEL* MESSES UP HE'S "FUNNY," AND WHEN **I** MESS UP I'M "BAD"?
darb
WELL, NOT ONLY ARE SATCHEL'S MESS-UPS *ACCIDENTS*, BUT THEY'VE NEVER RESULTED IN A SUBPOENA.
THAT COP WAS **PRO-DOG** AND YOU KNOW IT.

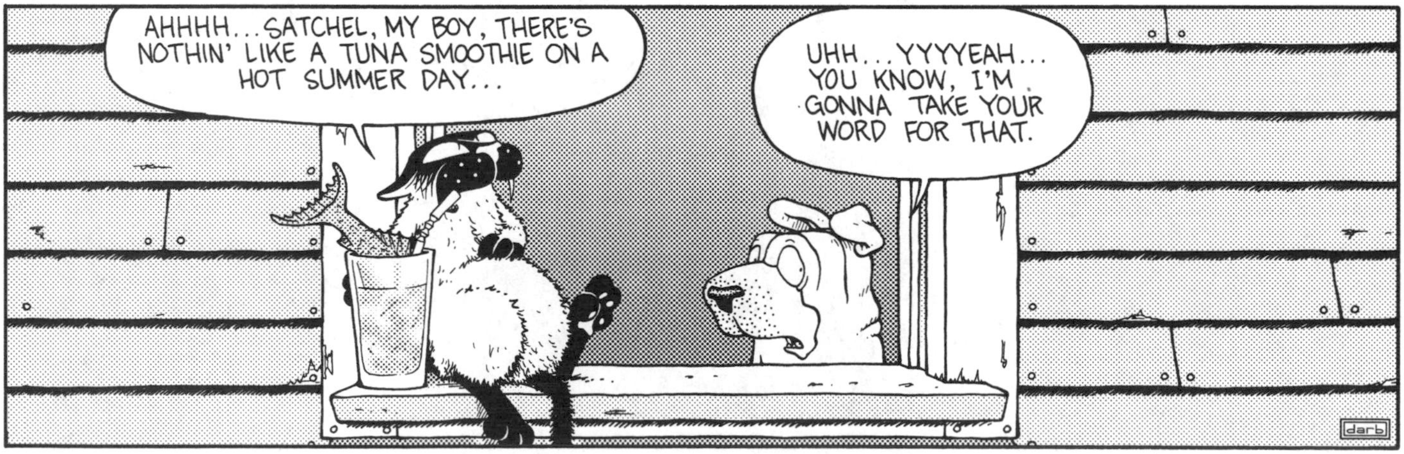
AHHHH...SATCHEL, MY BOY, THERE'S NOTHIN' LIKE A TUNA SMOOTHIE ON A HOT SUMMER DAY...
UHH...YYYYEAH... YOU KNOW, I'M GONNA TAKE YOUR WORD FOR THAT.
darb

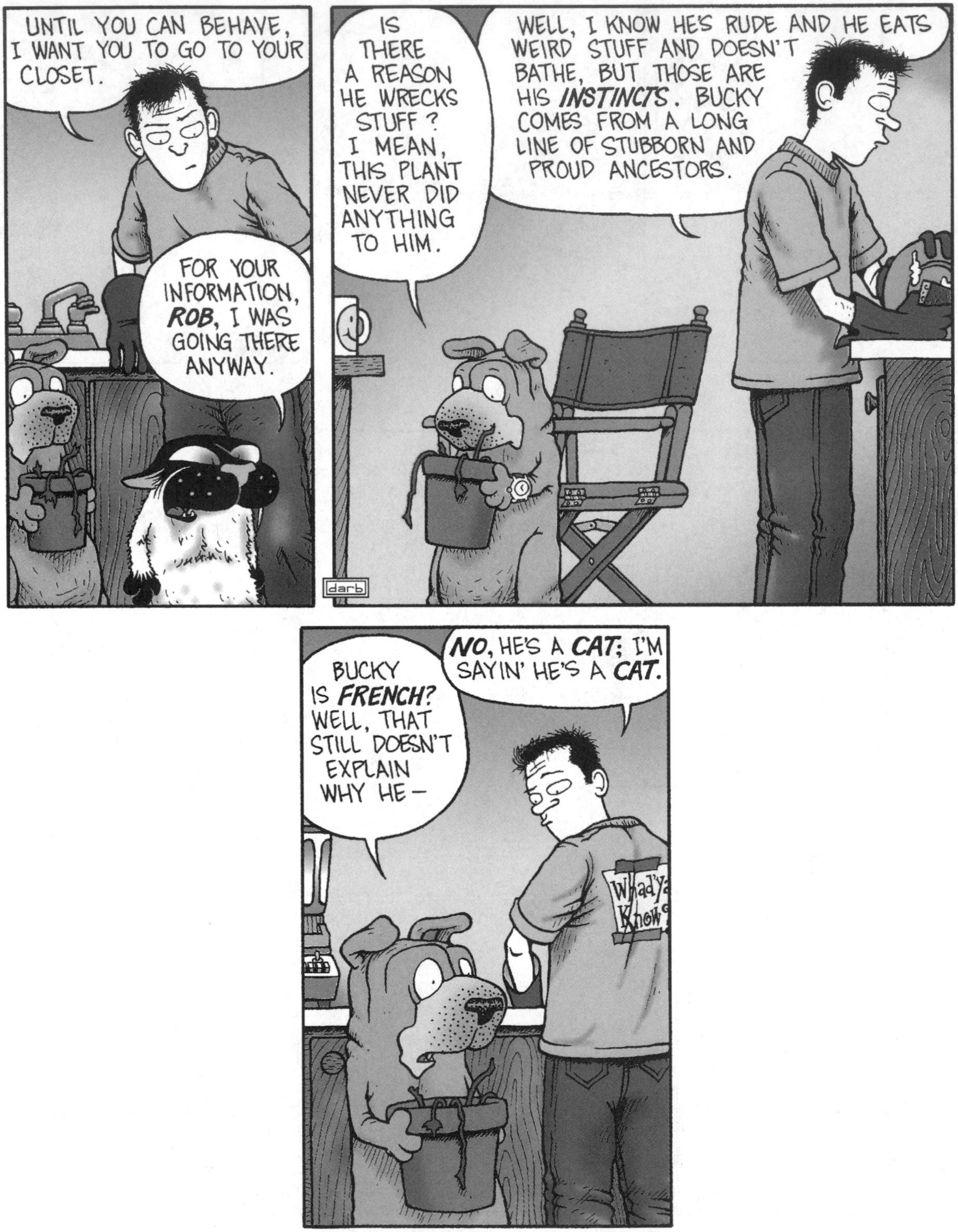
UNTIL YOU CAN BEHAVE, I WANT YOU TO GO TO YOUR CLOSET.
FOR YOUR INFORMATION, **ROB**, I WAS GOING THERE ANYWAY.
IS THERE A REASON HE WRECKS STUFF? I MEAN, THIS PLANT NEVER DID ANYTHING TO HIM.
WELL, I KNOW HE'S RUDE AND HE EATS WEIRD STUFF AND DOESN'T BATHE, BUT THOSE ARE HIS ***INSTINCTS***. BUCKY COMES FROM A LONG LINE OF STUBBORN AND PROUD ANCESTORS.
darb
BUCKY IS ***FRENCH***? WELL, THAT STILL DOESN'T EXPLAIN WHY HE—
NO, HE'S A ***CAT***; I'M SAYIN' HE'S A ***CAT***.

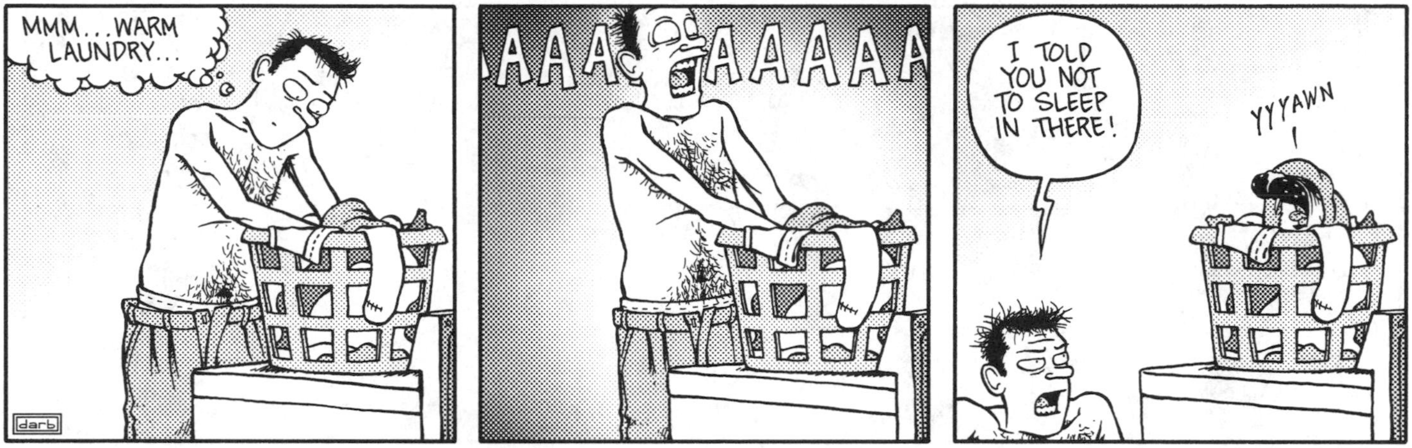
MMM...WARM LAUNDRY...
AAAAAAAAAA
I TOLD YOU NOT TO SLEEP IN THERE!
YYYAWN

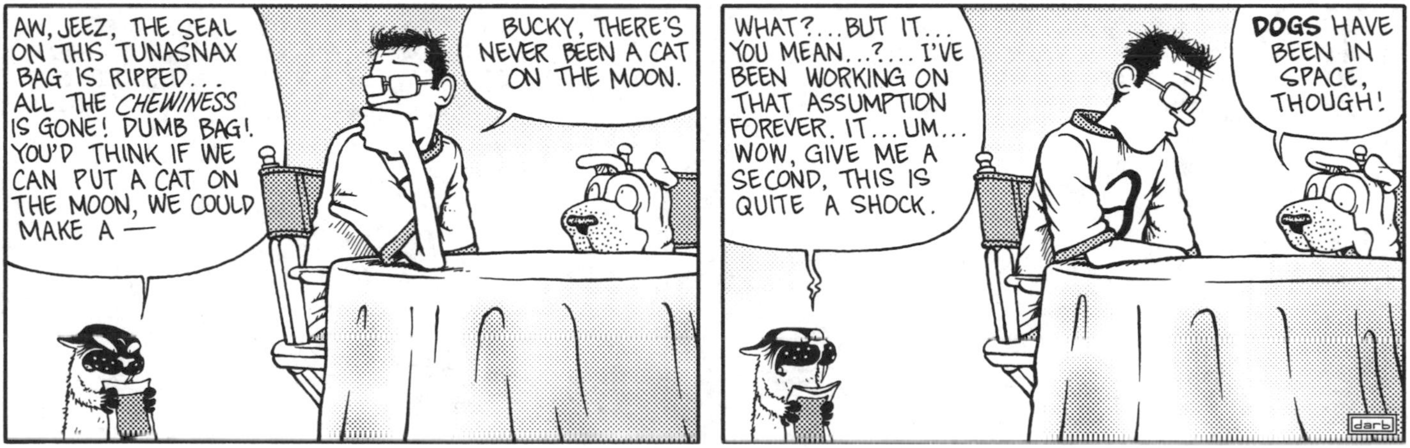
AW, JEEZ, THE SEAL ON THIS TUNASNAX BAG IS RIPPED... ALL THE *CHEWINESS* IS GONE! DUMB BAG! YOU'D THINK IF WE CAN PUT A CAT ON THE MOON, WE COULD MAKE A—
BUCKY, THERE'S NEVER BEEN A CAT ON THE MOON.
WHAT?...BUT IT... YOU MEAN...?... I'VE BEEN WORKING ON THAT ASSUMPTION FOREVER. IT... UM... WOW, GIVE ME A SECOND, THIS IS QUITE A SHOCK.
DOGS HAVE BEEN IN SPACE, THOUGH!

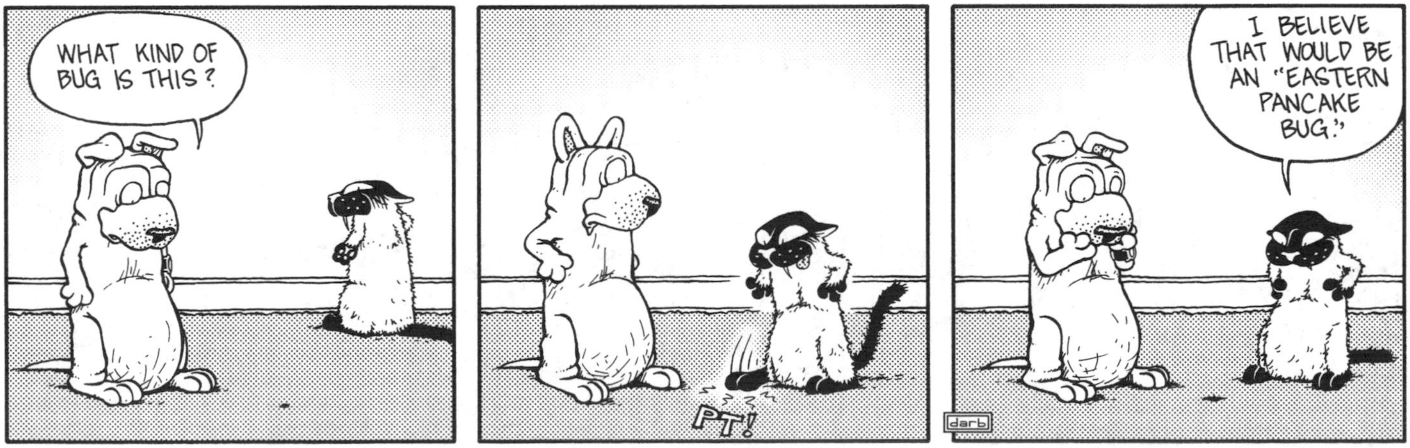
WHAT KIND OF BUG IS THIS?
PT!
I BELIEVE THAT WOULD BE AN "EASTERN PANCAKE BUG."

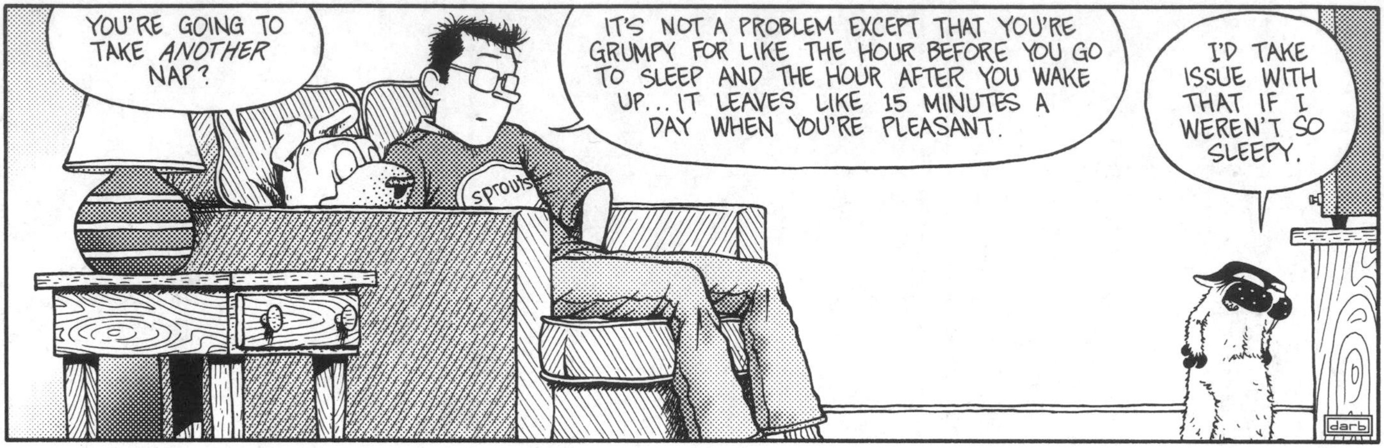
YOU'RE GOING TO TAKE *ANOTHER* NAP?
IT'S NOT A PROBLEM EXCEPT THAT YOU'RE GRUMPY FOR LIKE THE HOUR BEFORE YOU GO TO SLEEP AND THE HOUR AFTER YOU WAKE UP... IT LEAVES LIKE 15 MINUTES A DAY WHEN YOU'RE PLEASANT.
I'D TAKE ISSUE WITH THAT IF I WEREN'T SO SLEEPY.

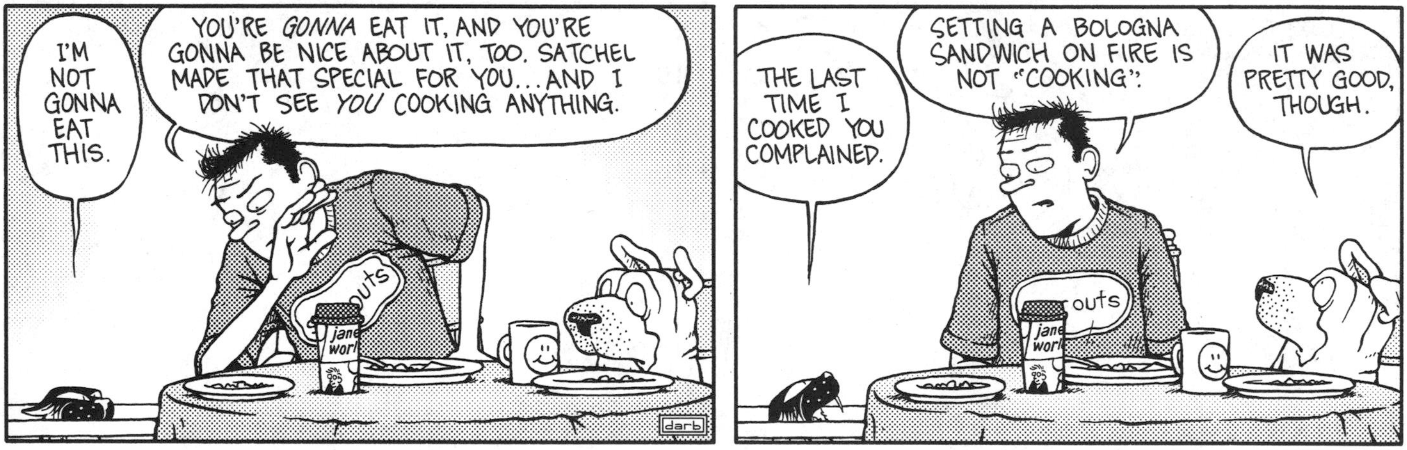
I'M NOT GONNA EAT THIS.
YOU'RE *GONNA* EAT IT, AND YOU'RE GONNA BE NICE ABOUT IT, TOO. SATCHEL MADE THAT SPECIAL FOR YOU... AND I DON'T SEE *YOU* COOKING ANYTHING.
THE LAST TIME I COOKED YOU COMPLAINED.
SETTING A BOLOGNA SANDWICH ON FIRE IS NOT "COOKING".
IT WAS PRETTY GOOD, THOUGH.

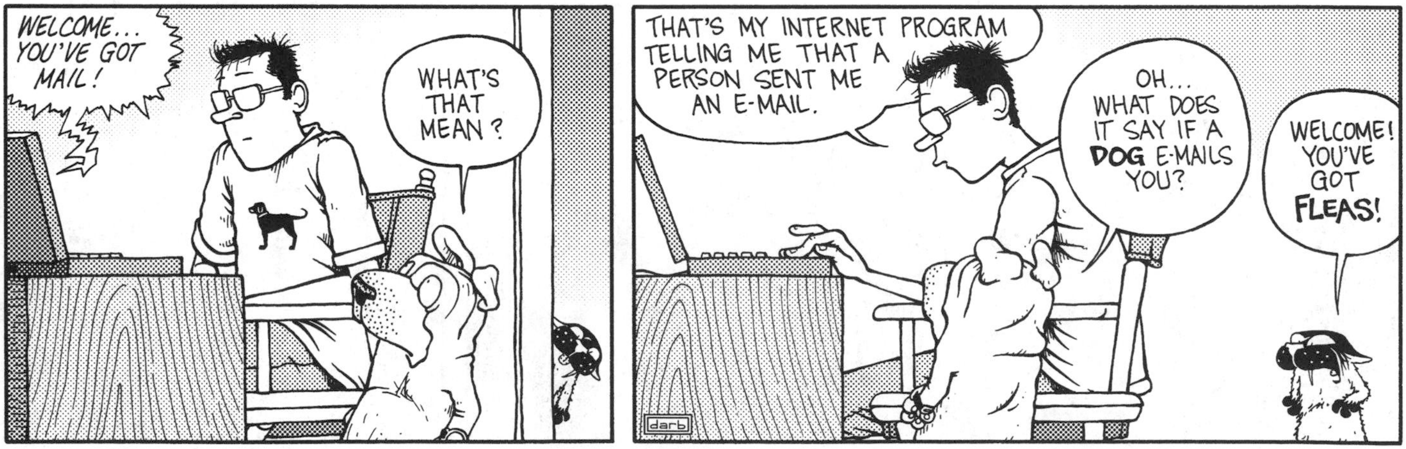
WELCOME... YOU'VE GOT MAIL!
WHAT'S THAT MEAN?
THAT'S MY INTERNET PROGRAM TELLING ME THAT A PERSON SENT ME AN E-MAIL.
OH... WHAT DOES IT SAY IF A **DOG** E-MAILS YOU?
WELCOME! YOU'VE GOT **FLEAS**!

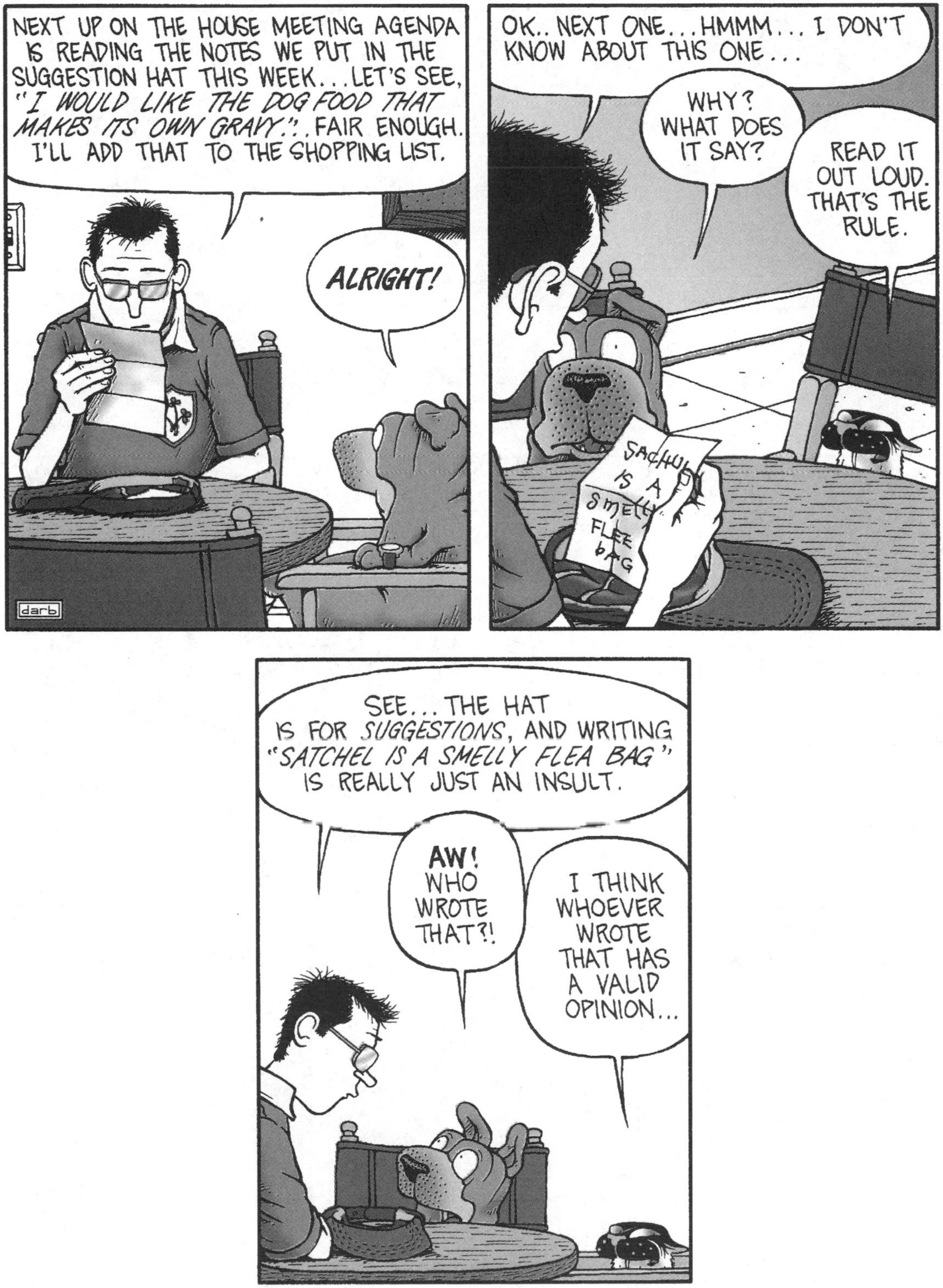
NEXT UP ON THE HOUSE MEETING AGENDA IS READING THE NOTES WE PUT IN THE SUGGESTION HAT THIS WEEK... LET'S SEE, "I WOULD LIKE THE DOG FOOD THAT MAKES ITS OWN GRAVY.". FAIR ENOUGH. I'LL ADD THAT TO THE SHOPPING LIST.
ALRIGHT!
OK.. NEXT ONE... HMMM... I DON'T KNOW ABOUT THIS ONE...
WHY? WHAT DOES IT SAY?
READ IT OUT LOUD. THAT'S THE RULE.
SEE... THE HAT IS FOR SUGGESTIONS, AND WRITING "SATCHEL IS A SMELLY FLEA BAG" IS REALLY JUST AN INSULT.
AW! WHO WROTE THAT?!
I THINK WHOEVER WROTE THAT HAS A VALID OPINION...

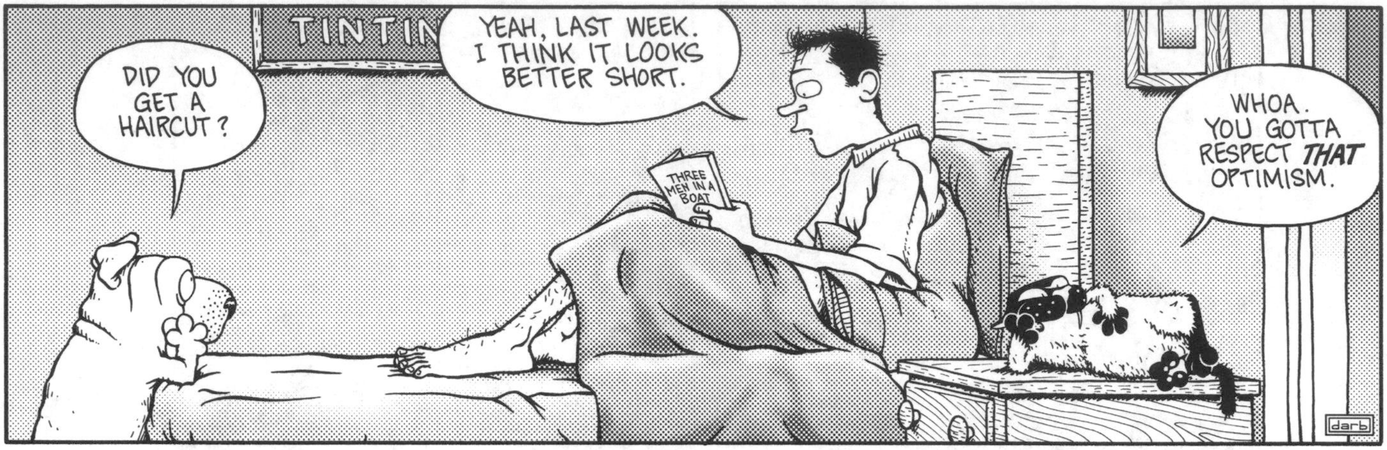
TINTIN
DID YOU GET A HAIRCUT?
YEAH, LAST WEEK. I THINK IT LOOKS BETTER SHORT.
THREE MEN IN A BOAT
WHOA. YOU GOTTA RESPECT **THAT** OPTIMISM.
darb

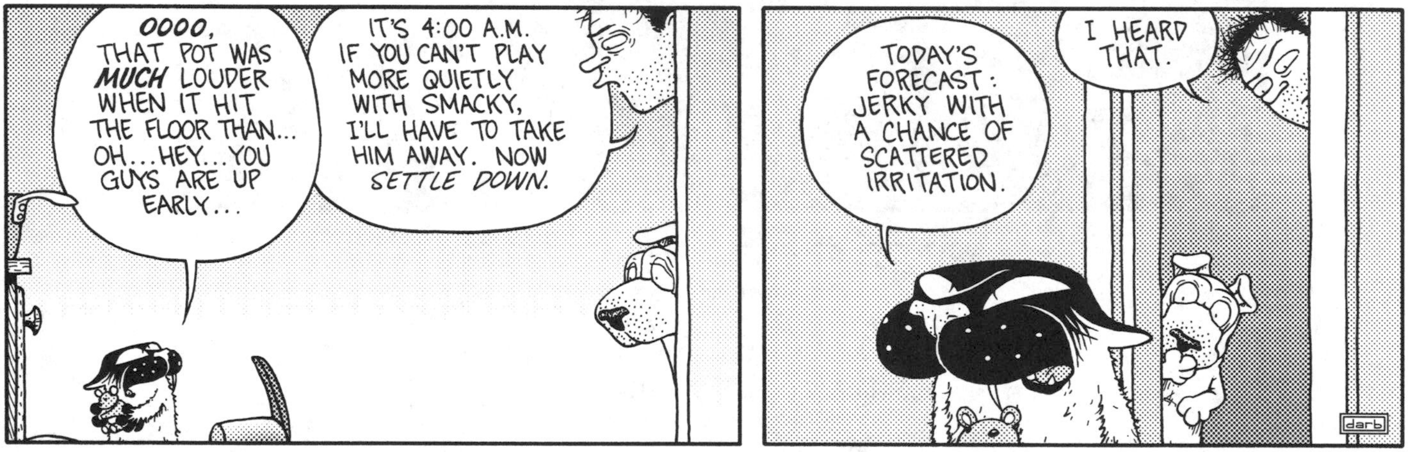
OOOO, THAT POT WAS **MUCH** LOUDER WHEN IT HIT THE FLOOR THAN... OH... HEY... YOU GUYS ARE UP EARLY...
IT'S 4:00 A.M. IF YOU CAN'T PLAY MORE QUIETLY WITH SMACKY, I'LL HAVE TO TAKE HIM AWAY. NOW *SETTLE DOWN.*
TODAY'S FORECAST: JERKY WITH A CHANCE OF SCATTERED IRRITATION.
I HEARD THAT.
darb

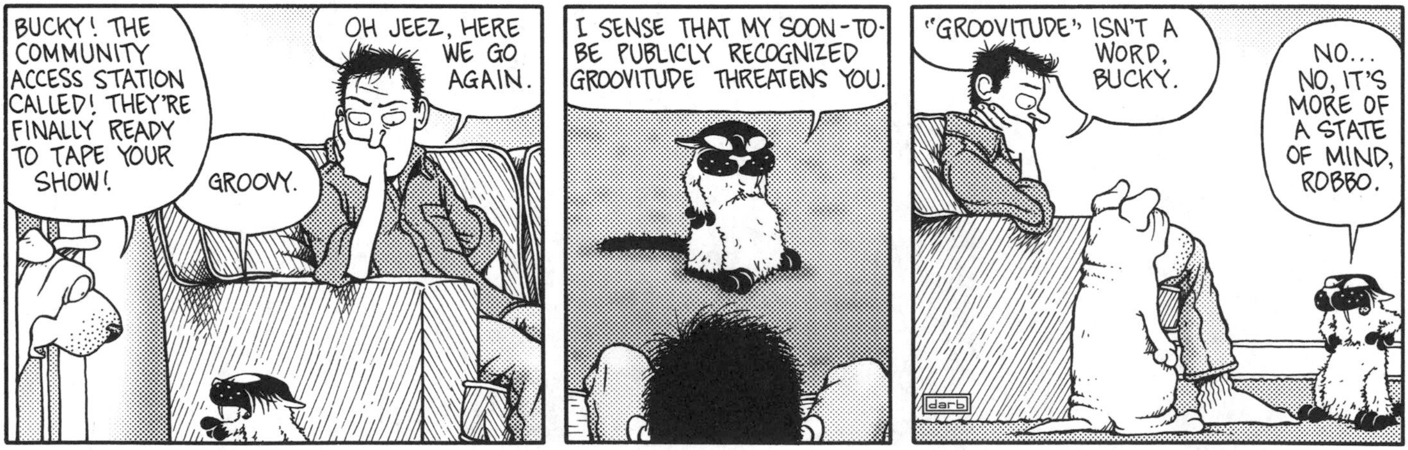
BUCKY! THE COMMUNITY ACCESS STATION CALLED! THEY'RE FINALLY READY TO TAPE YOUR SHOW!
OH JEEZ, HERE WE GO AGAIN.
GROOVY.
I SENSE THAT MY SOON-TO-BE PUBLICLY RECOGNIZED GROOVITUDE THREATENS YOU.
"GROOVITUDE" ISN'T A WORD, BUCKY.
NO... NO, IT'S MORE OF A STATE OF MIND, ROBBO.
darb

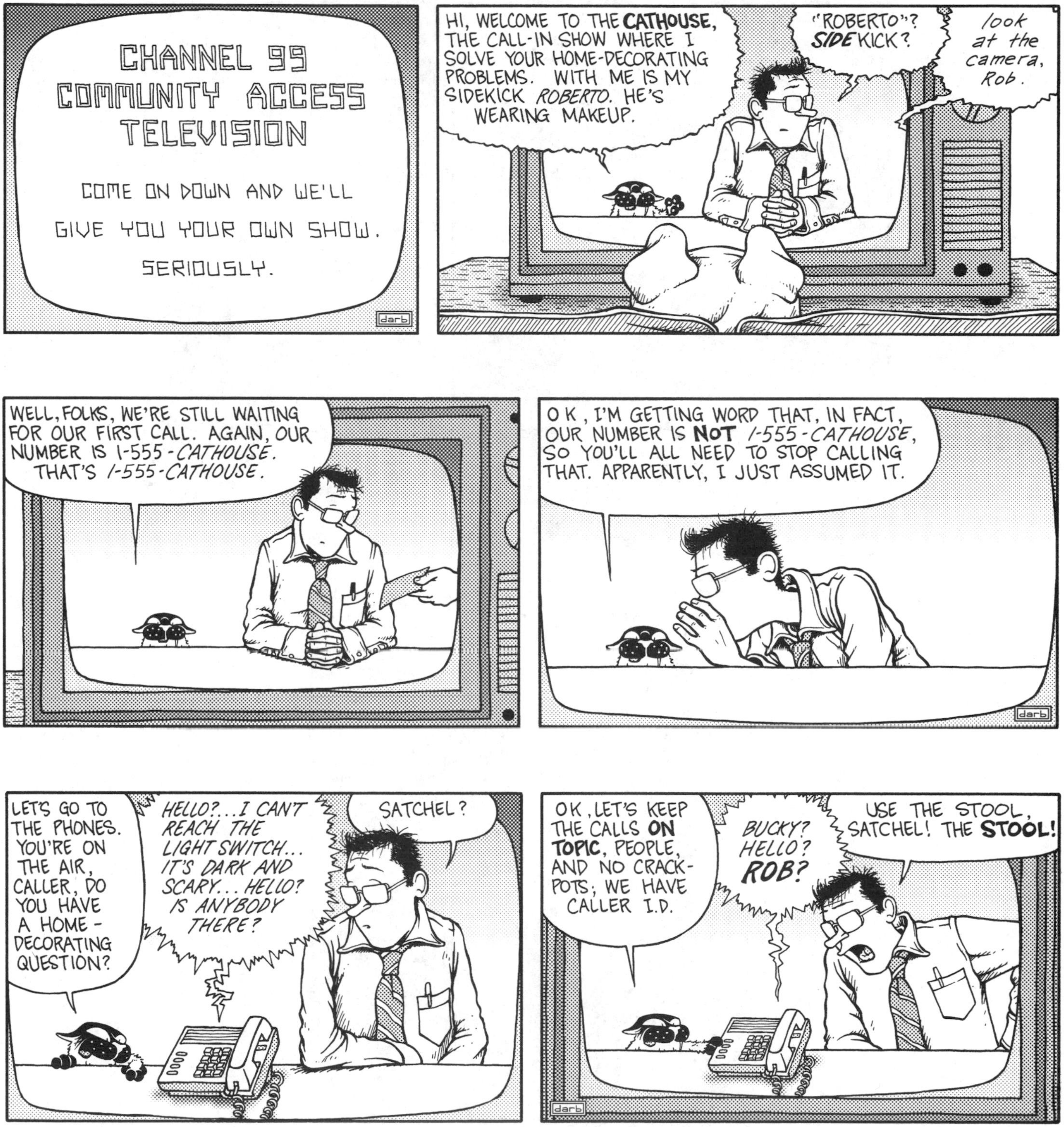
CHANNEL 99
COMMUNITY ACCESS
TELEVISION
COME ON DOWN AND WE'LL GIVE YOU YOUR OWN SHOW. SERIOUSLY.
darb
HI, WELCOME TO THE CATHOUSE, THE CALL-IN SHOW WHERE I SOLVE YOUR HOME-DECORATING PROBLEMS. WITH ME IS MY SIDEKICK ROBERTO. HE'S WEARING MAKEUP.
"ROBERTO"? SIDEKICK?
look at the camera, Rob.
WELL, FOLKS, WE'RE STILL WAITING FOR OUR FIRST CALL. AGAIN, OUR NUMBER IS 1-555-CATHOUSE. THAT'S 1-555-CATHOUSE.
OK, I'M GETTING WORD THAT, IN FACT, OUR NUMBER IS NOT 1-555-CATHOUSE, SO YOU'LL ALL NEED TO STOP CALLING THAT. APPARENTLY, I JUST ASSUMED IT.
darb
LET'S GO TO THE PHONES. YOU'RE ON THE AIR, CALLER. DO YOU HAVE A HOME-DECORATING QUESTION?
HELLO?... I CAN'T REACH THE LIGHT SWITCH... IT'S DARK AND SCARY... HELLO? IS ANYBODY THERE?
SATCHEL?
OK, LET'S KEEP THE CALLS ON TOPIC, PEOPLE, AND NO CRACK-POTS; WE HAVE CALLER I.D.
BUCKY? HELLO? ROB?
USE THE STOOL, SATCHEL! THE STOOL!
darb

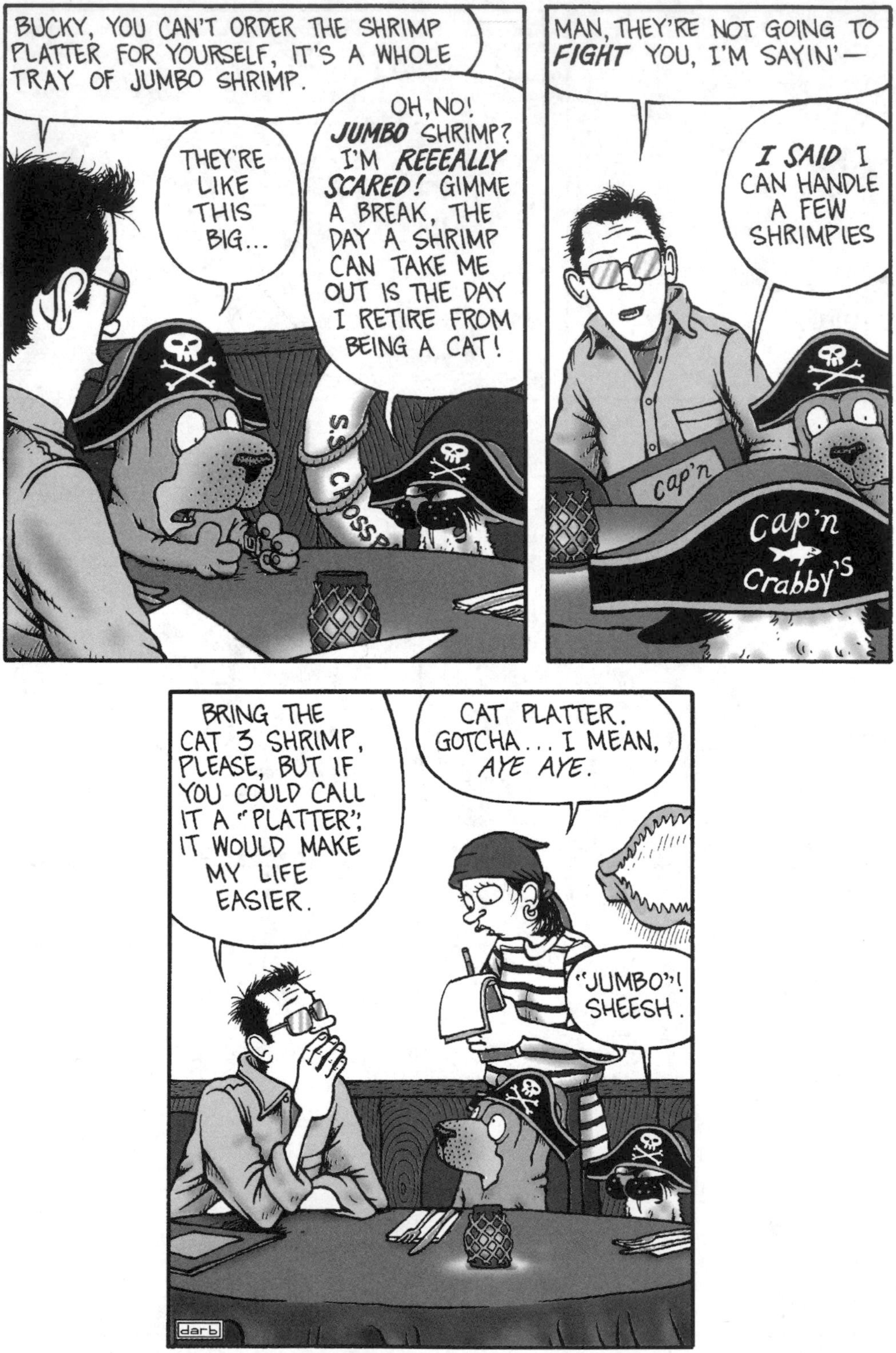
BUCKY, YOU CAN'T ORDER THE SHRIMP PLATTER FOR YOURSELF, IT'S A WHOLE TRAY OF JUMBO SHRIMP.
THEY'RE LIKE THIS BIG...
OH, NO! **JUMBO** SHRIMP? I'M ***REEEALLY SCARED!*** GIMME A BREAK, THE DAY A SHRIMP CAN TAKE ME OUT IS THE DAY I RETIRE FROM BEING A CAT!
S.S.
MAN, THEY'RE NOT GOING TO ***FIGHT*** YOU, I'M SAYIN'—
I SAID I CAN HANDLE A FEW SHRIMPIES
Cap'n
Cap'n Crabby's
BRING THE CAT 3 SHRIMP, PLEASE, BUT IF YOU COULD CALL IT A "PLATTER", IT WOULD MAKE MY LIFE EASIER.
CAT PLATTER. GOTCHA... I MEAN, *AYE AYE*.
"JUMBO"! SHEESH.
darb

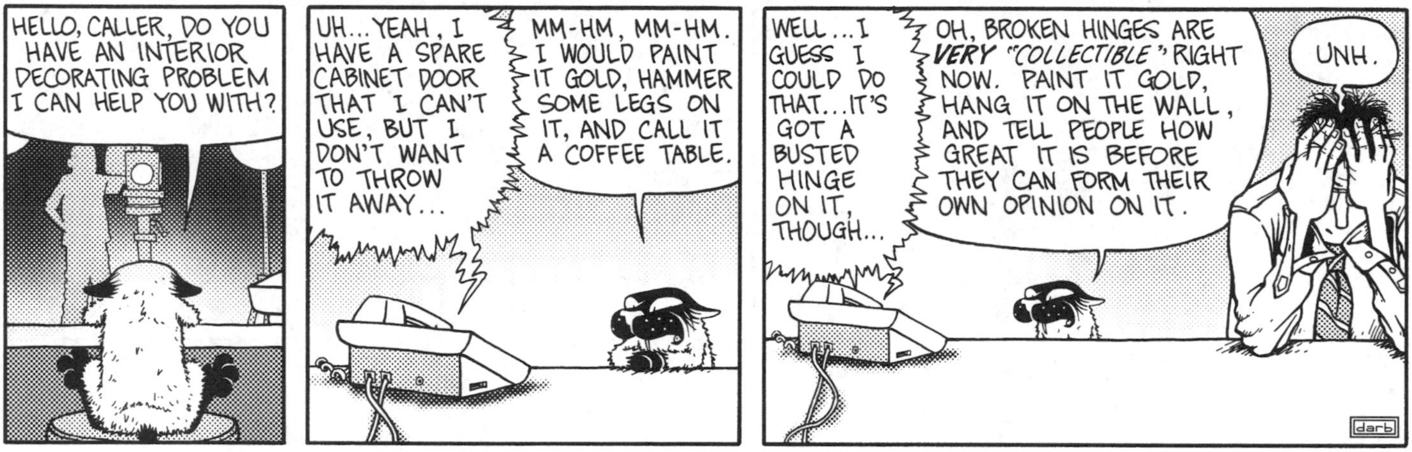
HELLO, CALLER, DO YOU HAVE AN INTERIOR DECORATING PROBLEM I CAN HELP YOU WITH?
UH... YEAH, I HAVE A SPARE CABINET DOOR THAT I CAN'T USE, BUT I DON'T WANT TO THROW IT AWAY...
MM-HM, MM-HM. I WOULD PAINT IT GOLD, HAMMER SOME LEGS ON IT, AND CALL IT A COFFEE TABLE.
WELL... I GUESS I COULD DO THAT... IT'S GOT A BUSTED HINGE ON IT, THOUGH...
OH, BROKEN HINGES ARE *VERY* "COLLECTIBLE" RIGHT NOW. PAINT IT GOLD, HANG IT ON THE WALL, AND TELL PEOPLE HOW GREAT IT IS BEFORE THEY CAN FORM THEIR OWN OPINION ON IT.
UNH.
darb

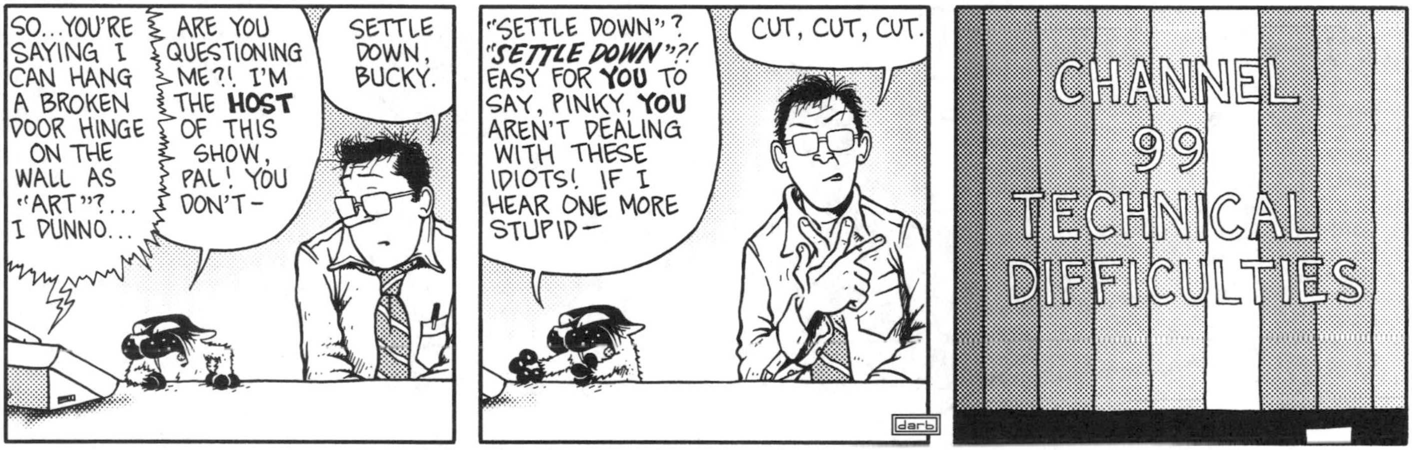
SO... YOU'RE SAYING I CAN HANG A BROKEN DOOR HINGE ON THE WALL AS "ART"?... I DUNNO...
ARE YOU QUESTIONING ME?! I'M THE **HOST** OF THIS SHOW, PAL! YOU DON'T-
SETTLE DOWN, BUCKY.
"SETTLE DOWN"? "***SETTLE DOWN***"?! EASY FOR **YOU** TO SAY, PINKY, **YOU** AREN'T DEALING WITH THESE IDIOTS! IF I HEAR ONE MORE STUPID—
CUT, CUT, CUT.
darb
CHANNEL 99 TECHNICAL DIFFICULTIES

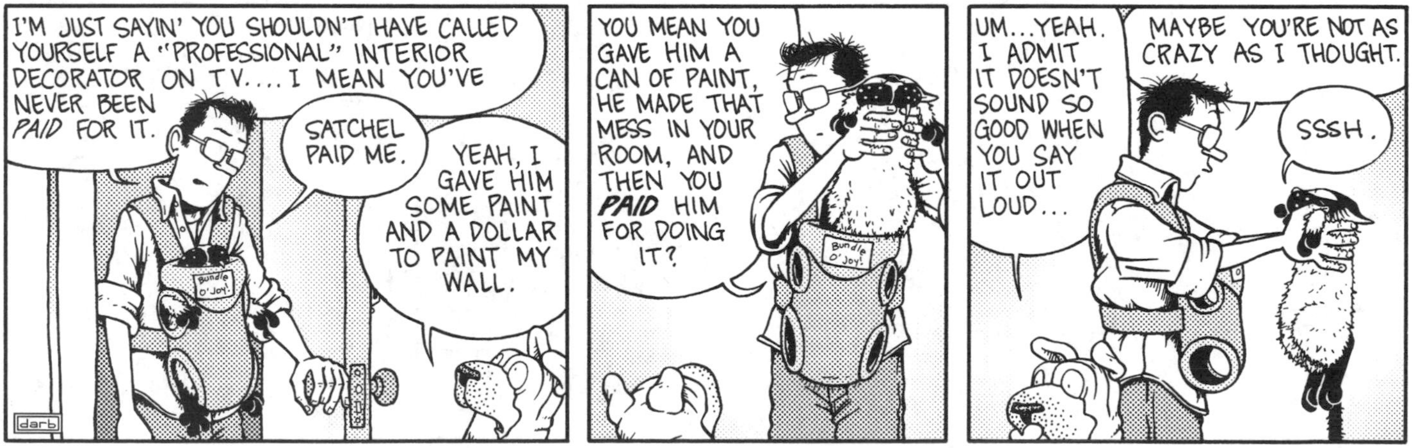
I'M JUST SAYIN' YOU SHOULDN'T HAVE CALLED YOURSELF A "PROFESSIONAL" INTERIOR DECORATOR ON TV.... I MEAN YOU'VE NEVER BEEN *PAID* FOR IT.
SATCHEL PAID ME.
YEAH, I GAVE HIM SOME PAINT AND A DOLLAR TO PAINT MY WALL.
Bundle O' Joy!
darb
YOU MEAN YOU GAVE HIM A CAN OF PAINT, HE MADE THAT MESS IN YOUR ROOM, AND THEN YOU ***PAID*** HIM FOR DOING IT?
Bundle O' Joy!
UM... YEAH. I ADMIT IT DOESN'T SOUND SO GOOD WHEN YOU SAY IT OUT LOUD...
MAYBE YOU'RE NOT AS CRAZY AS I THOUGHT.
SSSH.

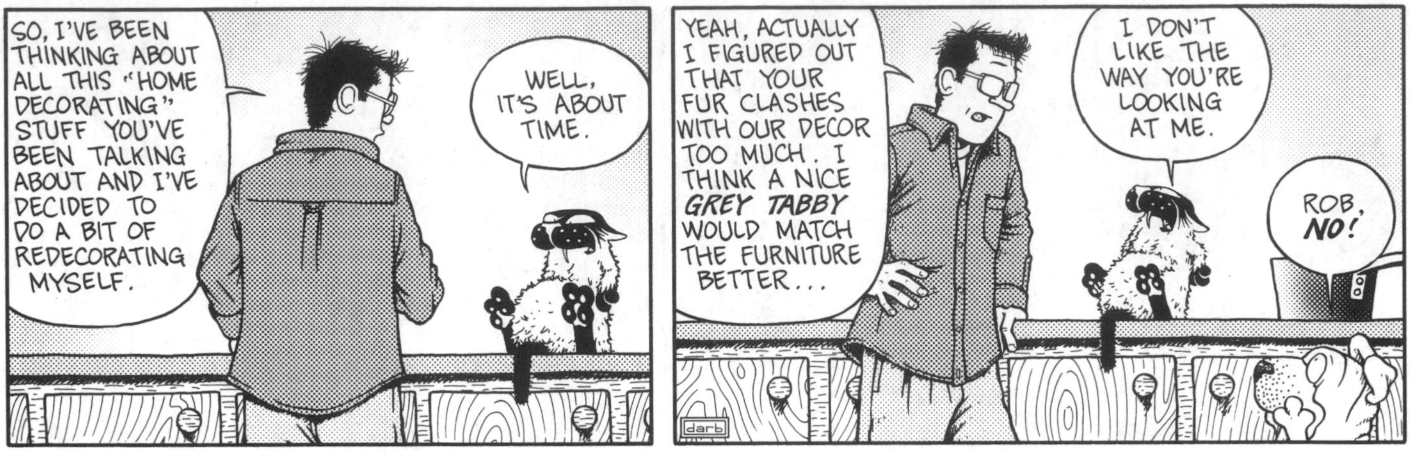
SO, I'VE BEEN THINKING ABOUT ALL THIS "HOME DECORATING" STUFF YOU'VE BEEN TALKING ABOUT AND I'VE DECIDED TO DO A BIT OF REDECORATING MYSELF.
WELL, IT'S ABOUT TIME.
YEAH, ACTUALLY I FIGURED OUT THAT YOUR FUR CLASHES WITH OUR DECOR TOO MUCH. I THINK A NICE GREY TABBY WOULD MATCH THE FURNITURE BETTER...
I DON'T LIKE THE WAY YOU'RE LOOKING AT ME.
ROB, NO!
darb

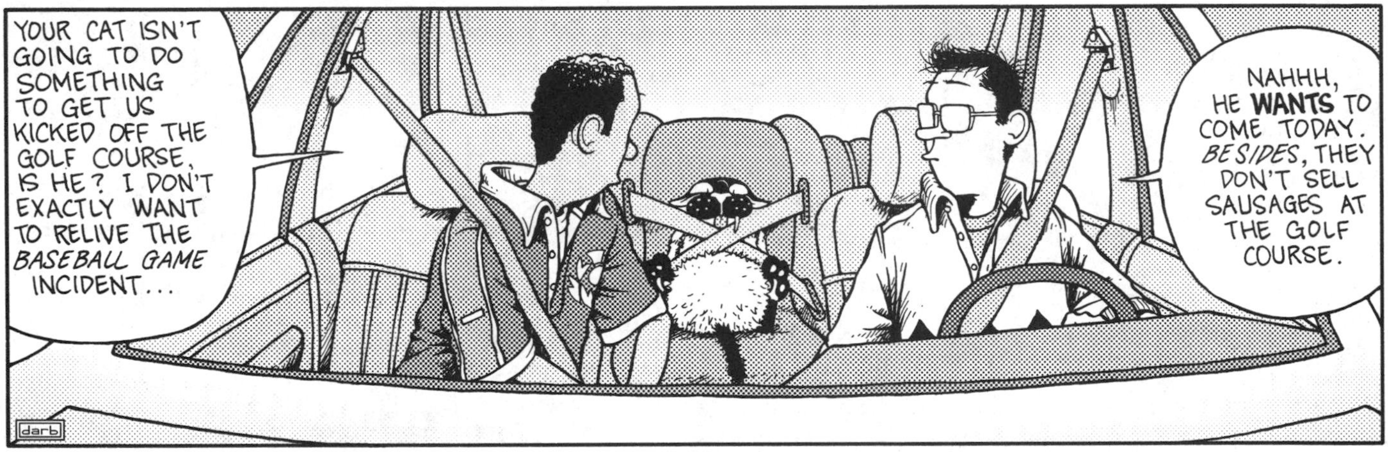
YOUR CAT ISN'T GOING TO DO SOMETHING TO GET US KICKED OFF THE GOLF COURSE, IS HE? I DON'T EXACTLY WANT TO RELIVE THE BASEBALL GAME INCIDENT...
NAHHH, HE WANTS TO COME TODAY. BESIDES, THEY DON'T SELL SAUSAGES AT THE GOLF COURSE.
darb

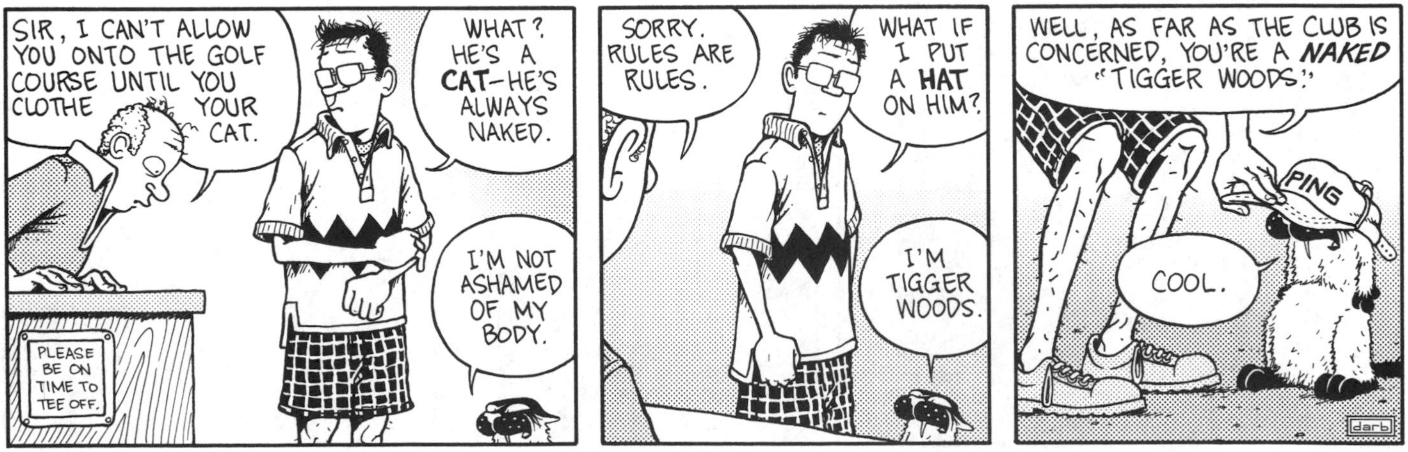
SIR, I CAN'T ALLOW YOU ONTO THE GOLF COURSE UNTIL YOU CLOTHE YOUR CAT.
WHAT? HE'S A CAT—HE'S ALWAYS NAKED.
I'M NOT ASHAMED OF MY BODY.
PLEASE BE ON TIME TO TEE OFF.
SORRY. RULES ARE RULES.
WHAT IF I PUT A HAT ON HIM?
I'M TIGGER WOODS.
WELL, AS FAR AS THE CLUB IS CONCERNED, YOU'RE A NAKED "TIGGER WOODS."
PING
COOL.
darb

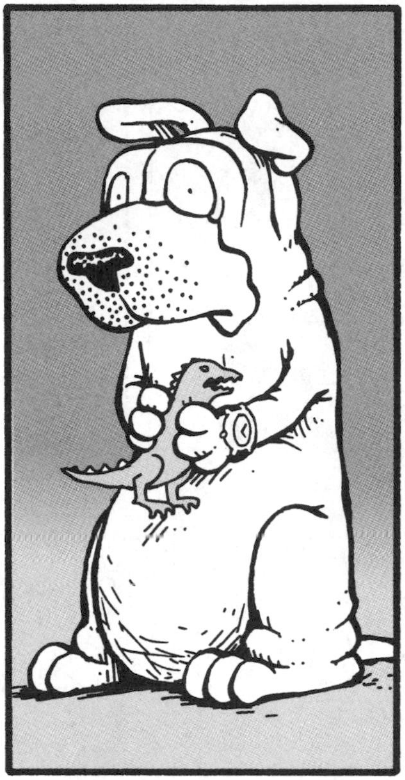

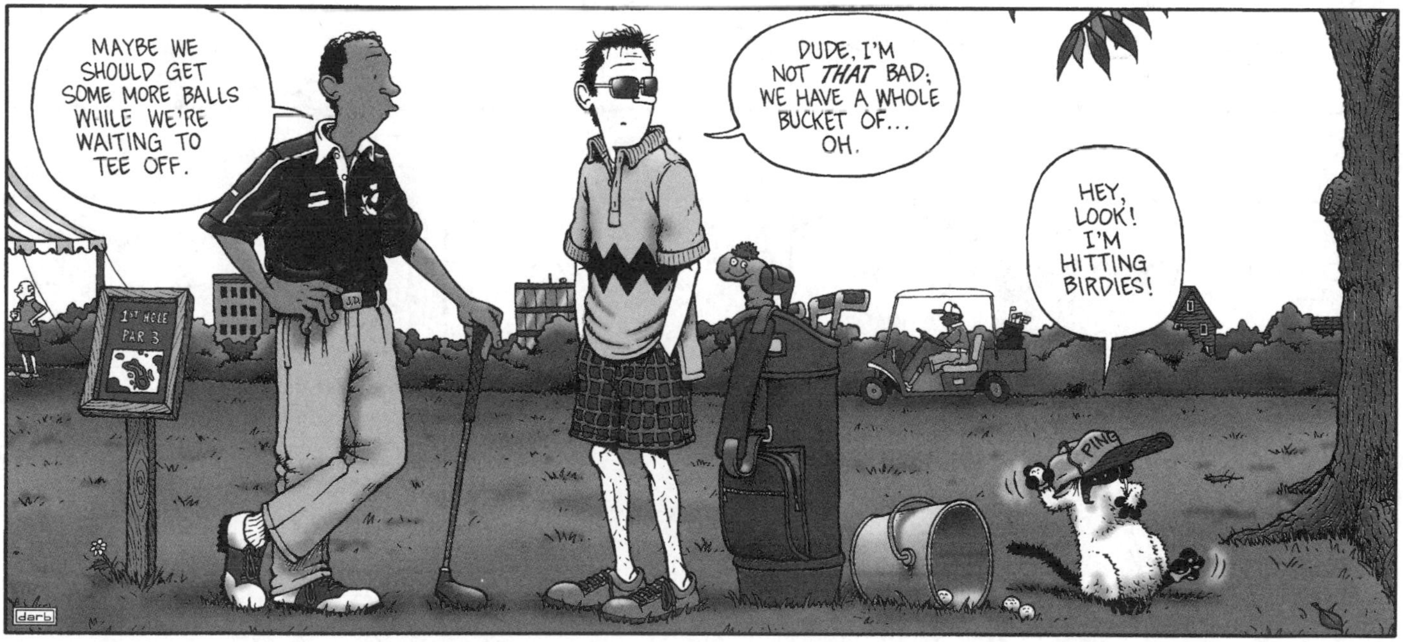
MAYBE WE SHOULD GET SOME MORE BALLS WHILE WE'RE WAITING TO TEE OFF.
DUDE, I'M NOT *THAT* BAD; WE HAVE A WHOLE BUCKET OF... OH.
HEY, LOOK! I'M HITTING BIRDIES!
1ST HOLE PAR 3
PING
darb

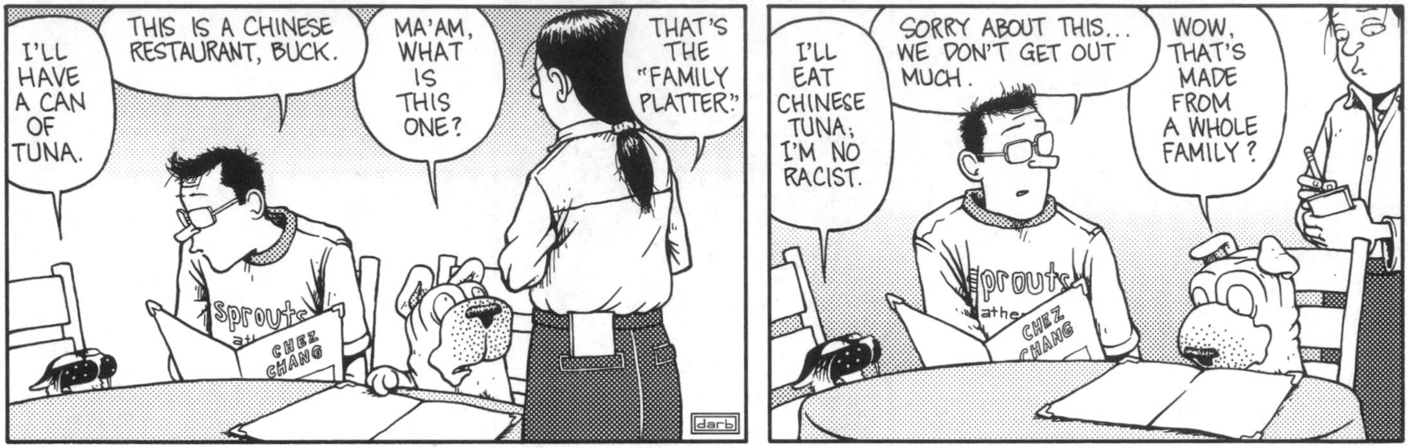
I'LL HAVE A CAN OF TUNA.
THIS IS A CHINESE RESTAURANT, BUCK.
MA'AM, WHAT IS THIS ONE?
THAT'S THE "FAMILY PLATTER."
SPROUTS athens
CHEZ CHANG
I'LL EAT CHINESE TUNA; I'M NO RACIST.
SORRY ABOUT THIS... WE DON'T GET OUT MUCH.
WOW, THAT'S MADE FROM A WHOLE FAMILY?
darb

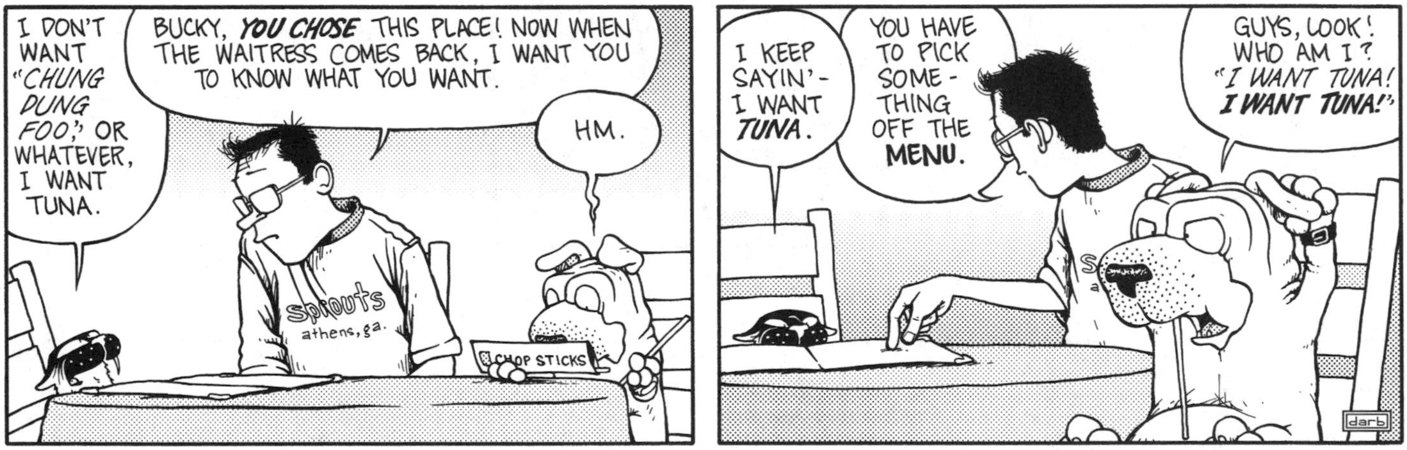
I DON'T WANT "CHUNG DUNG FOO," OR WHATEVER, I WANT TUNA.
BUCKY, YOU CHOSE THIS PLACE! NOW WHEN THE WAITRESS COMES BACK, I WANT YOU TO KNOW WHAT YOU WANT.
HM.
SPROUTS athens, ga.
CHOP STICKS
I KEEP SAYIN' - I WANT TUNA.
YOU HAVE TO PICK SOME-THING OFF THE MENU.
GUYS, LOOK! WHO AM I? "I WANT TUNA! I WANT TUNA!"
darb

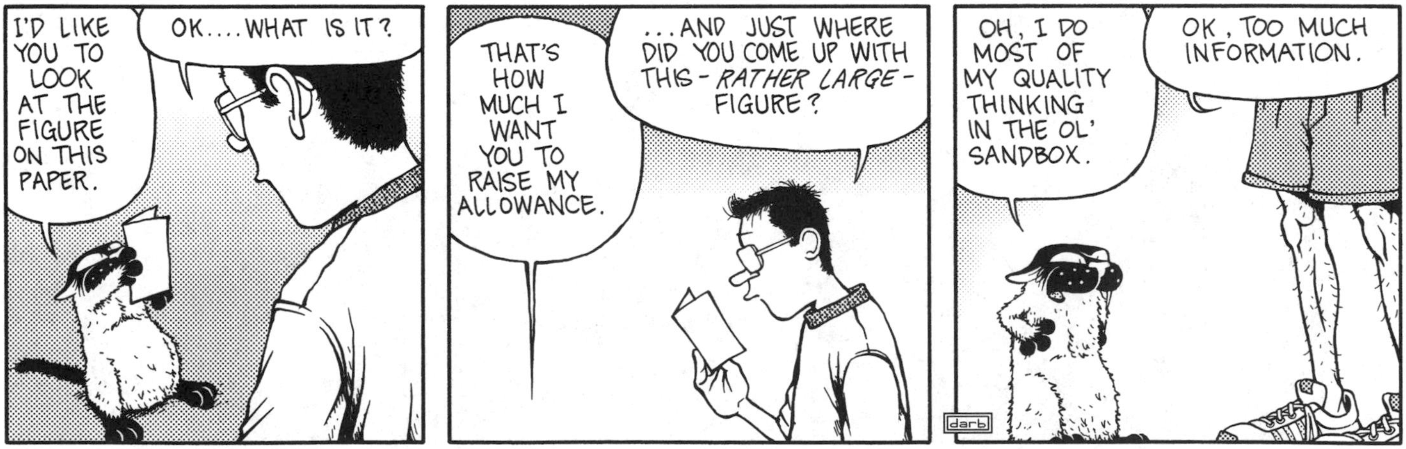
I'D LIKE YOU TO LOOK AT THE FIGURE ON THIS PAPER.
OK.... WHAT IS IT?
THAT'S HOW MUCH I WANT YOU TO RAISE MY ALLOWANCE.
...AND JUST WHERE DID YOU COME UP WITH THIS - RATHER LARGE - FIGURE?
darb
OH, I DO MOST OF MY QUALITY THINKING IN THE OL' SANDBOX.
OK, TOO MUCH INFORMATION.

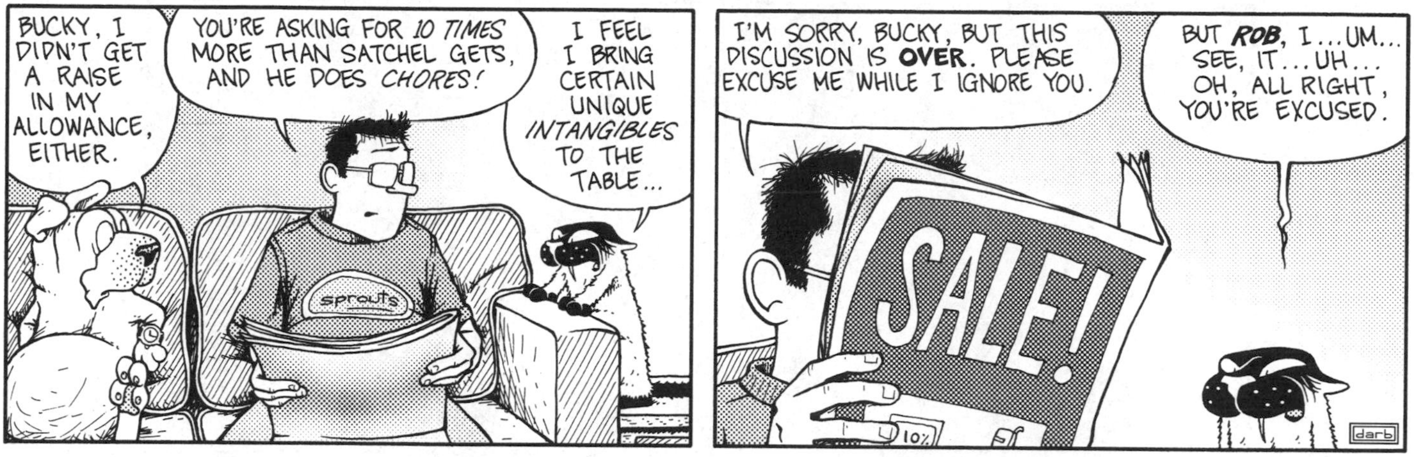
BUCKY, I DIDN'T GET A RAISE IN MY ALLOWANCE, EITHER.
YOU'RE ASKING FOR *10 TIMES* MORE THAN SATCHEL GETS, AND HE DOES *CHORES!*
I FEEL I BRING CERTAIN UNIQUE *INTANGIBLES* TO THE TABLE...
sprouts
I'M SORRY, BUCKY, BUT THIS DISCUSSION IS **OVER**. PLEASE EXCUSE ME WHILE I IGNORE YOU.
BUT ***ROB***, I...UM... SEE, IT...UH... OH, ALL RIGHT, YOU'RE EXCUSED.
SALE!
10%
darb

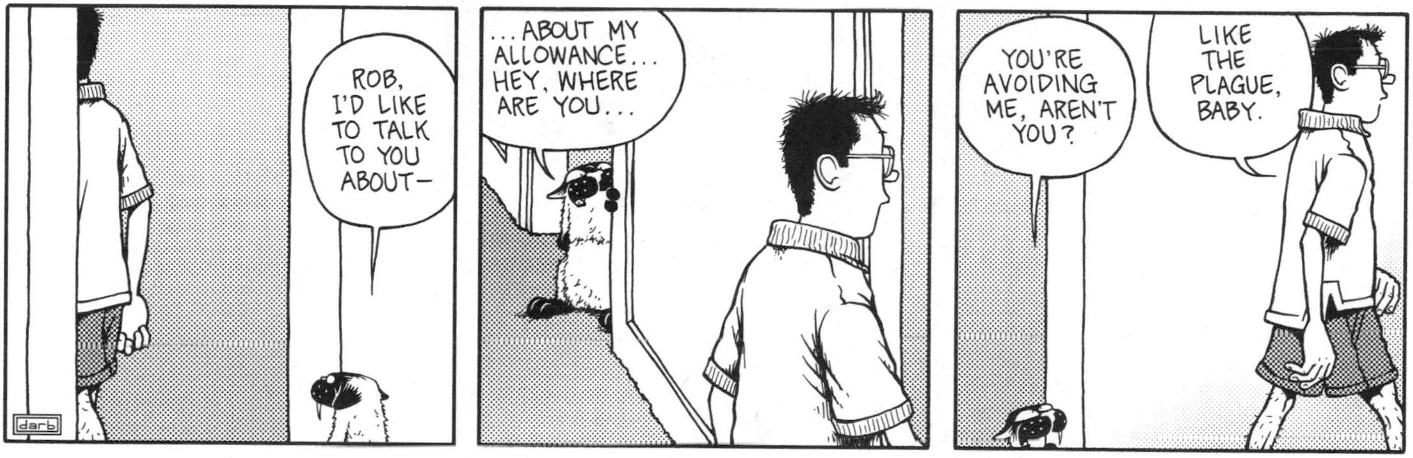
ROB, I'D LIKE TO TALK TO YOU ABOUT—
darb
...ABOUT MY ALLOWANCE... HEY, WHERE ARE YOU...
YOU'RE AVOIDING ME, AREN'T YOU?
LIKE THE PLAGUE, BABY.

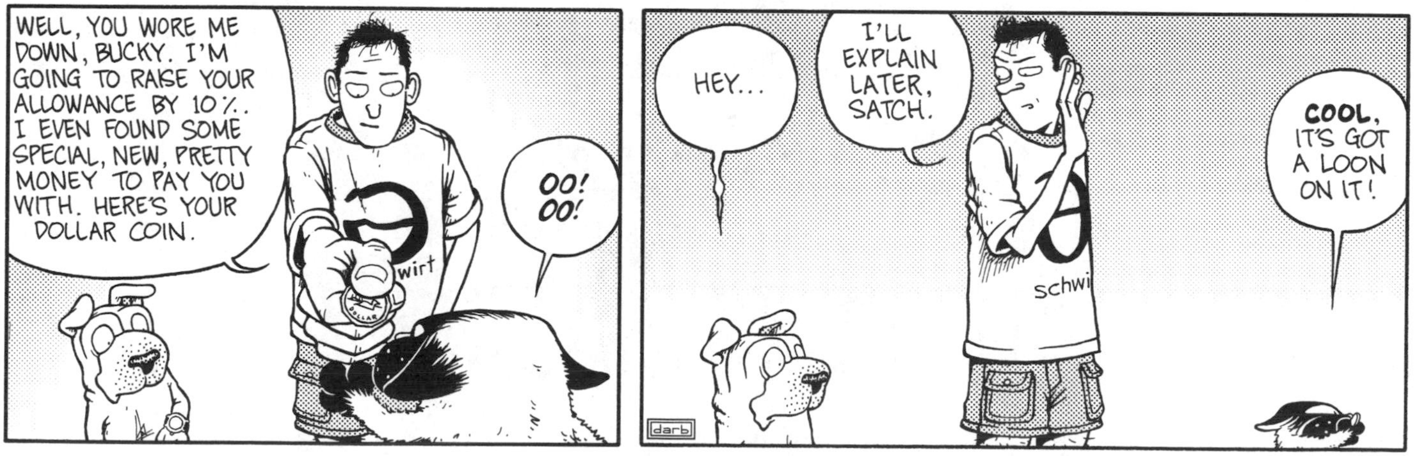
WELL, YOU WORE ME DOWN, BUCKY. I'M GOING TO RAISE YOUR ALLOWANCE BY 10%. I EVEN FOUND SOME SPECIAL, NEW, PRETTY MONEY TO PAY YOU WITH. HERE'S YOUR DOLLAR COIN.
OO! OO!
wirt
HEY...
I'LL EXPLAIN LATER, SATCH.
COOL, IT'S GOT A LOON ON IT!
schwi
darb

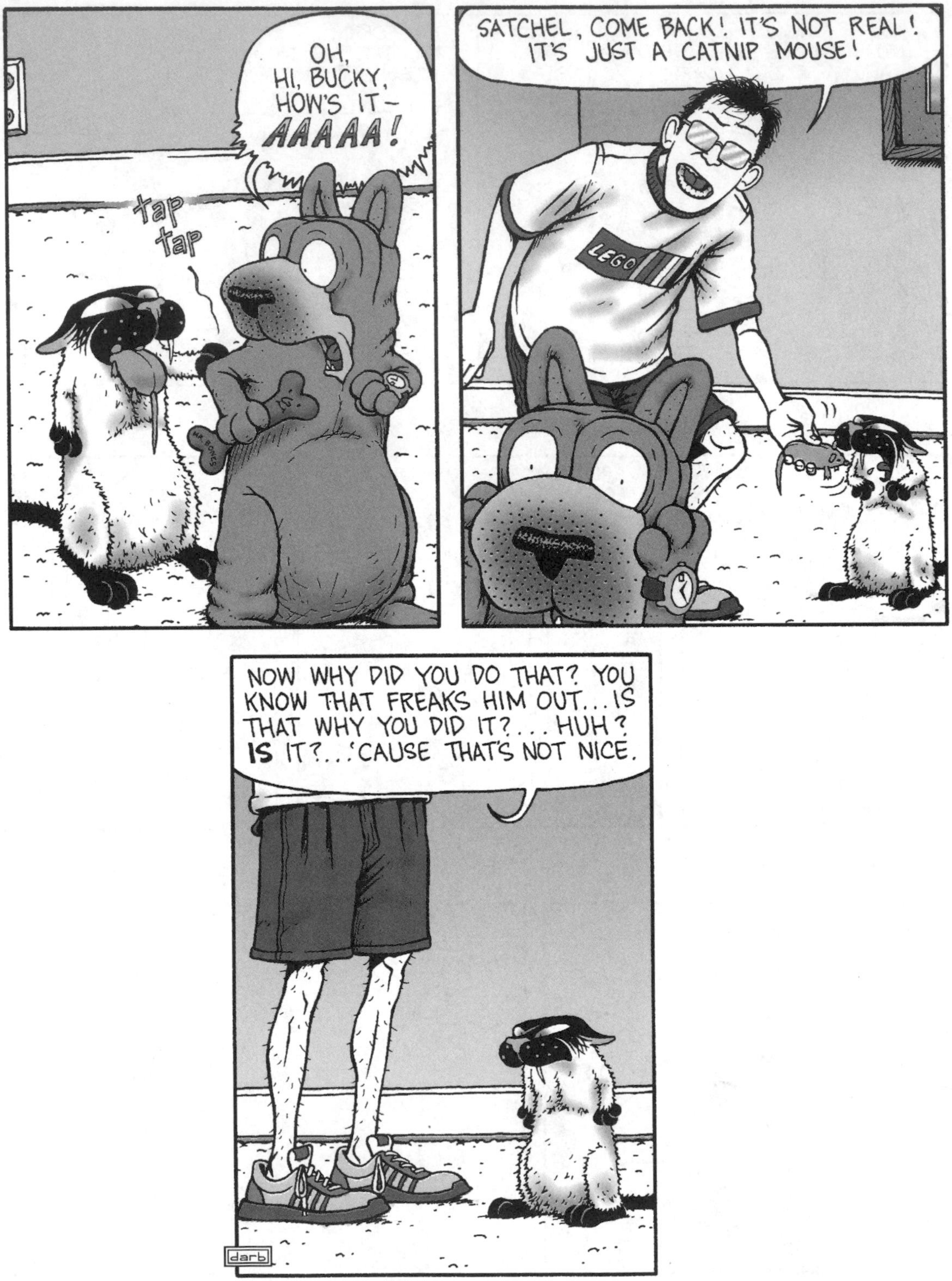
OH, HI, BUCKY, HOW'S IT— AAAAA!
tap tap
SATCHEL, COME BACK! IT'S NOT REAL! IT'S JUST A CATNIP MOUSE!
LEGO
NOW WHY DID YOU DO THAT? YOU KNOW THAT FREAKS HIM OUT... IS THAT WHY YOU DID IT?... HUH? IS IT?...'CAUSE THAT'S NOT NICE.
darb

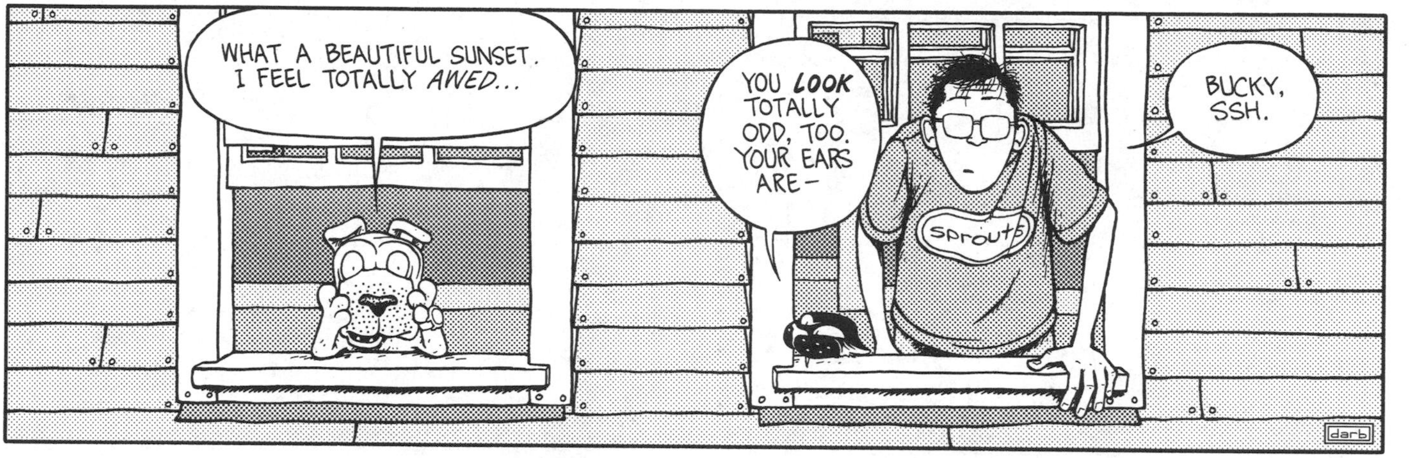
WHAT A BEAUTIFUL SUNSET. I FEEL TOTALLY *AWED...*
YOU ***LOOK*** TOTALLY ODD, TOO. YOUR EARS ARE–
BUCKY, SSH.
sprouts
darb

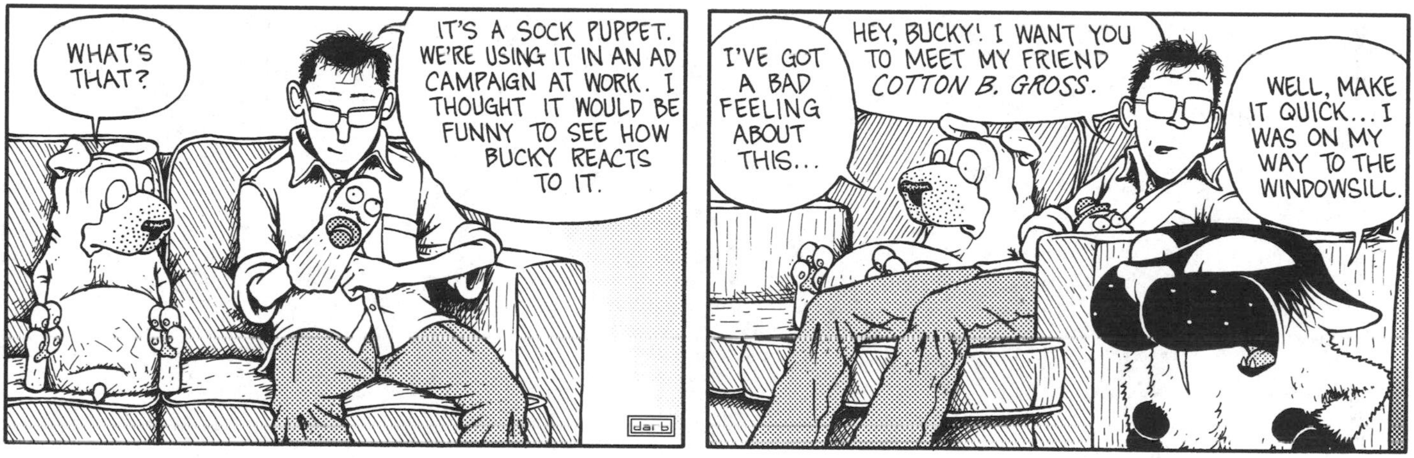
WHAT'S THAT?
IT'S A SOCK PUPPET. WE'RE USING IT IN AN AD CAMPAIGN AT WORK. I THOUGHT IT WOULD BE FUNNY TO SEE HOW BUCKY REACTS TO IT.
darb
I'VE GOT A BAD FEELING ABOUT THIS...
HEY, BUCKY! I WANT YOU TO MEET MY FRIEND *COTTON B. GROSS.*
WELL, MAKE IT QUICK... I WAS ON MY WAY TO THE WINDOWSILL.

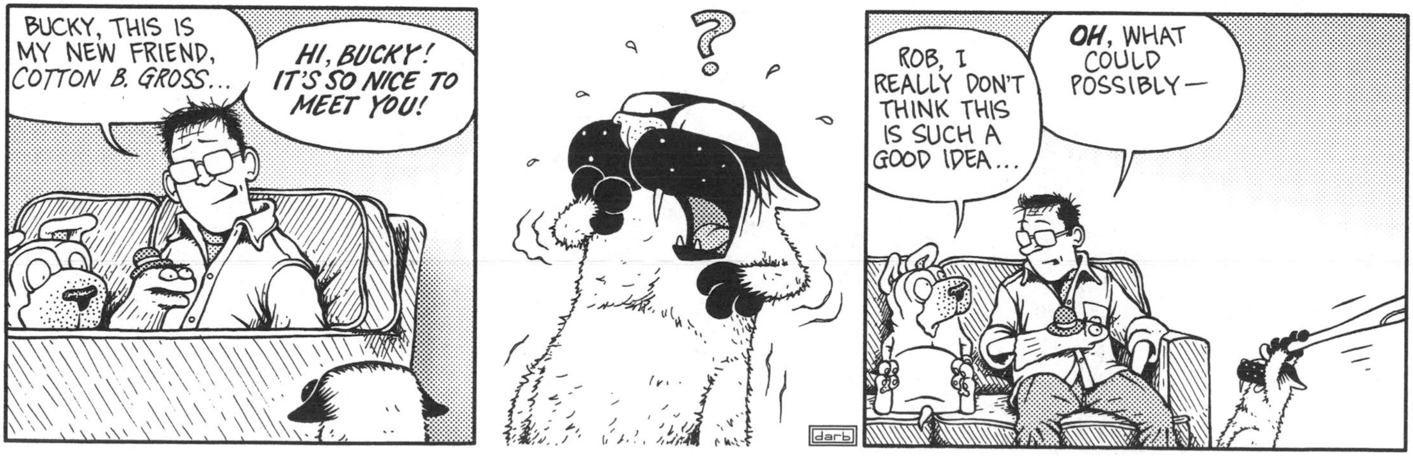
BUCKY, THIS IS MY NEW FRIEND, *COTTON B. GROSS...*
HI, BUCKY! IT'S SO NICE TO MEET YOU!
?
darb
ROB, I REALLY DON'T THINK THIS IS SUCH A GOOD IDEA...
OH, WHAT COULD POSSIBLY–

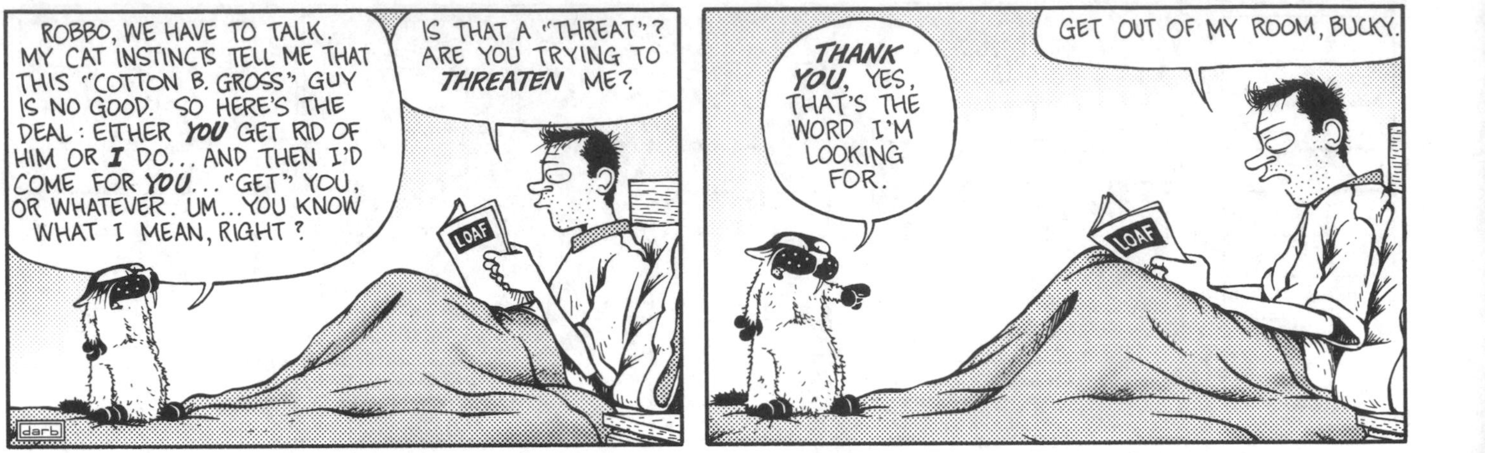
ROBBO, WE HAVE TO TALK. MY CAT INSTINCTS TELL ME THAT THIS "COTTON B. GROSS" GUY IS NO GOOD. SO HERE'S THE DEAL: EITHER YOU GET RID OF HIM OR I DO... AND THEN I'D COME FOR YOU... "GET" YOU, OR WHATEVER. UM... YOU KNOW WHAT I MEAN, RIGHT?
IS THAT A "THREAT"? ARE YOU TRYING TO THREATEN ME?
LOAF
darb
THANK YOU, YES, THAT'S THE WORD I'M LOOKING FOR.
GET OUT OF MY ROOM, BUCKY.
LOAF

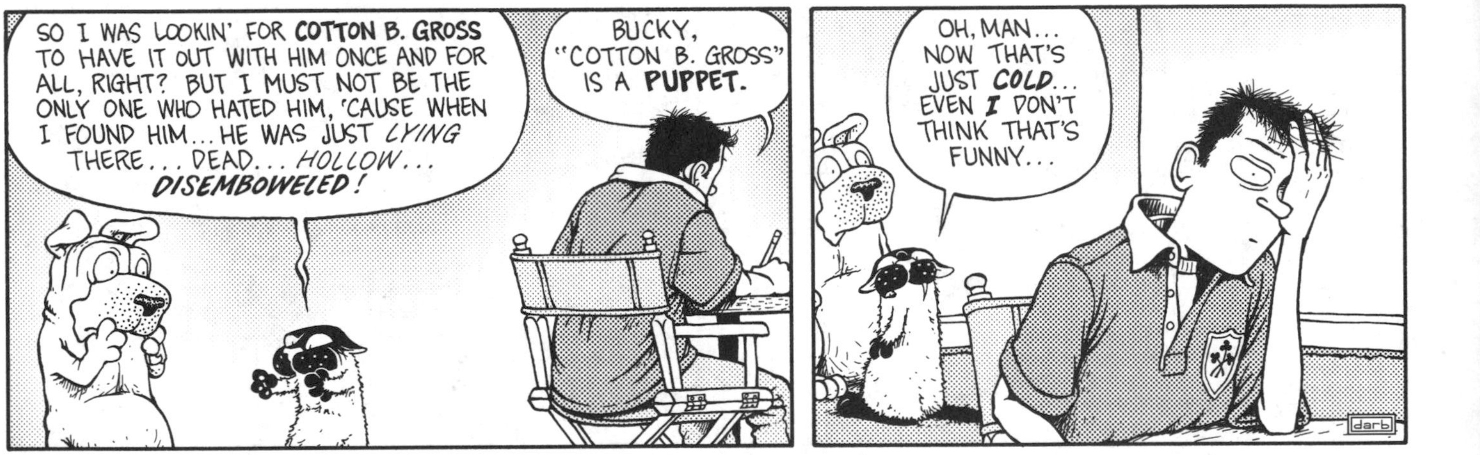
SO I WAS LOOKIN' FOR COTTON B. GROSS TO HAVE IT OUT WITH HIM ONCE AND FOR ALL, RIGHT? BUT I MUST NOT BE THE ONLY ONE WHO HATED HIM, 'CAUSE WHEN I FOUND HIM... HE WAS JUST LYING THERE... DEAD... HOLLOW... DISEMBOWELED!
BUCKY, "COTTON B. GROSS" IS A PUPPET.
OH, MAN... NOW THAT'S JUST COLD... EVEN I DON'T THINK THAT'S FUNNY...
darb

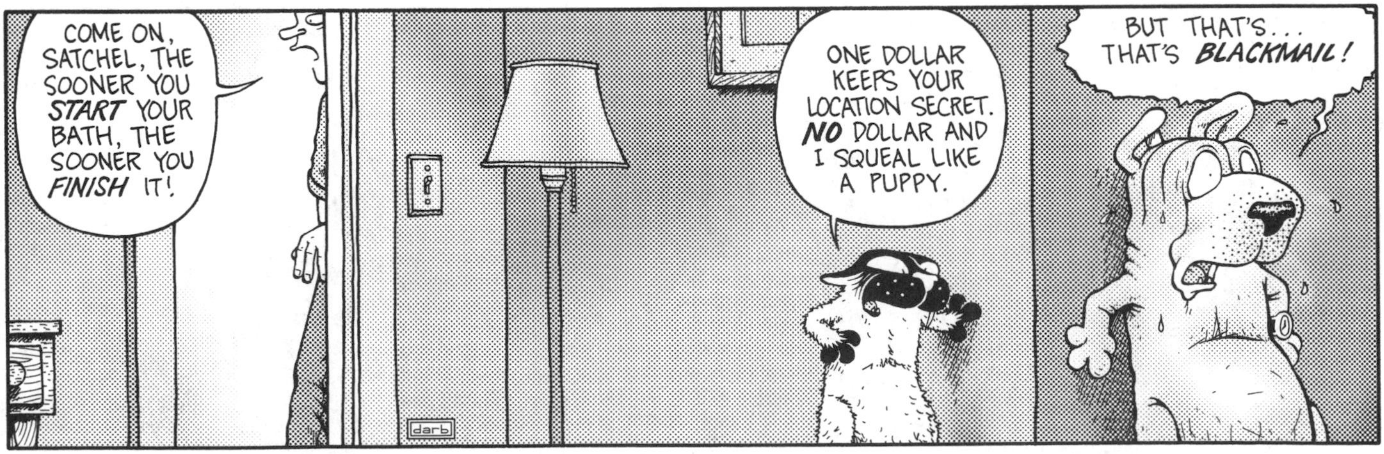
COME ON, SATCHEL, THE SOONER YOU START YOUR BATH, THE SOONER YOU FINISH IT!
darb
ONE DOLLAR KEEPS YOUR LOCATION SECRET. NO DOLLAR AND I SQUEAL LIKE A PUPPY.
BUT THAT'S... THAT'S BLACKMAIL!

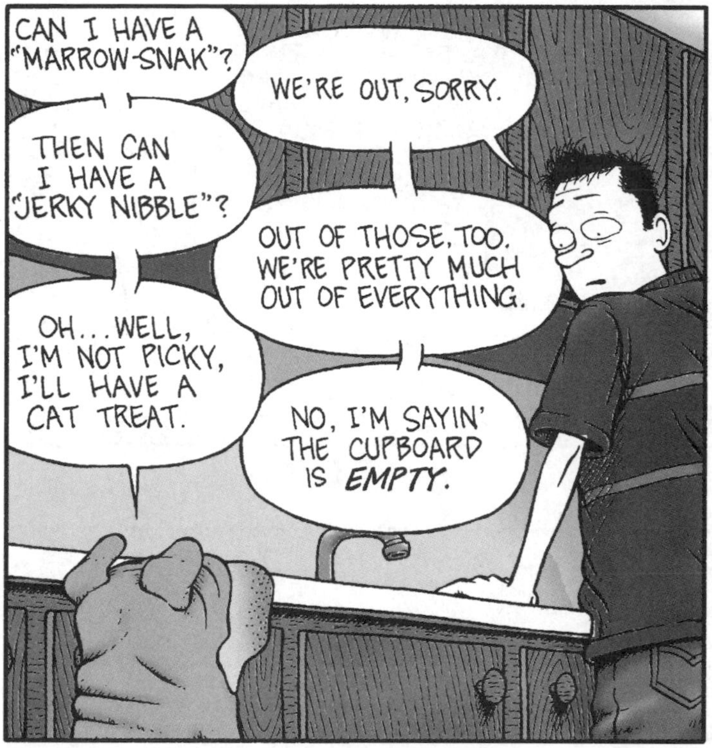
CAN I HAVE A "MARROW-SNAK"?
WE'RE OUT, SORRY.
THEN CAN I HAVE A "JERKY NIBBLE"?
OUT OF THOSE, TOO. WE'RE PRETTY MUCH OUT OF EVERYTHING.
OH... WELL, I'M NOT PICKY, I'LL HAVE A CAT TREAT.
NO, I'M SAYIN' THE CUPBOARD IS *EMPTY*.

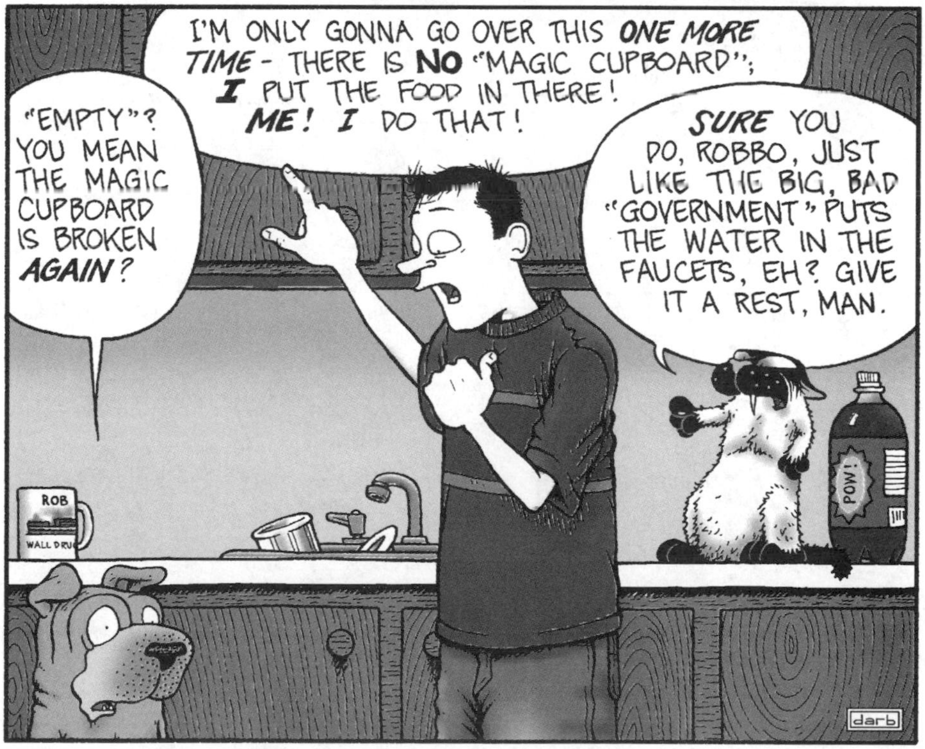
"EMPTY"? YOU MEAN THE MAGIC CUPBOARD IS BROKEN *AGAIN*?
I'M ONLY GONNA GO OVER THIS *ONE MORE TIME* - THERE IS **NO** "MAGIC CUPBOARD"; *I* PUT THE FOOD IN THERE! *ME! I* DO THAT!
SURE YOU DO, ROBBO, JUST LIKE THE BIG, BAD "GOVERNMENT" PUTS THE WATER IN THE FAUCETS, EH? GIVE IT A REST, MAN.
ROB
POW!
darb

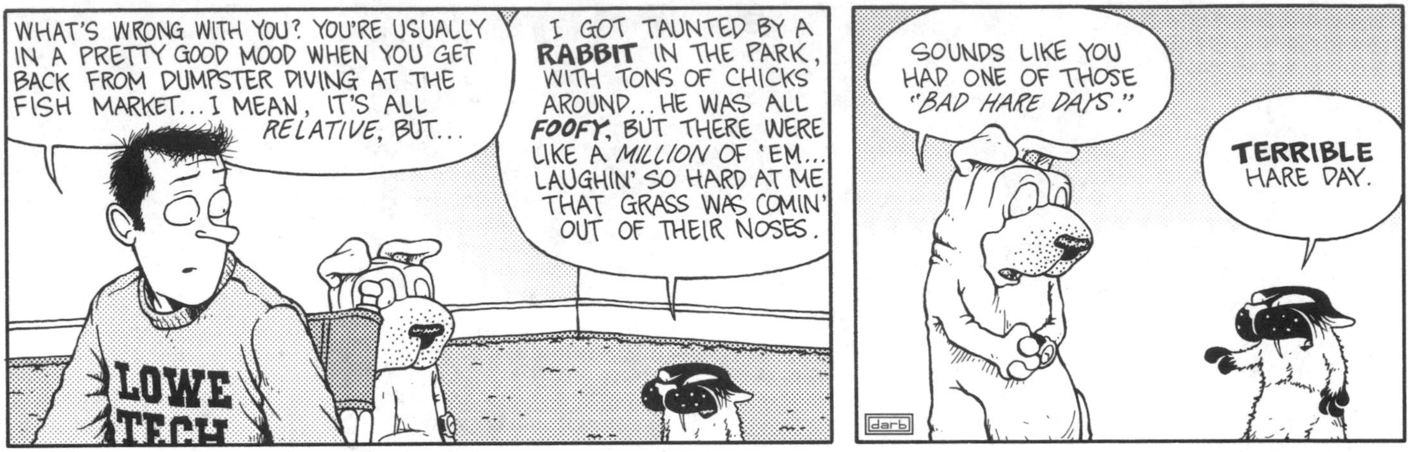
WHAT'S WRONG WITH YOU? YOU'RE USUALLY IN A PRETTY GOOD MOOD WHEN YOU GET BACK FROM DUMPSTER DIVING AT THE FISH MARKET... I MEAN, IT'S ALL *RELATIVE*, BUT...
I GOT TAUNTED BY A **RABBIT** IN THE PARK, WITH TONS OF CHICKS AROUND... HE WAS ALL ***FOOFY***, BUT THERE WERE LIKE A *MILLION* OF 'EM... LAUGHIN' SO HARD AT ME THAT GRASS WAS COMIN' OUT OF THEIR NOSES.
LOWE TECH
SOUNDS LIKE YOU HAD ONE OF THOSE *"BAD HARE DAYS."*
TERRIBLE HARE DAY.

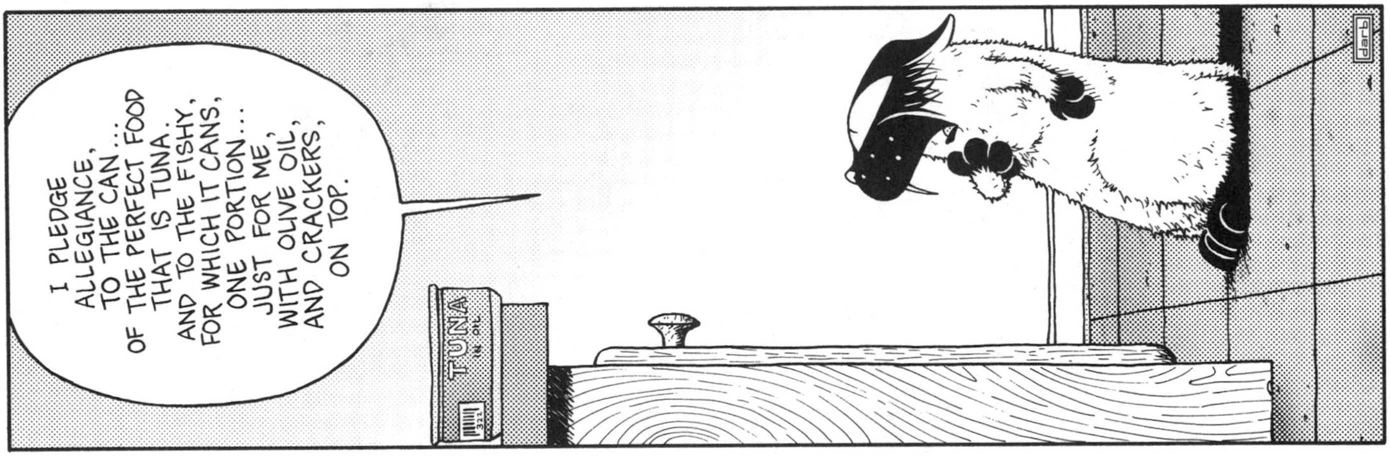
I PLEDGE ALLEGIANCE, TO THE CAN... OF THE PERFECT FOOD THAT IS TUNA. AND TO THE FISHY, FOR WHICH IT CANS, ONE PORTION... JUST FOR ME, WITH OLIVE OIL, AND CRACKERS, ON TOP.
TUNA IN OIL

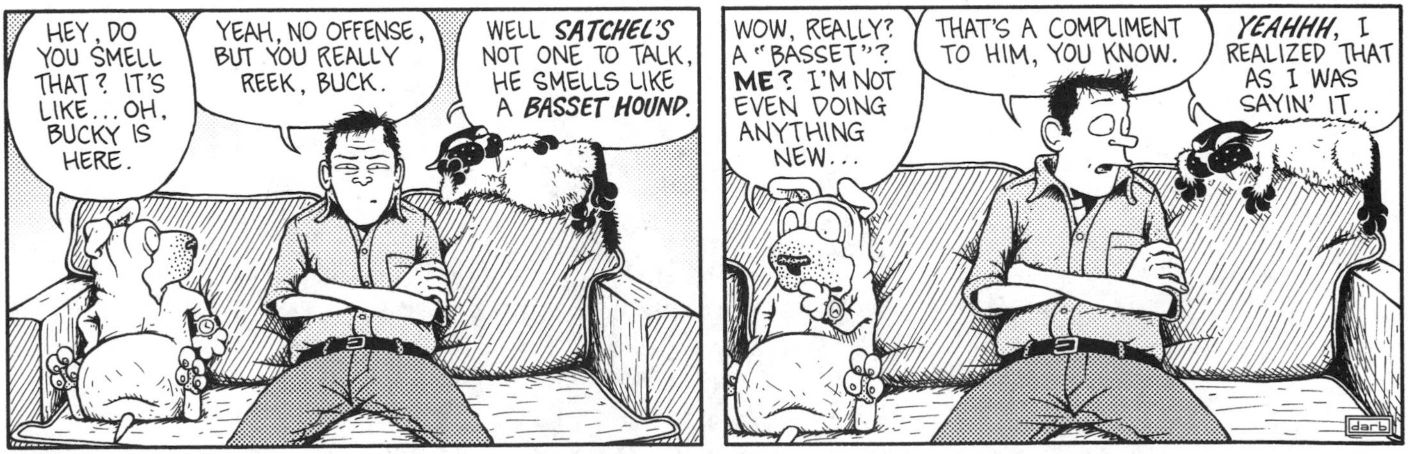
HEY, DO YOU SMELL THAT? IT'S LIKE... OH, BUCKY IS HERE.
YEAH, NO OFFENSE, BUT YOU REALLY REEK, BUCK.
WELL ***SATCHEL'S*** NOT ONE TO TALK, HE SMELLS LIKE A ***BASSET HOUND***.
WOW, REALLY? A "BASSET"? **ME**? I'M NOT EVEN DOING ANYTHING NEW...
THAT'S A COMPLIMENT TO HIM, YOU KNOW.
YEAHHH, I REALIZED THAT AS I WAS SAYIN' IT...

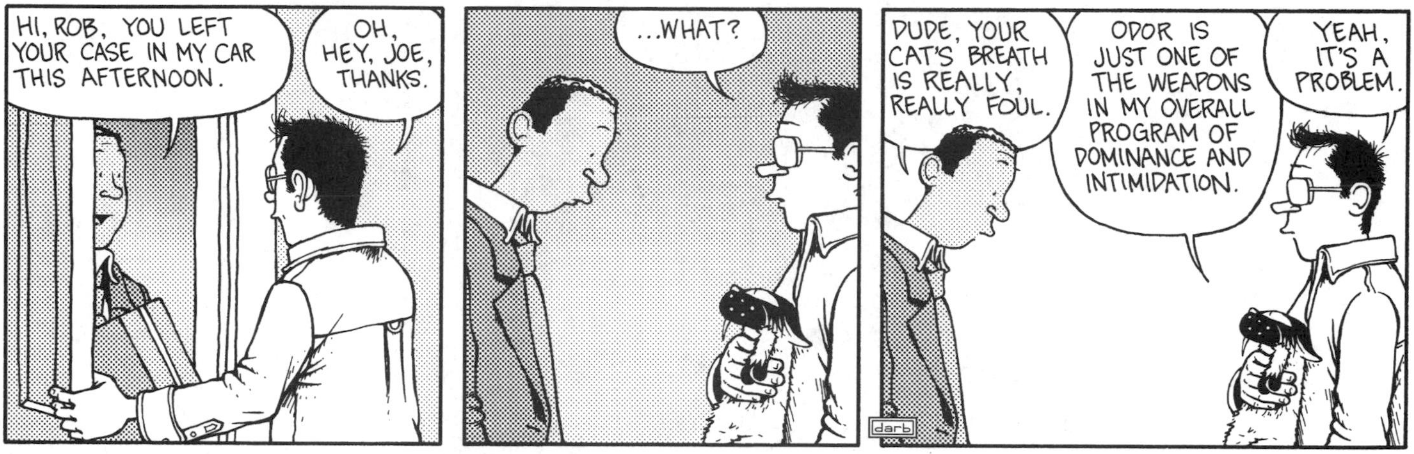
HI, ROB, YOU LEFT YOUR CASE IN MY CAR THIS AFTERNOON.
OH, HEY, JOE, THANKS.
...WHAT?
DUDE, YOUR CAT'S BREATH IS REALLY, REALLY FOUL.
ODOR IS JUST ONE OF THE WEAPONS IN MY OVERALL PROGRAM OF DOMINANCE AND INTIMIDATION.
YEAH, IT'S A PROBLEM.
darb

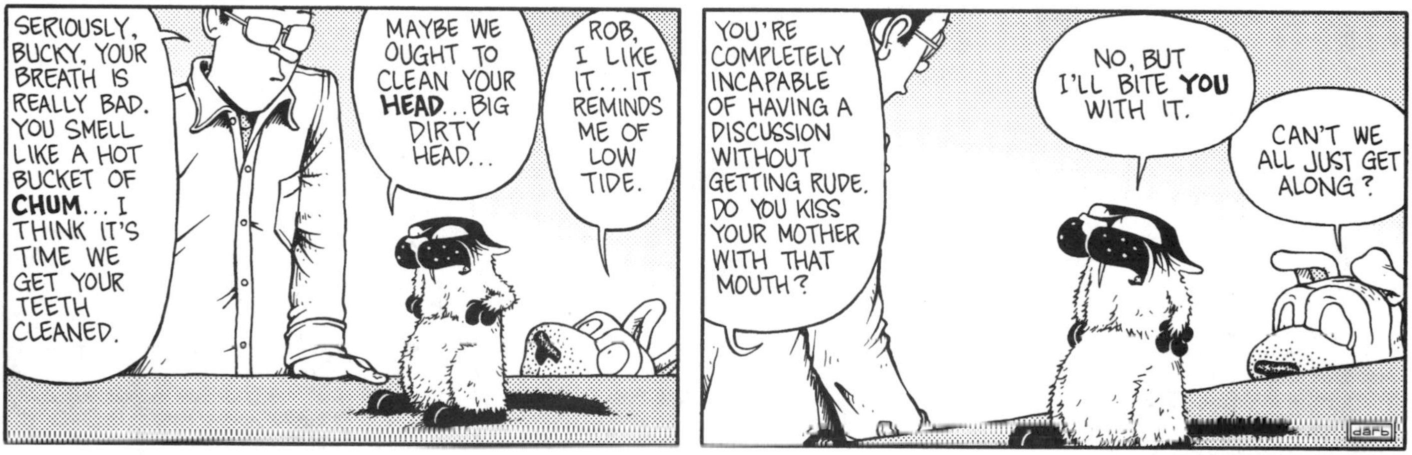
SERIOUSLY, BUCKY, YOUR BREATH IS REALLY BAD. YOU SMELL LIKE A HOT BUCKET OF **CHUM**... I THINK IT'S TIME WE GET YOUR TEETH CLEANED.
MAYBE WE OUGHT TO CLEAN YOUR **HEAD**...BIG DIRTY HEAD...
ROB, I LIKE IT...IT REMINDS ME OF LOW TIDE.
YOU'RE COMPLETELY INCAPABLE OF HAVING A DISCUSSION WITHOUT GETTING RUDE. DO YOU KISS YOUR MOTHER WITH THAT MOUTH?
NO, BUT I'LL BITE **YOU** WITH IT.
CAN'T WE ALL JUST GET ALONG?
darb

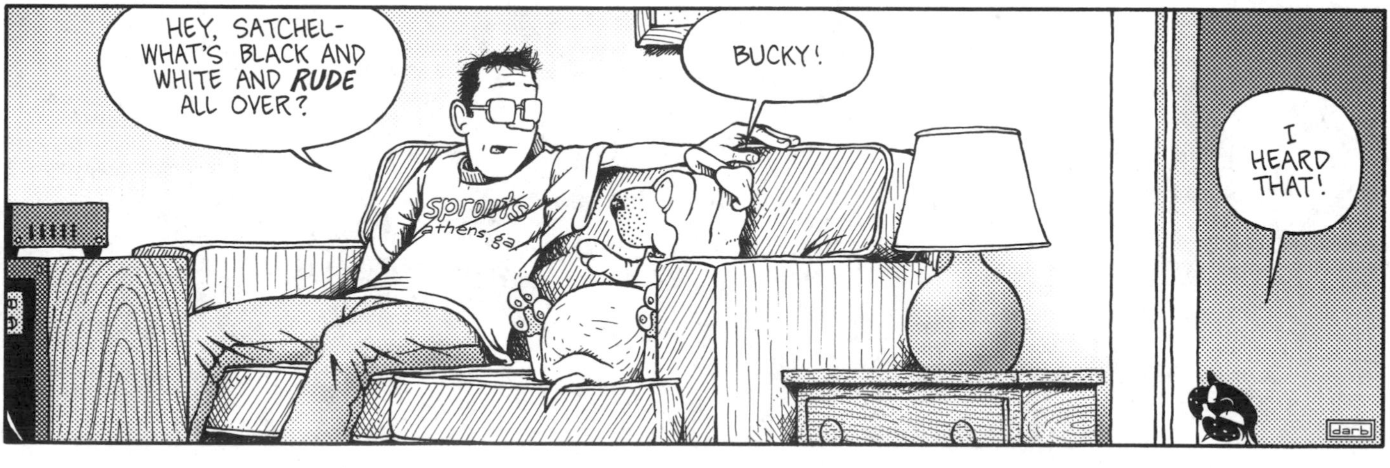
HEY, SATCHEL- WHAT'S BLACK AND WHITE AND ***RUDE*** ALL OVER?
BUCKY!
I HEARD THAT!
sprouts
athens, ga.
darb

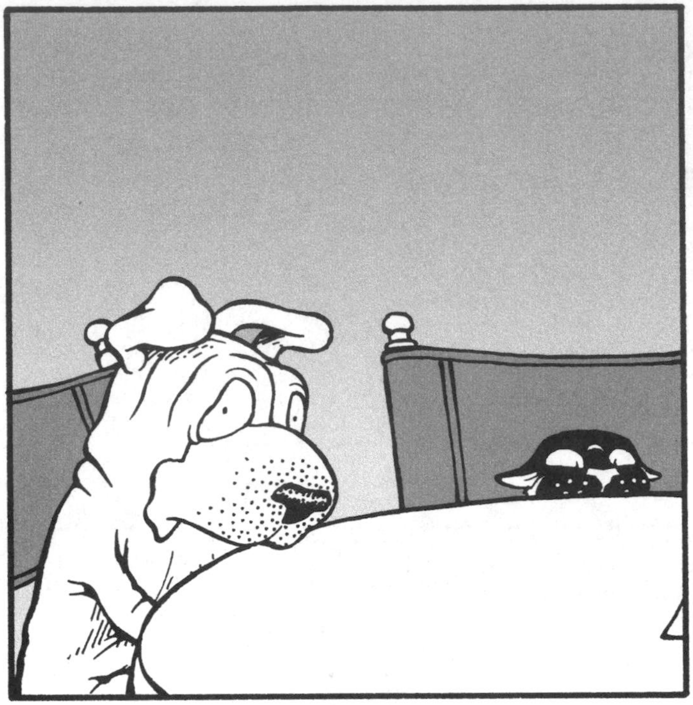

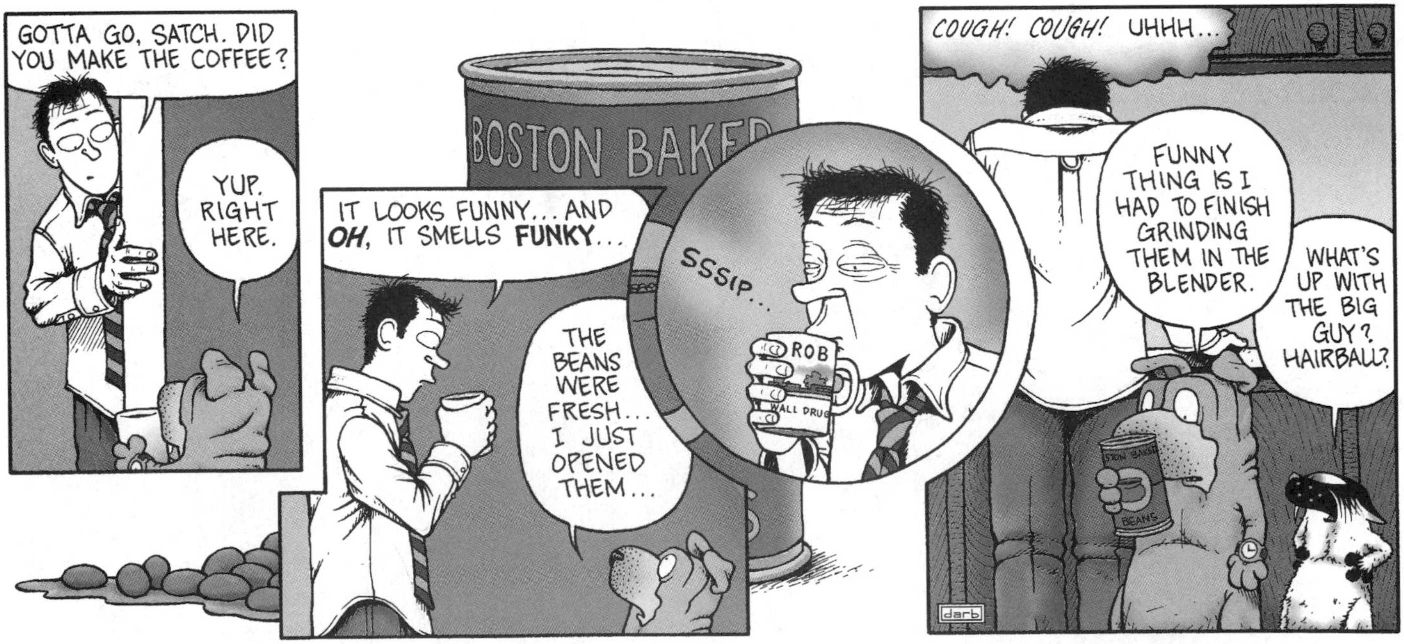

GOTTA GO, SATCH. DID YOU MAKE THE COFFEE?
YUP. RIGHT HERE.
BOSTON BAKED
IT LOOKS FUNNY... AND OH, IT SMELLS FUNKY...
THE BEANS WERE FRESH... I JUST OPENED THEM...
SSSIP...
ROB
WALL DRUG
COUGH! COUGH! UHHH...
FUNNY THING IS I HAD TO FINISH GRINDING THEM IN THE BLENDER.
WHAT'S UP WITH THE BIG GUY? HAIRBALL?
darb

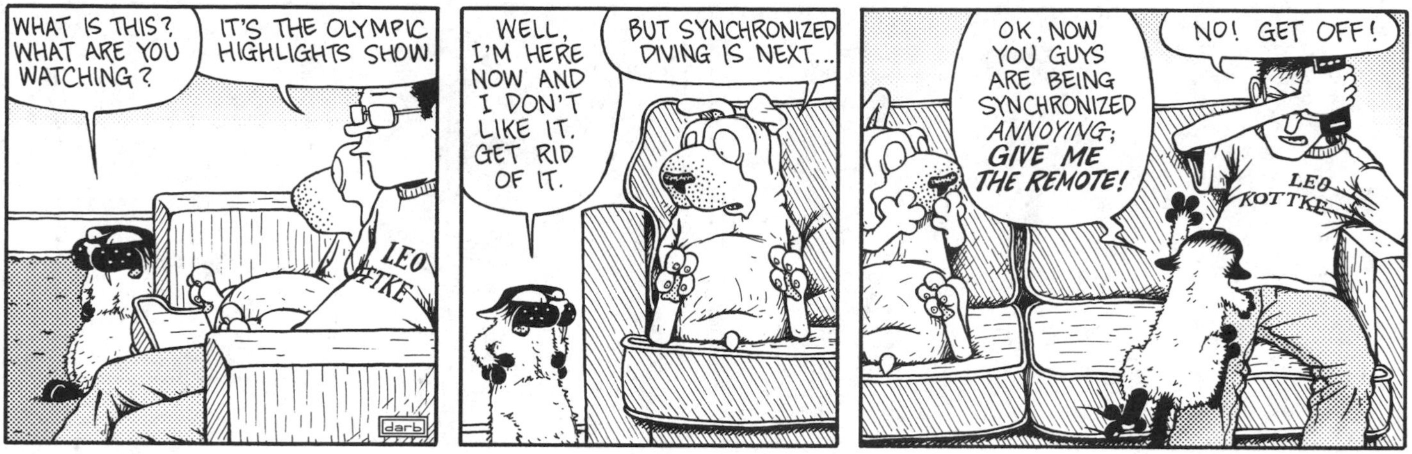
WHAT IS THIS? WHAT ARE YOU WATCHING?
IT'S THE OLYMPIC HIGHLIGHTS SHOW.
WELL, I'M HERE NOW AND I DON'T LIKE IT. GET RID OF IT.
BUT SYNCHRONIZED DIVING IS NEXT...
OK, NOW YOU GUYS ARE BEING SYNCHRONIZED *ANNOYING*; **GIVE ME THE REMOTE!**
NO! GET OFF!
LEO KOTTKE
darb

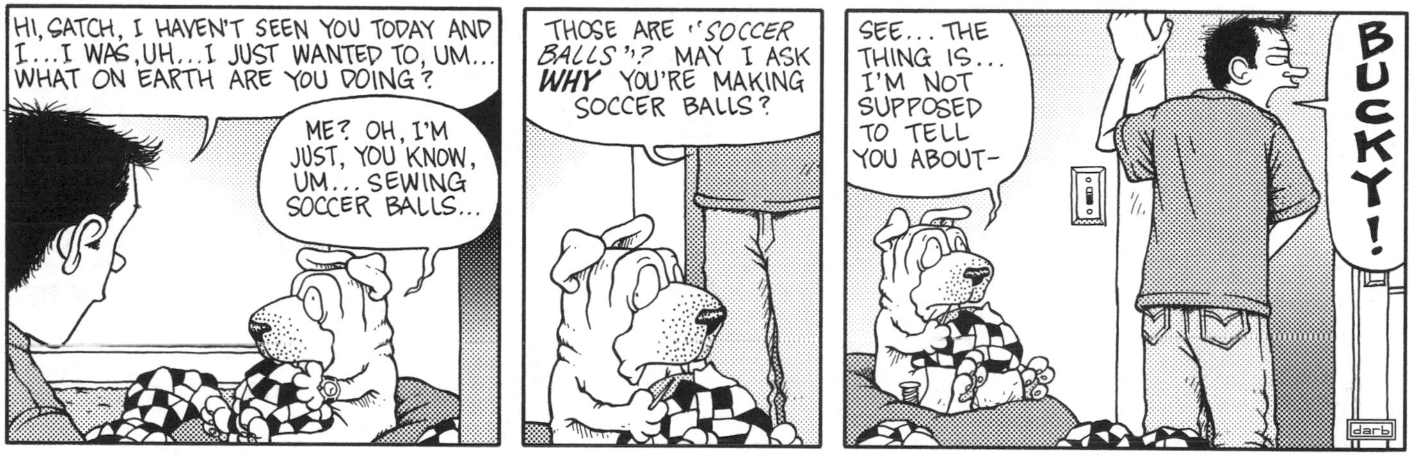
HI, SATCH, I HAVEN'T SEEN YOU TODAY AND I... I WAS, UH... I JUST WANTED TO, UM... WHAT ON EARTH ARE YOU DOING?
ME? OH, I'M JUST, YOU KNOW, UM... SEWING SOCCER BALLS...
THOSE ARE "*SOCCER BALLS*"? MAY I ASK **WHY** YOU'RE MAKING SOCCER BALLS?
SEE... THE THING IS... I'M NOT SUPPOSED TO TELL YOU ABOUT-
BUCKY!
darb

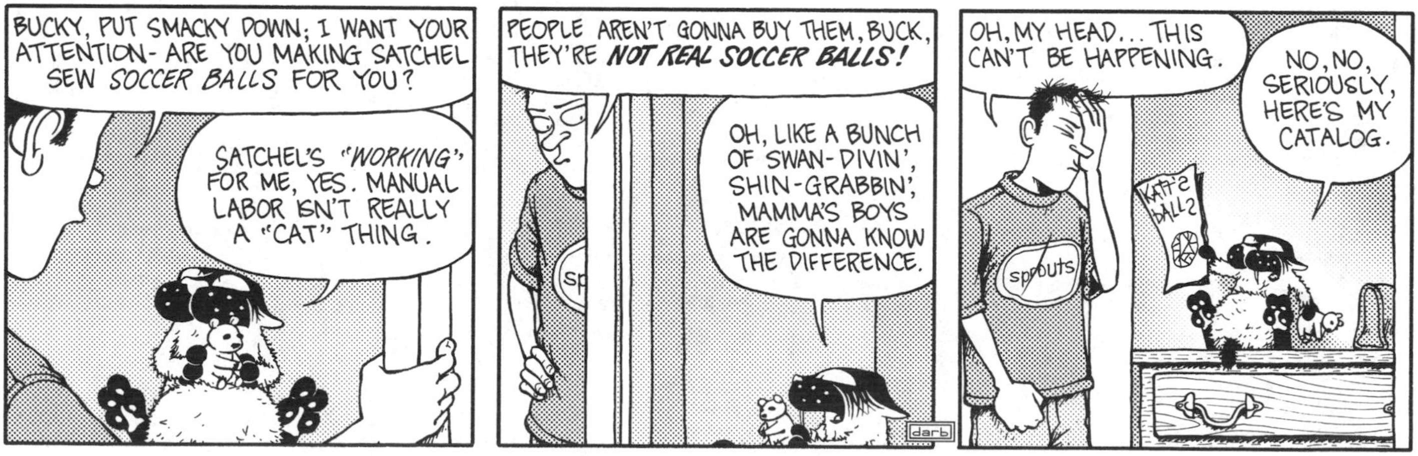
BUCKY, PUT SMACKY DOWN; I WANT YOUR ATTENTION- ARE YOU MAKING SATCHEL SEW *SOCCER BALLS* FOR YOU?
SATCHEL'S "*WORKING*" FOR ME, YES. MANUAL LABOR ISN'T REALLY A "CAT" THING.
PEOPLE AREN'T GONNA BUY THEM, BUCK, THEY'RE ***NOT REAL SOCCER BALLS!***
OH, LIKE A BUNCH OF SWAN-DIVIN', SHIN-GRABBIN', MAMMA'S BOYS ARE GONNA KNOW THE DIFFERENCE.
OH, MY HEAD... THIS CAN'T BE HAPPENING.
NO, NO, SERIOUSLY, HERE'S MY CATALOG.
sprouts
darb

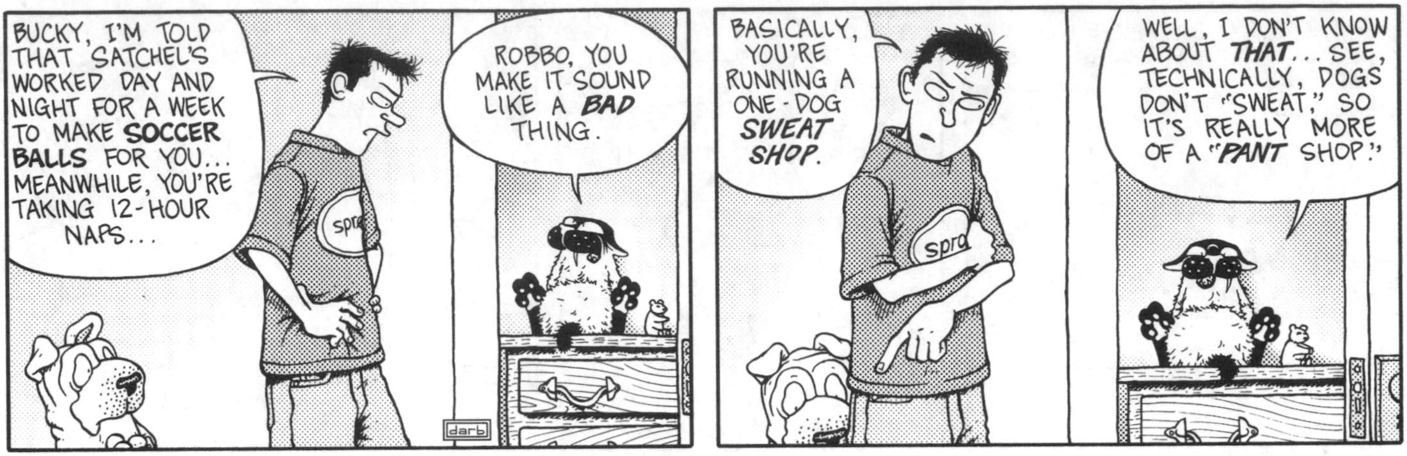
BUCKY, I'M TOLD THAT SATCHEL'S WORKED DAY AND NIGHT FOR A WEEK TO MAKE **SOCCER BALLS** FOR YOU... MEANWHILE, YOU'RE TAKING 12-HOUR NAPS...
ROBBO, YOU MAKE IT SOUND LIKE A ***BAD*** THING.
BASICALLY, YOU'RE RUNNING A ONE-DOG ***SWEAT SHOP.***
WELL, I DON'T KNOW ABOUT ***THAT***... SEE, TECHNICALLY, DOGS DON'T "SWEAT," SO IT'S REALLY MORE OF A "***PANT*** SHOP."

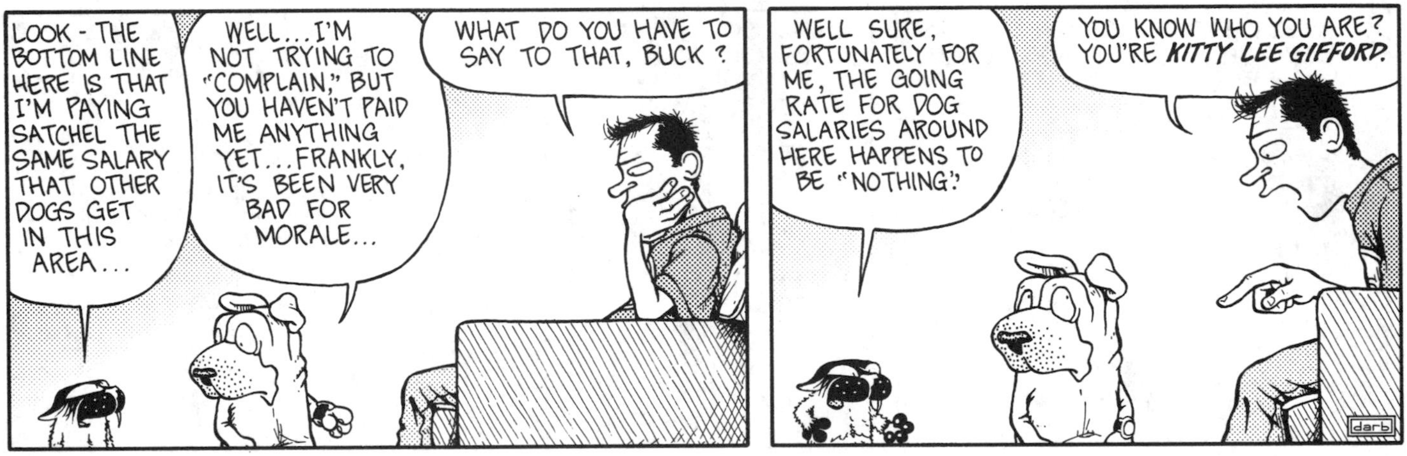
LOOK - THE BOTTOM LINE HERE IS THAT I'M PAYING SATCHEL THE SAME SALARY THAT OTHER DOGS GET IN THIS AREA...
WELL... I'M NOT TRYING TO "COMPLAIN," BUT YOU HAVEN'T PAID ME ANYTHING YET... FRANKLY, IT'S BEEN VERY BAD FOR MORALE...
WHAT DO YOU HAVE TO SAY TO THAT, BUCK?
WELL SURE, FORTUNATELY FOR ME, THE GOING RATE FOR DOG SALARIES AROUND HERE HAPPENS TO BE "NOTHING."
YOU KNOW WHO YOU ARE? YOU'RE ***KITTY LEE GIFFORD.***

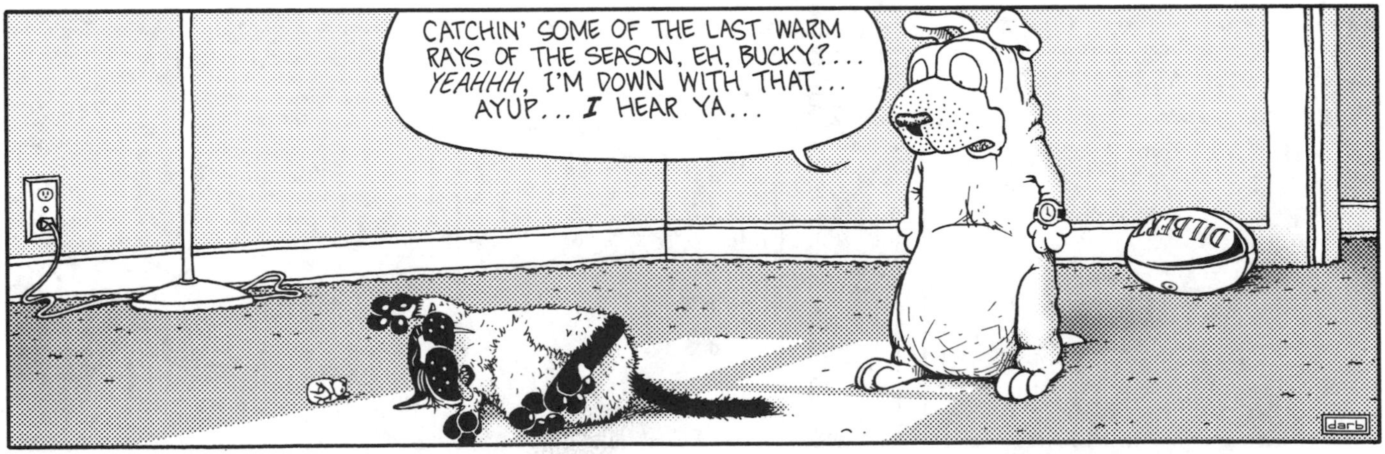
CATCHIN' SOME OF THE LAST WARM RAYS OF THE SEASON, EH, BUCKY?... *YEAHHH*, I'M DOWN WITH THAT... AYUP... ***I*** HEAR YA...

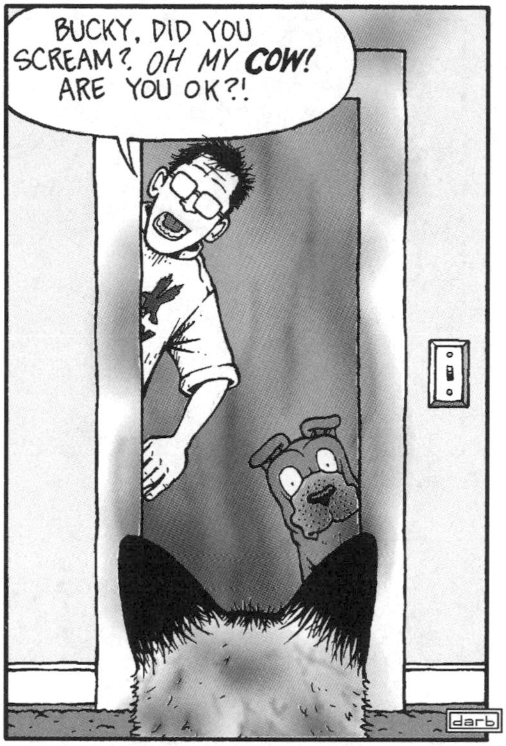
BUCKY, DID YOU SCREAM? OH MY COW! ARE YOU OK?!
darb

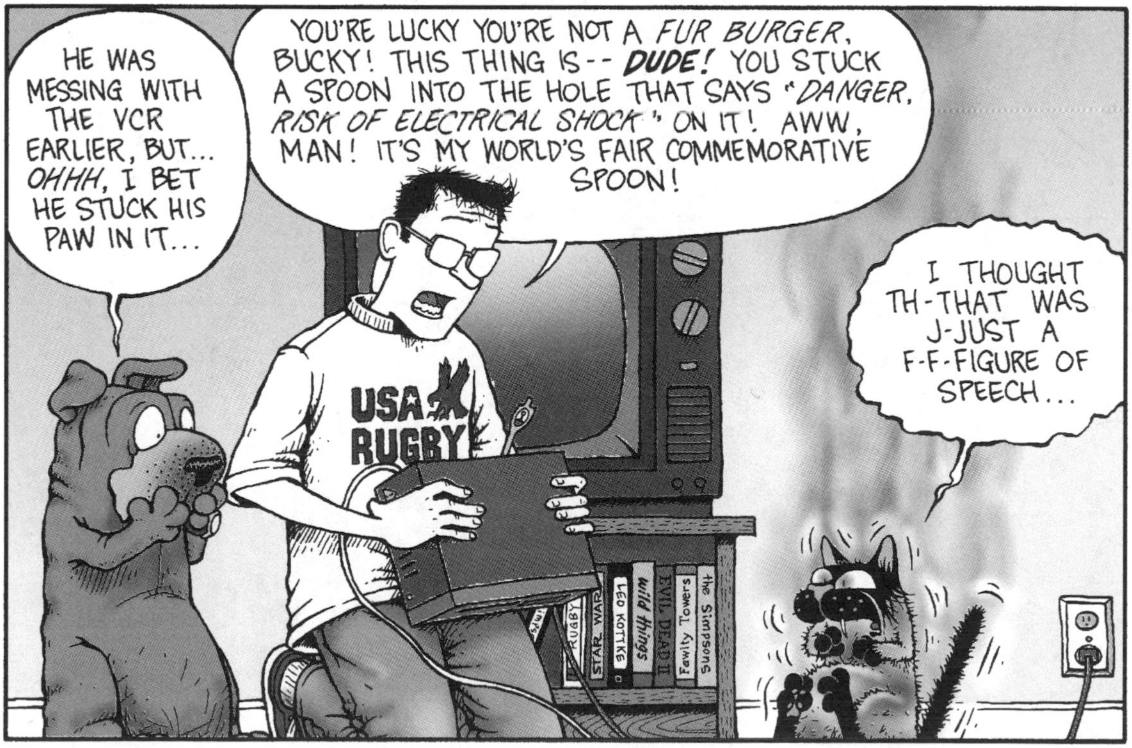
HE WAS MESSING WITH THE VCR EARLIER, BUT... OHHH, I BET HE STUCK HIS PAW IN IT...
YOU'RE LUCKY YOU'RE NOT A FUR BURGER, BUCKY! THIS THING IS-- DUDE! YOU STUCK A SPOON INTO THE HOLE THAT SAYS "DANGER, RISK OF ELECTRICAL SHOCK" ON IT! AWW, MAN! IT'S MY WORLD'S FAIR COMMEMORATIVE SPOON!
I THOUGHT TH-THAT WAS J-JUST A F-F-FIGURE OF SPEECH...
USA RUGBY
RUGBY
STAR WARS
LEO KOTTKE
wild things
EVIL DEAD II
Fawlty Towers
the Simpsons

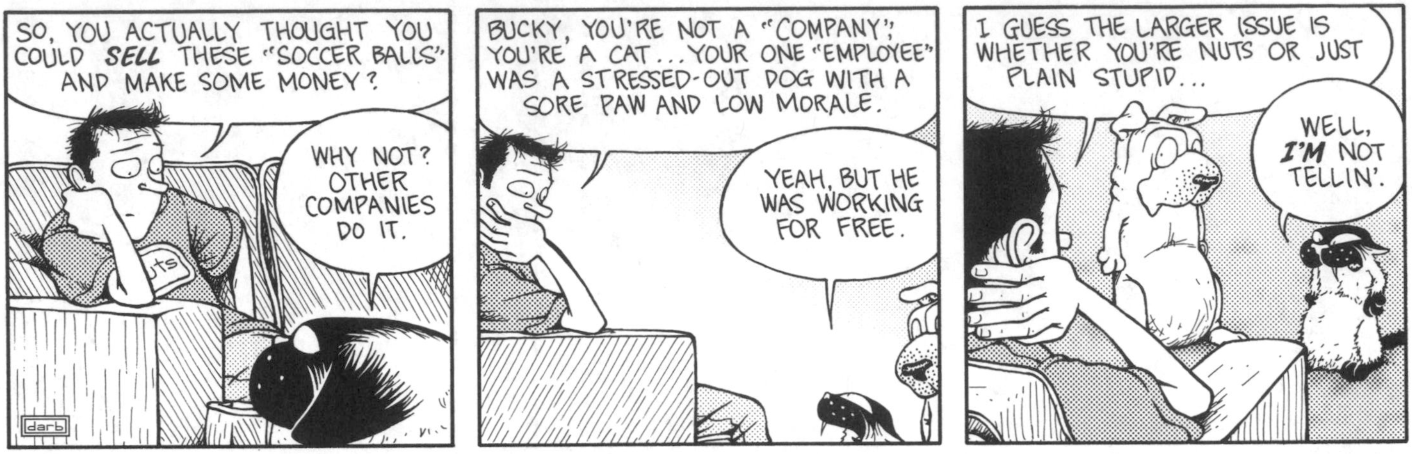
SO, YOU ACTUALLY THOUGHT YOU COULD **SELL** THESE "SOCCER BALLS" AND MAKE SOME MONEY?
WHY NOT? OTHER COMPANIES DO IT.
BUCKY, YOU'RE NOT A "COMPANY"; YOU'RE A CAT... YOUR ONE "EMPLOYEE" WAS A STRESSED-OUT DOG WITH A SORE PAW AND LOW MORALE.
YEAH, BUT HE WAS WORKING FOR FREE.
I GUESS THE LARGER ISSUE IS WHETHER YOU'RE NUTS OR JUST PLAIN STUPID...
WELL, ***I'M*** NOT TELLIN'.

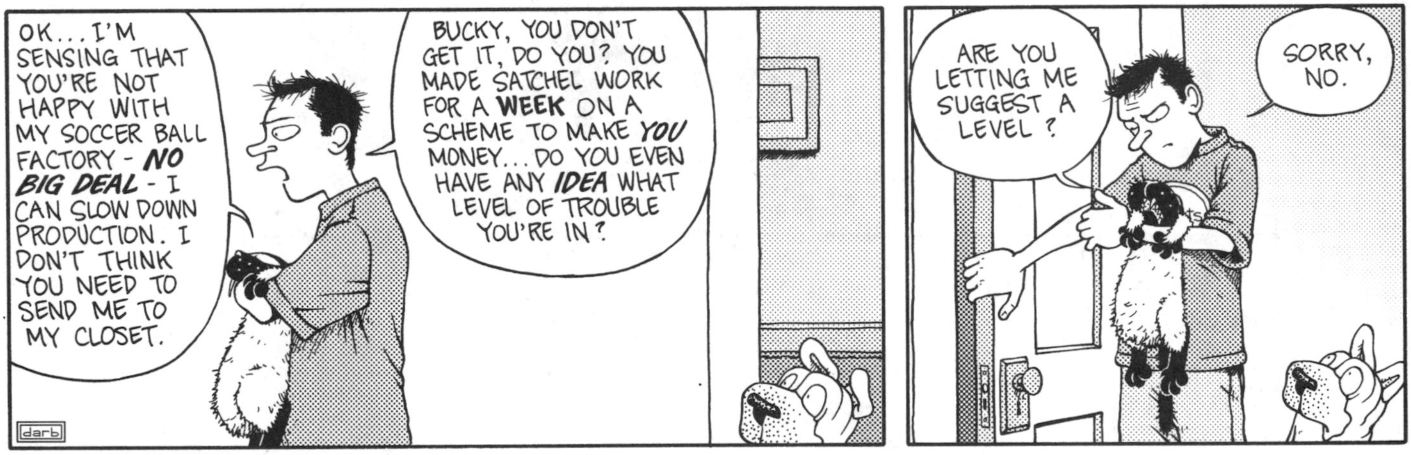
OK... I'M SENSING THAT YOU'RE NOT HAPPY WITH MY SOCCER BALL FACTORY - ***NO BIG DEAL*** - I CAN SLOW DOWN PRODUCTION. I DON'T THINK YOU NEED TO SEND ME TO MY CLOSET.
BUCKY, YOU DON'T GET IT, DO YOU? YOU MADE SATCHEL WORK FOR A **WEEK** ON A SCHEME TO MAKE ***YOU*** MONEY... DO YOU EVEN HAVE ANY ***IDEA*** WHAT LEVEL OF TROUBLE YOU'RE IN?
ARE YOU LETTING ME SUGGEST A LEVEL?
SORRY, NO.

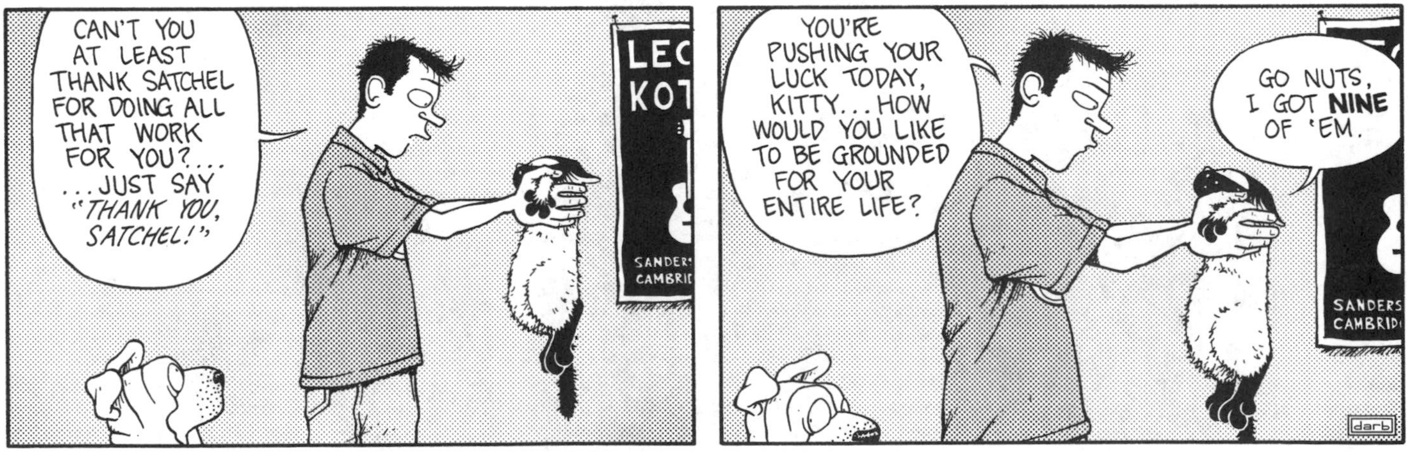
CAN'T YOU AT LEAST THANK SATCHEL FOR DOING ALL THAT WORK FOR YOU?... ...JUST SAY *"THANK YOU, SATCHEL!"*
YOU'RE PUSHING YOUR LUCK TODAY, KITTY... HOW WOULD YOU LIKE TO BE GROUNDED FOR YOUR ENTIRE LIFE?
GO NUTS, I GOT **NINE** OF 'EM.

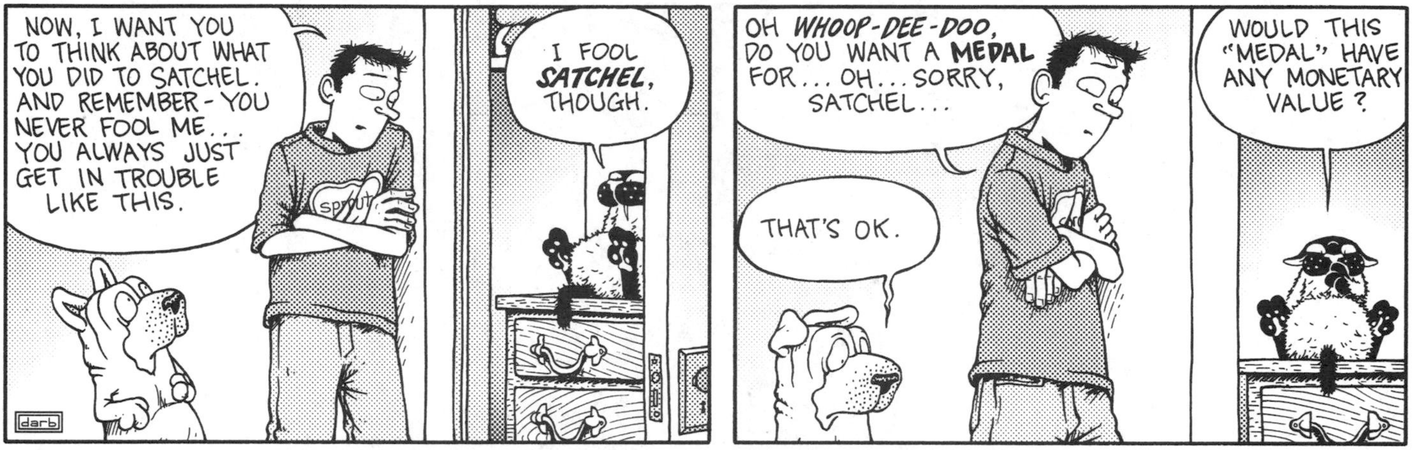
NOW, I WANT YOU TO THINK ABOUT WHAT YOU DID TO SATCHEL. AND REMEMBER - YOU NEVER FOOL ME... YOU ALWAYS JUST GET IN TROUBLE LIKE THIS.
I FOOL ***SATCHEL***, THOUGH.
OH ***WHOOP-DEE-DOO***, DO YOU WANT A **MEDAL** FOR... OH... SORRY, SATCHEL...
THAT'S OK.
WOULD THIS "MEDAL" HAVE ANY MONETARY VALUE?

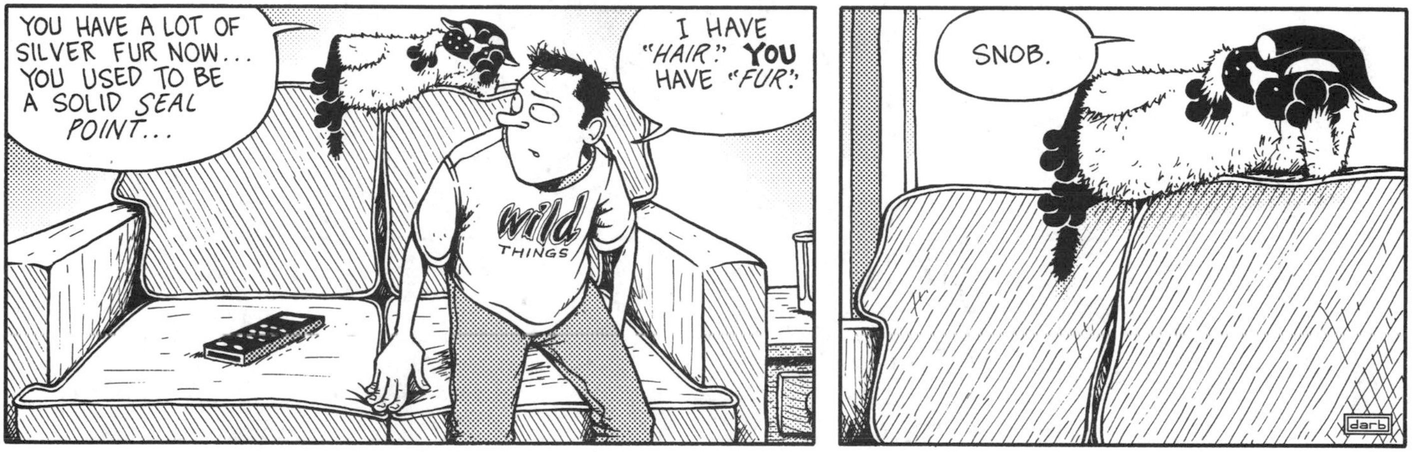
YOU HAVE A LOT OF SILVER FUR NOW... YOU USED TO BE A SOLID *SEAL POINT*...
I HAVE "*HAIR*." **YOU** HAVE "*FUR*."
wild THINGS
SNOB.

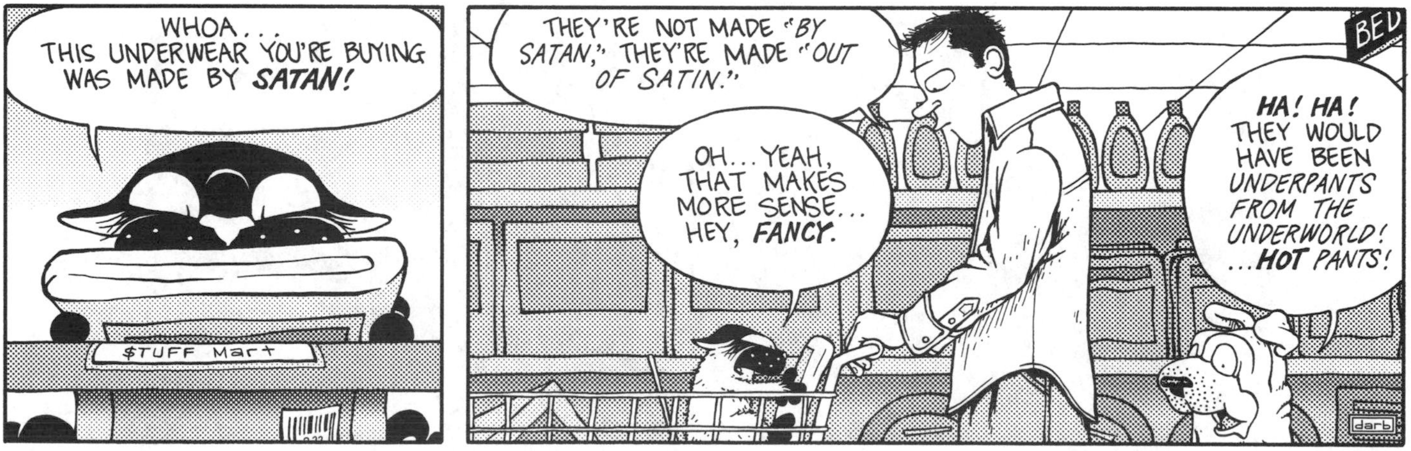
WHOA... THIS UNDERWEAR YOU'RE BUYING WAS MADE BY ***SATAN!***
$TUFF Mart
THEY'RE NOT MADE "*BY SATAN*," THEY'RE MADE "*OUT OF SATIN*."
BED
OH... YEAH, THAT MAKES MORE SENSE... HEY, ***FANCY***.
HA! HA! THEY WOULD HAVE BEEN *UNDERPANTS FROM THE UNDERWORLD!* ...***HOT*** *PANTS!*

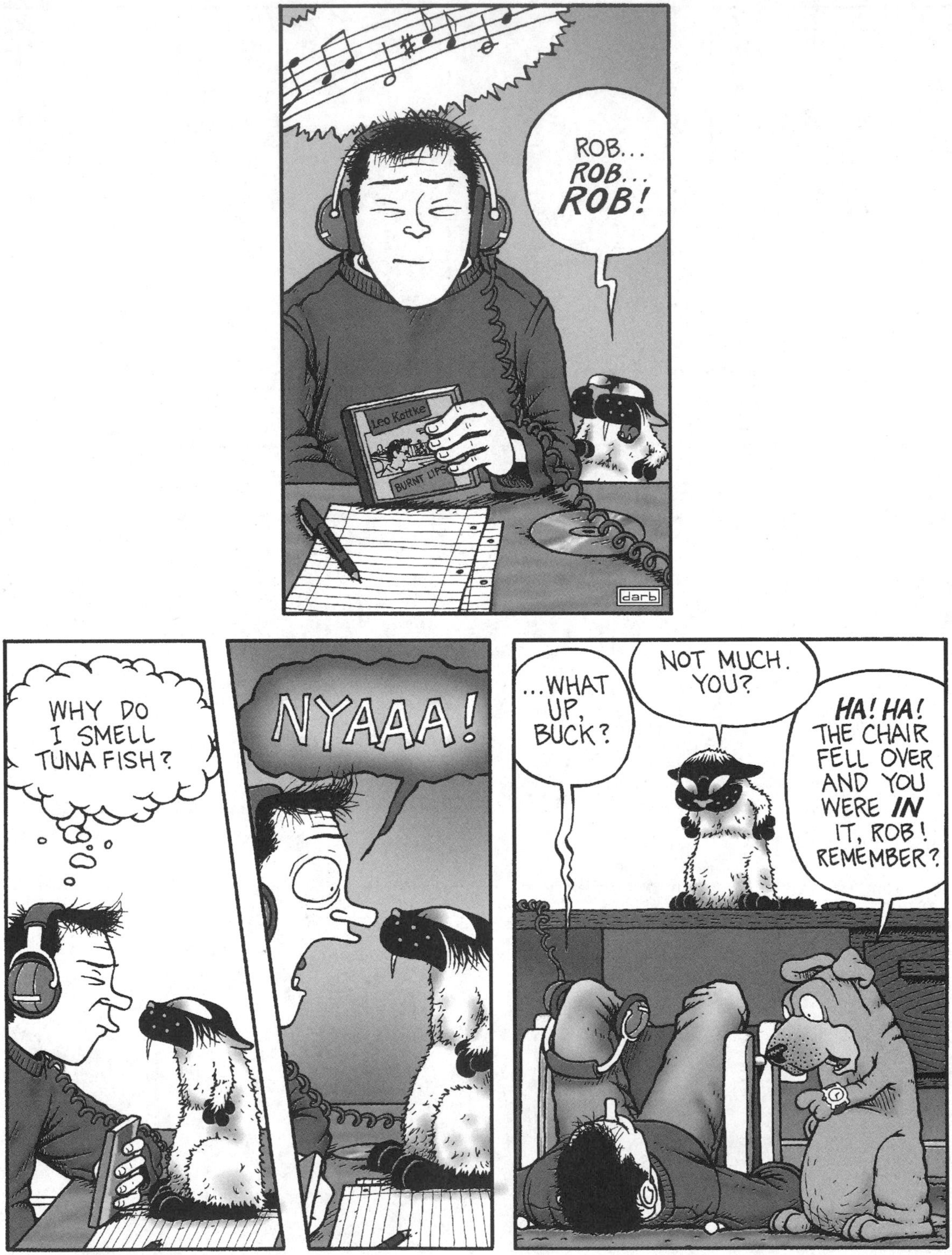

ROB... ROB... ROB!
Leo Kottke
BURNT LIPS
darb
WHY DO I SMELL TUNA FISH?
NYAAA!
...WHAT UP, BUCK?
NOT MUCH. YOU?
HA! HA! THE CHAIR FELL OVER AND YOU WERE IN IT, ROB! REMEMBER?

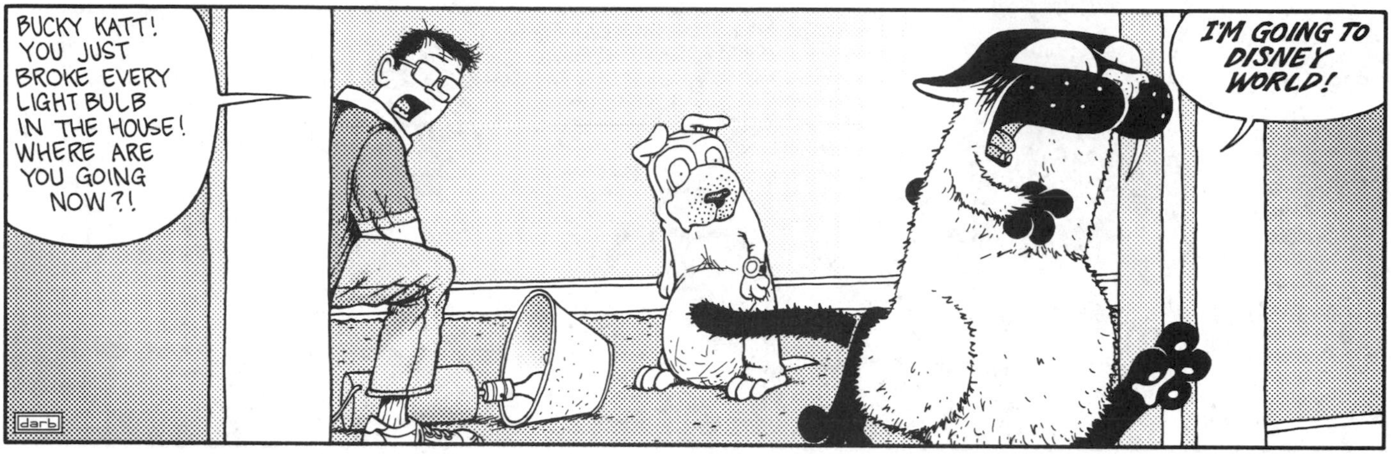
BUCKY KATT! YOU JUST BROKE EVERY LIGHT BULB IN THE HOUSE! WHERE ARE YOU GOING NOW?!
I'M GOING TO DISNEY WORLD!
darb

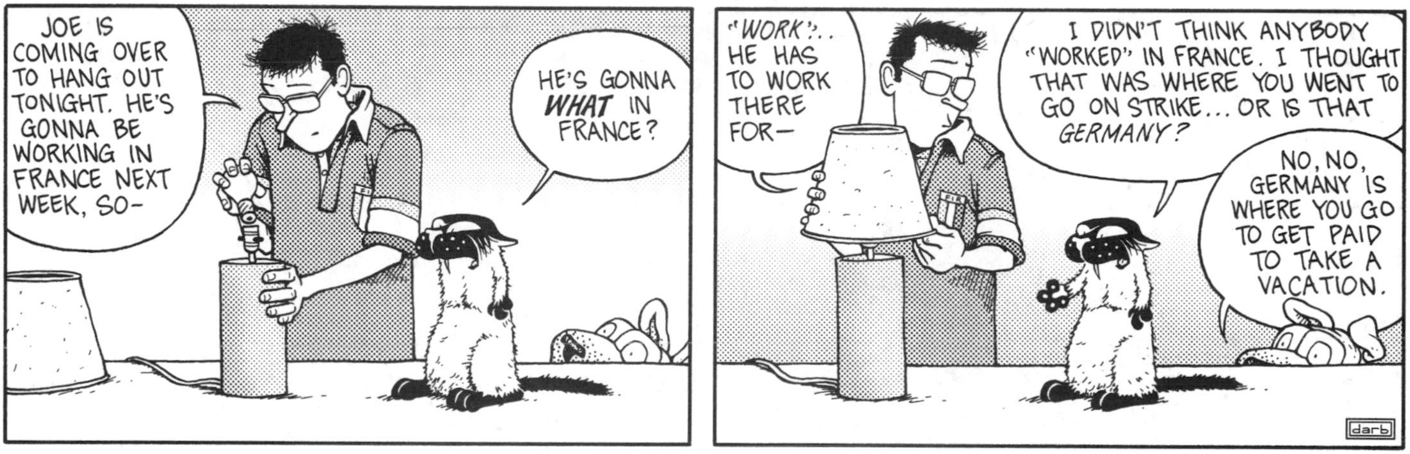
JOE IS COMING OVER TO HANG OUT TONIGHT. HE'S GONNA BE WORKING IN FRANCE NEXT WEEK, SO-
HE'S GONNA WHAT IN FRANCE?
"WORK"... HE HAS TO WORK THERE FOR—
I DIDN'T THINK ANYBODY "WORKED" IN FRANCE. I THOUGHT THAT WAS WHERE YOU WENT TO GO ON STRIKE... OR IS THAT GERMANY?
NO, NO, GERMANY IS WHERE YOU GO TO GET PAID TO TAKE A VACATION.
darb

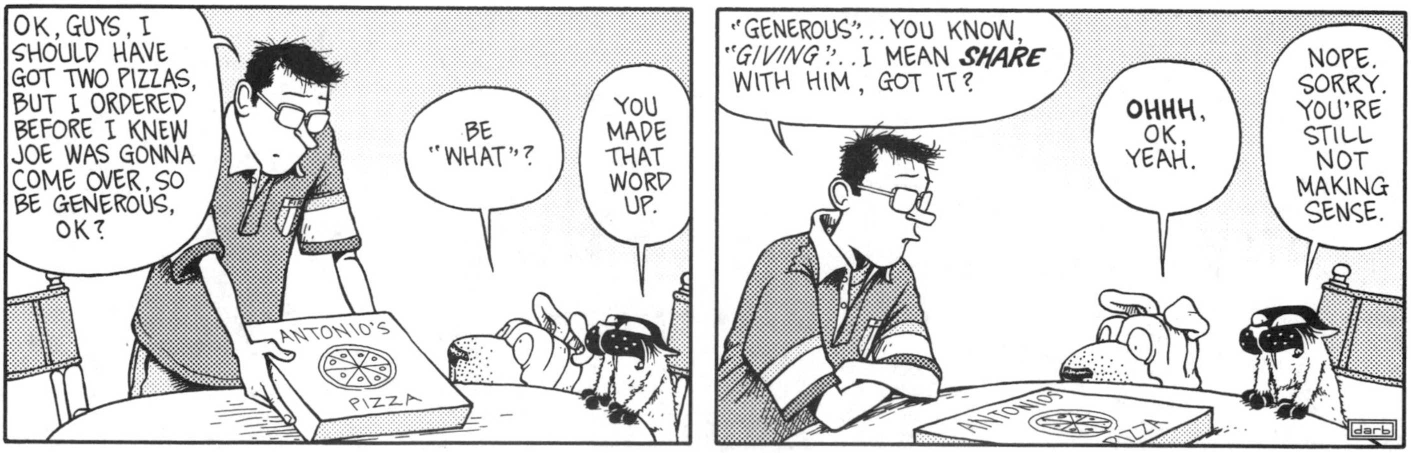
OK, GUYS, I SHOULD HAVE GOT TWO PIZZAS, BUT I ORDERED BEFORE I KNEW JOE WAS GONNA COME OVER, SO BE GENEROUS, OK?
BE "WHAT"?
YOU MADE THAT WORD UP.
ANTONIO'S PIZZA
"GENEROUS"... YOU KNOW, "GIVING"... I MEAN SHARE WITH HIM, GOT IT?
OHHH, OK, YEAH.
NOPE. SORRY. YOU'RE STILL NOT MAKING SENSE.
ANTONIO'S PIZZA
darb

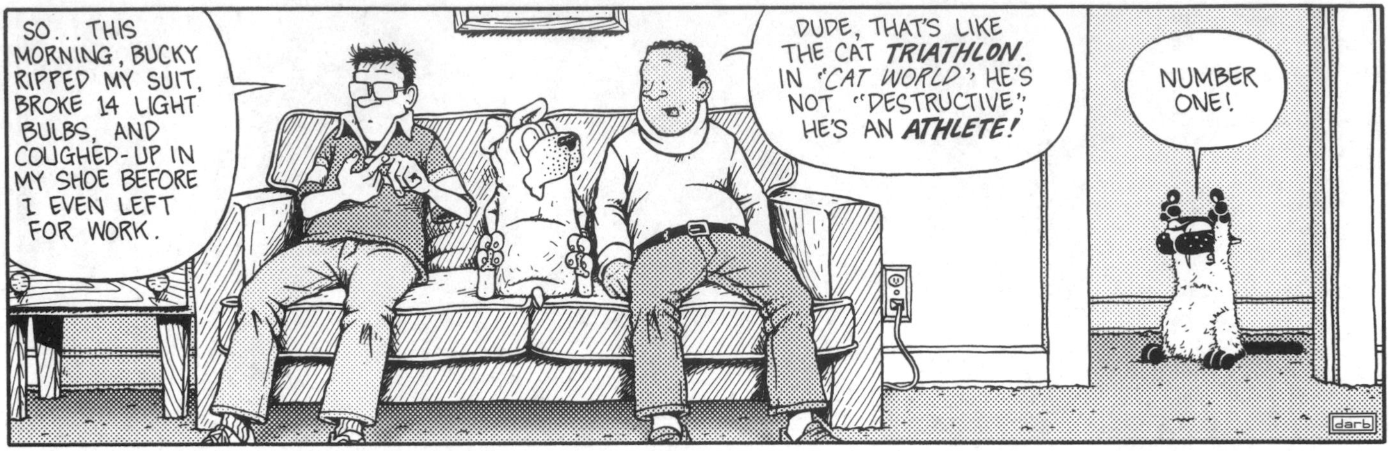
SO... THIS MORNING, BUCKY RIPPED MY SUIT, BROKE 14 LIGHT BULBS, AND COUGHED-UP IN MY SHOE BEFORE I EVEN LEFT FOR WORK.
DUDE, THAT'S LIKE THE CAT *TRIATHLON*. IN "CAT WORLD" HE'S NOT "DESTRUCTIVE"; HE'S AN *ATHLETE!*
NUMBER ONE!
darb

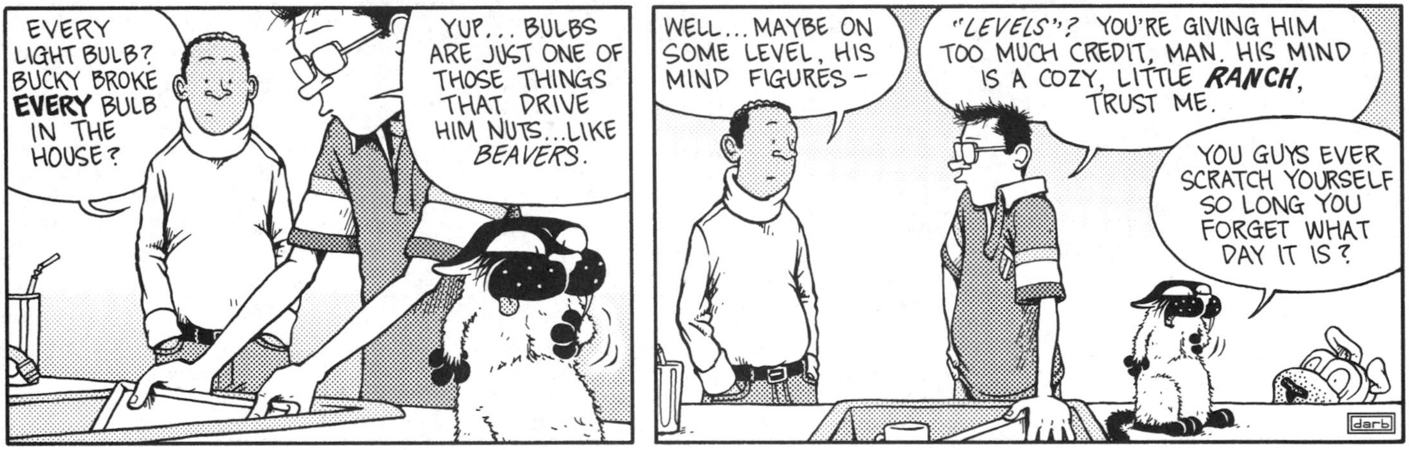
EVERY LIGHT BULB? BUCKY BROKE **EVERY** BULB IN THE HOUSE?
YUP... BULBS ARE JUST ONE OF THOSE THINGS THAT DRIVE HIM NUTS...LIKE *BEAVERS*.
WELL... MAYBE ON SOME LEVEL, HIS MIND FIGURES–
"LEVELS"? YOU'RE GIVING HIM TOO MUCH CREDIT, MAN. HIS MIND IS A COZY, LITTLE *RANCH*, TRUST ME.
YOU GUYS EVER SCRATCH YOURSELF SO LONG YOU FORGET WHAT DAY IT IS?
darb

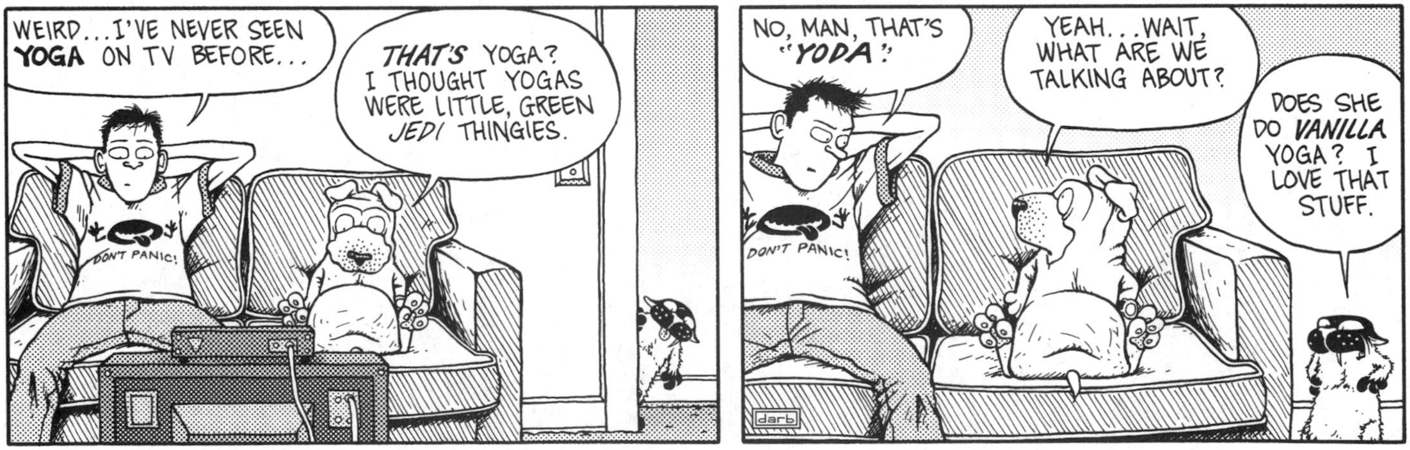
WEIRD...I'VE NEVER SEEN **YOGA** ON TV BEFORE...
THAT'S YOGA? I THOUGHT YOGAS WERE LITTLE, GREEN *JEDI* THINGIES.
DON'T PANIC!
NO, MAN, THAT'S "*YODA*."
YEAH...WAIT, WHAT ARE WE TALKING ABOUT?
DOES SHE DO *VANILLA* YOGA? I LOVE THAT STUFF.
darb

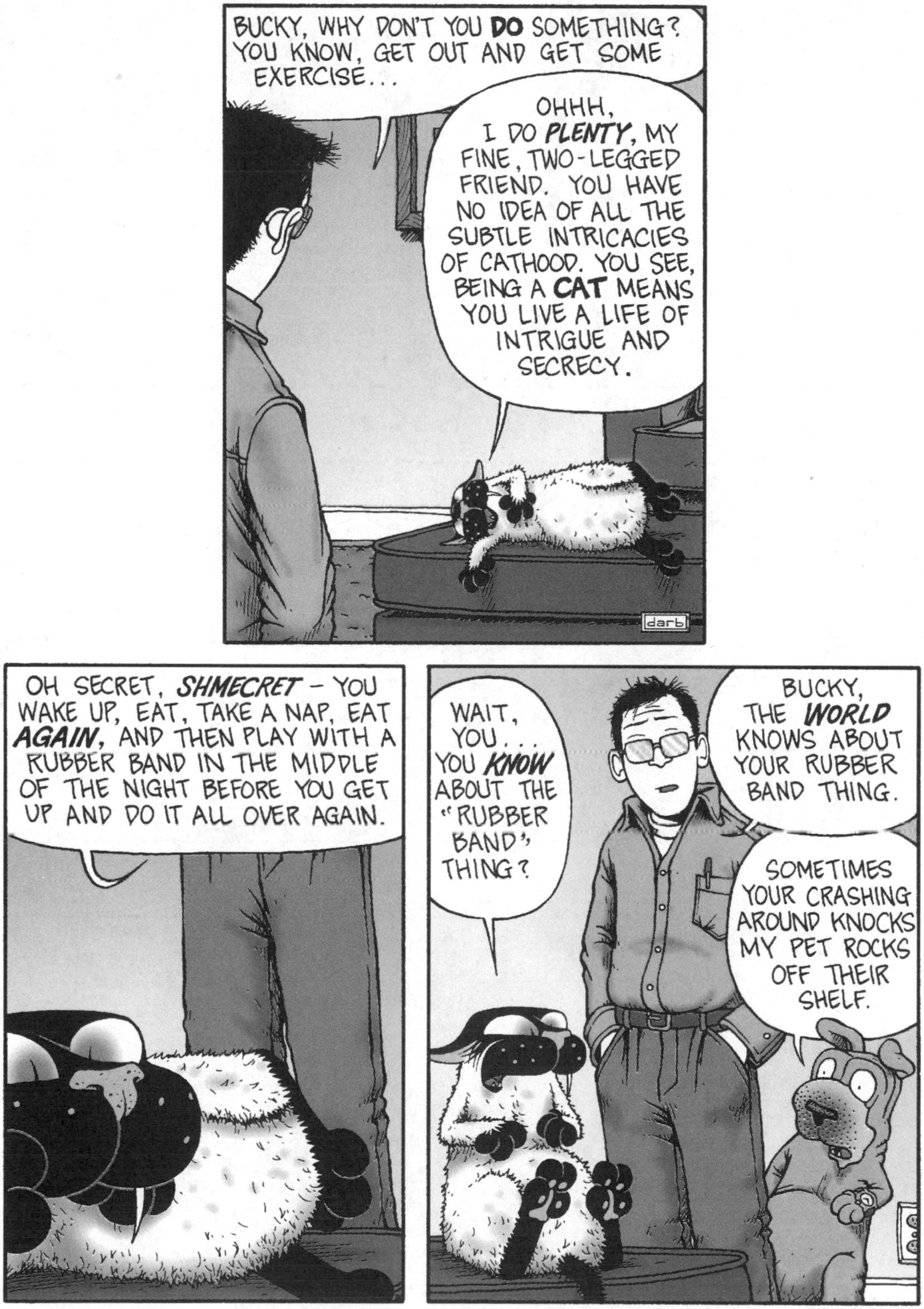
BUCKY, WHY DON'T YOU **DO** SOMETHING? YOU KNOW, GET OUT AND GET SOME EXERCISE...
OHHH, I DO ***PLENTY***, MY FINE, TWO-LEGGED FRIEND. YOU HAVE NO IDEA OF ALL THE SUBTLE INTRICACIES OF CATHOOD. YOU SEE, BEING A **CAT** MEANS YOU LIVE A LIFE OF INTRIGUE AND SECRECY.
darb
OH SECRET, ***SHMECRET*** – YOU WAKE UP, EAT, TAKE A NAP, EAT ***AGAIN***, AND THEN PLAY WITH A RUBBER BAND IN THE MIDDLE OF THE NIGHT BEFORE YOU GET UP AND DO IT ALL OVER AGAIN.
WAIT, YOU... YOU ***KNOW*** ABOUT THE "RUBBER BAND" THING?
BUCKY, THE ***WORLD*** KNOWS ABOUT YOUR RUBBER BAND THING.
SOMETIMES YOUR CRASHING AROUND KNOCKS MY PET ROCKS OFF THEIR SHELF.

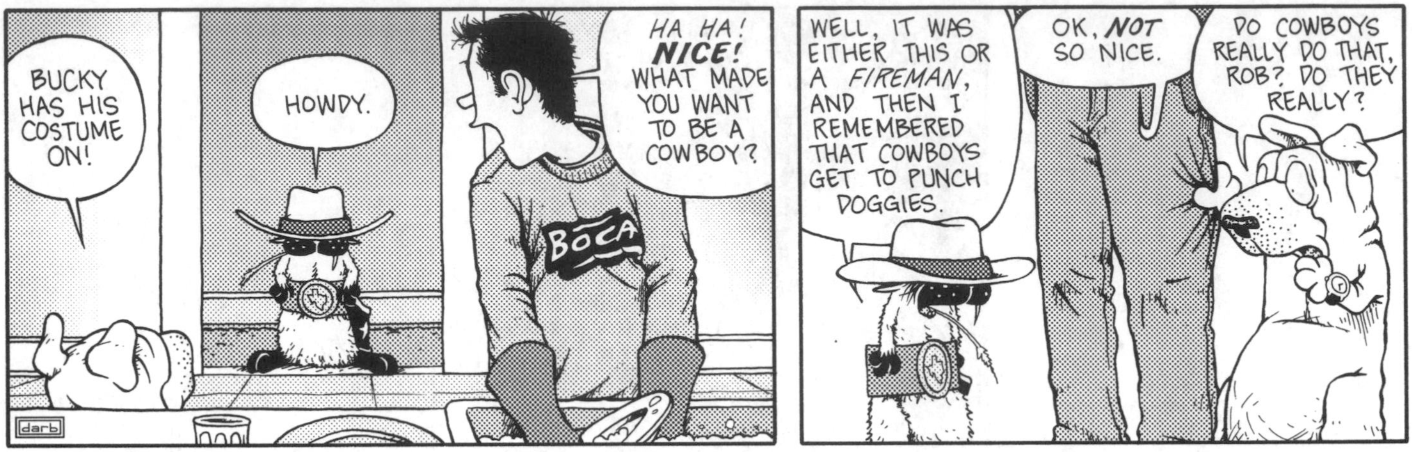
BUCKY HAS HIS COSTUME ON!
HOWDY.
HA HA! NICE! WHAT MADE YOU WANT TO BE A COWBOY?
BOCA
WELL, IT WAS EITHER THIS OR A FIREMAN, AND THEN I REMEMBERED THAT COWBOYS GET TO PUNCH DOGGIES.
OK, NOT SO NICE.
DO COWBOYS REALLY DO THAT, ROB? DO THEY REALLY?

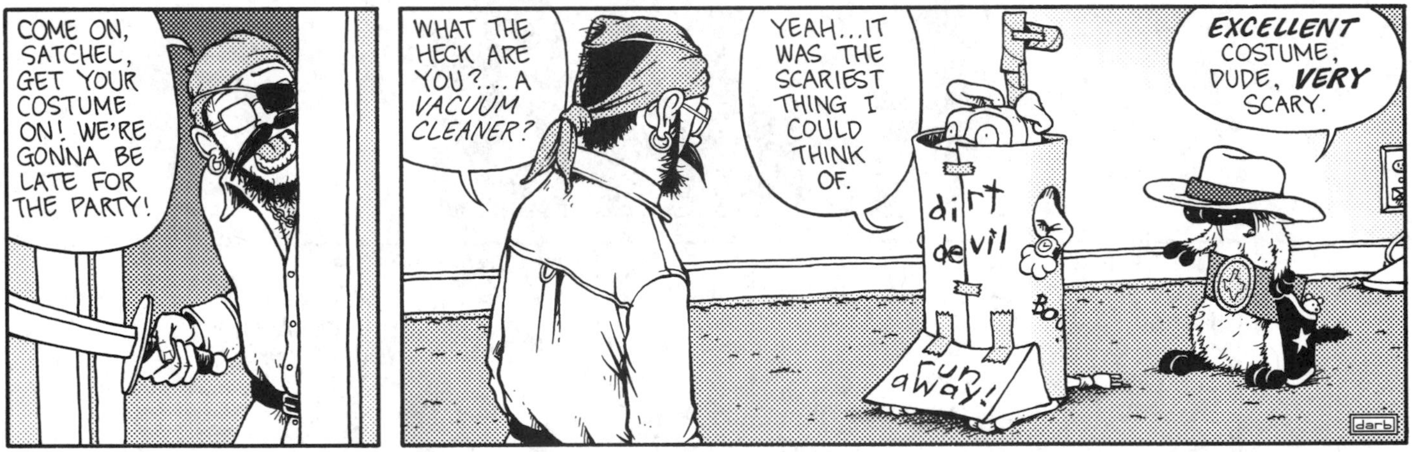
COME ON, SATCHEL, GET YOUR COSTUME ON! WE'RE GONNA BE LATE FOR THE PARTY!
WHAT THE HECK ARE YOU?... A VACUUM CLEANER?
YEAH... IT WAS THE SCARIEST THING I COULD THINK OF.
dirt devil
Boo
run away!
EXCELLENT COSTUME, DUDE, VERY SCARY.

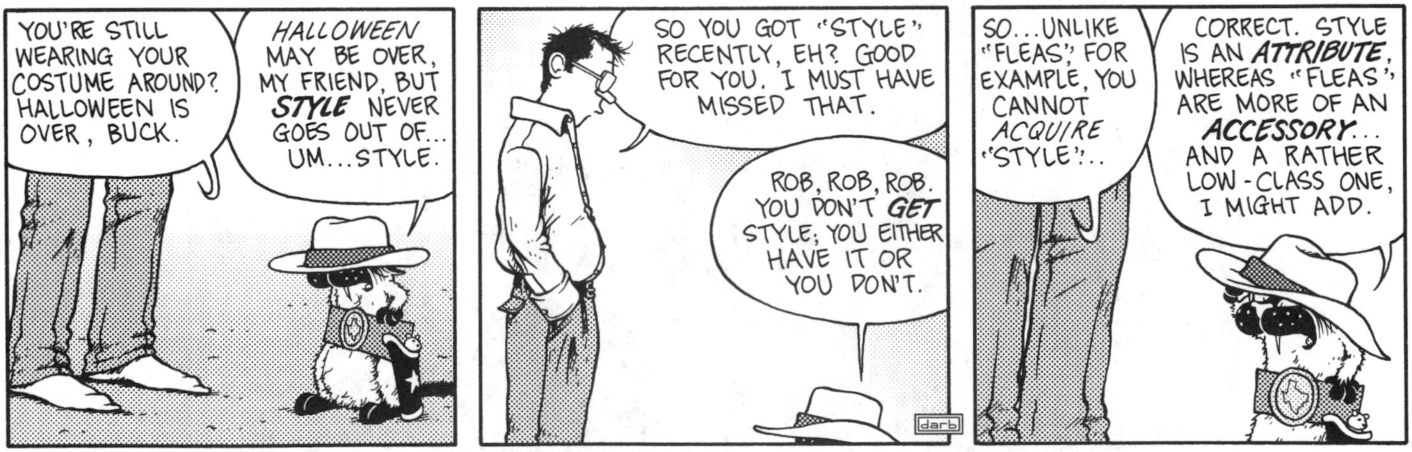
YOU'RE STILL WEARING YOUR COSTUME AROUND? HALLOWEEN IS OVER, BUCK.
HALLOWEEN MAY BE OVER, MY FRIEND, BUT STYLE NEVER GOES OUT OF... UM... STYLE.
SO YOU GOT "STYLE" RECENTLY, EH? GOOD FOR YOU. I MUST HAVE MISSED THAT.
ROB, ROB, ROB. YOU DON'T GET STYLE; YOU EITHER HAVE IT OR YOU DON'T.
SO... UNLIKE "FLEAS," FOR EXAMPLE, YOU CANNOT ACQUIRE "STYLE"?..
CORRECT. STYLE IS AN ATTRIBUTE, WHEREAS "FLEAS" ARE MORE OF AN ACCESSORY... AND A RATHER LOW-CLASS ONE, I MIGHT ADD.

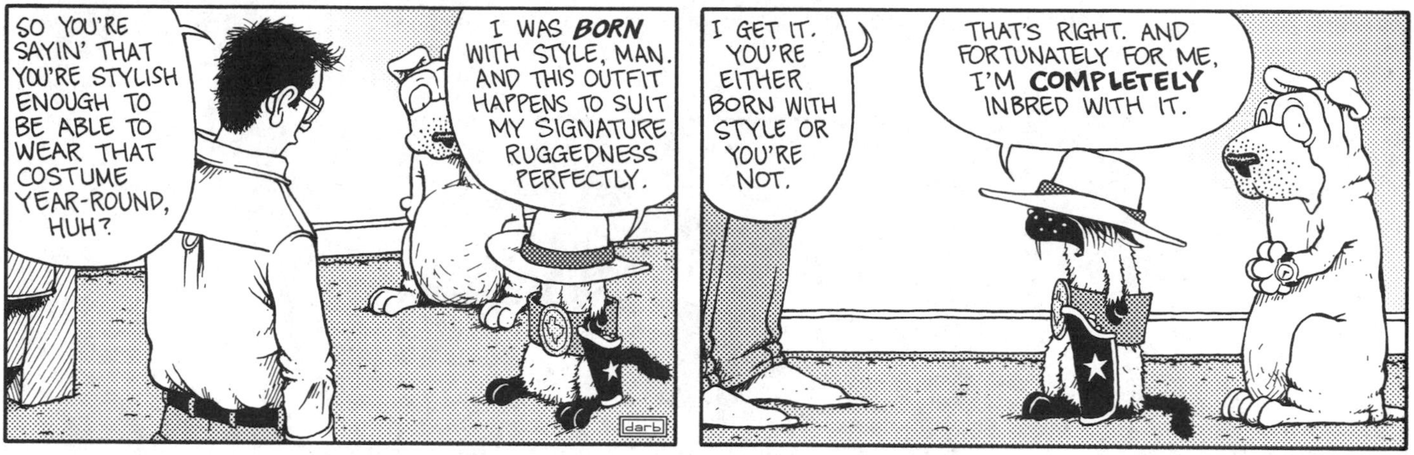
SO YOU'RE SAYIN' THAT YOU'RE STYLISH ENOUGH TO BE ABLE TO WEAR THAT COSTUME YEAR-ROUND, HUH?
I WAS **BORN** WITH STYLE, MAN. AND THIS OUTFIT HAPPENS TO SUIT MY SIGNATURE RUGGEDNESS PERFECTLY.
I GET IT. YOU'RE EITHER BORN WITH STYLE OR YOU'RE NOT.
THAT'S RIGHT. AND FORTUNATELY FOR ME, I'M **COMPLETELY** INBRED WITH IT.
darb

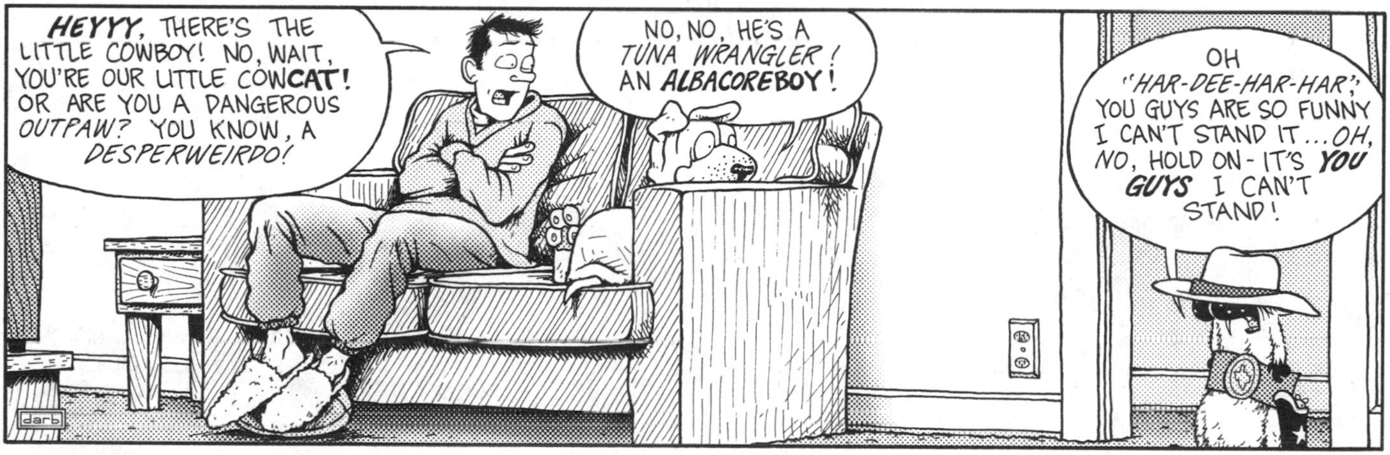
HEYYY, THERE'S THE LITTLE COWBOY! NO, WAIT, YOU'RE OUR LITTLE COW**CAT**! OR ARE YOU A DANGEROUS *OUTPAW?* YOU KNOW, A *DESPERWEIRDO!*
NO, NO, HE'S A *TUNA WRANGLER!* AN ***ALBACOREBOY!***
OH *"HAR-DEE-HAR-HAR,"* YOU GUYS ARE SO FUNNY I CAN'T STAND IT... *OH, NO,* HOLD ON - IT'S ***YOU GUYS*** I CAN'T STAND!
darb

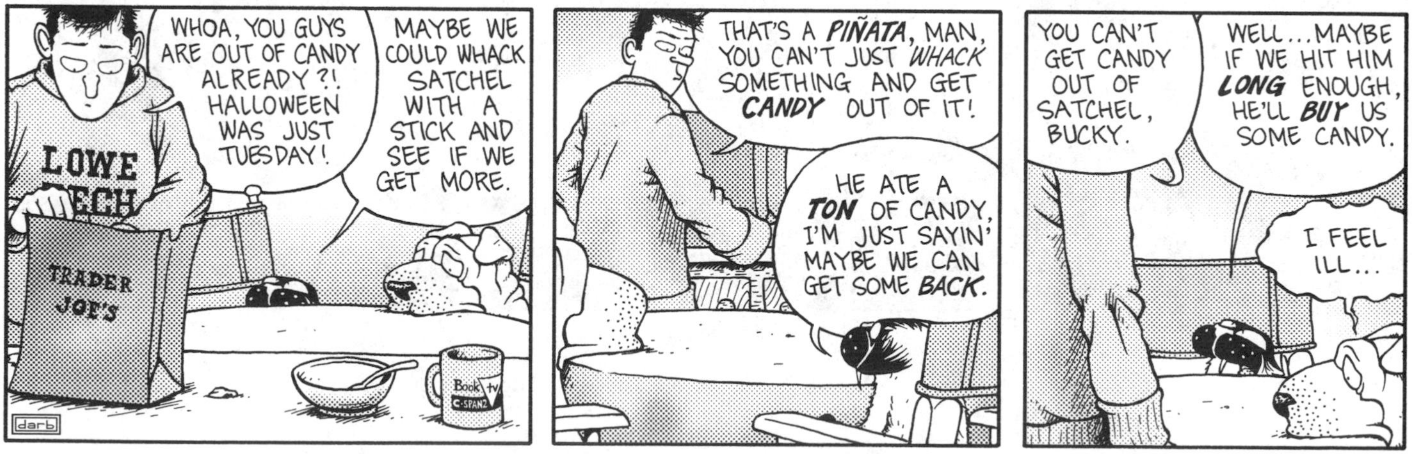
WHOA, YOU GUYS ARE OUT OF CANDY ALREADY?! HALLOWEEN WAS JUST TUESDAY!
MAYBE WE COULD WHACK SATCHEL WITH A STICK AND SEE IF WE GET MORE.
LOWE
TRADER JOE'S
Book tv C-SPAN2
darb
THAT'S A ***PIÑATA,*** MAN, YOU CAN'T JUST *WHACK* SOMETHING AND GET ***CANDY*** OUT OF IT!
HE ATE A ***TON*** OF CANDY, I'M JUST SAYIN' MAYBE WE CAN GET SOME ***BACK.***
YOU CAN'T GET CANDY OUT OF SATCHEL, BUCKY.
WELL... MAYBE IF WE HIT HIM ***LONG*** ENOUGH, HE'LL ***BUY*** US SOME CANDY.
I FEEL ILL...

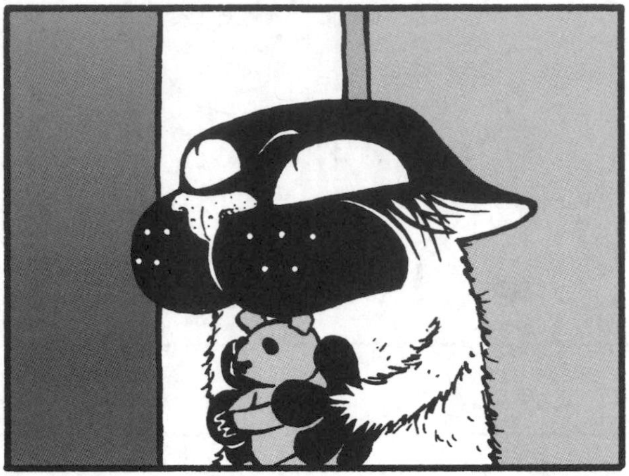

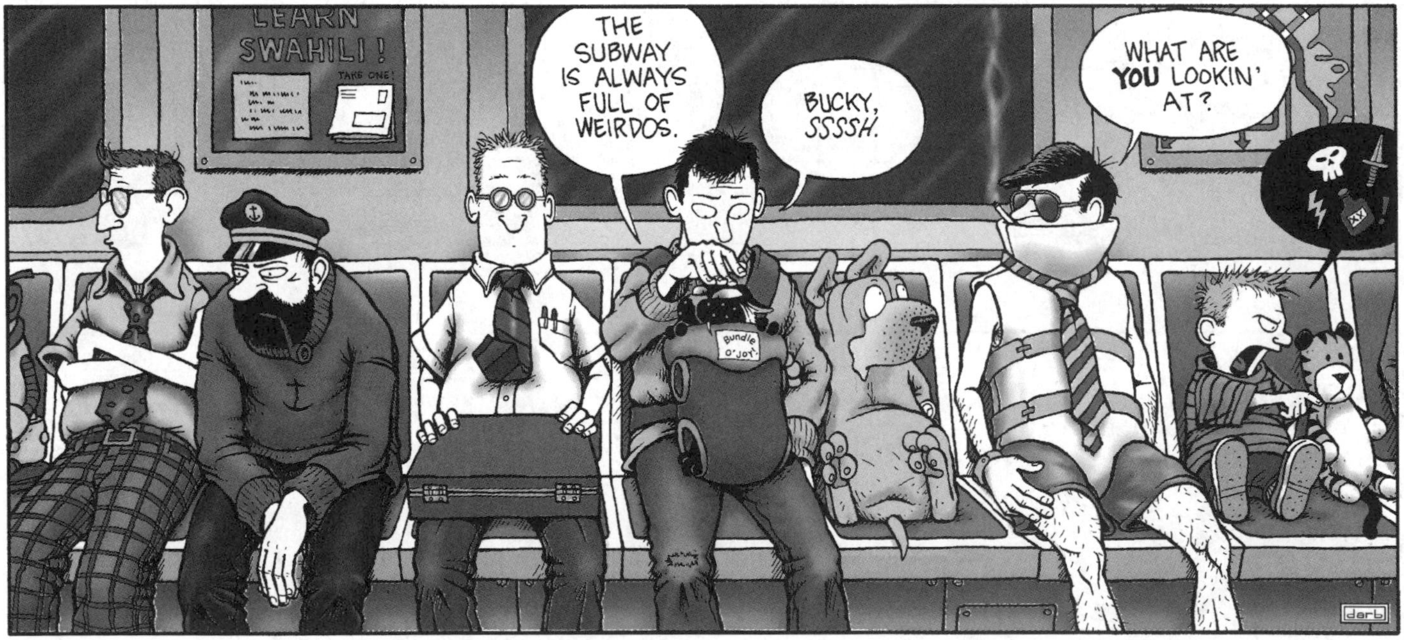
LEARN SWAHILI!
TAKE ONE!
THE SUBWAY IS ALWAYS FULL OF WEIRDOS.
BUCKY, SSSSH.
WHAT ARE **YOU** LOOKIN' AT?
Bundle O' Joy
darb

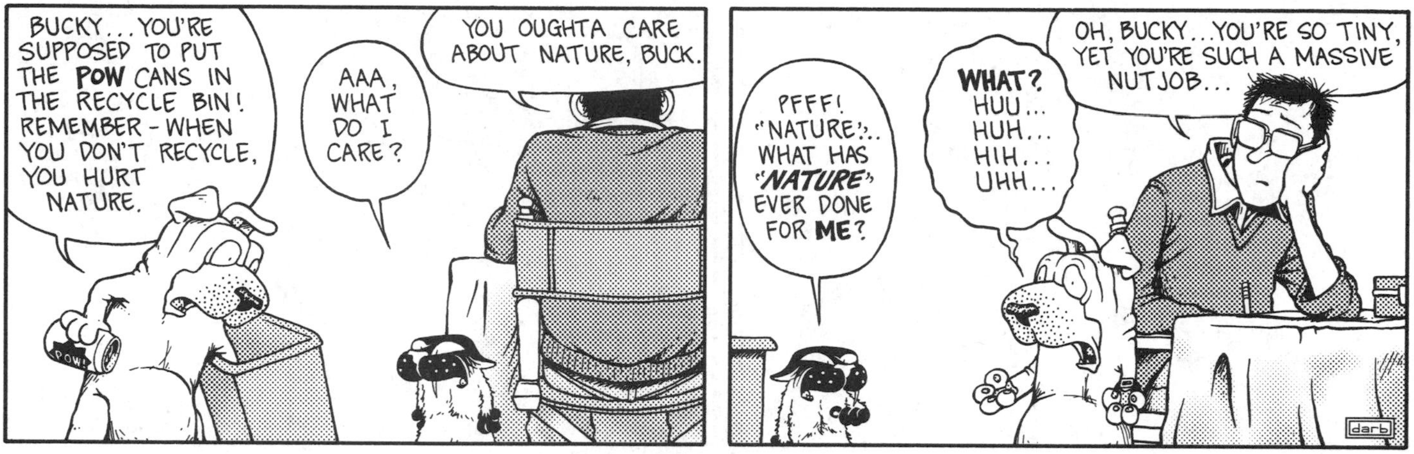
BUCKY... YOU'RE SUPPOSED TO PUT THE **POW** CANS IN THE RECYCLE BIN! REMEMBER - WHEN YOU DON'T RECYCLE, YOU HURT NATURE.
AAA, WHAT DO I CARE?
YOU OUGHTA CARE ABOUT NATURE, BUCK.
PFFF! "NATURE"... WHAT HAS "***NATURE***" EVER DONE FOR **ME**?
WHAT? HUU... HUH... HIH... UHH...
OH, BUCKY... YOU'RE SO TINY, YET YOU'RE SUCH A MASSIVE NUTJOB...
darb

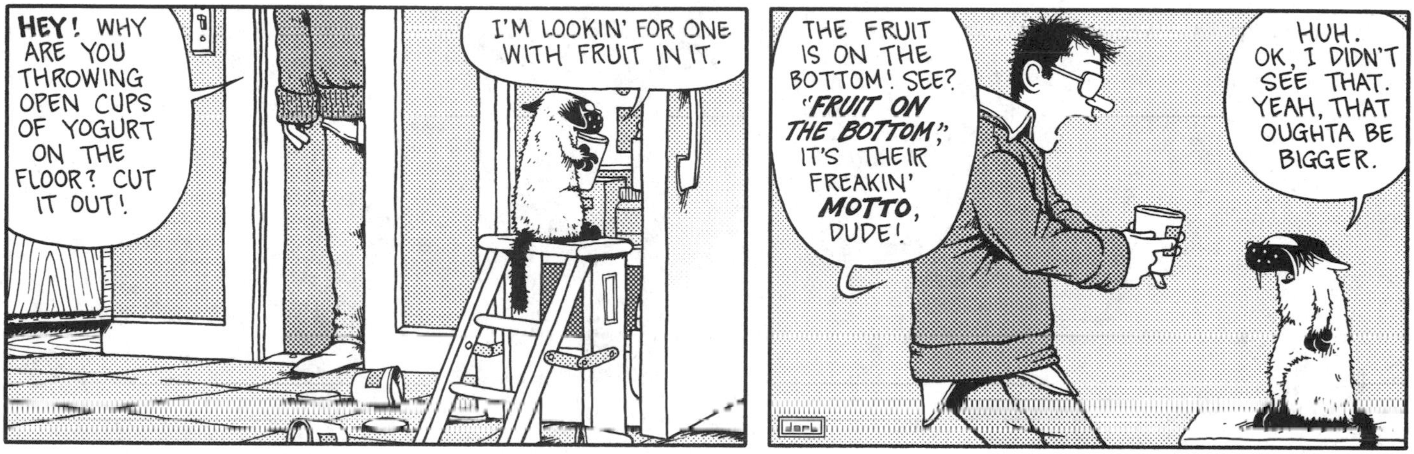
HEY! WHY ARE YOU THROWING OPEN CUPS OF YOGURT ON THE FLOOR? CUT IT OUT!
I'M LOOKIN' FOR ONE WITH FRUIT IN IT.
THE FRUIT IS ON THE BOTTOM! SEE? "***FRUIT ON THE BOTTOM***," IT'S THEIR FREAKIN' ***MOTTO***, DUDE!
HUH. OK, I DIDN'T SEE THAT. YEAH, THAT OUGHTA BE BIGGER.
darb

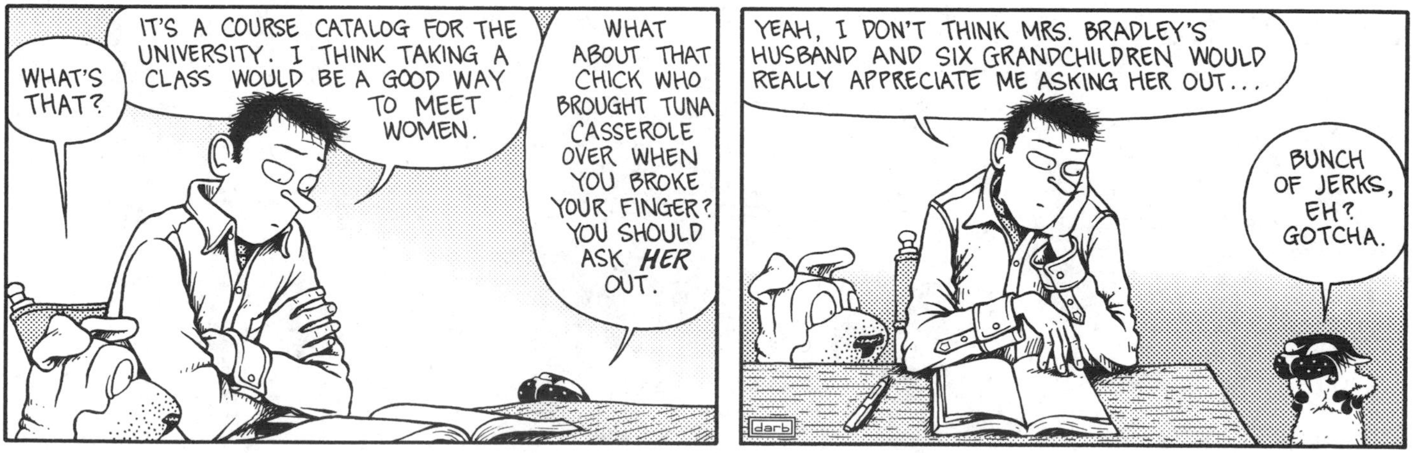
WHAT'S THAT?
IT'S A COURSE CATALOG FOR THE UNIVERSITY. I THINK TAKING A CLASS WOULD BE A GOOD WAY TO MEET WOMEN.
WHAT ABOUT THAT CHICK WHO BROUGHT TUNA CASSEROLE OVER WHEN YOU BROKE YOUR FINGER? YOU SHOULD ASK ***HER*** OUT.
YEAH, I DON'T THINK MRS. BRADLEY'S HUSBAND AND SIX GRANDCHILDREN WOULD REALLY APPRECIATE ME ASKING HER OUT...
BUNCH OF JERKS, EH? GOTCHA.
darb

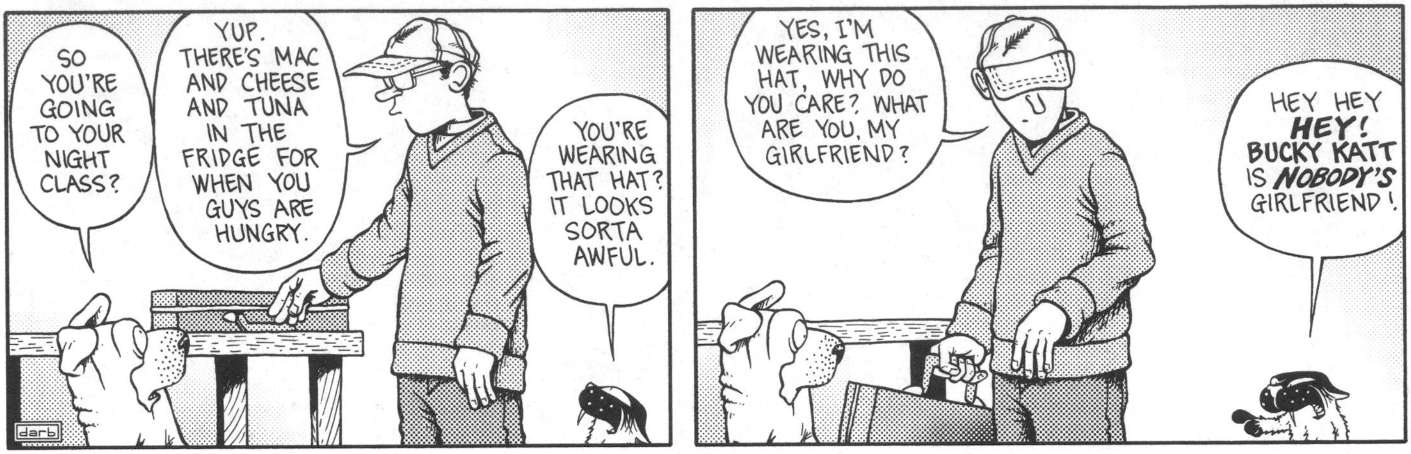
SO YOU'RE GOING TO YOUR NIGHT CLASS?
YUP. THERE'S MAC AND CHEESE AND TUNA IN THE FRIDGE FOR WHEN YOU GUYS ARE HUNGRY.
YOU'RE WEARING THAT HAT? IT LOOKS SORTA AWFUL.
YES, I'M WEARING THIS HAT, WHY DO YOU CARE? WHAT ARE YOU, MY GIRLFRIEND?
HEY HEY HEY! BUCKY KATT IS NOBODY'S GIRLFRIEND!
darb

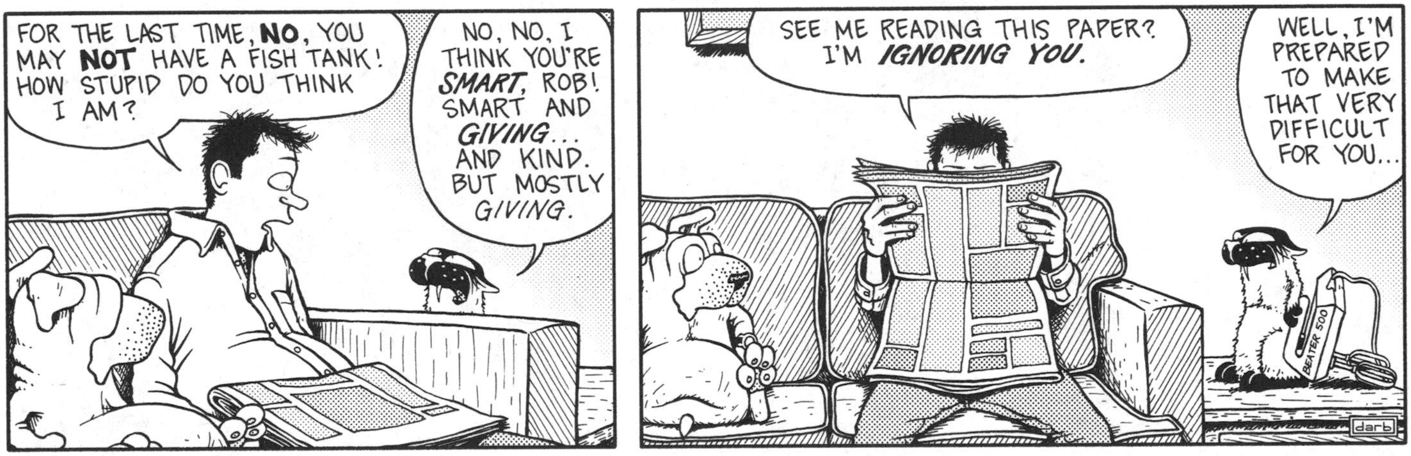
FOR THE LAST TIME, NO, YOU MAY NOT HAVE A FISH TANK! HOW STUPID DO YOU THINK I AM?
NO, NO, I THINK YOU'RE SMART, ROB! SMART AND GIVING... AND KIND. BUT MOSTLY GIVING.
SEE ME READING THIS PAPER? I'M IGNORING YOU.
WELL, I'M PREPARED TO MAKE THAT VERY DIFFICULT FOR YOU...
BEATER 500
darb

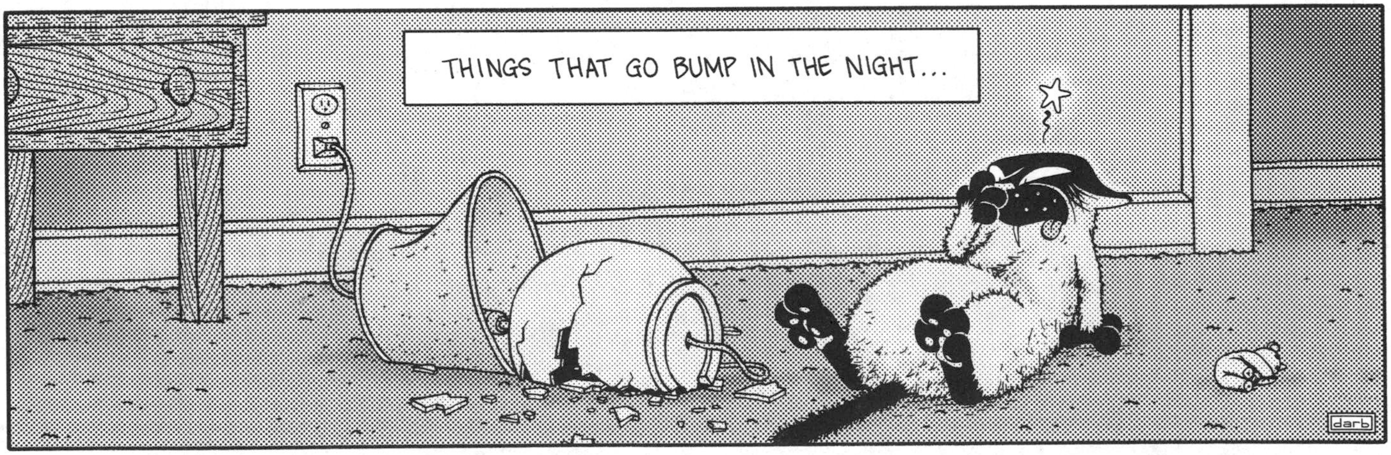
THINGS THAT GO BUMP IN THE NIGHT...
darb

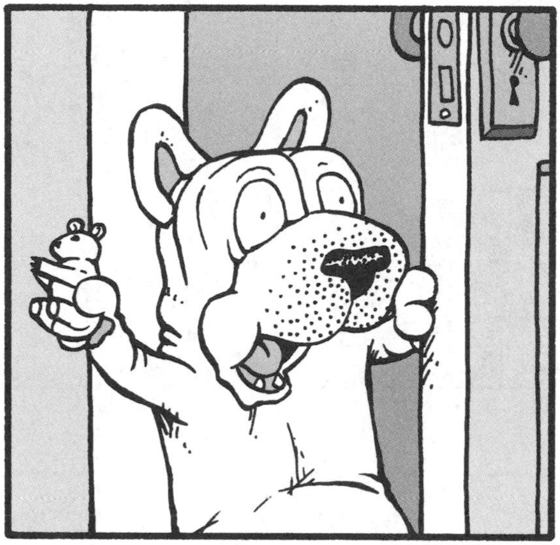

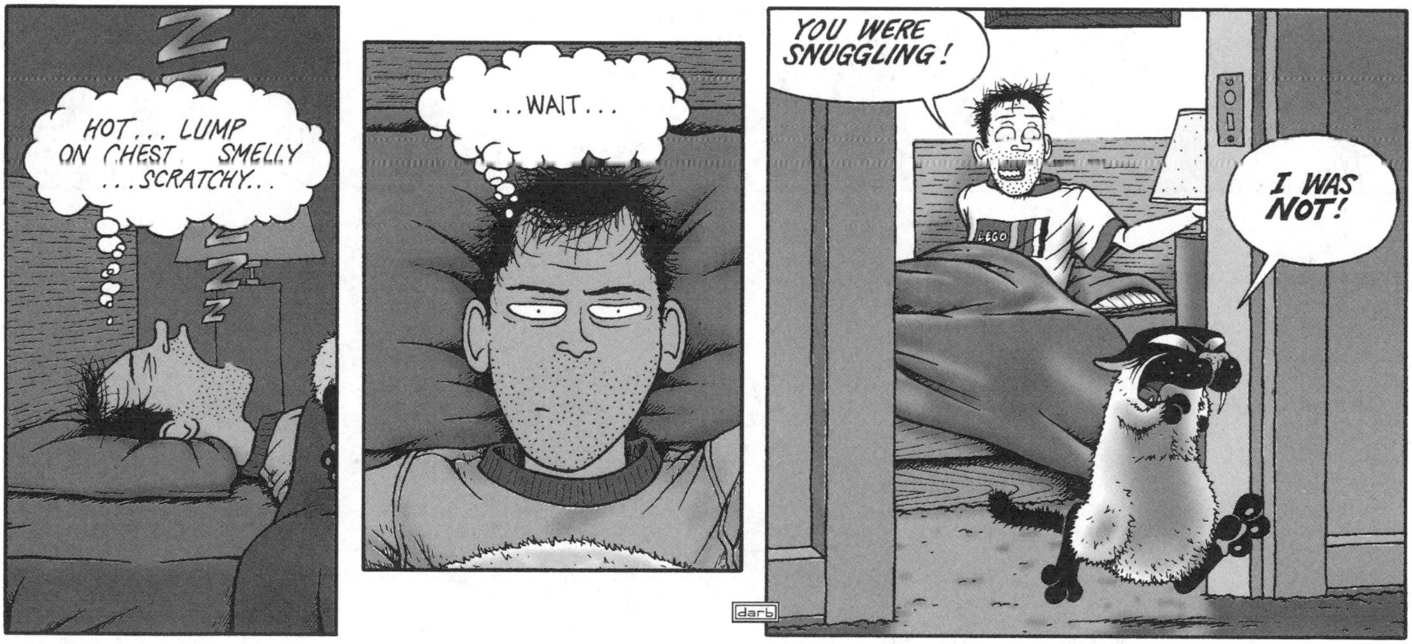

HOT... LUMP ON CHEST. SMELLY ...SCRATCHY...
...WAIT...
YOU WERE SNUGGLING!
I WAS NOT!

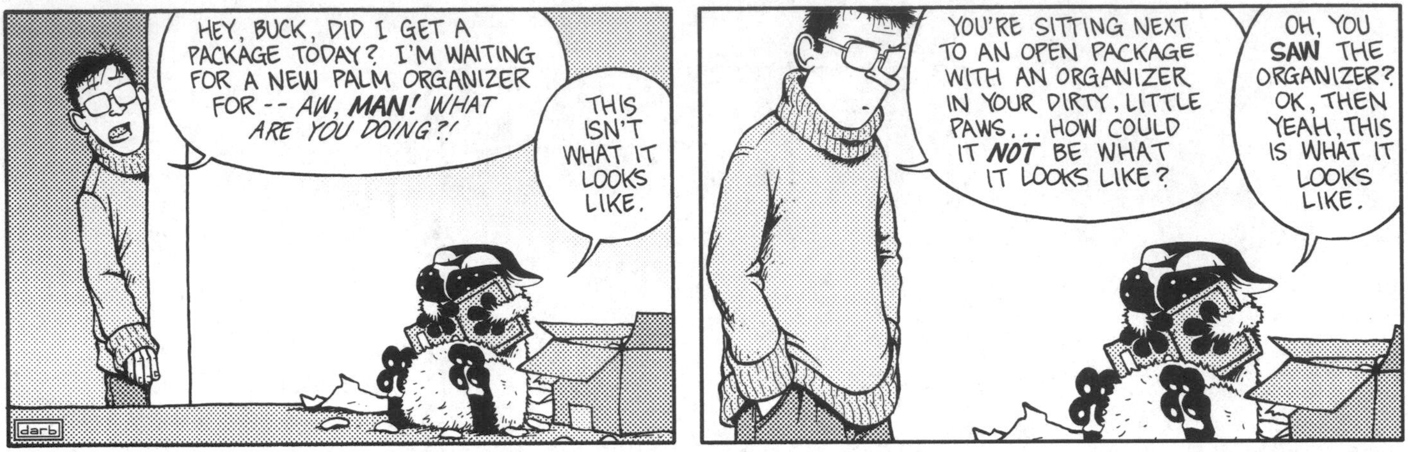
HEY, BUCK, DID I GET A PACKAGE TODAY? I'M WAITING FOR A NEW PALM ORGANIZER FOR -- AW, MAN! WHAT ARE YOU DOING?!
THIS ISN'T WHAT IT LOOKS LIKE.
darb
YOU'RE SITTING NEXT TO AN OPEN PACKAGE WITH AN ORGANIZER IN YOUR DIRTY, LITTLE PAWS... HOW COULD IT NOT BE WHAT IT LOOKS LIKE?
OH, YOU SAW THE ORGANIZER? OK, THEN YEAH, THIS IS WHAT IT LOOKS LIKE.

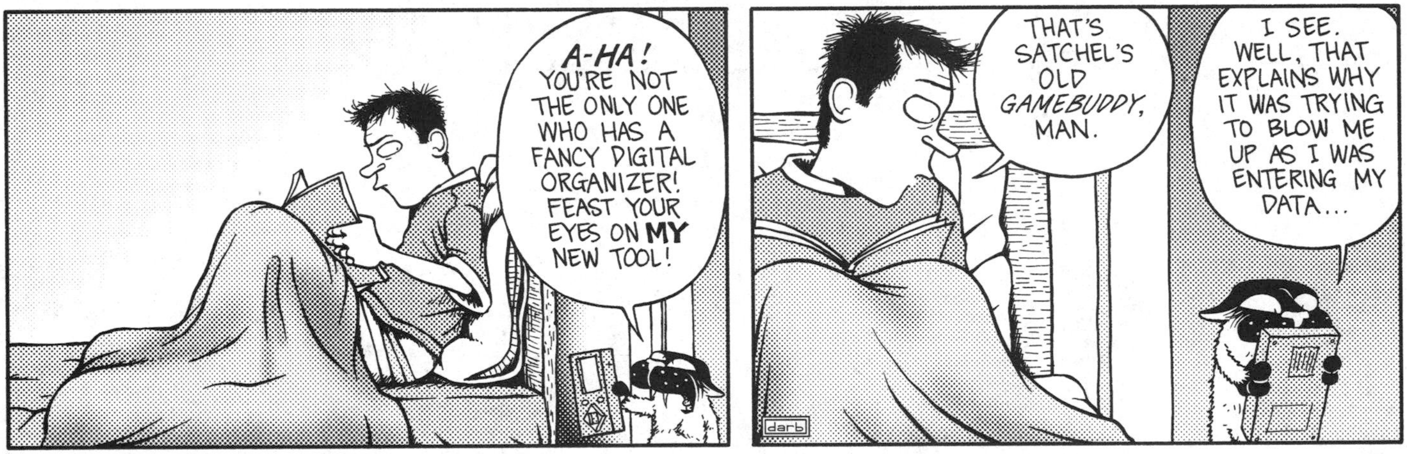
A-HA! YOU'RE NOT THE ONLY ONE WHO HAS A FANCY DIGITAL ORGANIZER! FEAST YOUR EYES ON MY NEW TOOL!
THAT'S SATCHEL'S OLD GAMEBUDDY, MAN.
I SEE. WELL, THAT EXPLAINS WHY IT WAS TRYING TO BLOW ME UP AS I WAS ENTERING MY DATA...
darb

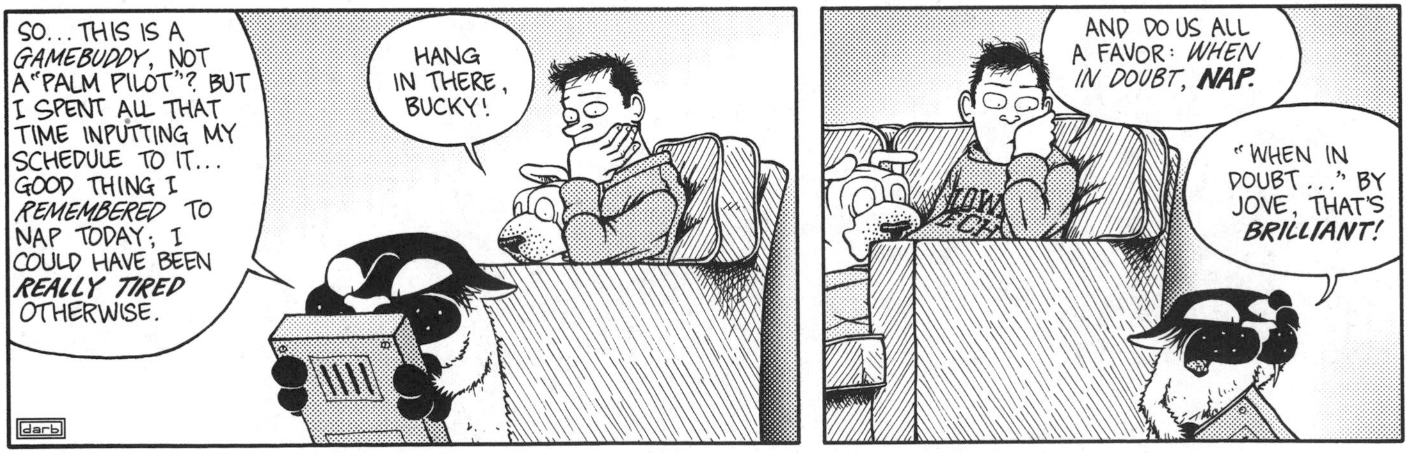
SO... THIS IS A GAMEBUDDY, NOT A "PALM PILOT"? BUT I SPENT ALL THAT TIME INPUTTING MY SCHEDULE TO IT... GOOD THING I REMEMBERED TO NAP TODAY; I COULD HAVE BEEN REALLY TIRED OTHERWISE.
HANG IN THERE, BUCKY!
darb
AND DO US ALL A FAVOR: WHEN IN DOUBT, NAP.
"WHEN IN DOUBT..." BY JOVE, THAT'S BRILLIANT!

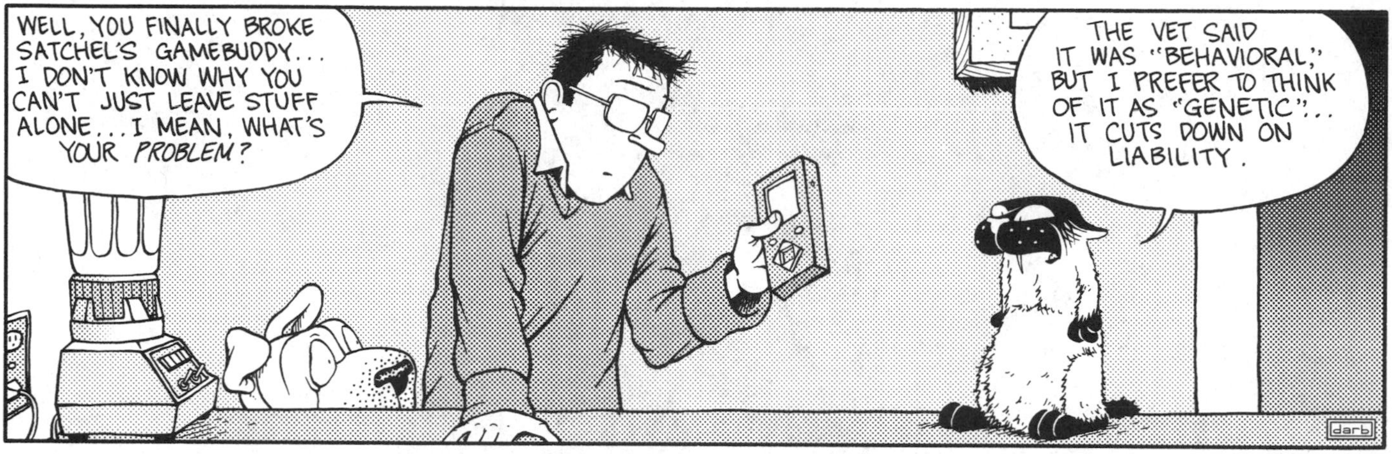
WELL, YOU FINALLY BROKE SATCHEL'S GAMEBUDDY... I DON'T KNOW WHY YOU CAN'T JUST LEAVE STUFF ALONE... I MEAN, WHAT'S YOUR *PROBLEM*?
THE VET SAID IT WAS "BEHAVIORAL," BUT I PREFER TO THINK OF IT AS "GENETIC"... IT CUTS DOWN ON LIABILITY.
darb

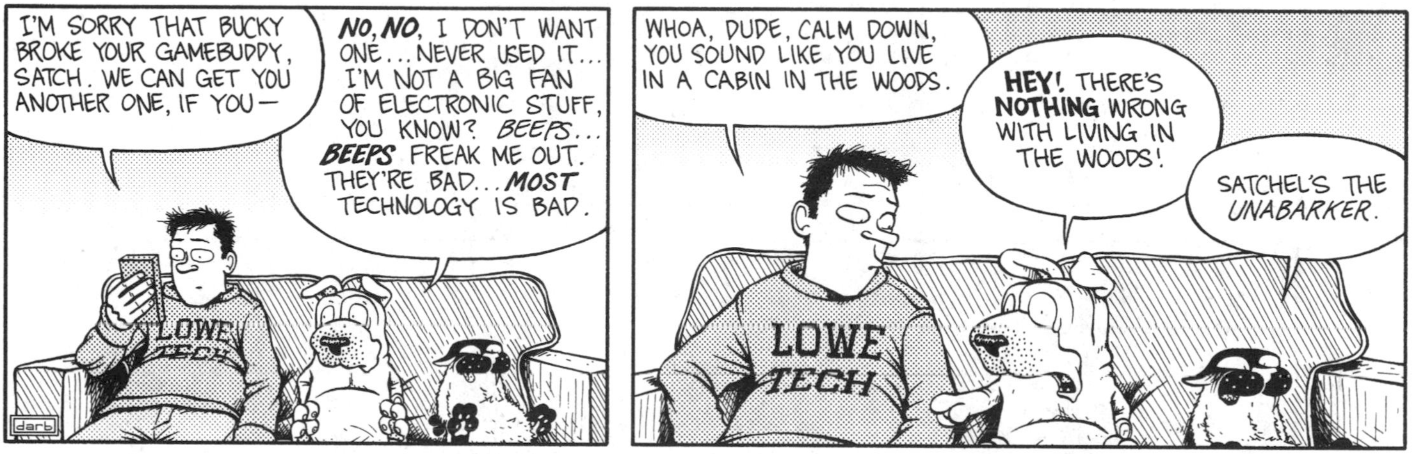
I'M SORRY THAT BUCKY BROKE YOUR GAMEBUDDY, SATCH. WE CAN GET YOU ANOTHER ONE, IF YOU—
NO, NO, I DON'T WANT ONE... NEVER USED IT... I'M NOT A BIG FAN OF ELECTRONIC STUFF, YOU KNOW? *BEEPS*... ***BEEPS*** FREAK ME OUT. THEY'RE BAD... ***MOST*** TECHNOLOGY IS BAD.
LOWE TECH
darb
WHOA, DUDE, CALM DOWN, YOU SOUND LIKE YOU LIVE IN A CABIN IN THE WOODS.
HEY! THERE'S **NOTHING** WRONG WITH LIVING IN THE WOODS!
SATCHEL'S THE *UNABARKER*.
LOWE TECH

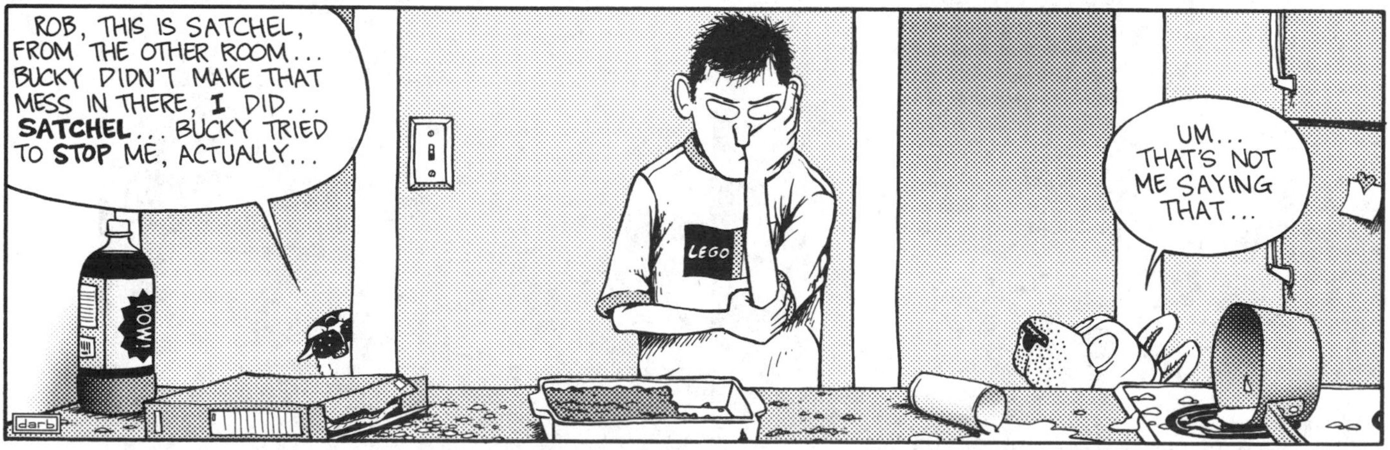
ROB, THIS IS SATCHEL, FROM THE OTHER ROOM... BUCKY DIDN'T MAKE THAT MESS IN THERE, **I** DID... **SATCHEL**... BUCKY TRIED TO **STOP** ME, ACTUALLY...
UM... THAT'S NOT ME SAYING THAT...
LEGO
POW!
darb

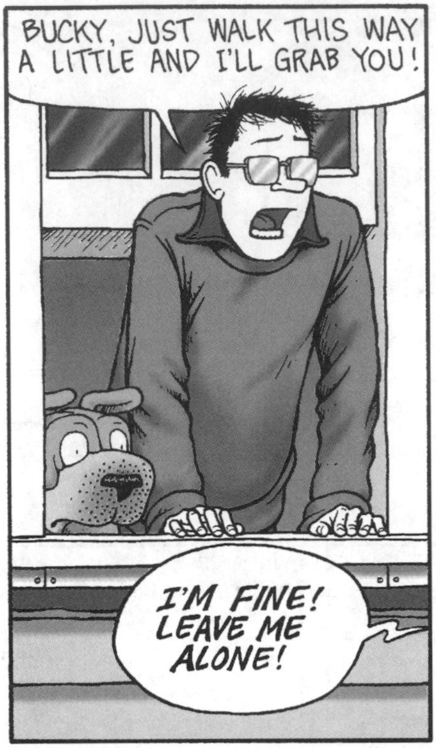
BUCKY, JUST WALK THIS WAY A LITTLE AND I'LL GRAB YOU!
I'M FINE! LEAVE ME ALONE!

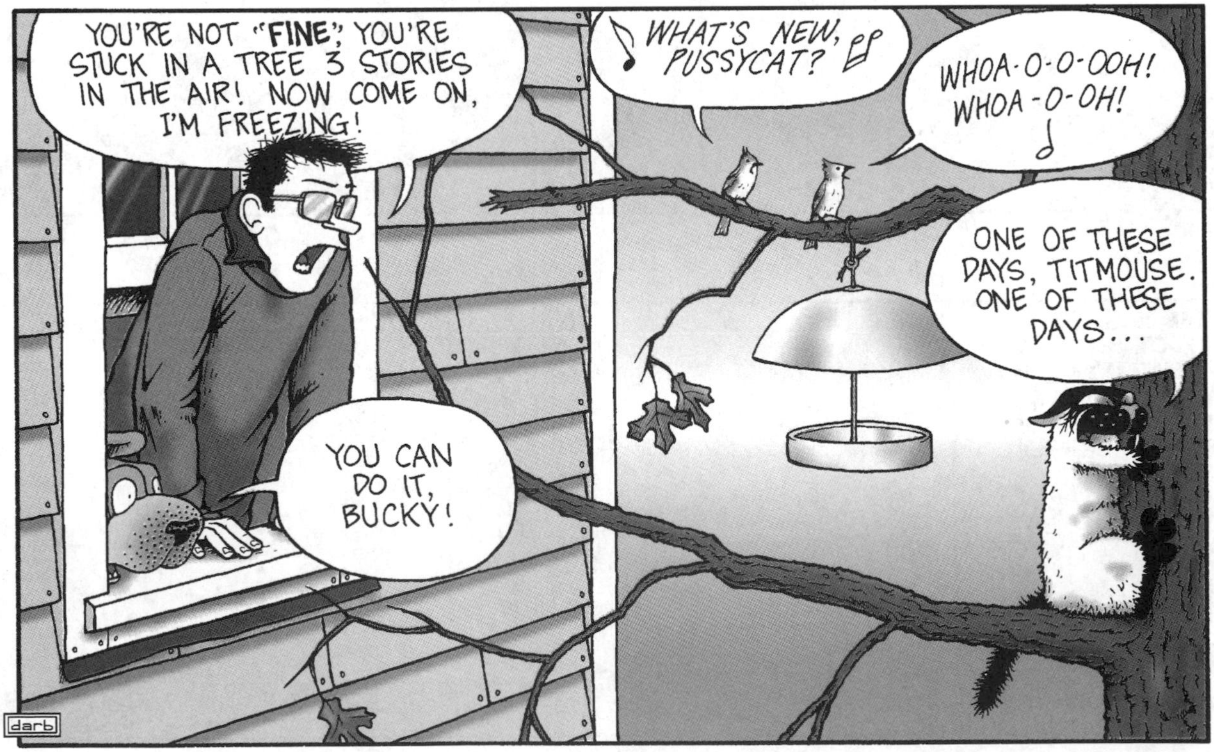
YOU'RE NOT "FINE"; YOU'RE STUCK IN A TREE 3 STORIES IN THE AIR! NOW COME ON, I'M FREEZING!
YOU CAN DO IT, BUCKY!
WHAT'S NEW, PUSSYCAT?
WHOA-O-O-OOH! WHOA-O-OH!
ONE OF THESE DAYS, TITMOUSE. ONE OF THESE DAYS...
darb

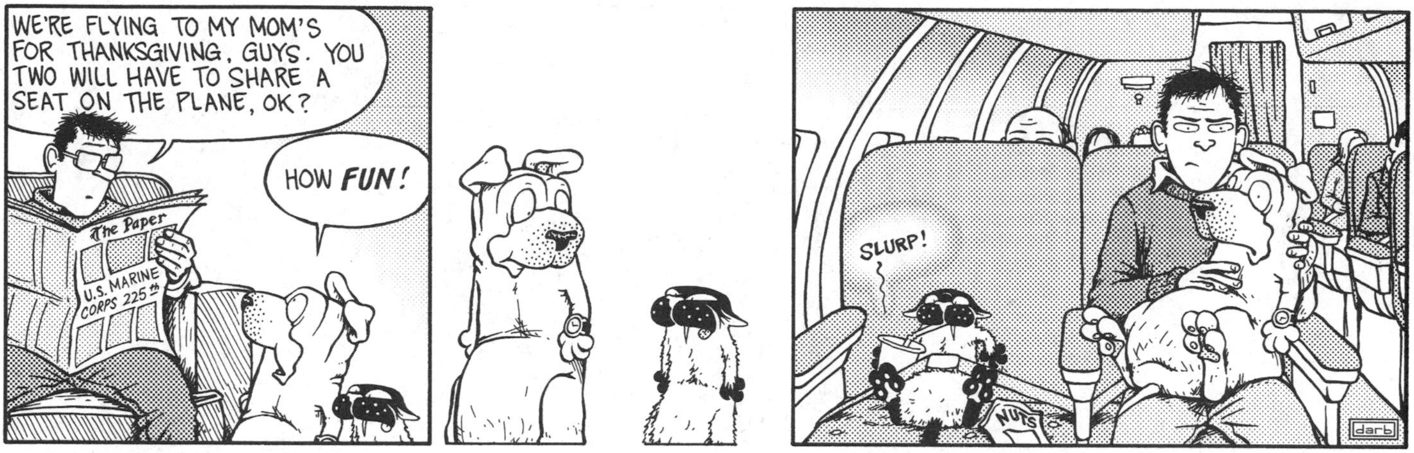
WE'RE FLYING TO MY MOM'S FOR THANKSGIVING, GUYS. YOU TWO WILL HAVE TO SHARE A SEAT ON THE PLANE, OK?
The Paper
U.S. MARINE CORPS 225th
HOW **FUN**!
SLURP!
NUTS
darb

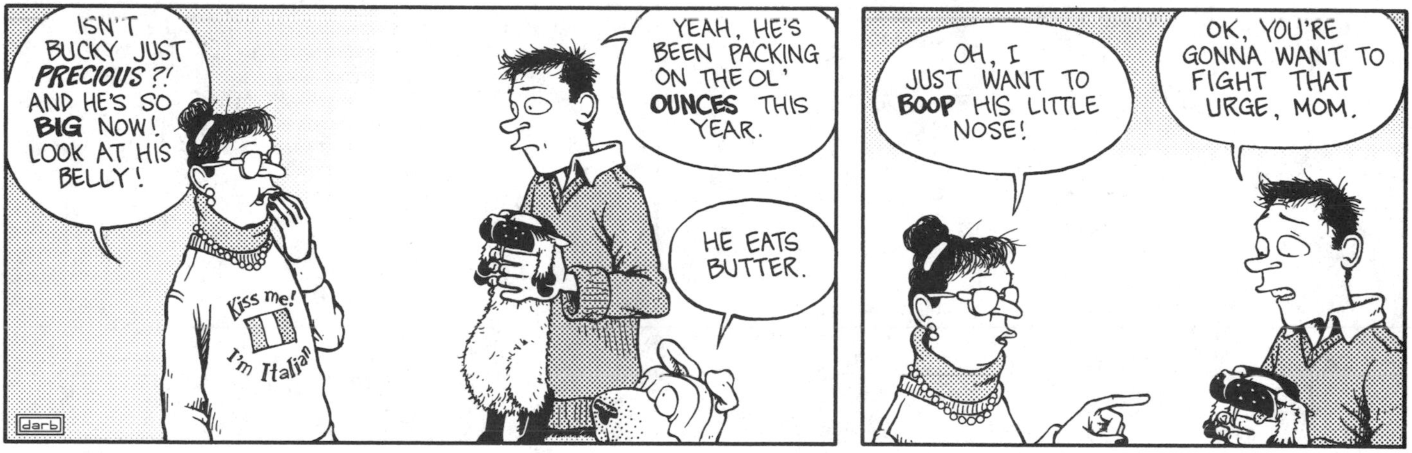
ISN'T BUCKY JUST ***PRECIOUS***?! AND HE'S SO **BIG** NOW! LOOK AT HIS BELLY!
YEAH, HE'S BEEN PACKING ON THE OL' **OUNCES** THIS YEAR.
HE EATS BUTTER.
Kiss me! I'm Italian
darb
OH, I JUST WANT TO **BOOP** HIS LITTLE NOSE!
OK, YOU'RE GONNA WANT TO FIGHT THAT URGE, MOM.

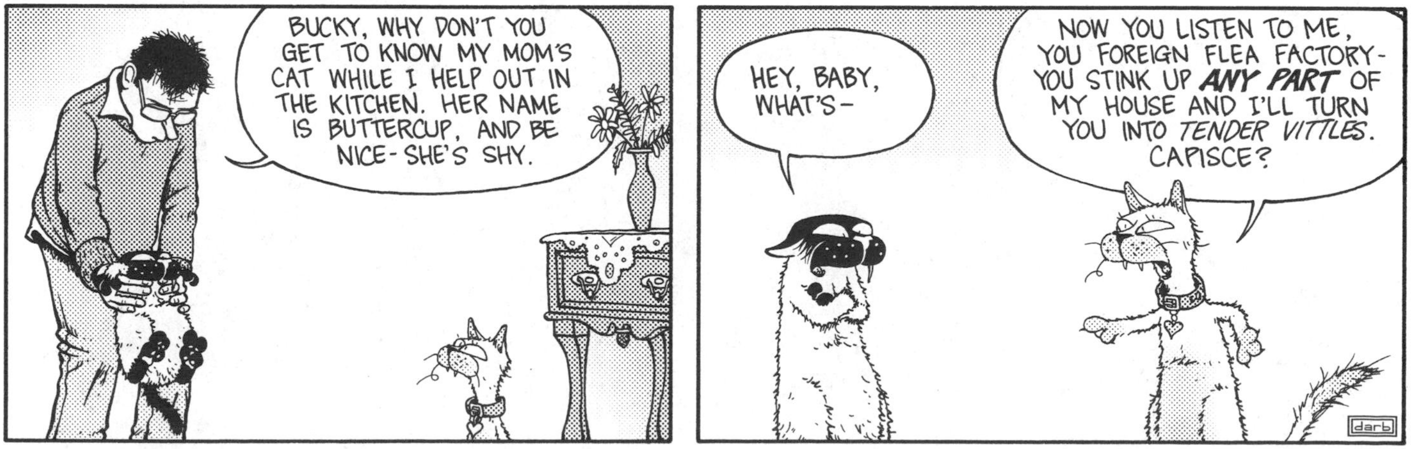
BUCKY, WHY DON'T YOU GET TO KNOW MY MOM'S CAT WHILE I HELP OUT IN THE KITCHEN. HER NAME IS BUTTERCUP, AND BE NICE- SHE'S SHY.
HEY, BABY, WHAT'S-
NOW YOU LISTEN TO ME, YOU FOREIGN FLEA FACTORY- YOU STINK UP ***ANY PART*** OF MY HOUSE AND I'LL TURN YOU INTO *TENDER VITTLES*. CAPISCE?
darb

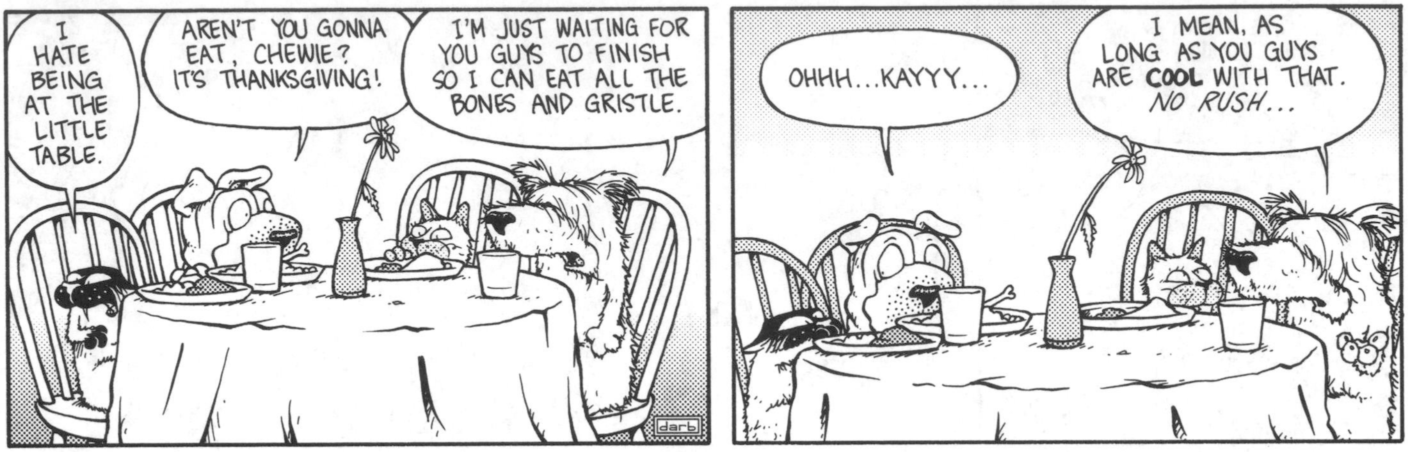
I HATE BEING AT THE LITTLE TABLE.
AREN'T YOU GONNA EAT, CHEWIE? IT'S THANKSGIVING!
I'M JUST WAITING FOR YOU GUYS TO FINISH SO I CAN EAT ALL THE BONES AND GRISTLE.
OHHH...KAYYY...
I MEAN, AS LONG AS YOU GUYS ARE **COOL** WITH THAT. *NO RUSH...*
darb

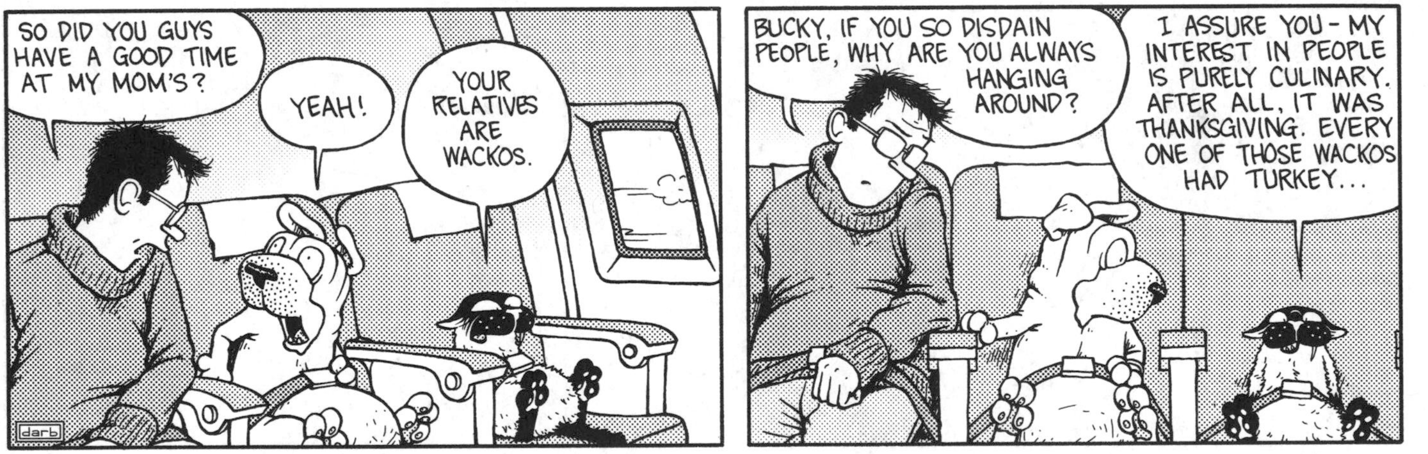
SO DID YOU GUYS HAVE A GOOD TIME AT MY MOM'S?
YEAH!
YOUR RELATIVES ARE WACKOS.
BUCKY, IF YOU SO DISDAIN PEOPLE, WHY ARE YOU ALWAYS HANGING AROUND?
I ASSURE YOU - MY INTEREST IN PEOPLE IS PURELY CULINARY. AFTER ALL, IT WAS THANKSGIVING. EVERY ONE OF THOSE WACKOS HAD TURKEY...
darb

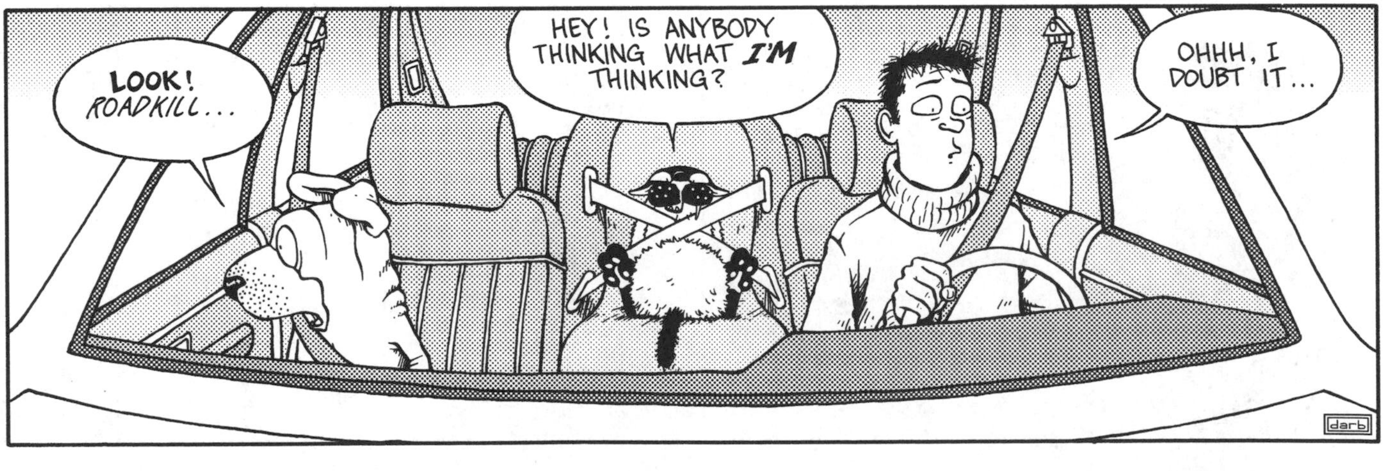
LOOK! *ROADKILL...*
HEY! IS ANYBODY THINKING WHAT ***I'M*** THINKING?
OHHH, I DOUBT IT...
darb

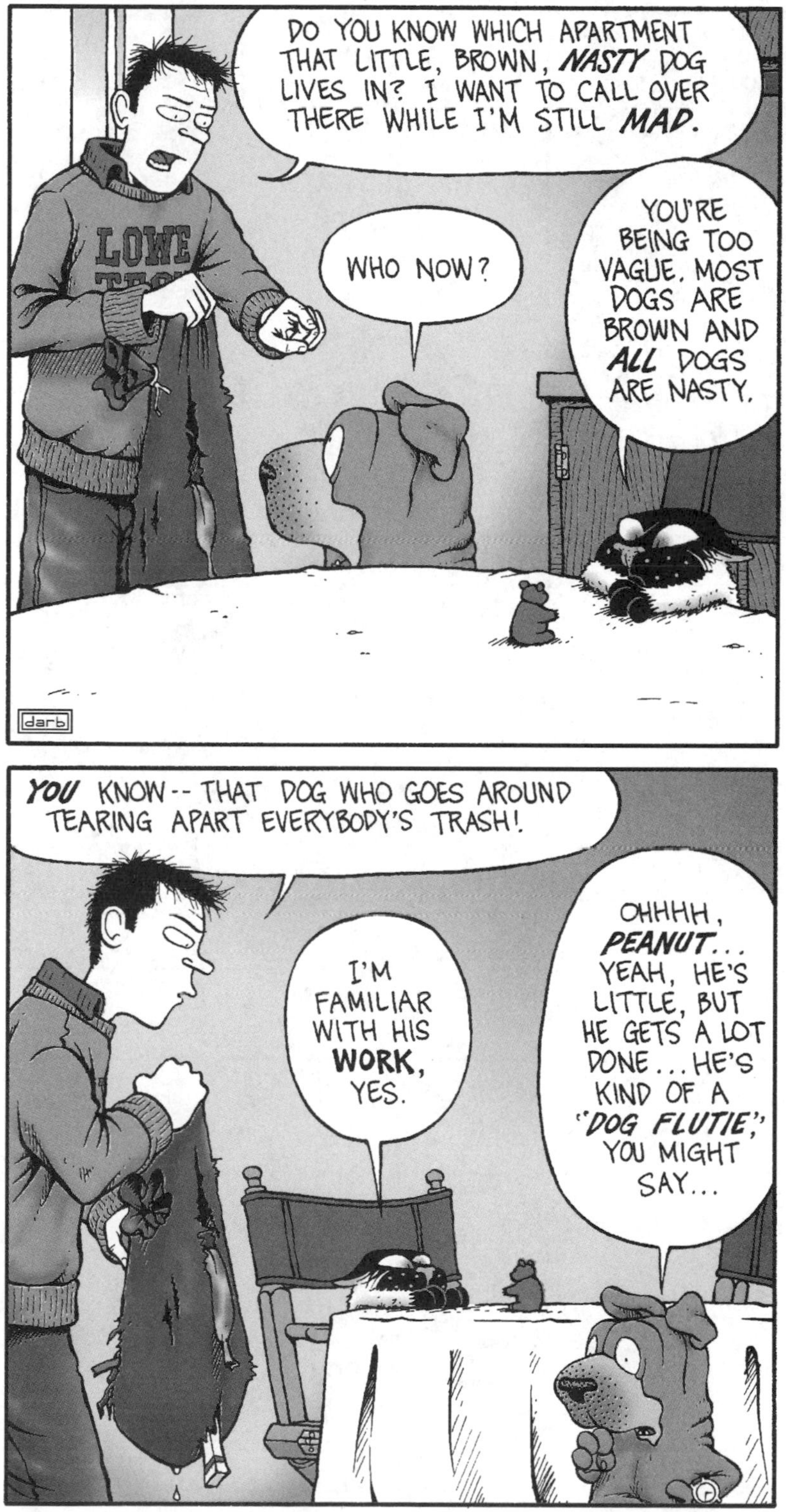
DO YOU KNOW WHICH APARTMENT THAT LITTLE, BROWN, NASTY DOG LIVES IN? I WANT TO CALL OVER THERE WHILE I'M STILL MAD.
WHO NOW?
YOU'RE BEING TOO VAGUE. MOST DOGS ARE BROWN AND ALL DOGS ARE NASTY.
darb
YOU KNOW -- THAT DOG WHO GOES AROUND TEARING APART EVERYBODY'S TRASH!
I'M FAMILIAR WITH HIS WORK, YES.
OHHHH, PEANUT... YEAH, HE'S LITTLE, BUT HE GETS A LOT DONE... HE'S KIND OF A "DOG FLUTIE," YOU MIGHT SAY...

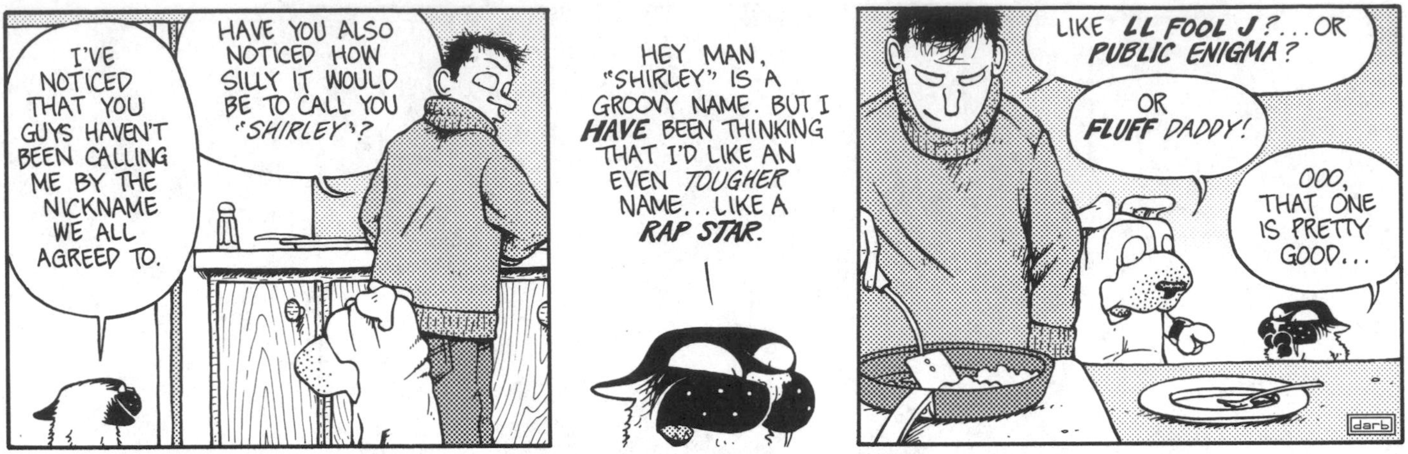
I'VE NOTICED THAT YOU GUYS HAVEN'T BEEN CALLING ME BY THE NICKNAME WE ALL AGREED TO.
HAVE YOU ALSO NOTICED HOW SILLY IT WOULD BE TO CALL YOU "SHIRLEY"?
HEY MAN, "SHIRLEY" IS A GROOVY NAME. BUT I HAVE BEEN THINKING THAT I'D LIKE AN EVEN TOUGHER NAME... LIKE A RAP STAR.
LIKE LL FOOL J?... OR PUBLIC ENIGMA?
OR FLUFF DADDY!
OOO, THAT ONE IS PRETTY GOOD...
darb

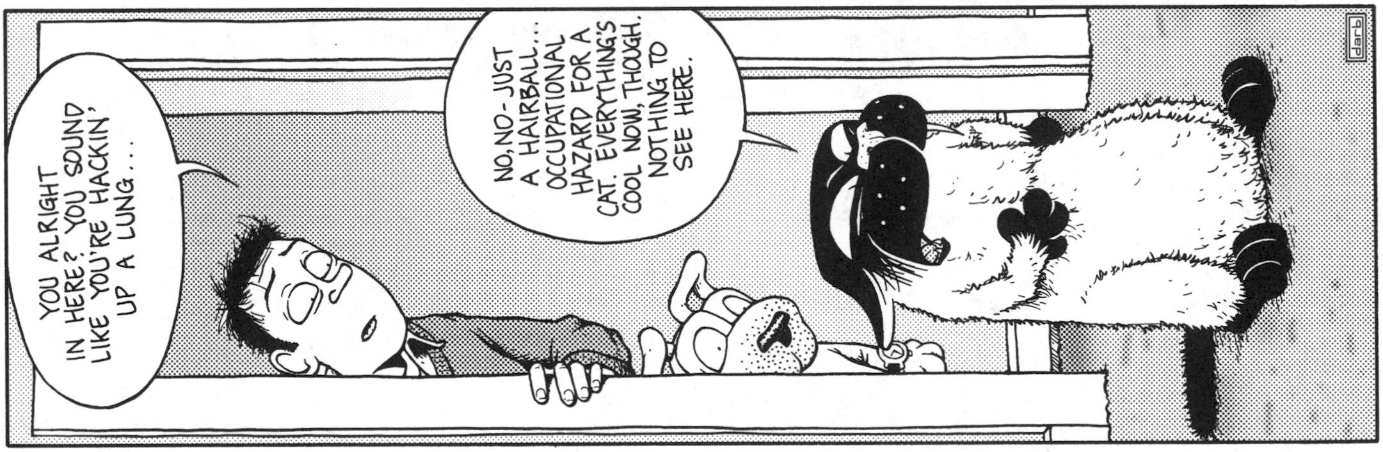
YOU ALRIGHT IN HERE? YOU SOUND LIKE YOU'RE HACKIN' UP A LUNG...
NO, NO- JUST A HAIRBALL... OCCUPATIONAL HAZARD FOR A CAT. EVERYTHING'S COOL NOW, THOUGH. NOTHING TO SEE HERE.
darb

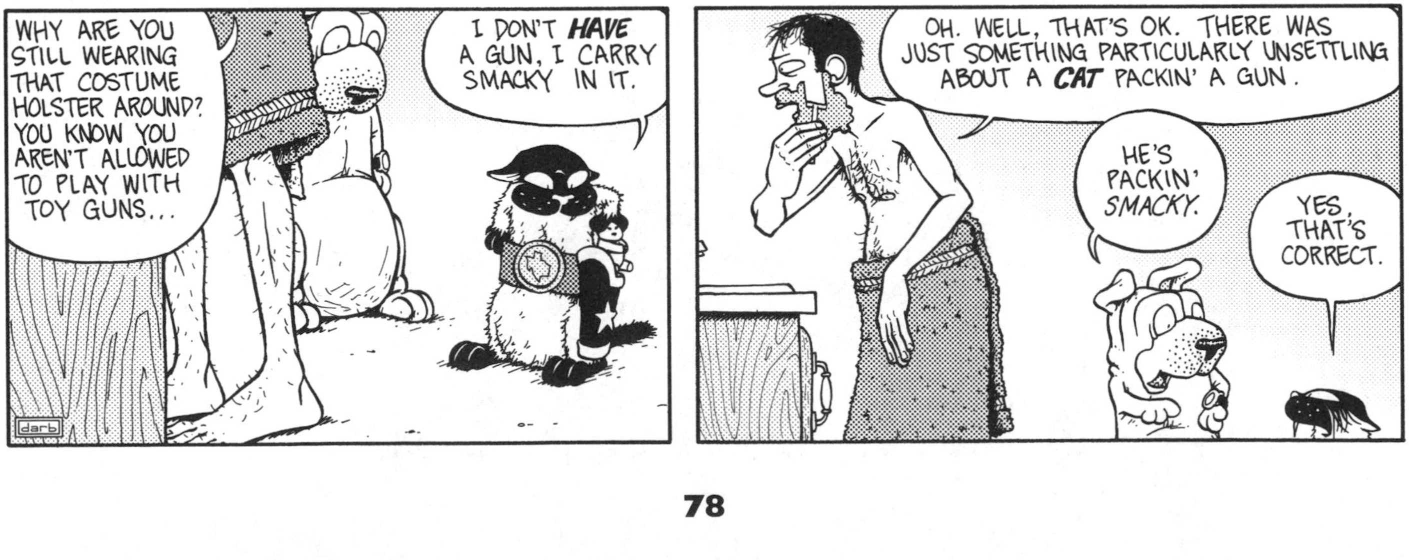
WHY ARE YOU STILL WEARING THAT COSTUME HOLSTER AROUND? YOU KNOW YOU AREN'T ALLOWED TO PLAY WITH TOY GUNS...
I DON'T HAVE A GUN, I CARRY SMACKY IN IT.
darb
OH. WELL, THAT'S OK. THERE WAS JUST SOMETHING PARTICULARLY UNSETTLING ABOUT A CAT PACKIN' A GUN.
HE'S PACKIN' SMACKY.
YES, THAT'S CORRECT.

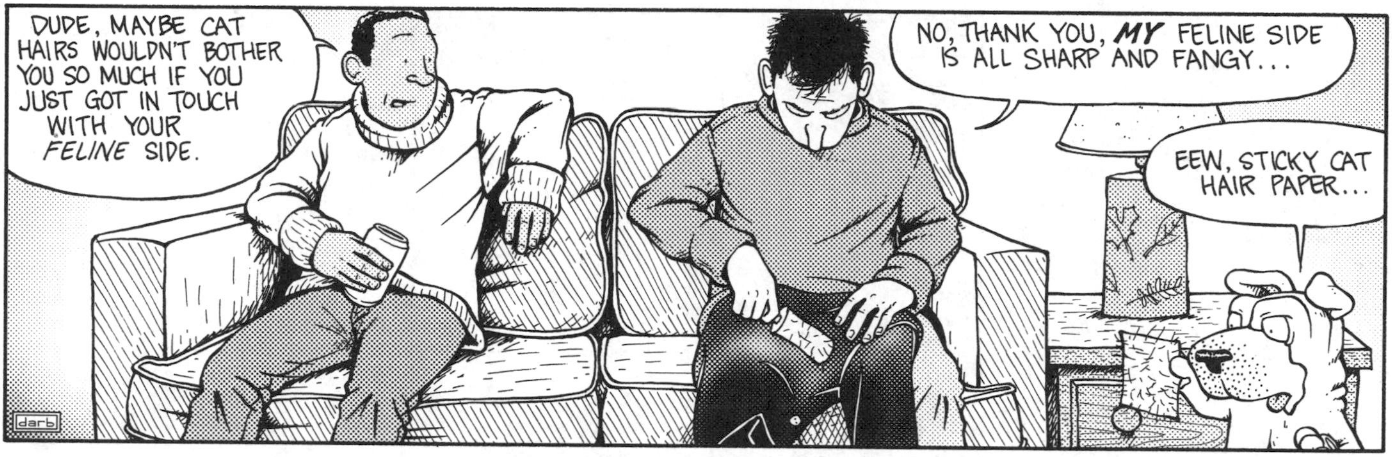
DUDE, MAYBE CAT HAIRS WOULDN'T BOTHER YOU SO MUCH IF YOU JUST GOT IN TOUCH WITH YOUR *FELINE* SIDE.
NO, THANK YOU, ***MY*** FELINE SIDE IS ALL SHARP AND FANGY...
EEW, STICKY CAT HAIR PAPER...
darb

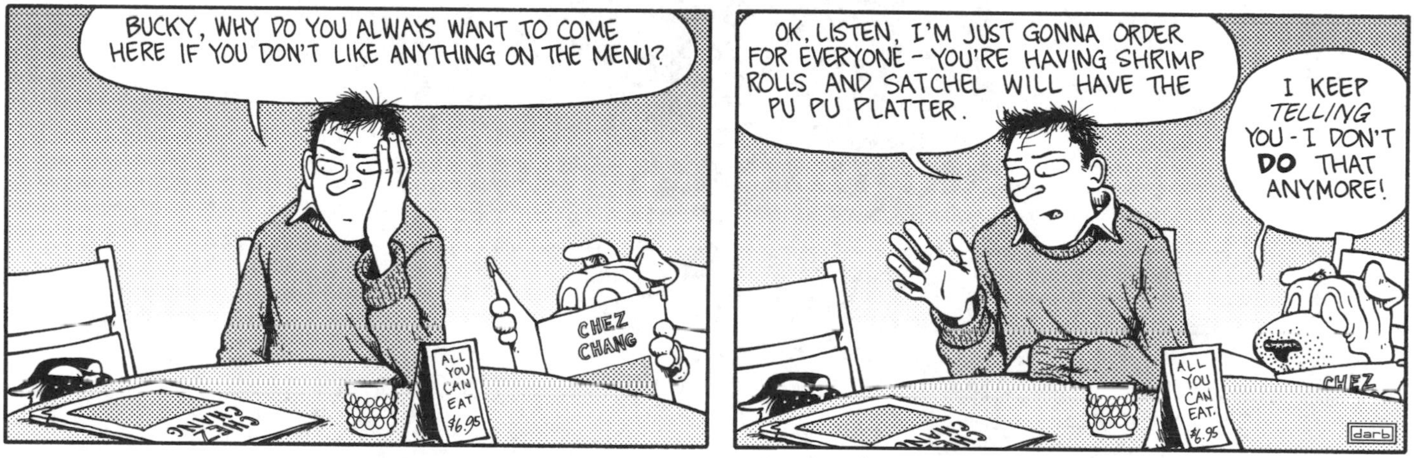
BUCKY, WHY DO YOU ALWAYS WANT TO COME HERE IF YOU DON'T LIKE ANYTHING ON THE MENU?
CHEZ CHANG
ALL YOU CAN EAT $6.95
OK, LISTEN, I'M JUST GONNA ORDER FOR EVERYONE - YOU'RE HAVING SHRIMP ROLLS AND SATCHEL WILL HAVE THE PU PU PLATTER.
I KEEP *TELLING* YOU - I DON'T **DO** THAT ANYMORE!
ALL YOU CAN EAT. $6.95
darb

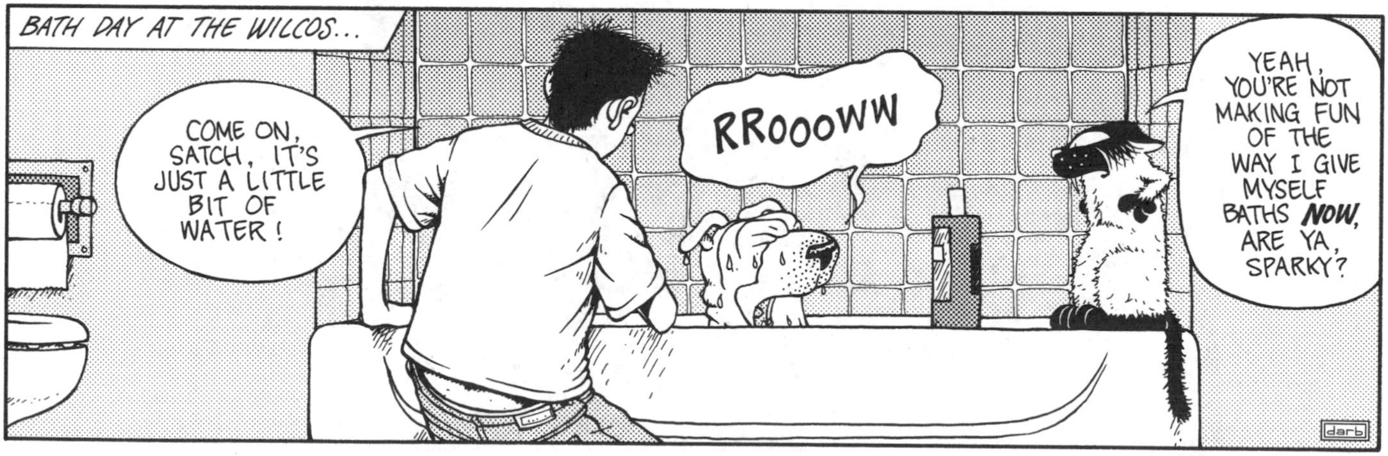
BATH DAY AT THE WILCOS...
COME ON, SATCH, IT'S JUST A LITTLE BIT OF WATER!
RROOOWW
YEAH, YOU'RE NOT MAKING FUN OF THE WAY I GIVE MYSELF BATHS ***NOW***, ARE YA, SPARKY?
darb

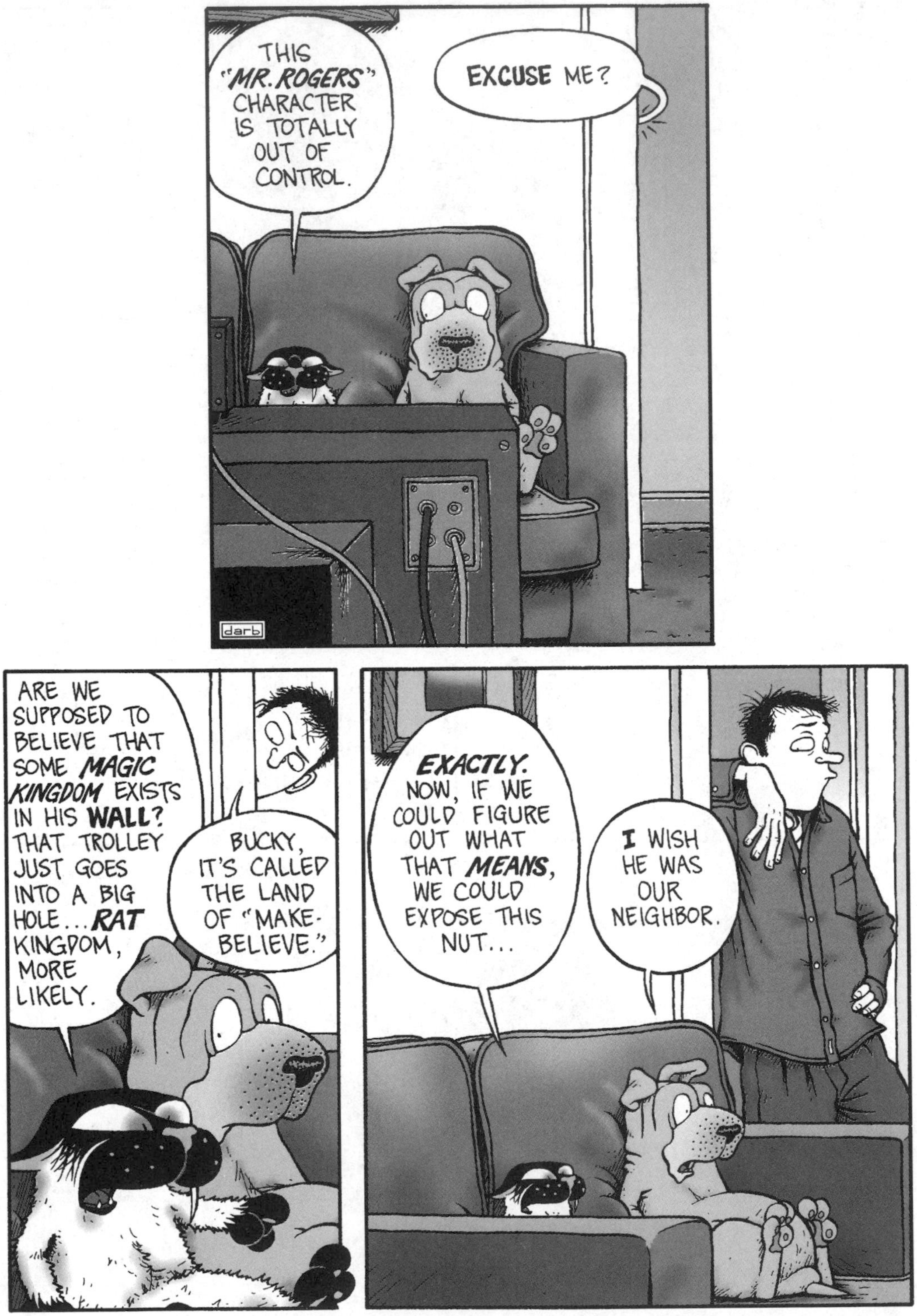
THIS "MR. ROGERS" CHARACTER IS TOTALLY OUT OF CONTROL.
EXCUSE ME?
darb
ARE WE SUPPOSED TO BELIEVE THAT SOME MAGIC KINGDOM EXISTS IN HIS WALL? THAT TROLLEY JUST GOES INTO A BIG HOLE... RAT KINGDOM, MORE LIKELY.
BUCKY, IT'S CALLED THE LAND OF "MAKE-BELIEVE."
EXACTLY. NOW, IF WE COULD FIGURE OUT WHAT THAT MEANS, WE COULD EXPOSE THIS NUT...
I WISH HE WAS OUR NEIGHBOR.

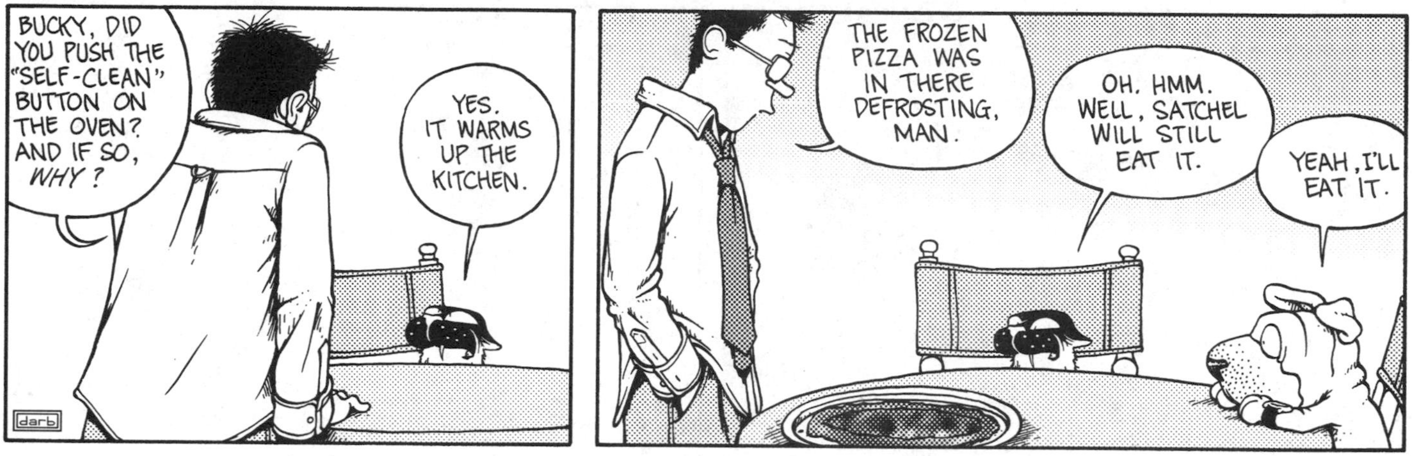
BUCKY, DID YOU PUSH THE "SELF-CLEAN" BUTTON ON THE OVEN? AND IF SO, *WHY*?
YES. IT WARMS UP THE KITCHEN.
THE FROZEN PIZZA WAS IN THERE DEFROSTING, MAN.
OH. HMM. WELL, SATCHEL WILL STILL EAT IT.
YEAH, I'LL EAT IT.

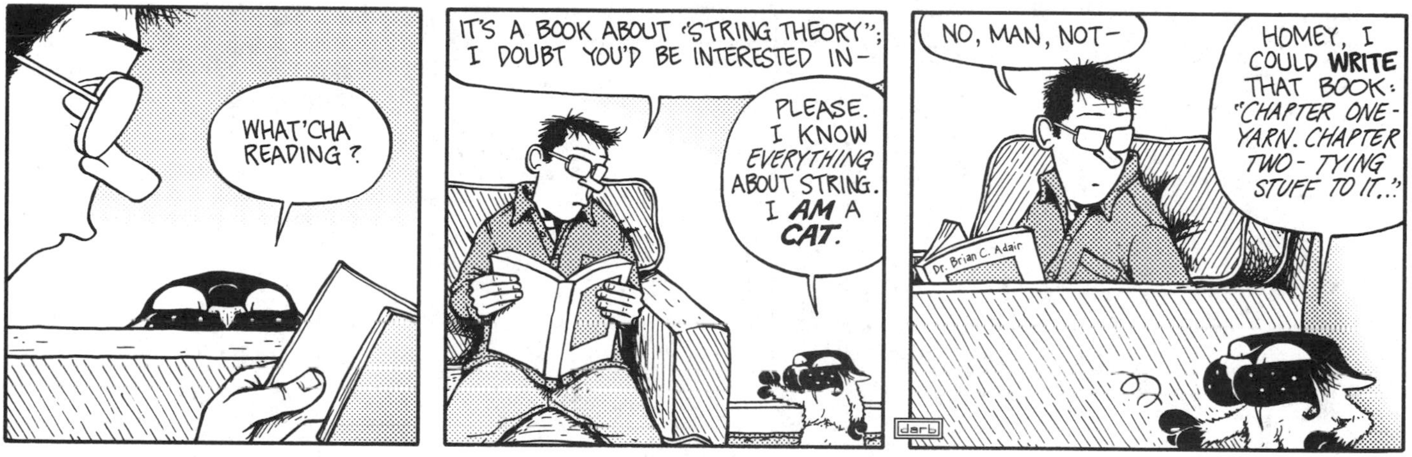
WHAT'CHA READING?
IT'S A BOOK ABOUT "STRING THEORY"; I DOUBT YOU'D BE INTERESTED IN-
PLEASE. I KNOW *EVERYTHING* ABOUT STRING. I **AM** A **CAT**.
NO, MAN, NOT-
HOMEY, I COULD **WRITE** THAT BOOK: *"CHAPTER ONE- YARN. CHAPTER TWO- TYING STUFF TO IT..."*
Dr. Brian C. Adair

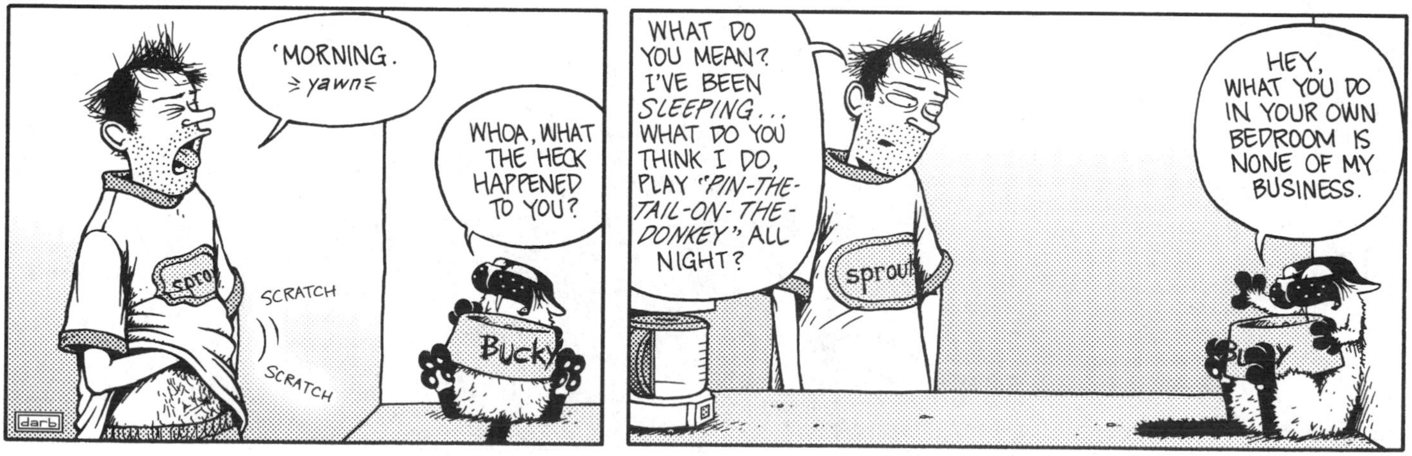
'MORNING.
yawn
SCRATCH
SCRATCH
WHOA, WHAT THE HECK HAPPENED TO YOU?
WHAT DO YOU MEAN? I'VE BEEN *SLEEPING*... WHAT DO YOU THINK I DO, PLAY *"PIN-THE-TAIL-ON-THE-DONKEY"* ALL NIGHT?
HEY, WHAT YOU DO IN YOUR OWN BEDROOM IS NONE OF MY BUSINESS.

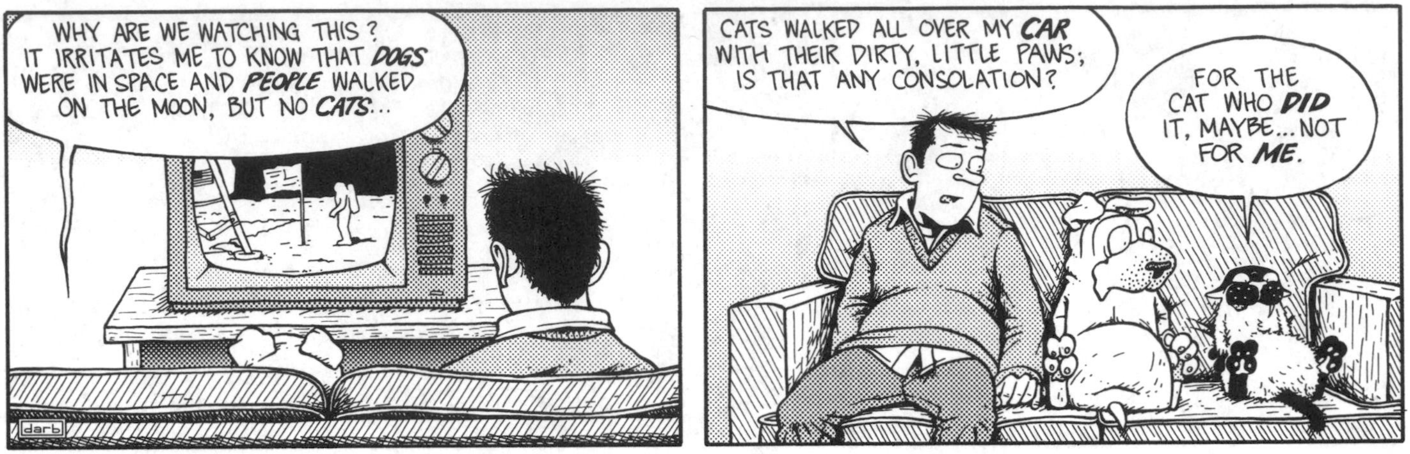
WHY ARE WE WATCHING THIS? IT IRRITATES ME TO KNOW THAT DOGS WERE IN SPACE AND PEOPLE WALKED ON THE MOON, BUT NO CATS...
darb
CATS WALKED ALL OVER MY CAR WITH THEIR DIRTY, LITTLE PAWS; IS THAT ANY CONSOLATION?
FOR THE CAT WHO DID IT, MAYBE... NOT FOR ME.

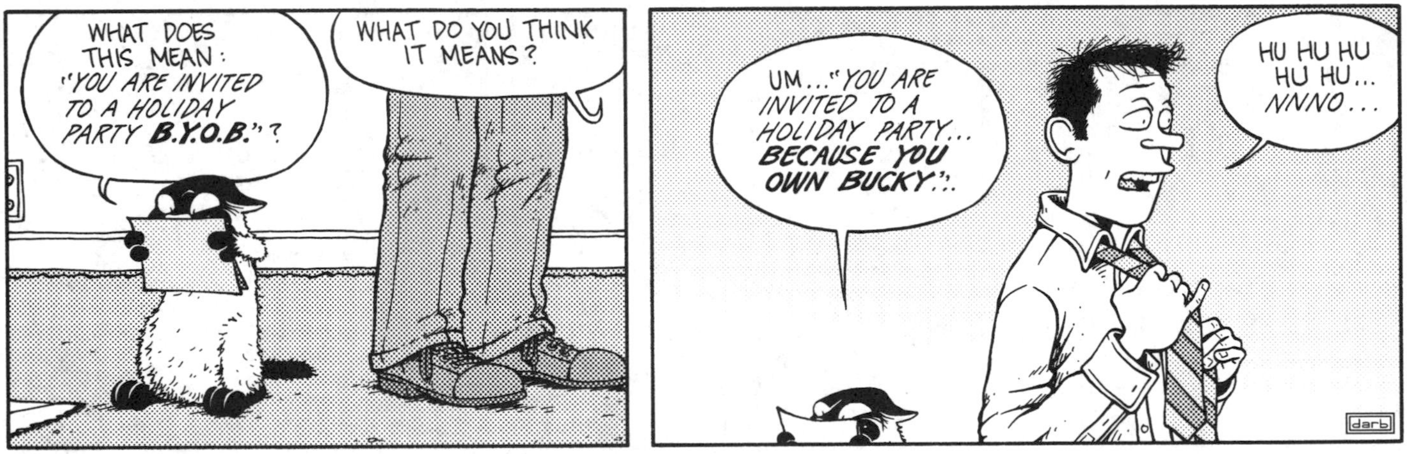
WHAT DOES THIS MEAN: "YOU ARE INVITED TO A HOLIDAY PARTY B.Y.O.B."?
WHAT DO YOU THINK IT MEANS?
UM... "YOU ARE INVITED TO A HOLIDAY PARTY... BECAUSE YOU OWN BUCKY."
HU HU HU HU HU... NNNO...
darb

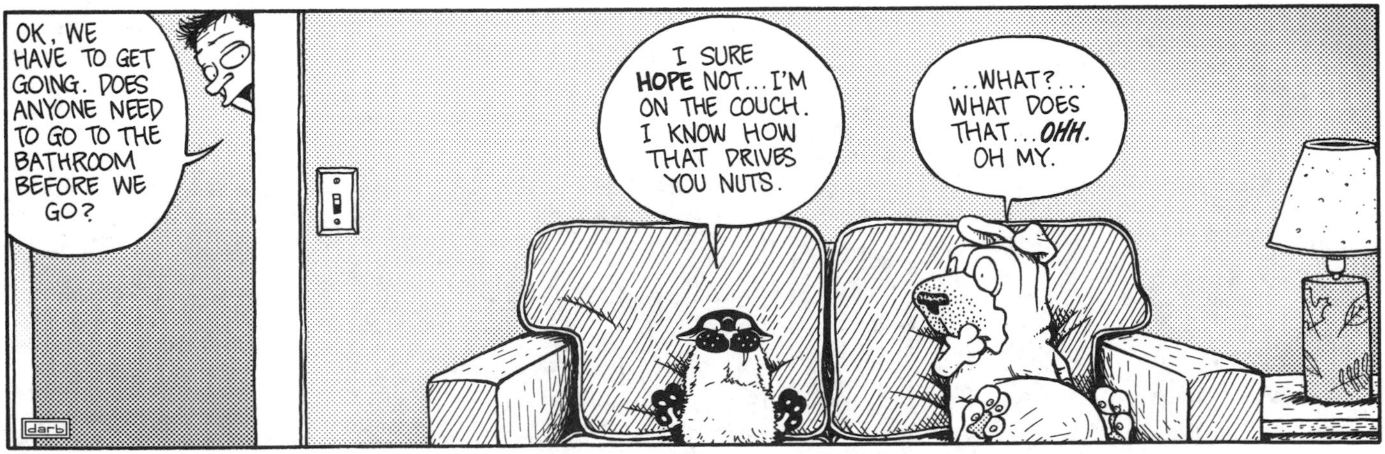
OK, WE HAVE TO GET GOING. DOES ANYONE NEED TO GO TO THE BATHROOM BEFORE WE GO?
I SURE HOPE NOT... I'M ON THE COUCH. I KNOW HOW THAT DRIVES YOU NUTS.
...WHAT?... WHAT DOES THAT... OHH. OH MY.
darb

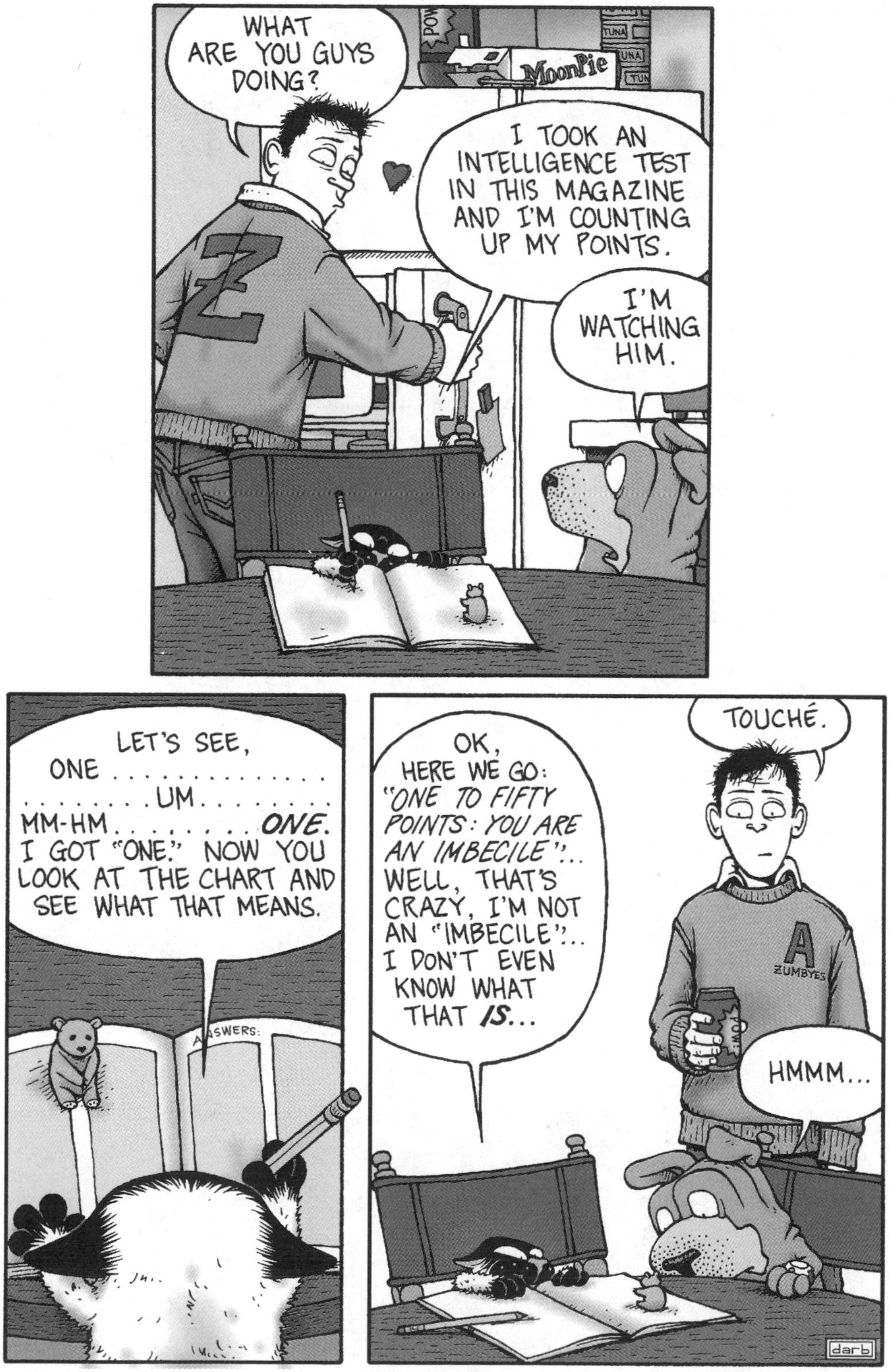
POW
MoonPie
TUNA
WHAT ARE YOU GUYS DOING?
I TOOK AN INTELLIGENCE TEST IN THIS MAGAZINE AND I'M COUNTING UP MY POINTS.
I'M WATCHING HIM.
LET'S SEE, ONE ....UM......... MM-HM........***ONE***. I GOT "ONE." NOW YOU LOOK AT THE CHART AND SEE WHAT THAT MEANS.
ANSWERS:
OK, HERE WE GO: "*ONE TO FIFTY POINTS: YOU ARE AN IMBECILE*"... WELL, THAT'S CRAZY, I'M NOT AN "IMBECILE"... I DON'T EVEN KNOW WHAT THAT ***IS***...
TOUCHÉ.
ZUMBYES
HMMM...
darb

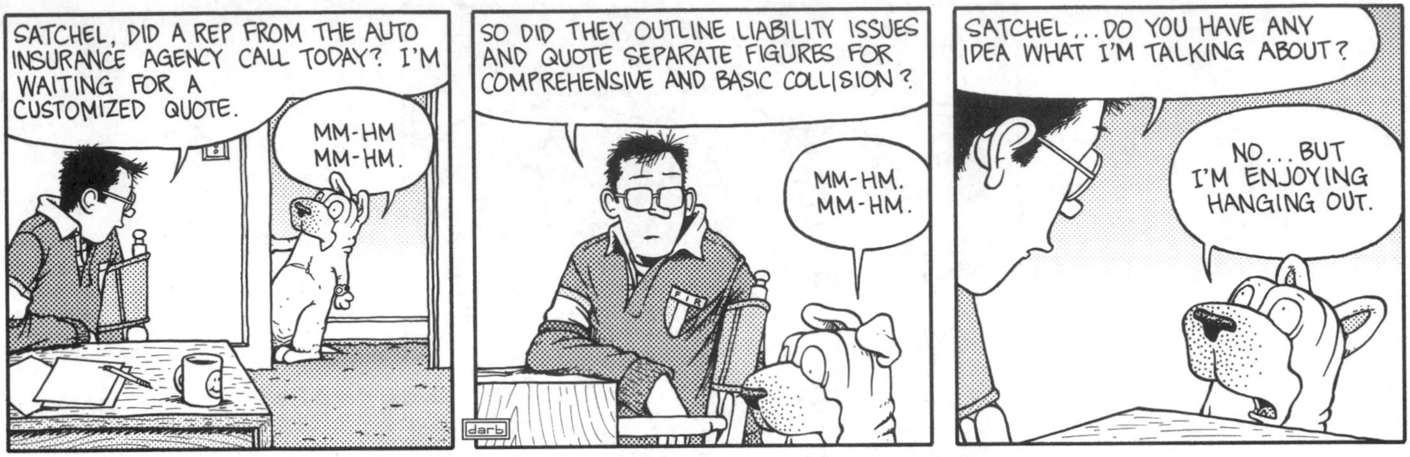
SATCHEL, DID A REP FROM THE AUTO INSURANCE AGENCY CALL TODAY? I'M WAITING FOR A CUSTOMIZED QUOTE.
MM-HM MM-HM.
SO DID THEY OUTLINE LIABILITY ISSUES AND QUOTE SEPARATE FIGURES FOR COMPREHENSIVE AND BASIC COLLISION?
MM-HM. MM-HM.
SATCHEL... DO YOU HAVE ANY IDEA WHAT I'M TALKING ABOUT?
NO... BUT I'M ENJOYING HANGING OUT.

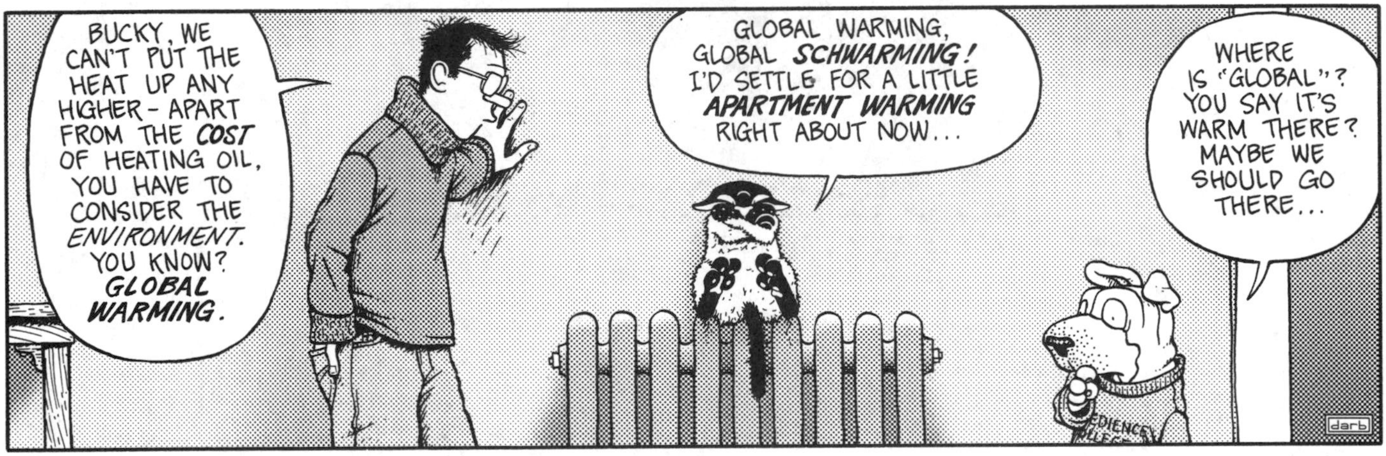
BUCKY, WE CAN'T PUT THE HEAT UP ANY HIGHER - APART FROM THE *COST* OF HEATING OIL, YOU HAVE TO CONSIDER THE *ENVIRONMENT.* YOU KNOW? **GLOBAL WARMING.**
GLOBAL WARMING, GLOBAL **SCHWARMING!** I'D SETTLE FOR A LITTLE **APARTMENT WARMING** RIGHT ABOUT NOW...
WHERE IS "GLOBAL"? YOU SAY IT'S WARM THERE? MAYBE WE SHOULD GO THERE...

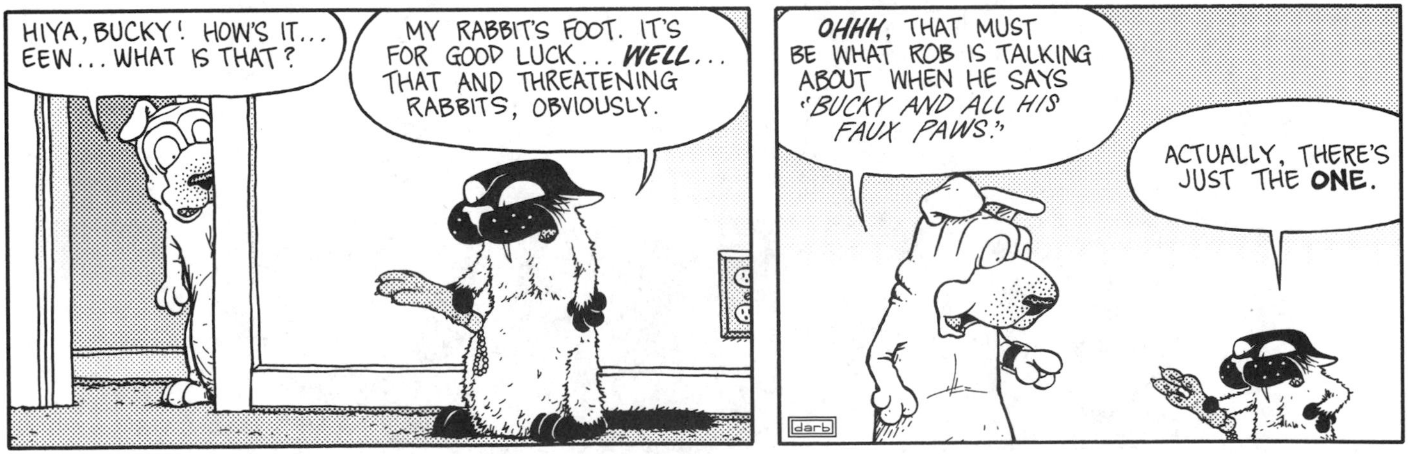
HIYA, BUCKY! HOW'S IT... EEW... WHAT IS THAT?
MY RABBIT'S FOOT. IT'S FOR GOOD LUCK... **WELL**... THAT AND THREATENING RABBITS, OBVIOUSLY.
OHHH, THAT MUST BE WHAT ROB IS TALKING ABOUT WHEN HE SAYS "*BUCKY AND ALL HIS FAUX PAWS.*"
ACTUALLY, THERE'S JUST THE **ONE.**

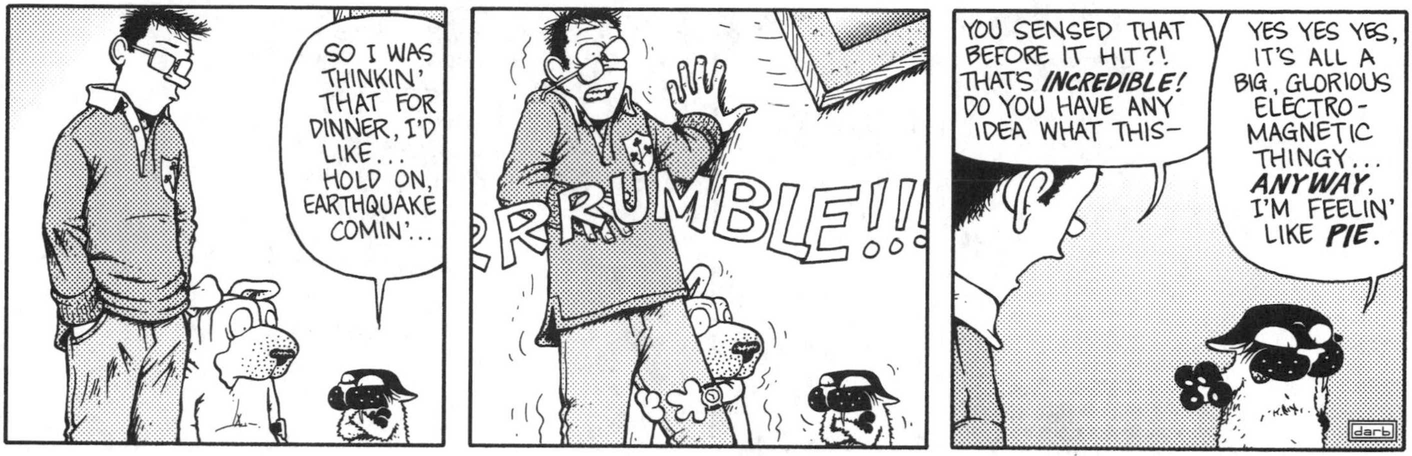
SO I WAS THINKIN' THAT FOR DINNER, I'D LIKE... HOLD ON, EARTHQUAKE COMIN'...
RRUMBLE!!!
YOU SENSED THAT BEFORE IT HIT?! THAT'S **INCREDIBLE!** DO YOU HAVE ANY IDEA WHAT THIS—
YES YES YES, IT'S ALL A BIG, GLORIOUS ELECTRO-MAGNETIC THINGY... **ANYWAY**, I'M FEELIN' LIKE **PIE**.

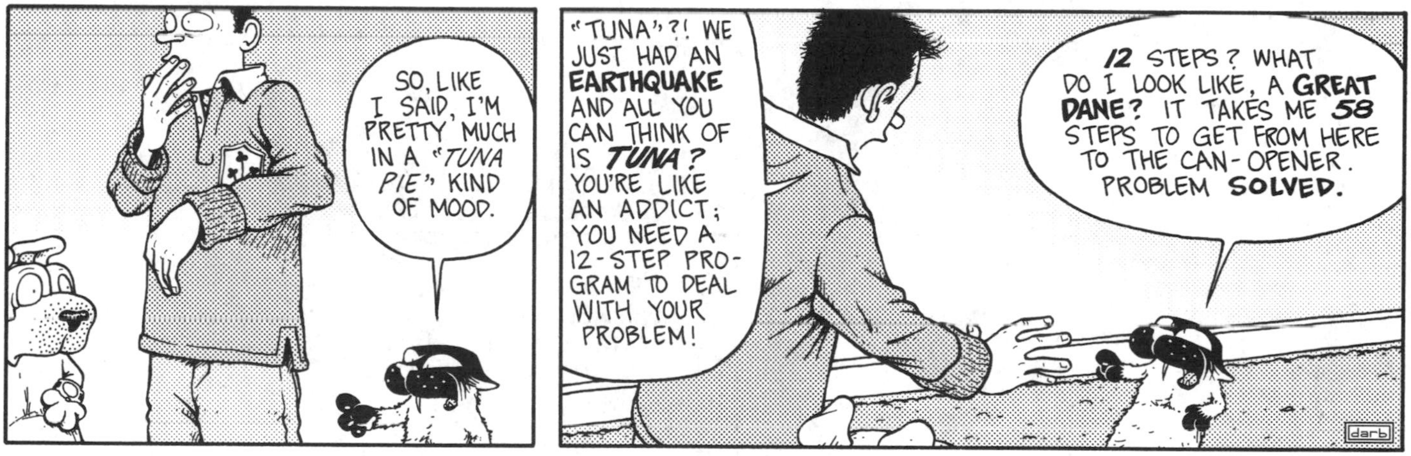
SO, LIKE I SAID, I'M PRETTY MUCH IN A "*TUNA PIE*" KIND OF MOOD.
"TUNA"?! WE JUST HAD AN **EARTHQUAKE** AND ALL YOU CAN THINK OF IS ***TUNA?*** YOU'RE LIKE AN ADDICT; YOU NEED A 12-STEP PROGRAM TO DEAL WITH YOUR PROBLEM!
12 STEPS? WHAT DO I LOOK LIKE, A **GREAT DANE**? IT TAKES ME ***58*** STEPS TO GET FROM HERE TO THE CAN-OPENER. PROBLEM **SOLVED**.

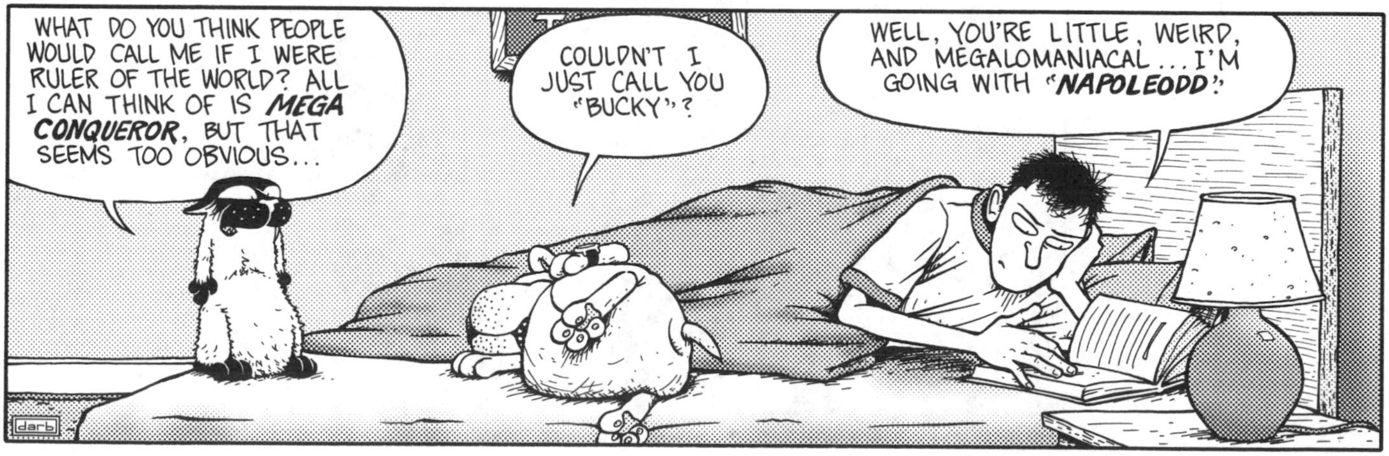
WHAT DO YOU THINK PEOPLE WOULD CALL ME IF I WERE RULER OF THE WORLD? ALL I CAN THINK OF IS ***MEGA CONQUEROR***, BUT THAT SEEMS TOO OBVIOUS...
COULDN'T I JUST CALL YOU "BUCKY"?
WELL, YOU'RE LITTLE, WEIRD, AND MEGALOMANIACAL... I'M GOING WITH "***NAPOLEODD***".

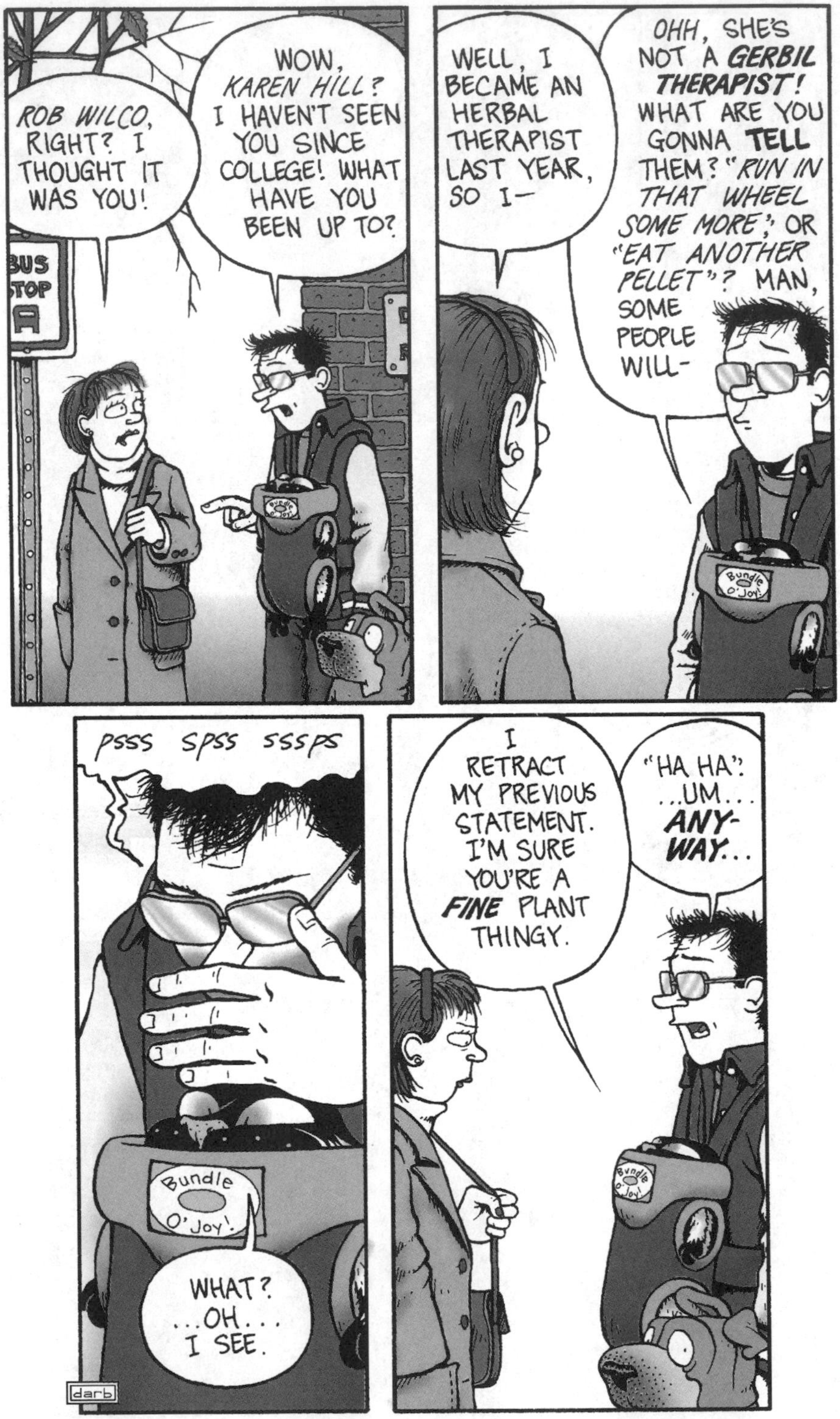
ROB WILCO, RIGHT? I THOUGHT IT WAS YOU!
WOW, KAREN HILL? I HAVEN'T SEEN YOU SINCE COLLEGE! WHAT HAVE YOU BEEN UP TO?
BUS STOP
Bundle O'Joy!
WELL, I BECAME AN HERBAL THERAPIST LAST YEAR, SO I—
OHH, SHE'S NOT A GERBIL THERAPIST! WHAT ARE YOU GONNA TELL THEM? "RUN IN THAT WHEEL SOME MORE", OR "EAT ANOTHER PELLET"? MAN, SOME PEOPLE WILL-
Bundle O'Joy!
psss spss sssps
Bundle O'Joy!
WHAT? ...OH... I SEE.
darb
I RETRACT MY PREVIOUS STATEMENT. I'M SURE YOU'RE A FINE PLANT THINGY.
"HA HA". ...UM... ANY-WAY...
Bundle O'Joy!

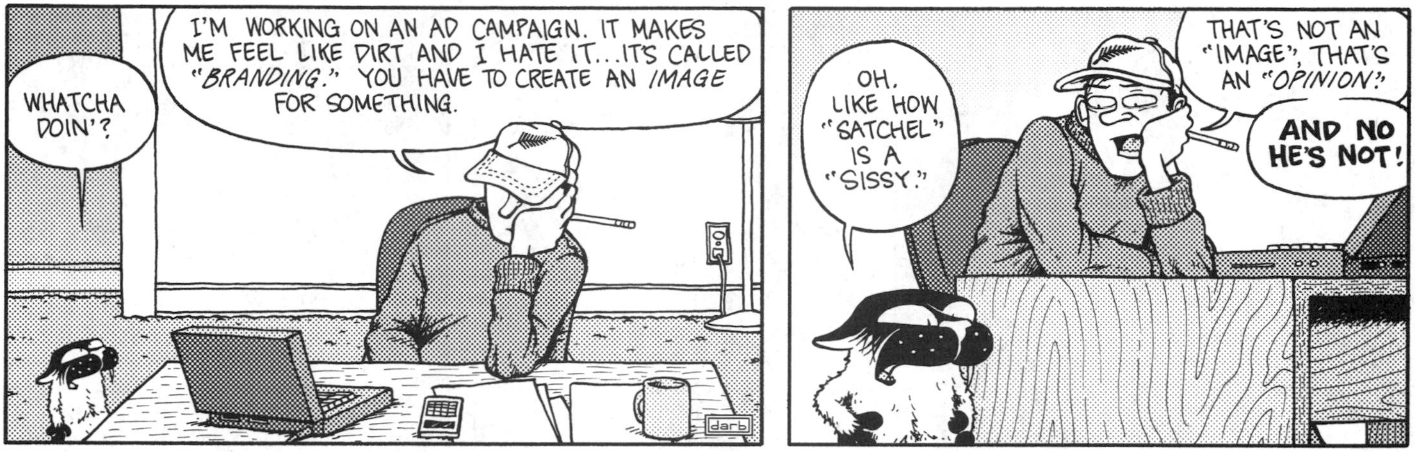
WHATCHA DOIN'?
I'M WORKING ON AN AD CAMPAIGN. IT MAKES ME FEEL LIKE DIRT AND I HATE IT...IT'S CALLED "*BRANDING.*" YOU HAVE TO CREATE AN *IMAGE* FOR SOMETHING.
OH. LIKE HOW "SATCHEL" IS A "SISSY."
THAT'S NOT AN "IMAGE", THAT'S AN "*OPINION*."
AND NO HE'S NOT!
darb

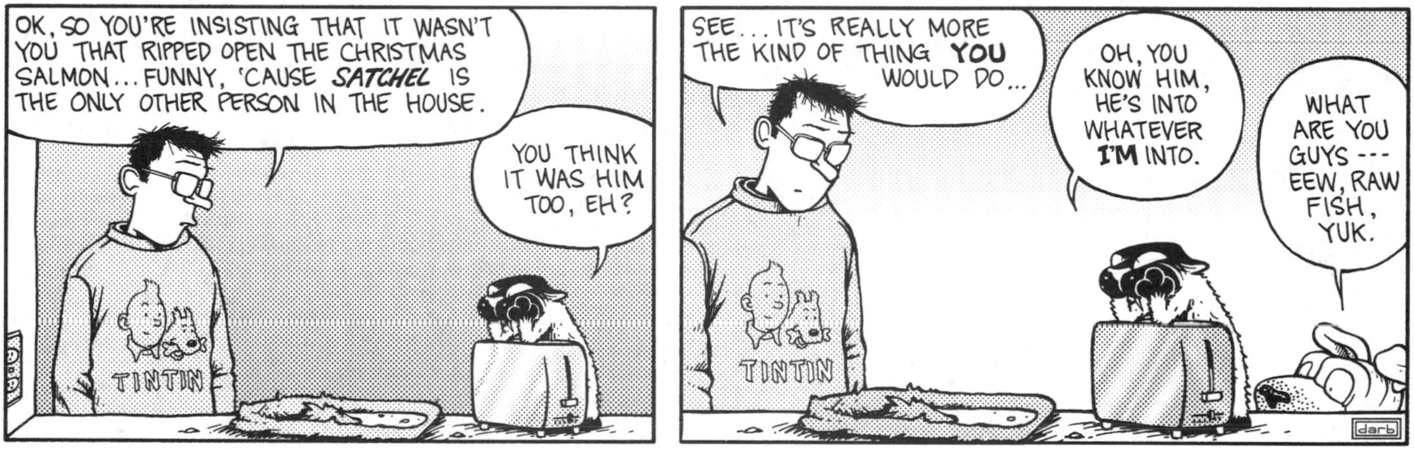
OK, SO YOU'RE INSISTING THAT IT WASN'T YOU THAT RIPPED OPEN THE CHRISTMAS SALMON... FUNNY, 'CAUSE ***SATCHEL*** IS THE ONLY OTHER PERSON IN THE HOUSE.
YOU THINK IT WAS HIM TOO, EH?
TINTIN
SEE... IT'S REALLY MORE THE KIND OF THING **YOU** WOULD DO...
OH, YOU KNOW HIM, HE'S INTO WHATEVER **I'M** INTO.
WHAT ARE YOU GUYS --- EEW, RAW FISH, YUK.
TINTIN
darb

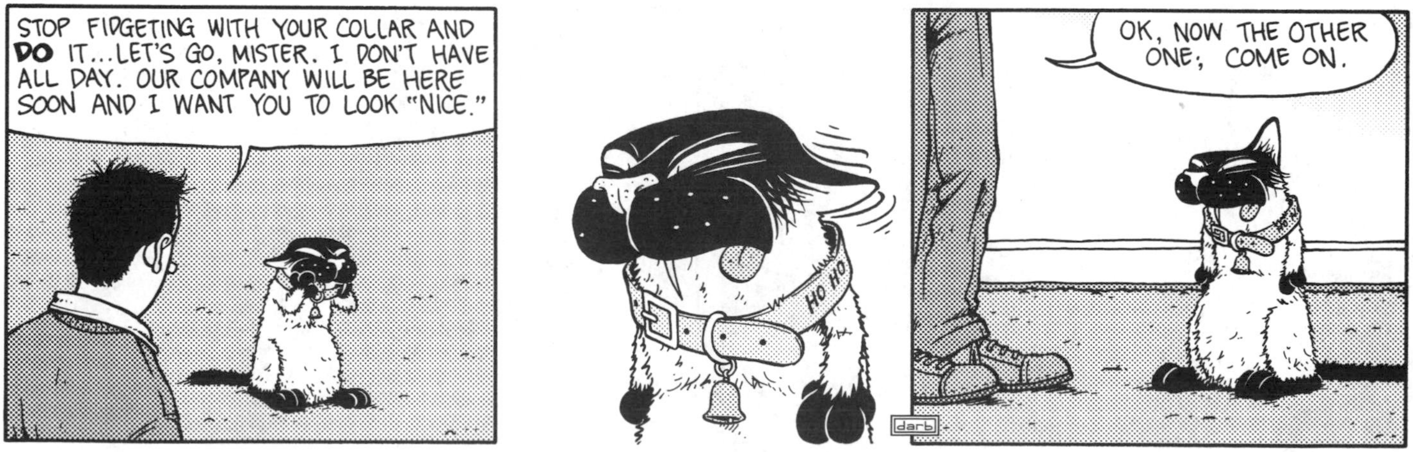
STOP FIDGETING WITH YOUR COLLAR AND **DO** IT...LET'S GO, MISTER. I DON'T HAVE ALL DAY. OUR COMPANY WILL BE HERE SOON AND I WANT YOU TO LOOK "NICE."
HO HO
darb
OK, NOW THE OTHER ONE; COME ON.

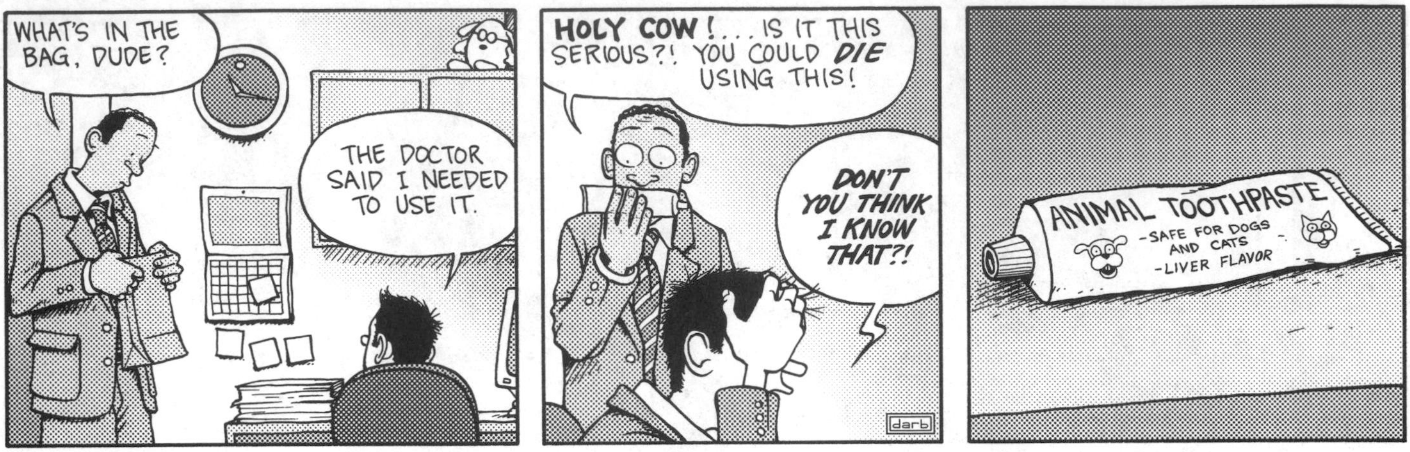
WHAT'S IN THE BAG, DUDE?
THE DOCTOR SAID I NEEDED TO USE IT.
HOLY COW!... IS IT THIS SERIOUS?! YOU COULD DIE USING THIS!
DON'T YOU THINK I KNOW THAT?!
ANIMAL TOOTHPASTE
-SAFE FOR DOGS AND CATS
-LIVER FLAVOR

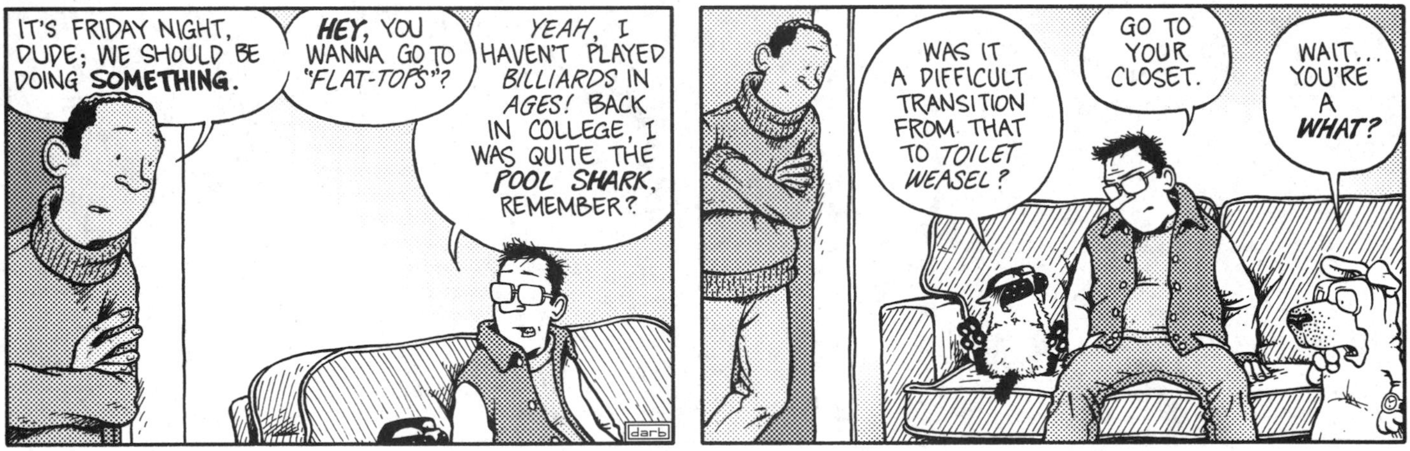
IT'S FRIDAY NIGHT, DUDE; WE SHOULD BE DOING SOMETHING.
HEY, YOU WANNA GO TO "FLAT-TOPS"?
YEAH, I HAVEN'T PLAYED BILLIARDS IN AGES! BACK IN COLLEGE, I WAS QUITE THE POOL SHARK, REMEMBER?
WAS IT A DIFFICULT TRANSITION FROM THAT TO TOILET WEASEL?
GO TO YOUR CLOSET.
WAIT... YOU'RE A WHAT?

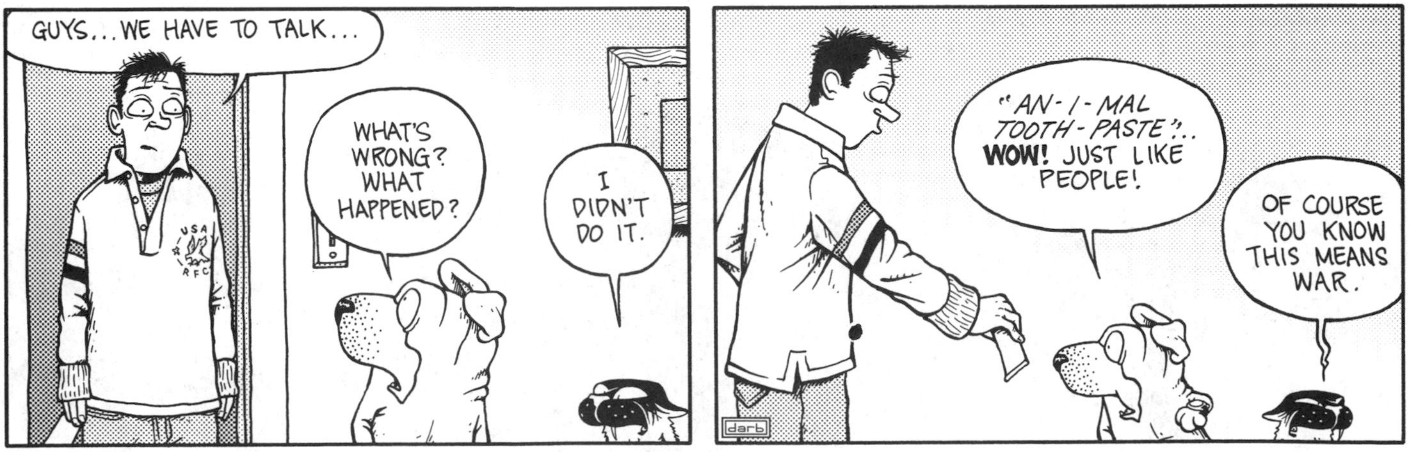
GUYS... WE HAVE TO TALK...
WHAT'S WRONG? WHAT HAPPENED?
I DIDN'T DO IT.
"AN-I-MAL TOOTH-PASTE"... WOW! JUST LIKE PEOPLE!
OF COURSE YOU KNOW THIS MEANS WAR.

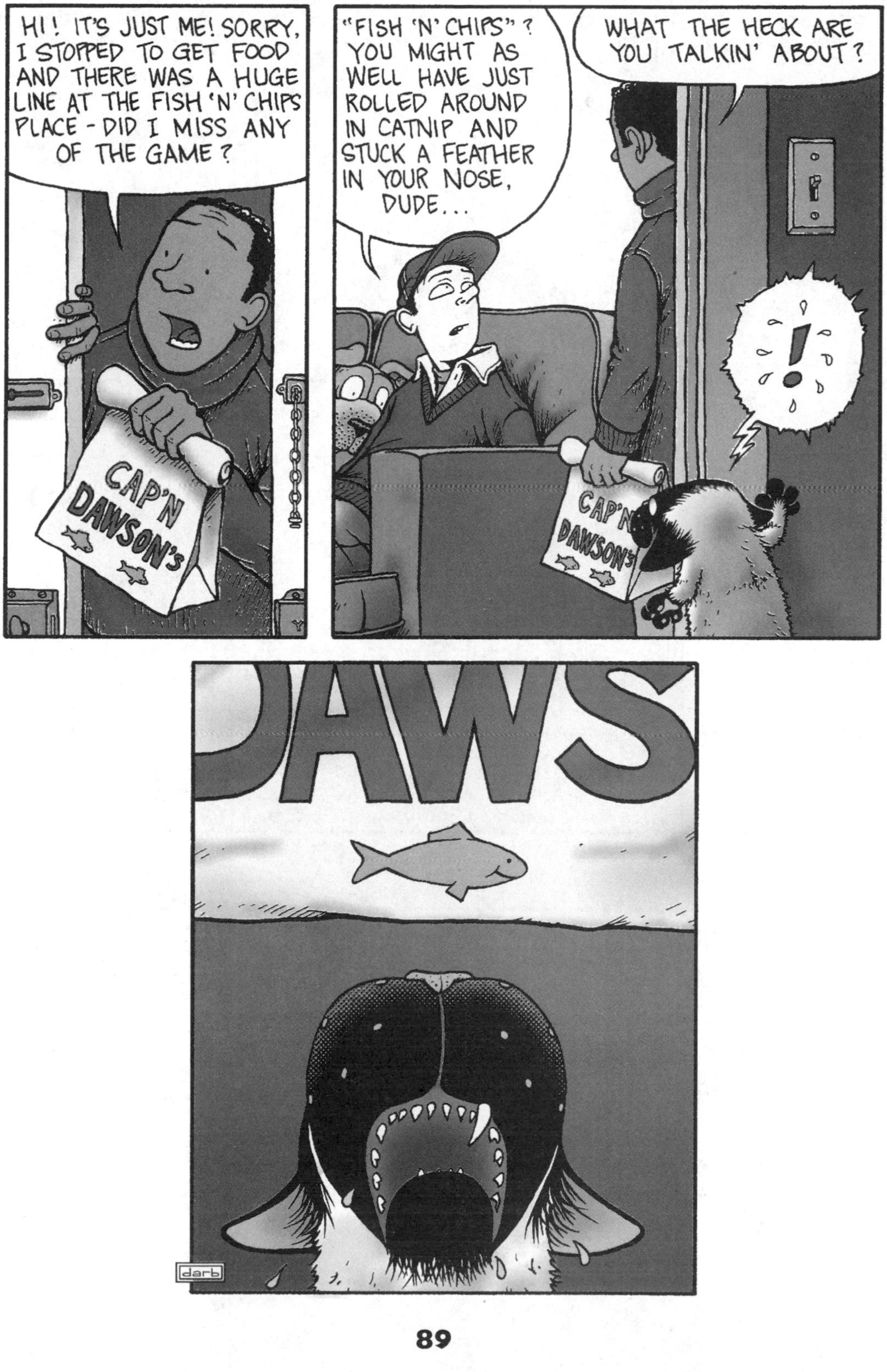
HI! IT'S JUST ME! SORRY, I STOPPED TO GET FOOD AND THERE WAS A HUGE LINE AT THE FISH 'N' CHIPS PLACE - DID I MISS ANY OF THE GAME?
CAP'N DAWSON'S
"FISH 'N' CHIPS"? YOU MIGHT AS WELL HAVE JUST ROLLED AROUND IN CATNIP AND STUCK A FEATHER IN YOUR NOSE, DUDE...
WHAT THE HECK ARE YOU TALKIN' ABOUT?
!
CAP'N DAWSON'S
DAWS
darb

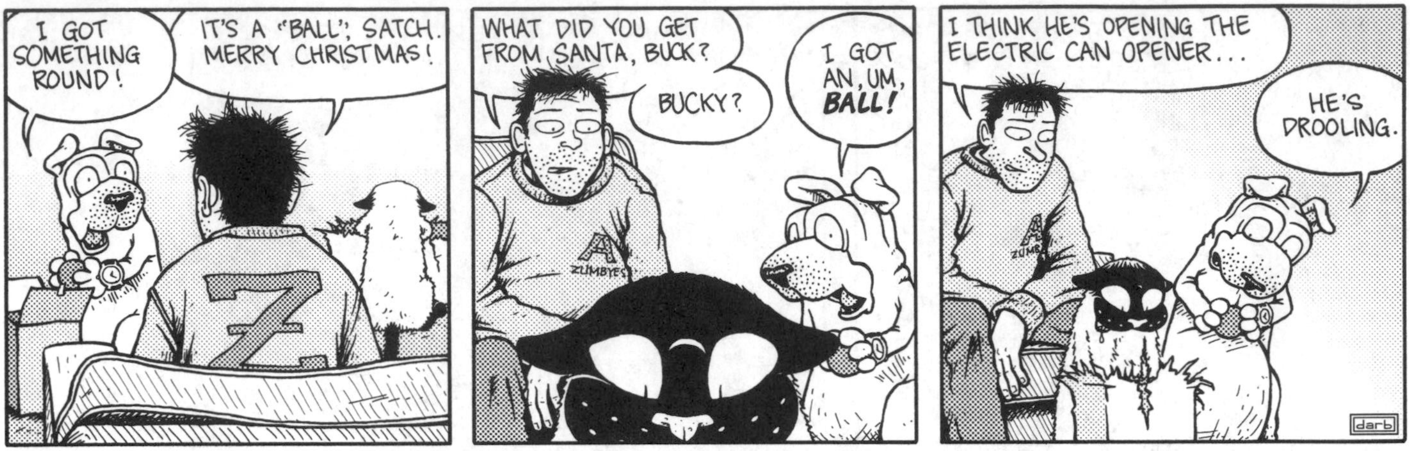
I GOT SOMETHING ROUND!
IT'S A "BALL", SATCH. MERRY CHRISTMAS!
WHAT DID YOU GET FROM SANTA, BUCK?
BUCKY?
I GOT AN, UM, **BALL!**
I THINK HE'S OPENING THE ELECTRIC CAN OPENER...
HE'S DROOLING.
darb

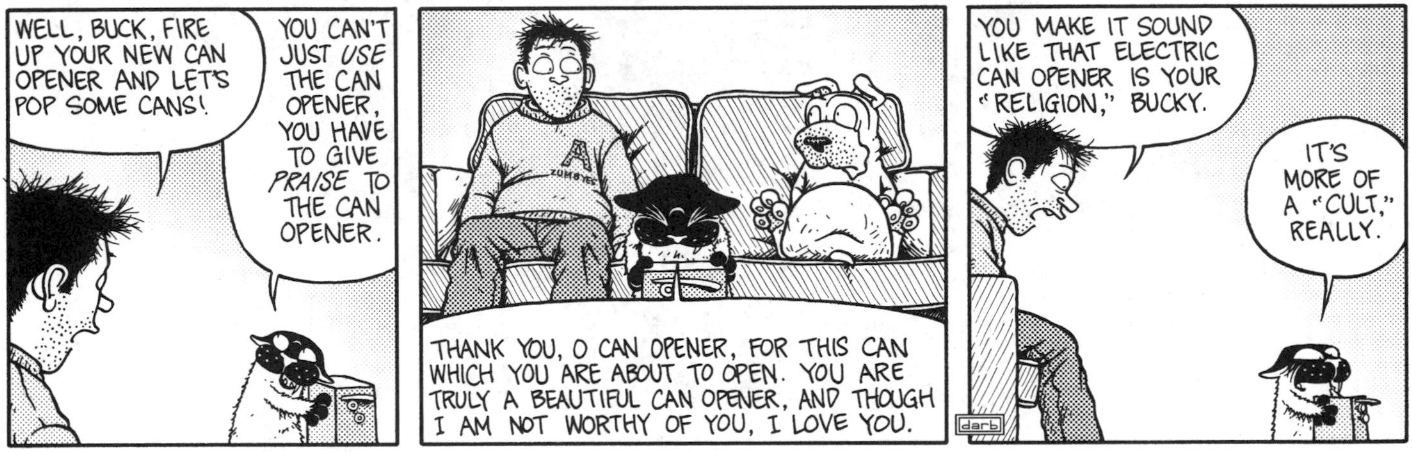
WELL, BUCK, FIRE UP YOUR NEW CAN OPENER AND LET'S POP SOME CANS!
YOU CAN'T JUST *USE* THE CAN OPENER, YOU HAVE TO GIVE *PRAISE* TO THE CAN OPENER.
THANK YOU, O CAN OPENER, FOR THIS CAN WHICH YOU ARE ABOUT TO OPEN. YOU ARE TRULY A BEAUTIFUL CAN OPENER, AND THOUGH I AM NOT WORTHY OF YOU, I LOVE YOU.
darb
YOU MAKE IT SOUND LIKE THAT ELECTRIC CAN OPENER IS YOUR "RELIGION," BUCKY.
IT'S MORE OF A "CULT," REALLY.

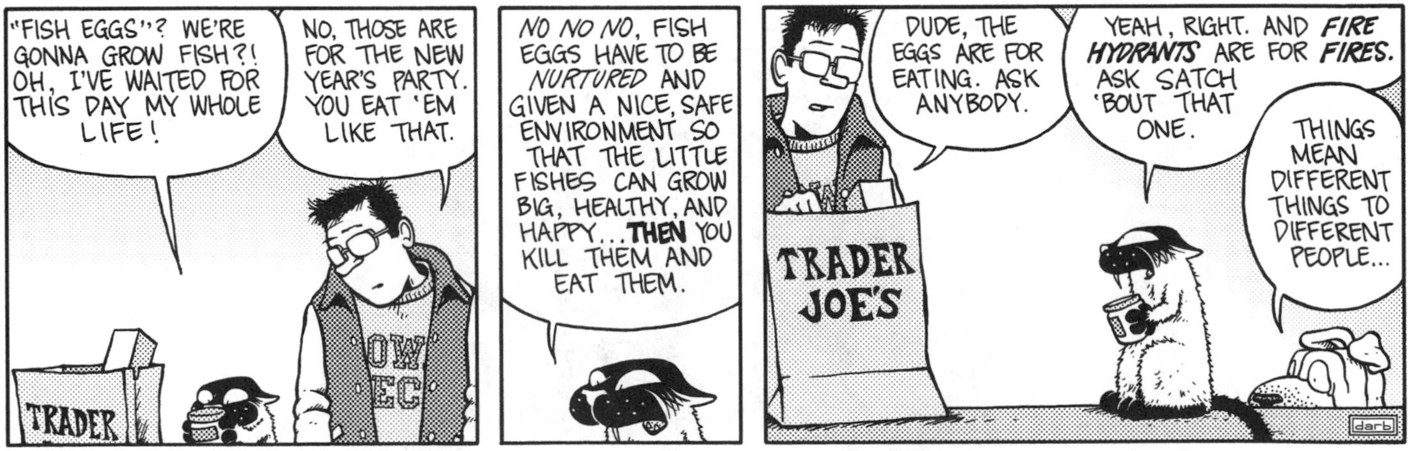
"FISH EGGS"? WE'RE GONNA GROW FISH?! OH, I'VE WAITED FOR THIS DAY MY WHOLE LIFE!
NO, THOSE ARE FOR THE NEW YEAR'S PARTY. YOU EAT 'EM LIKE THAT.
TRADER
NO NO NO, FISH EGGS HAVE TO BE *NURTURED* AND GIVEN A NICE, SAFE ENVIRONMENT SO THAT THE LITTLE FISHES CAN GROW BIG, HEALTHY, AND HAPPY... **THEN** YOU KILL THEM AND EAT THEM.
DUDE, THE EGGS ARE FOR EATING. ASK ANYBODY.
TRADER JOE'S
YEAH, RIGHT. AND ***FIRE HYDRANTS*** ARE FOR ***FIRES.*** ASK SATCH 'BOUT THAT ONE.
THINGS MEAN DIFFERENT THINGS TO DIFFERENT PEOPLE...
darb

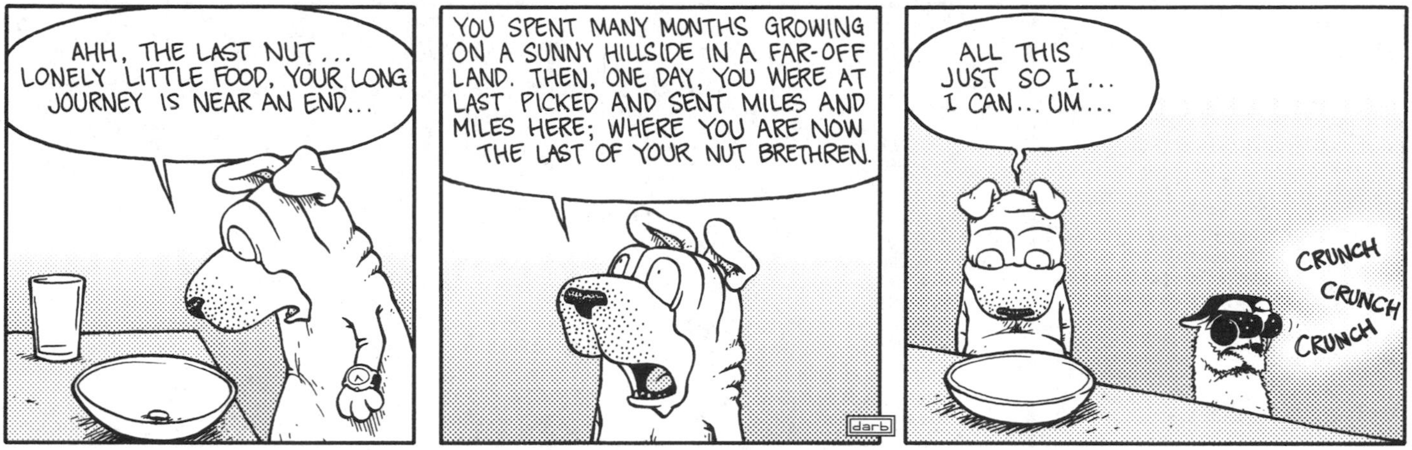
AHH, THE LAST NUT... LONELY LITTLE FOOD, YOUR LONG JOURNEY IS NEAR AN END...
YOU SPENT MANY MONTHS GROWING ON A SUNNY HILLSIDE IN A FAR-OFF LAND. THEN, ONE DAY, YOU WERE AT LAST PICKED AND SENT MILES AND MILES HERE; WHERE YOU ARE NOW THE LAST OF YOUR NUT BRETHREN.
darb
ALL THIS JUST SO I... I CAN... UM...
CRUNCH
CRUNCH
CRUNCH

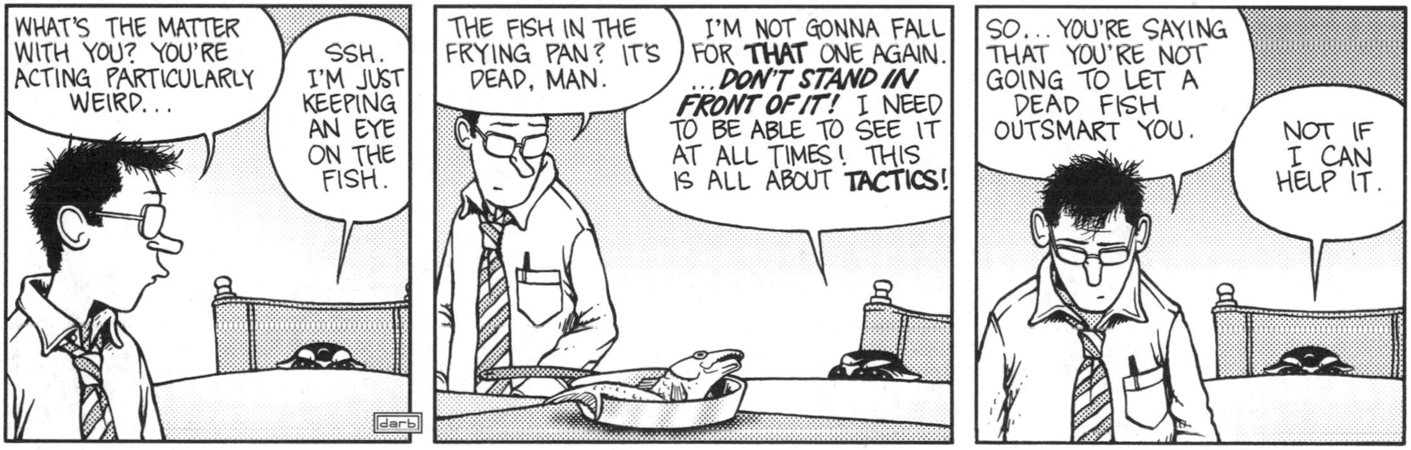
WHAT'S THE MATTER WITH YOU? YOU'RE ACTING PARTICULARLY WEIRD...
SSH. I'M JUST KEEPING AN EYE ON THE FISH.
darb
THE FISH IN THE FRYING PAN? IT'S DEAD, MAN.
I'M NOT GONNA FALL FOR **THAT** ONE AGAIN. ...***DON'T STAND IN FRONT OF IT!*** I NEED TO BE ABLE TO SEE IT AT ALL TIMES! THIS IS ALL ABOUT **TACTICS**!
SO... YOU'RE SAYING THAT YOU'RE NOT GOING TO LET A DEAD FISH OUTSMART YOU.
NOT IF I CAN HELP IT.

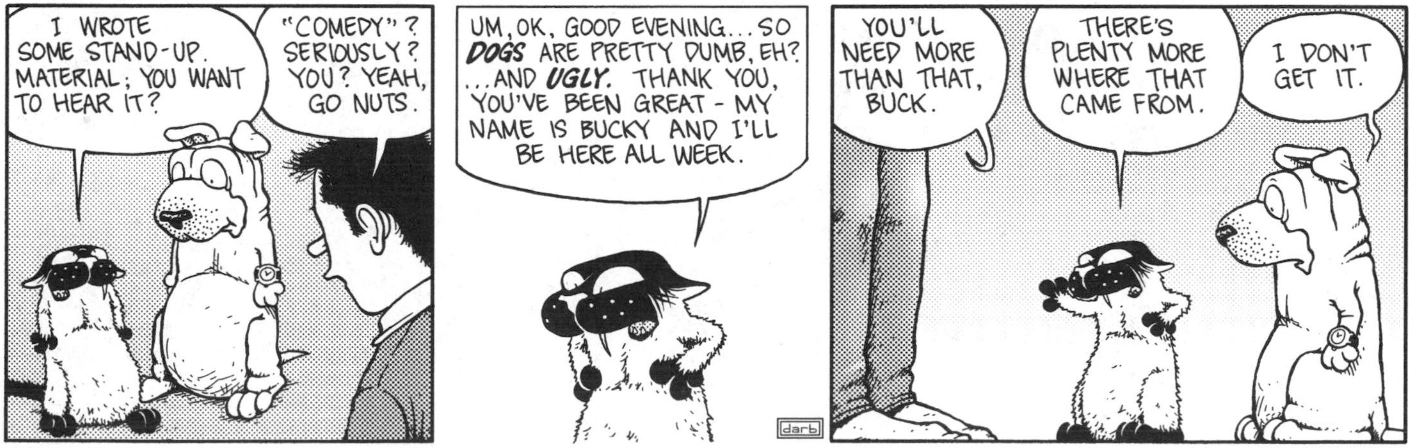
I WROTE SOME STAND-UP. MATERIAL; YOU WANT TO HEAR IT?
"COMEDY"? SERIOUSLY? YOU? YEAH, GO NUTS.
UM, OK, GOOD EVENING... SO ***DOGS*** ARE PRETTY DUMB, EH? ...AND ***UGLY.*** THANK YOU, YOU'VE BEEN GREAT - MY NAME IS BUCKY AND I'LL BE HERE ALL WEEK.
darb
YOU'LL NEED MORE THAN THAT, BUCK.
THERE'S PLENTY MORE WHERE THAT CAME FROM.
I DON'T GET IT.

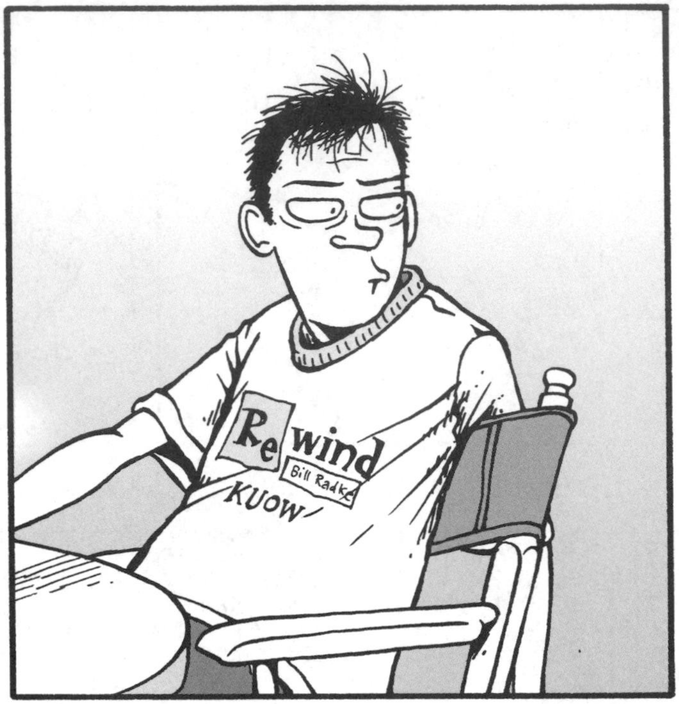
Rewind
Bill Radke
KUOW

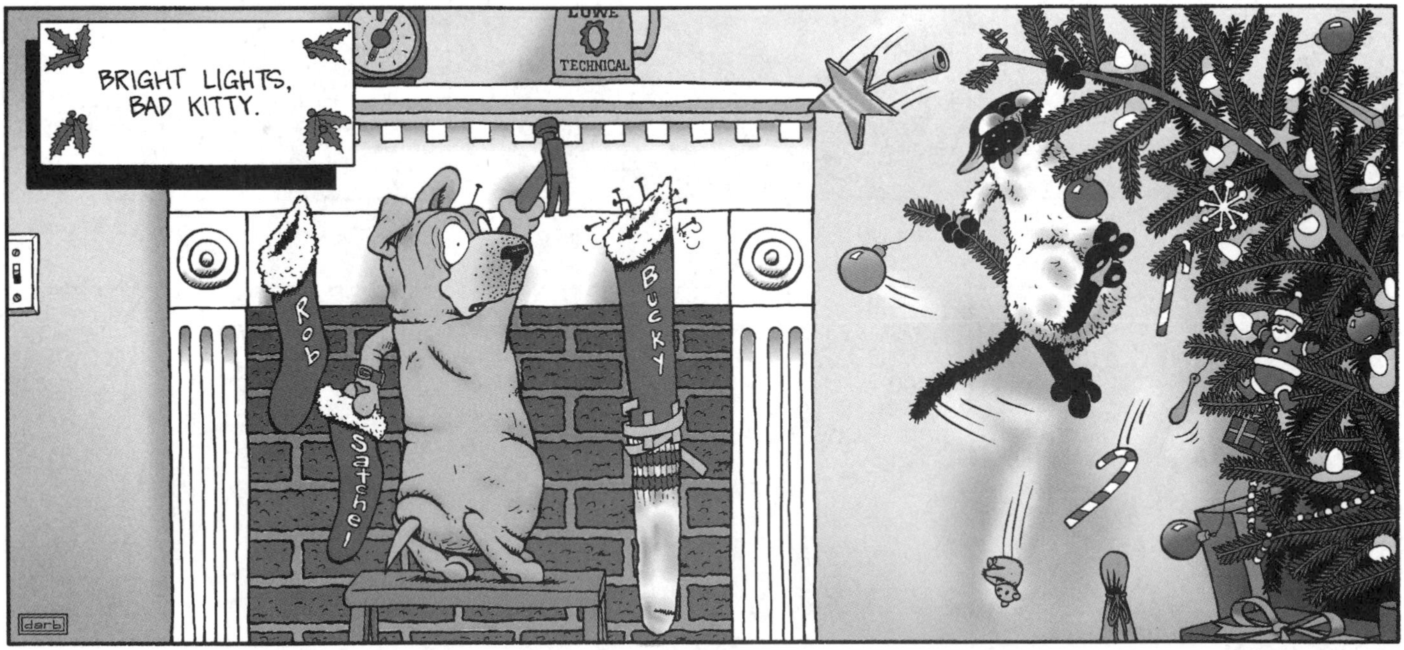
BRIGHT LIGHTS, BAD KITTY.
LOWE
TECHNICAL
Rob
Satchel
Bucky
darb

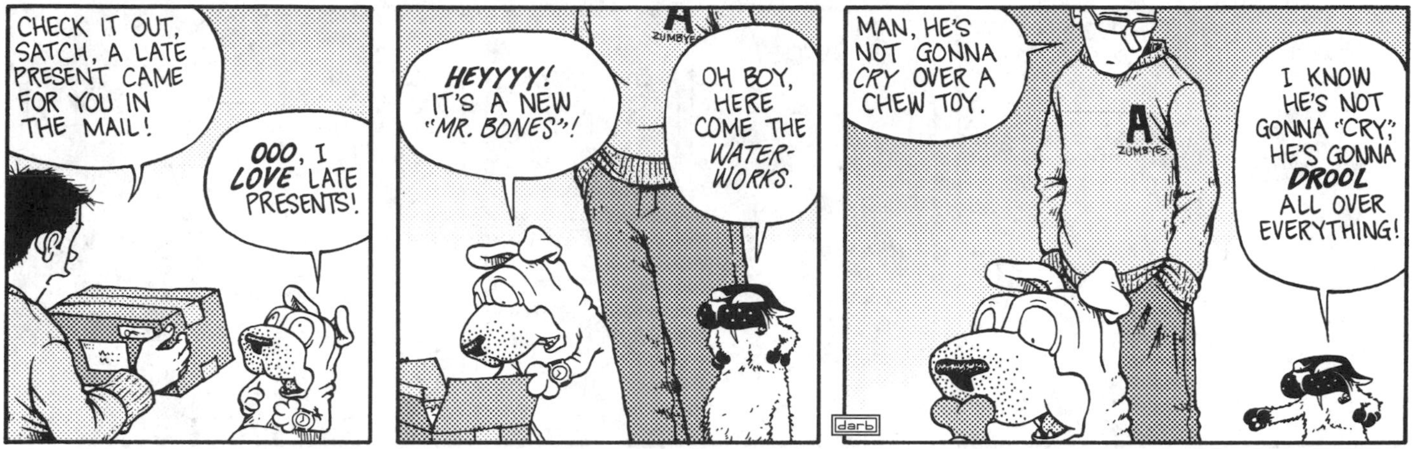
CHECK IT OUT, SATCH, A LATE PRESENT CAME FOR YOU IN THE MAIL!
OOO, I LOVE LATE PRESENTS!
HEYYYY! IT'S A NEW "MR. BONES"!
OH BOY, HERE COME THE WATER-WORKS.
MAN, HE'S NOT GONNA CRY OVER A CHEW TOY.
I KNOW HE'S NOT GONNA "CRY"; HE'S GONNA DROOL ALL OVER EVERYTHING!
darb
ZUMBYES

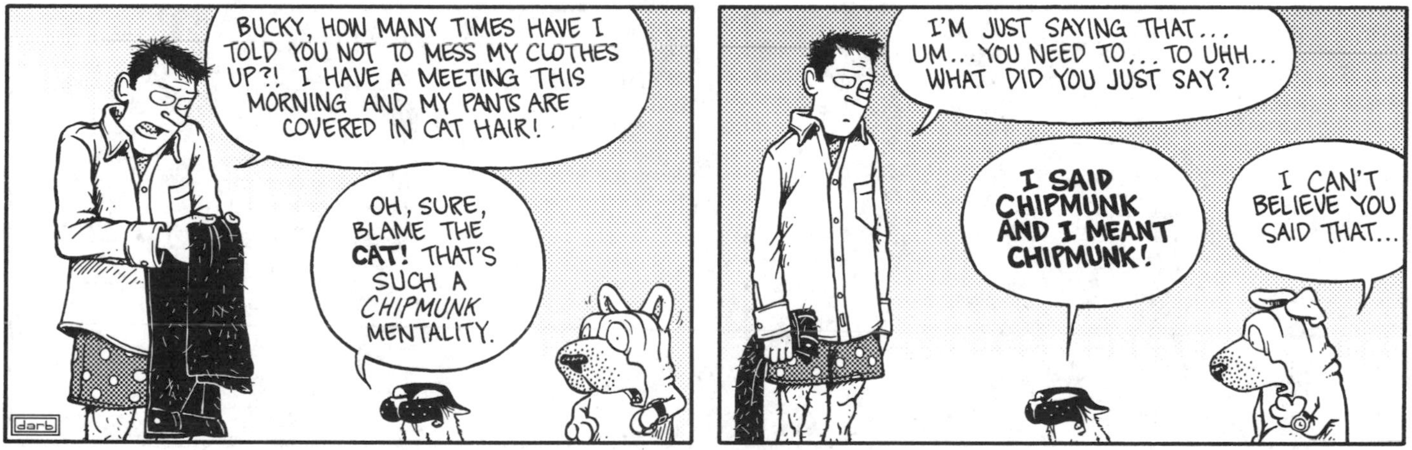
BUCKY, HOW MANY TIMES HAVE I TOLD YOU NOT TO MESS MY CLOTHES UP?! I HAVE A MEETING THIS MORNING AND MY PANTS ARE COVERED IN CAT HAIR!
OH, SURE, BLAME THE CAT! THAT'S SUCH A CHIPMUNK MENTALITY.
I'M JUST SAYING THAT... UM... YOU NEED TO... TO UHH... WHAT DID YOU JUST SAY?
I SAID CHIPMUNK AND I MEANT CHIPMUNK!
I CAN'T BELIEVE YOU SAID THAT...
darb

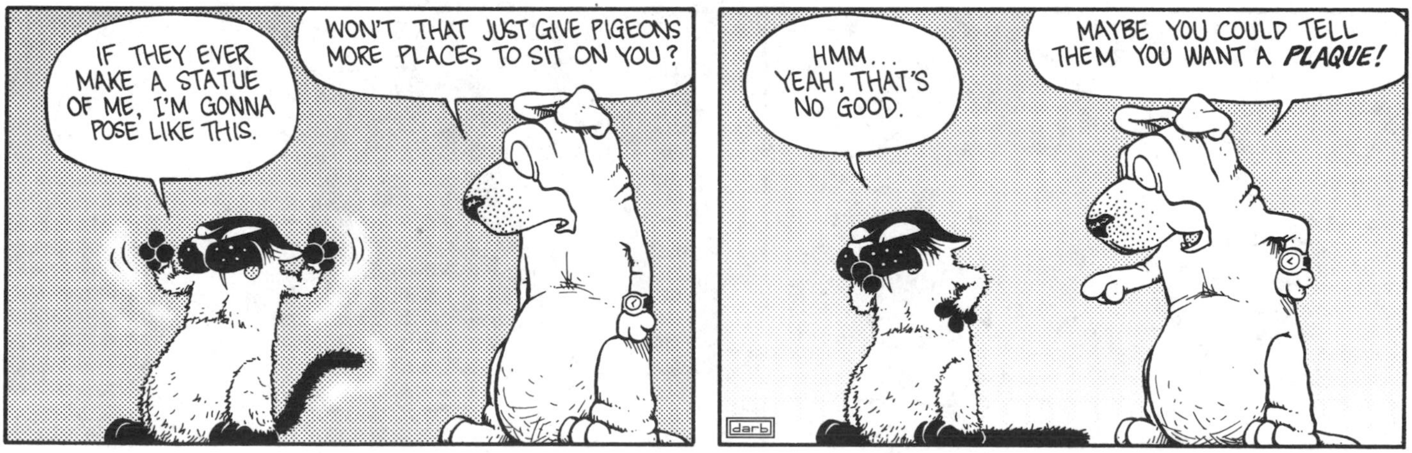
IF THEY EVER MAKE A STATUE OF ME, I'M GONNA POSE LIKE THIS.
WON'T THAT JUST GIVE PIGEONS MORE PLACES TO SIT ON YOU?
HMM... YEAH, THAT'S NO GOOD.
MAYBE YOU COULD TELL THEM YOU WANT A PLAQUE!
darb

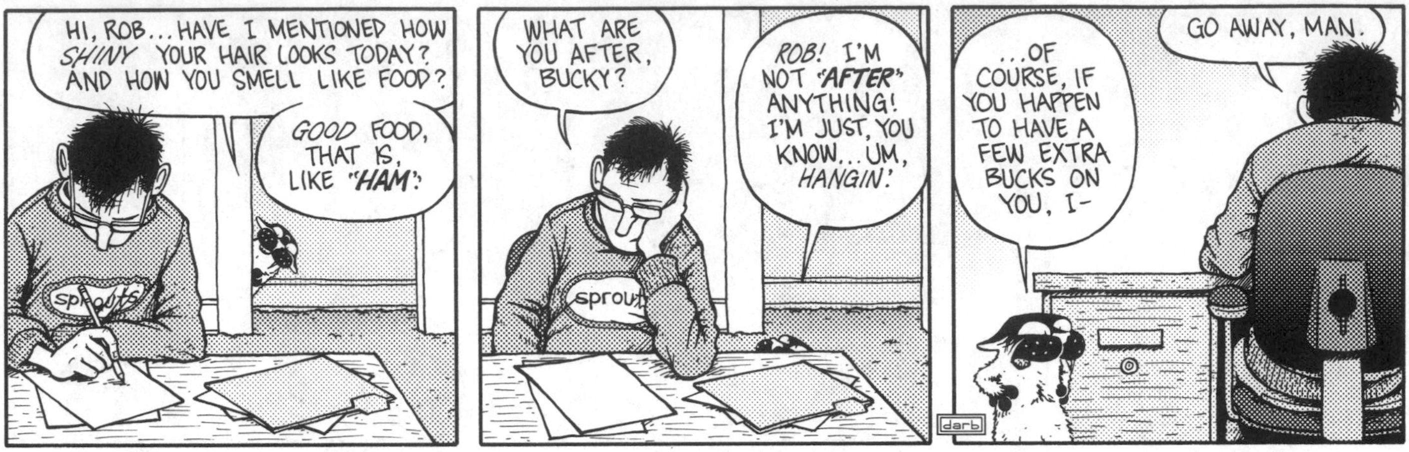
HI, ROB... HAVE I MENTIONED HOW *SHINY* YOUR HAIR LOOKS TODAY? AND HOW YOU SMELL LIKE FOOD?
GOOD FOOD, THAT IS, LIKE "***HAM***".
sprouts
WHAT ARE YOU AFTER, BUCKY?
ROB! I'M NOT "***AFTER***" ANYTHING! I'M JUST, YOU KNOW... UM, *HANGIN'!*
sprout
...OF COURSE, IF YOU HAPPEN TO HAVE A FEW EXTRA BUCKS ON YOU, I-
GO AWAY, MAN.
darb

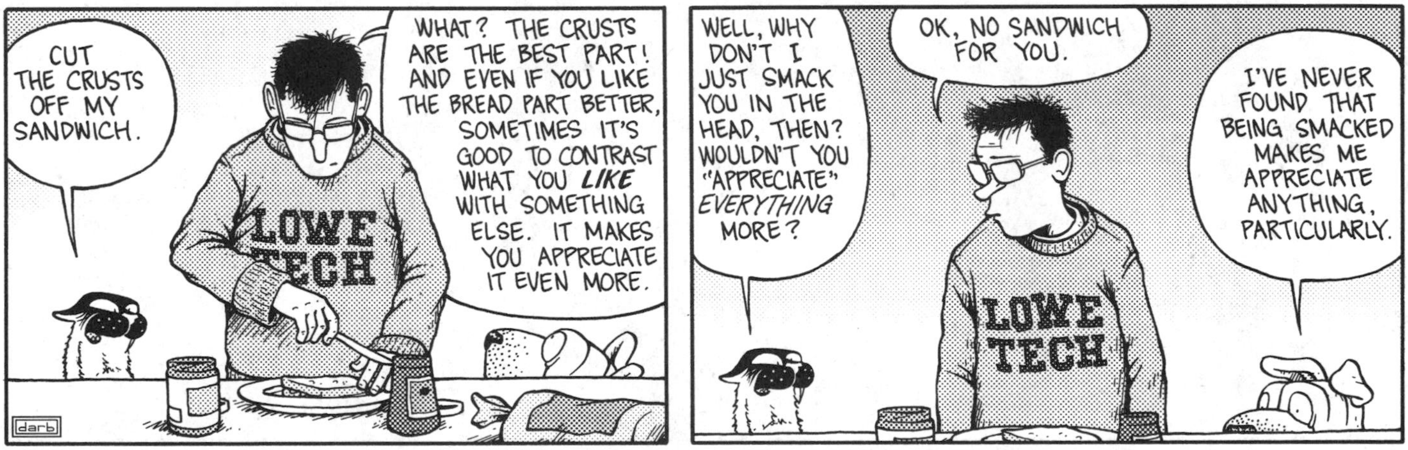
CUT THE CRUSTS OFF MY SANDWICH.
WHAT? THE CRUSTS ARE THE BEST PART! AND EVEN IF YOU LIKE THE BREAD PART BETTER, SOMETIMES IT'S GOOD TO CONTRAST WHAT YOU ***LIKE*** WITH SOMETHING ELSE. IT MAKES YOU APPRECIATE IT EVEN MORE.
LOWE TECH
darb
WELL, WHY DON'T I JUST SMACK YOU IN THE HEAD, THEN? WOULDN'T YOU "APPRECIATE" *EVERYTHING* MORE?
OK, NO SANDWICH FOR YOU.
I'VE NEVER FOUND THAT BEING SMACKED MAKES ME APPRECIATE ANYTHING, PARTICULARLY.
LOWE TECH

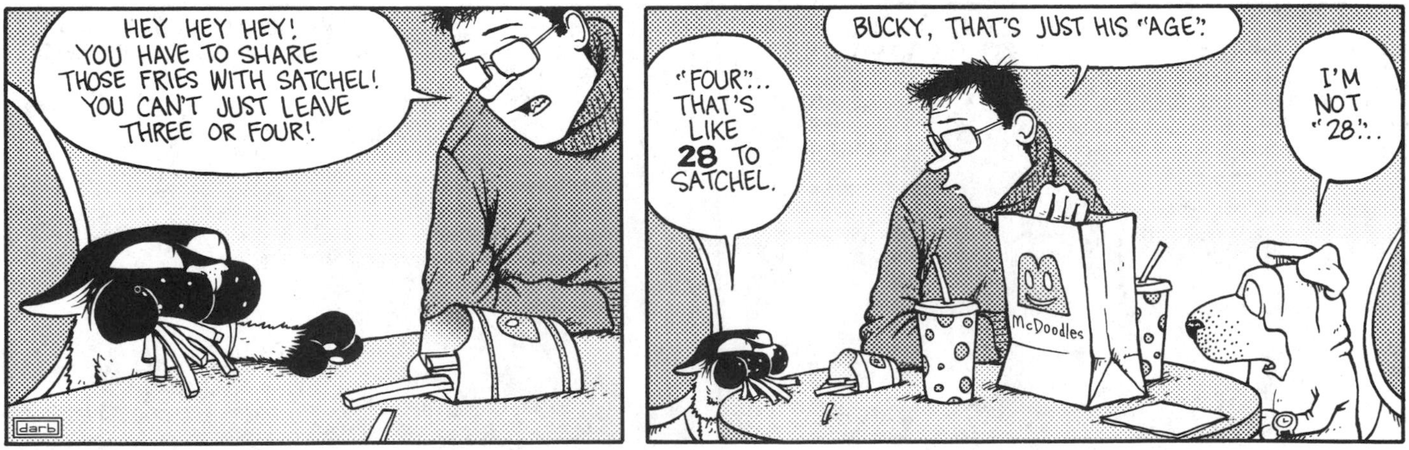
HEY HEY HEY! YOU HAVE TO SHARE THOSE FRIES WITH SATCHEL! YOU CAN'T JUST LEAVE THREE OR FOUR!
darb
"FOUR"... THAT'S LIKE **28** TO SATCHEL.
BUCKY, THAT'S JUST HIS "AGE".
I'M NOT "28"...
McDoodles

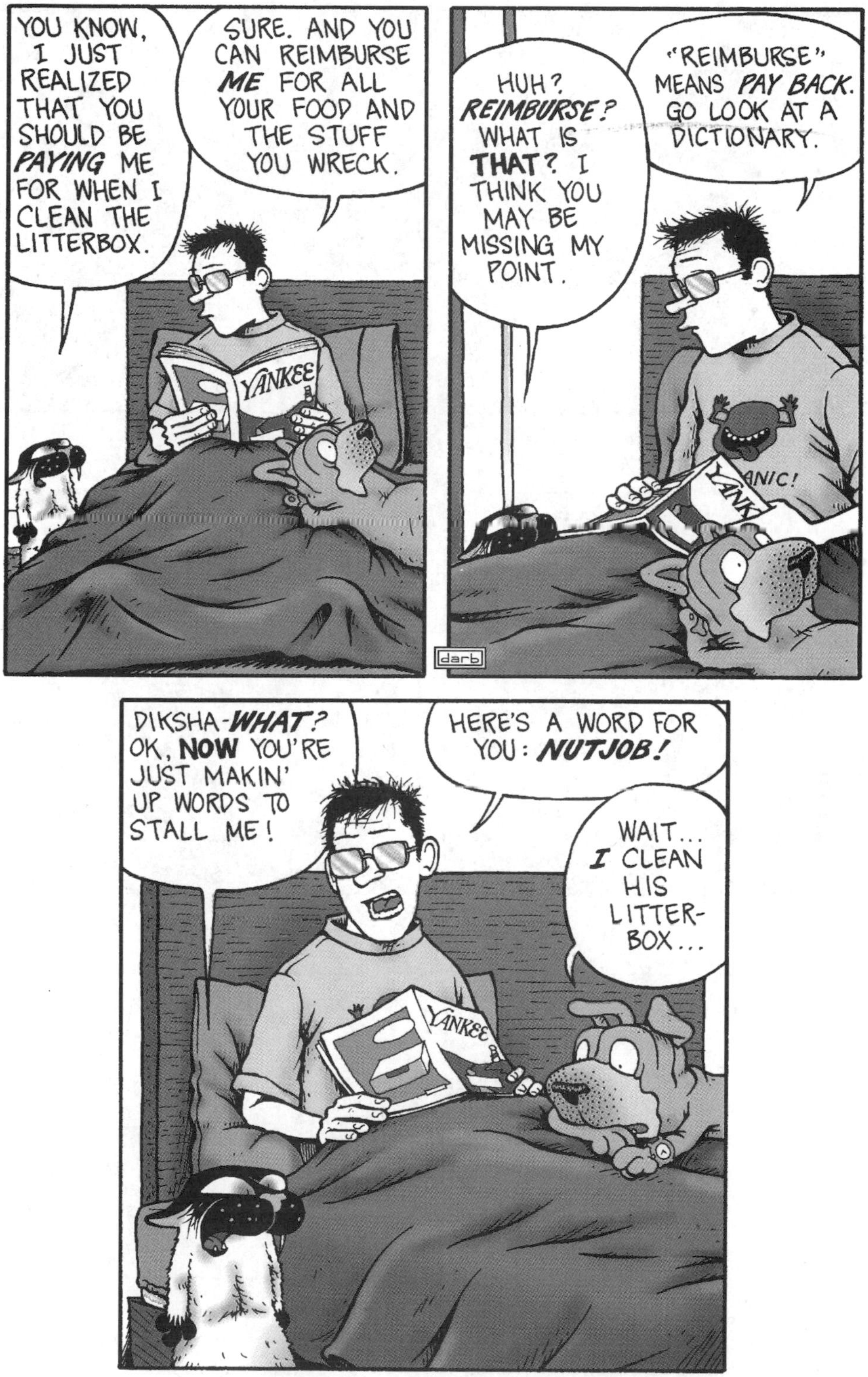
YOU KNOW, I JUST REALIZED THAT YOU SHOULD BE *PAYING* ME FOR WHEN I CLEAN THE LITTERBOX.
SURE. AND YOU CAN REIMBURSE *ME* FOR ALL YOUR FOOD AND THE STUFF YOU WRECK.
YANKEE
HUH? *REIMBURSE?* WHAT IS **THAT**? I THINK YOU MAY BE MISSING MY POINT.
"REIMBURSE" MEANS *PAY BACK*. GO LOOK AT A DICTIONARY.
ANIC!
YANK
darb
DIKSHA-*WHAT?* OK, **NOW** YOU'RE JUST MAKIN' UP WORDS TO STALL ME!
HERE'S A WORD FOR YOU: *NUTJOB!*
WAIT... *I* CLEAN HIS LITTER-BOX...
YANKEE

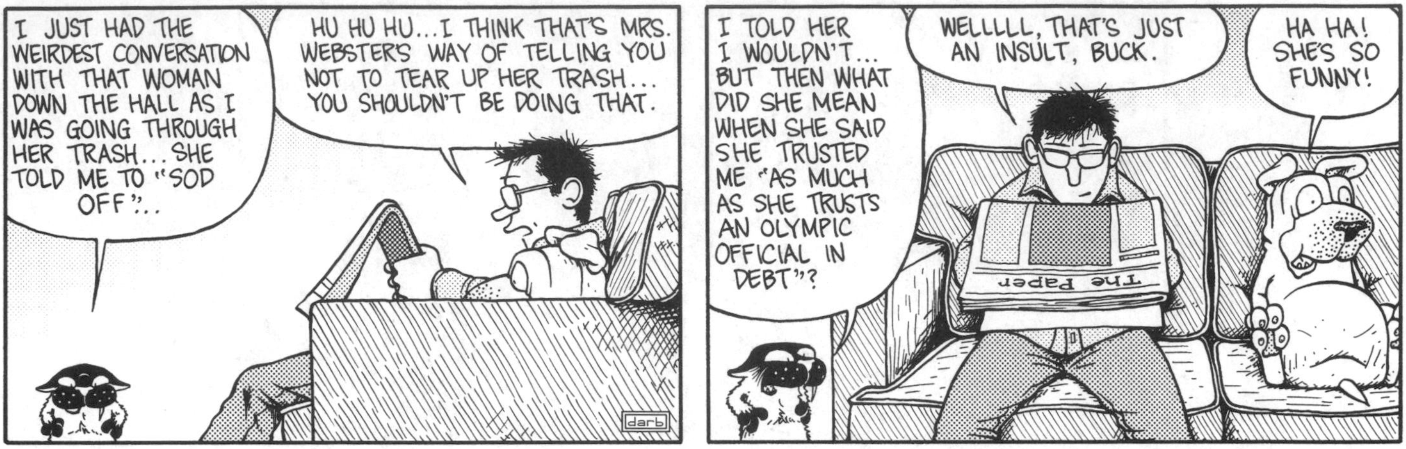
I JUST HAD THE WEIRDEST CONVERSATION WITH THAT WOMAN DOWN THE HALL AS I WAS GOING THROUGH HER TRASH... SHE TOLD ME TO "SOD OFF"...
HU HU HU... I THINK THAT'S MRS. WEBSTER'S WAY OF TELLING YOU NOT TO TEAR UP HER TRASH... YOU SHOULDN'T BE DOING THAT.
I TOLD HER I WOULDN'T... BUT THEN WHAT DID SHE MEAN WHEN SHE SAID SHE TRUSTED ME "AS MUCH AS SHE TRUSTS AN OLYMPIC OFFICIAL IN DEBT"?
WELLLLL, THAT'S JUST AN INSULT, BUCK.
HA HA! SHE'S SO FUNNY!
The Paper

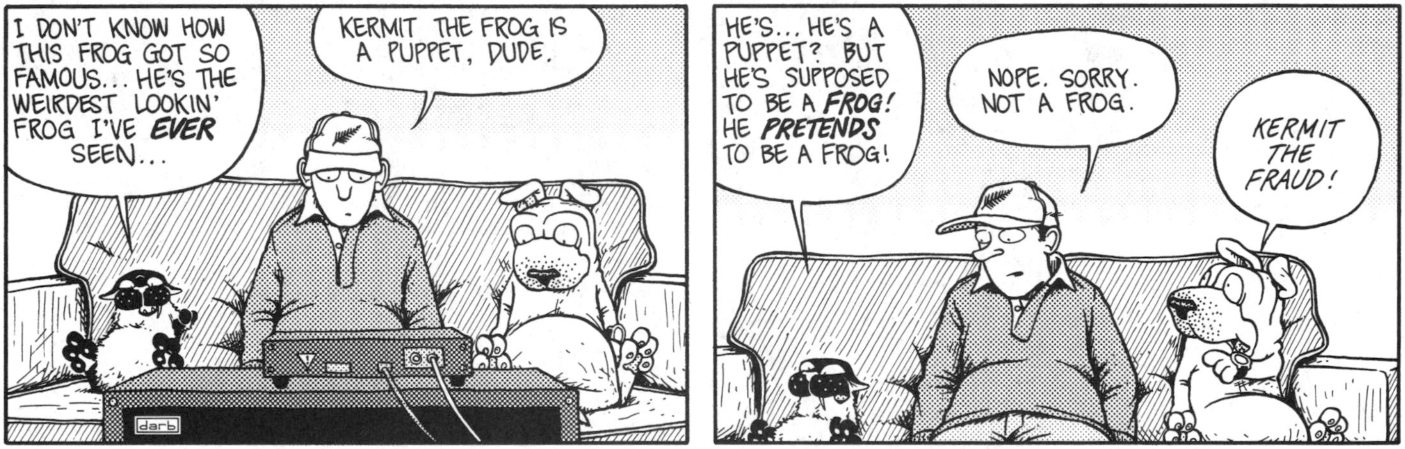
I DON'T KNOW HOW THIS FROG GOT SO FAMOUS... HE'S THE WEIRDEST LOOKIN' FROG I'VE **EVER** SEEN...
KERMIT THE FROG IS A PUPPET, DUDE.
HE'S... HE'S A PUPPET? BUT HE'S SUPPOSED TO BE A ***FROG!*** HE ***PRETENDS*** TO BE A FROG!
NOPE. SORRY. NOT A FROG.
KERMIT THE FRAUD!

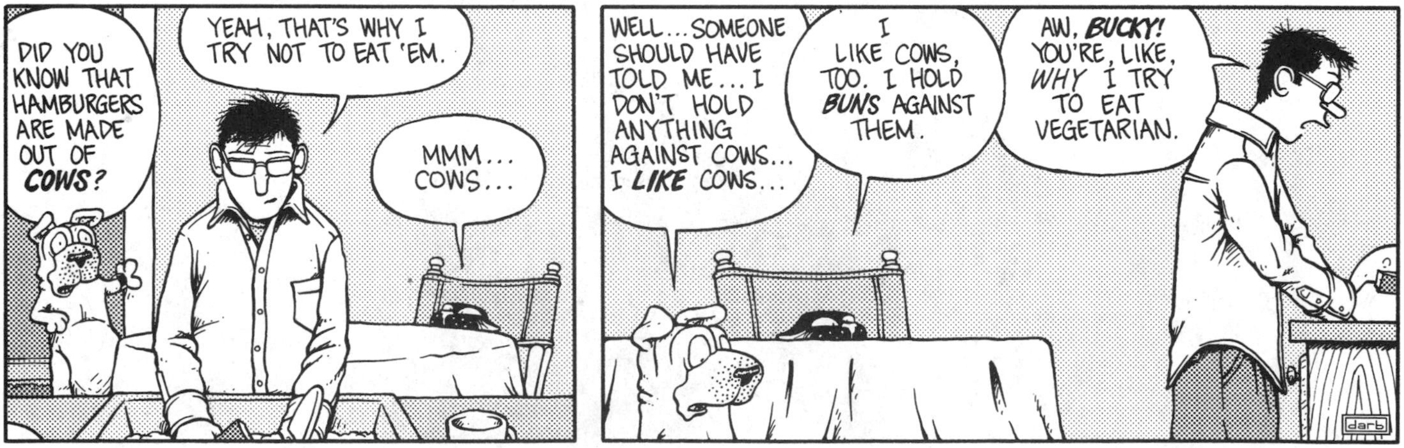
DID YOU KNOW THAT HAMBURGERS ARE MADE OUT OF ***COWS?***
YEAH, THAT'S WHY I TRY NOT TO EAT 'EM.
MMM... COWS...
WELL... SOMEONE SHOULD HAVE TOLD ME... I DON'T HOLD ANYTHING AGAINST COWS... I ***LIKE*** COWS...
I LIKE COWS, TOO. I HOLD ***BUNS*** AGAINST THEM.
AW, ***BUCKY!*** YOU'RE, LIKE, *WHY* I TRY TO EAT VEGETARIAN.

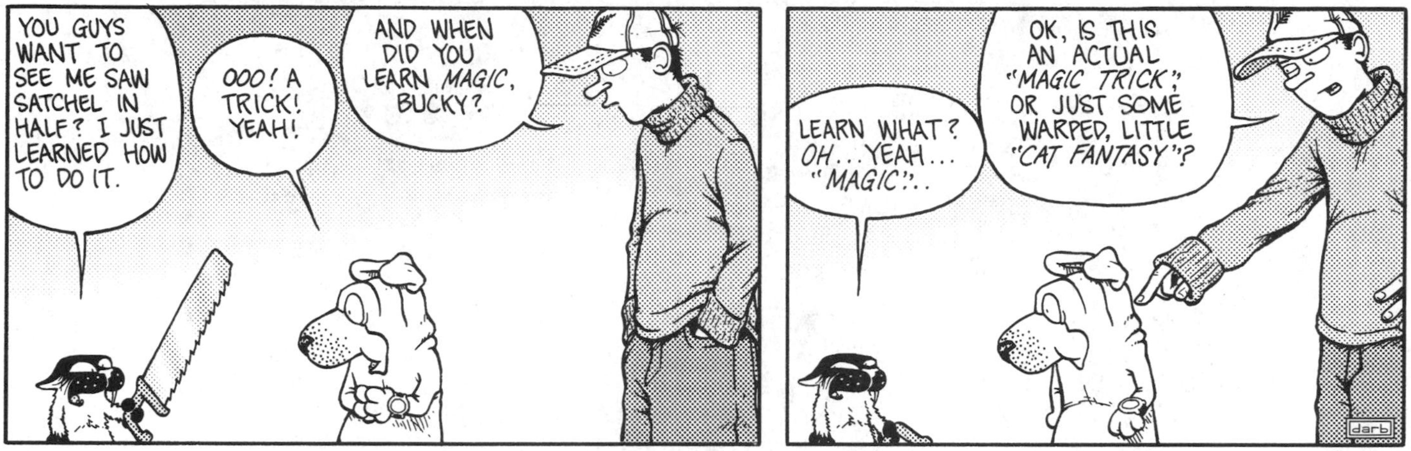
YOU GUYS WANT TO SEE ME SAW SATCHEL IN HALF? I JUST LEARNED HOW TO DO IT.
OOO! A TRICK! YEAH!
AND WHEN DID YOU LEARN *MAGIC*, BUCKY?
LEARN WHAT? *OH*... YEAH... *"MAGIC"*...
OK, IS THIS AN ACTUAL *"MAGIC TRICK"*, OR JUST SOME WARPED, LITTLE *"CAT FANTASY"*?
darb

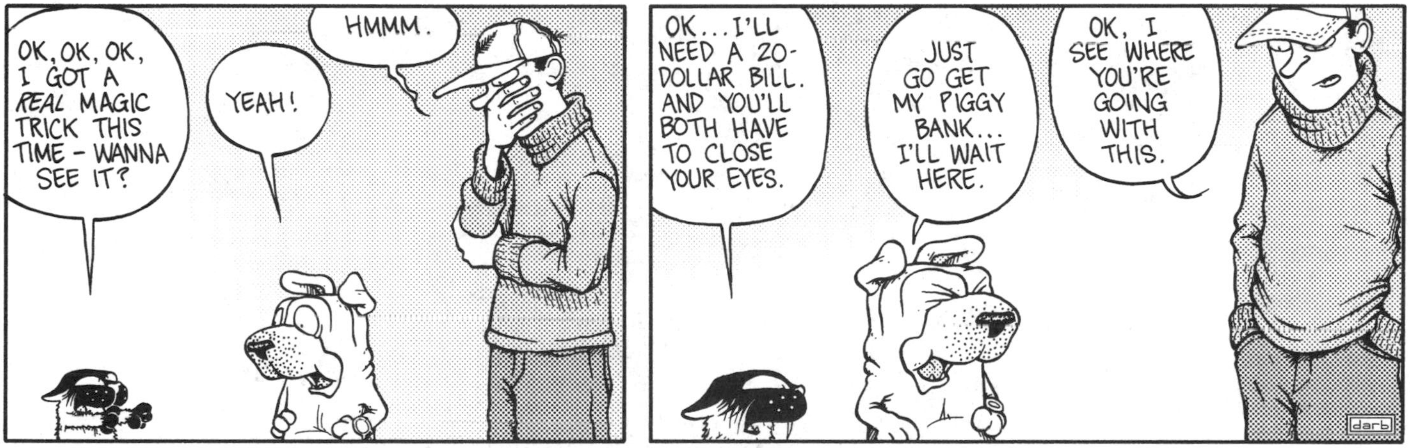
OK, OK, OK, I GOT A *REAL* MAGIC TRICK THIS TIME - WANNA SEE IT?
YEAH!
HMMM.
OK... I'LL NEED A 20-DOLLAR BILL. AND YOU'LL BOTH HAVE TO CLOSE YOUR EYES.
JUST GO GET MY PIGGY BANK... I'LL WAIT HERE.
OK, I SEE WHERE YOU'RE GOING WITH THIS.
darb

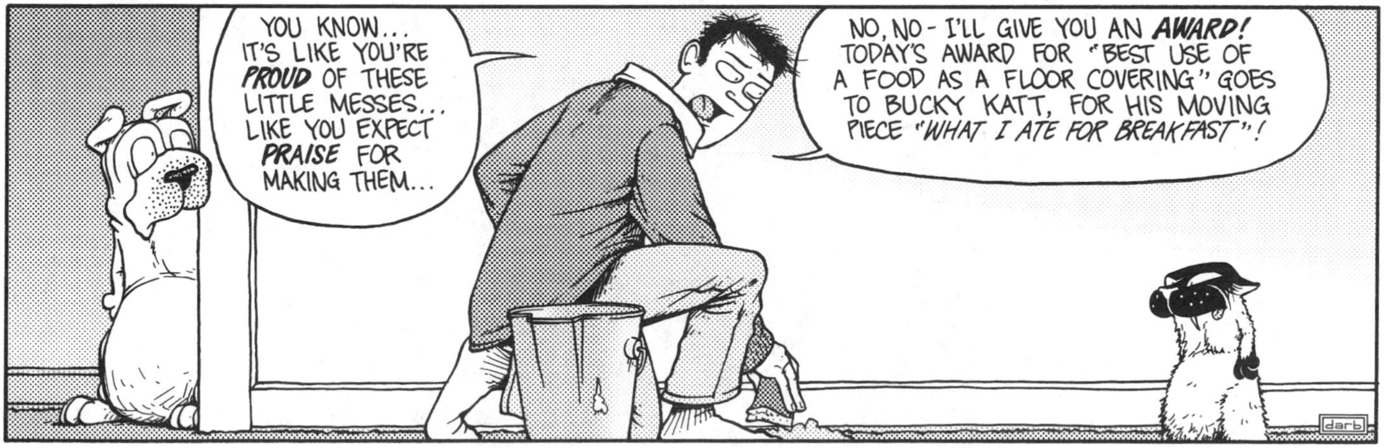
YOU KNOW... IT'S LIKE YOU'RE ***PROUD*** OF THESE LITTLE MESSES... LIKE YOU EXPECT ***PRAISE*** FOR MAKING THEM...
NO, NO - I'LL GIVE YOU AN ***AWARD!*** TODAY'S AWARD FOR "BEST USE OF A FOOD AS A FLOOR COVERING" GOES TO BUCKY KATT, FOR HIS MOVING PIECE *"WHAT I ATE FOR BREAKFAST"*!
darb

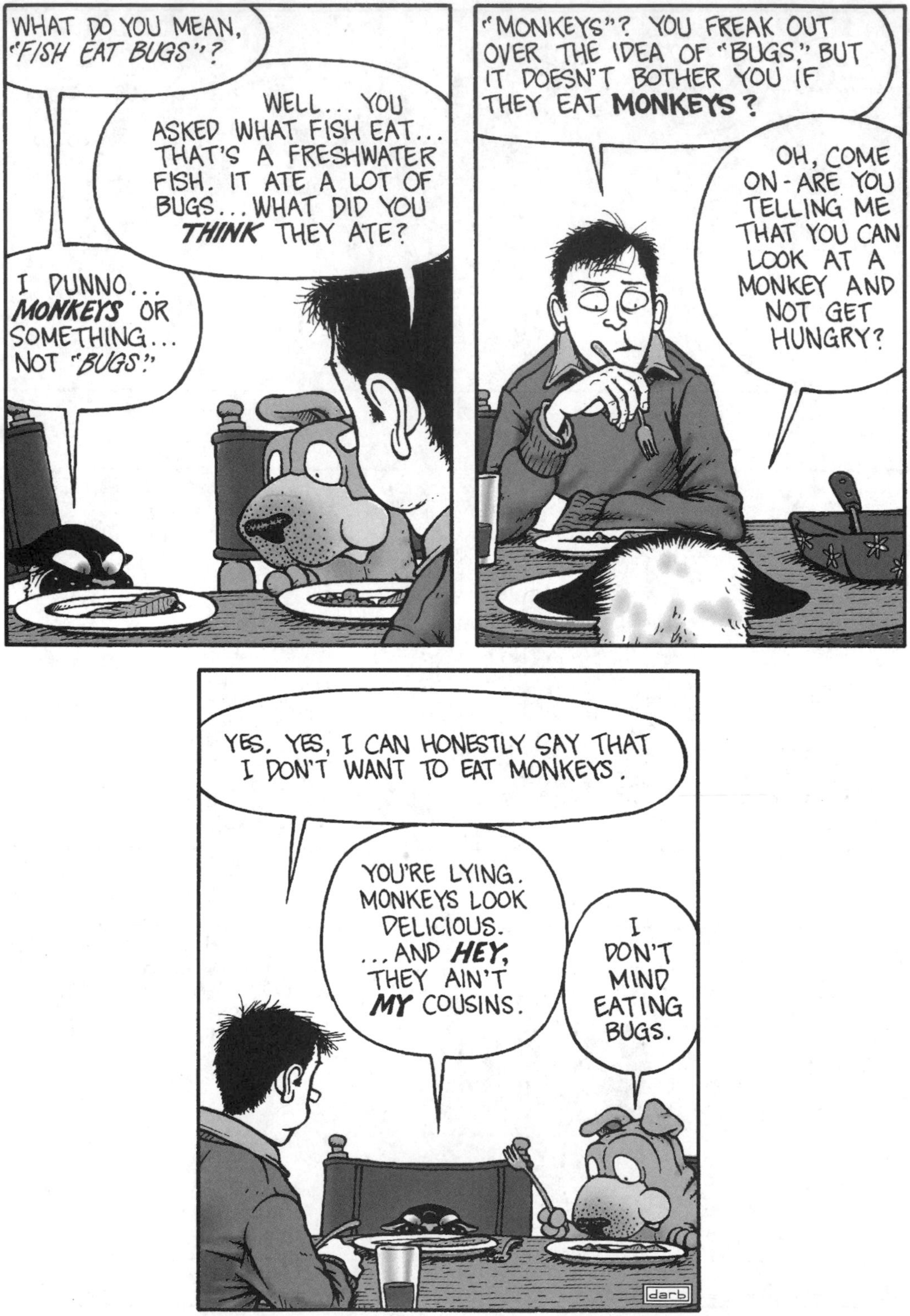
WHAT DO YOU MEAN, "FISH EAT BUGS"?
WELL... YOU ASKED WHAT FISH EAT... THAT'S A FRESHWATER FISH. IT ATE A LOT OF BUGS... WHAT DID YOU *THINK* THEY ATE?
I DUNNO... *MONKEYS* OR SOMETHING... NOT "*BUGS*."
"MONKEYS"? YOU FREAK OUT OVER THE IDEA OF "BUGS," BUT IT DOESN'T BOTHER YOU IF THEY EAT **MONKEYS**?
OH, COME ON - ARE YOU TELLING ME THAT YOU CAN LOOK AT A MONKEY AND NOT GET HUNGRY?
YES. YES, I CAN HONESTLY SAY THAT I DON'T WANT TO EAT MONKEYS.
YOU'RE LYING. MONKEYS LOOK DELICIOUS. ...AND *HEY*, THEY AIN'T *MY* COUSINS.
I DON'T MIND EATING BUGS.
darb

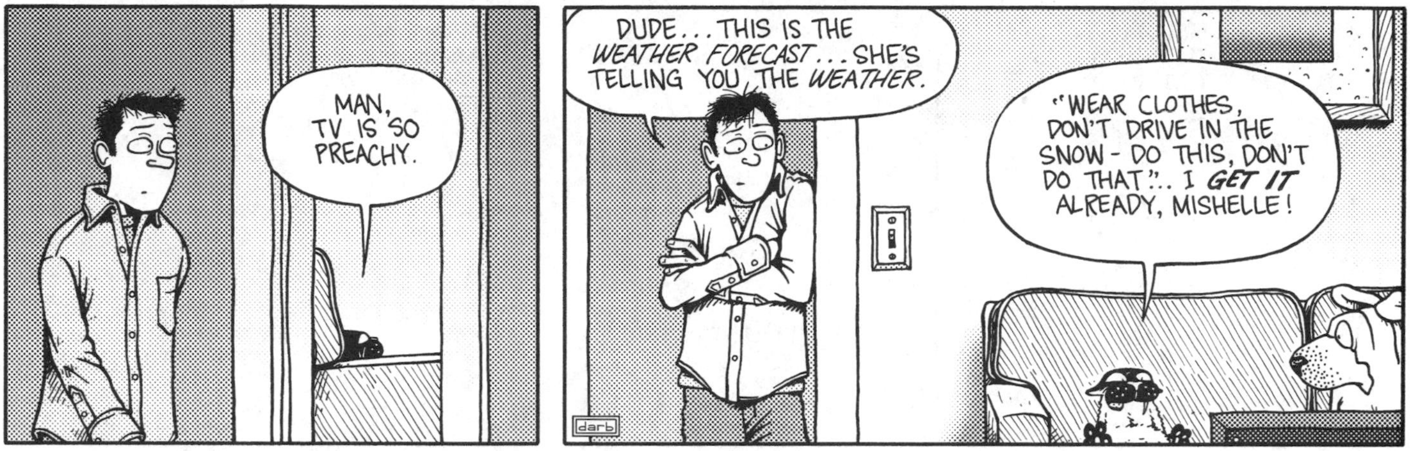
MAN, TV IS SO PREACHY.
DUDE... THIS IS THE *WEATHER FORECAST*... SHE'S TELLING YOU THE *WEATHER*.
"WEAR CLOTHES, DON'T DRIVE IN THE SNOW - DO THIS, DON'T DO THAT"... I ***GET IT*** ALREADY, MISHELLE!
darb

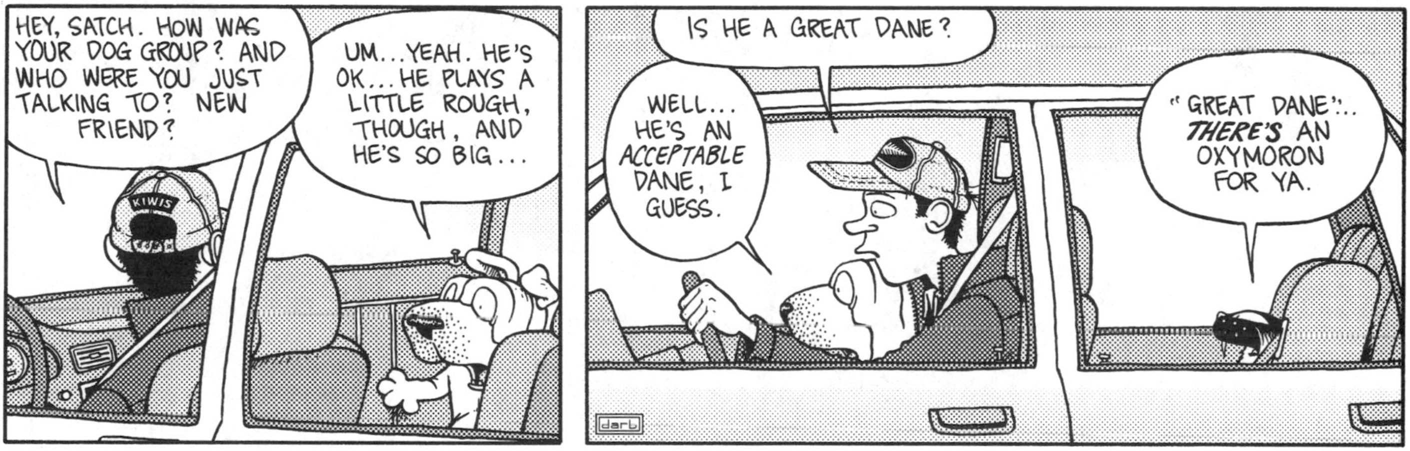
HEY, SATCH. HOW WAS YOUR DOG GROUP? AND WHO WERE YOU JUST TALKING TO? NEW FRIEND?
UM...YEAH. HE'S OK... HE PLAYS A LITTLE ROUGH, THOUGH, AND HE'S SO BIG...
KIWIS
IS HE A GREAT DANE?
WELL... HE'S AN *ACCEPTABLE* DANE, I GUESS.
"GREAT DANE"... ***THERE'S*** AN OXYMORON FOR YA.
darb

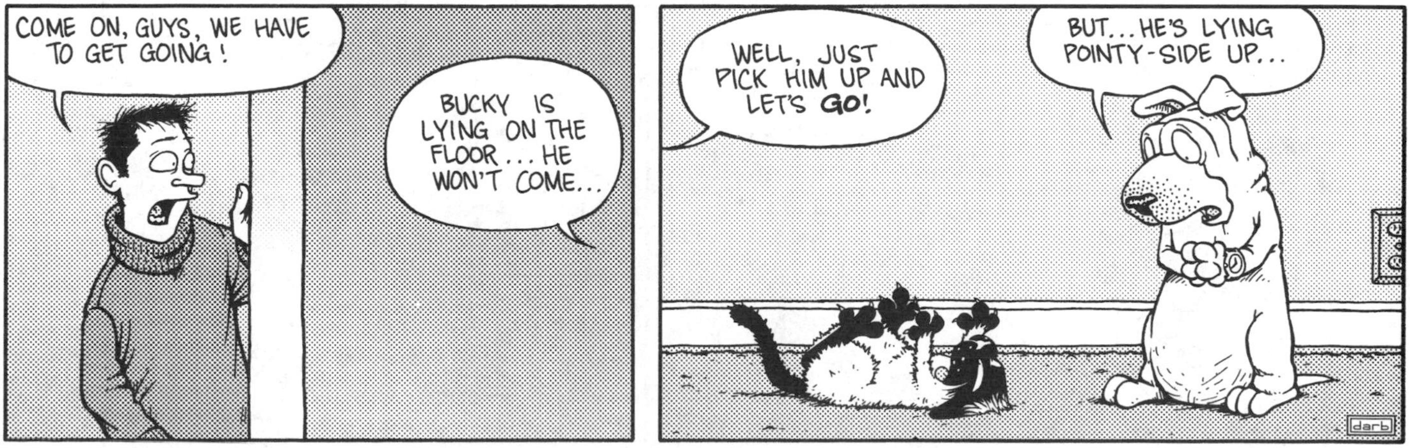
COME ON, GUYS, WE HAVE TO GET GOING!
BUCKY IS LYING ON THE FLOOR... HE WON'T COME...
WELL, JUST PICK HIM UP AND LET'S **GO**!
BUT... HE'S LYING POINTY-SIDE UP...
darb

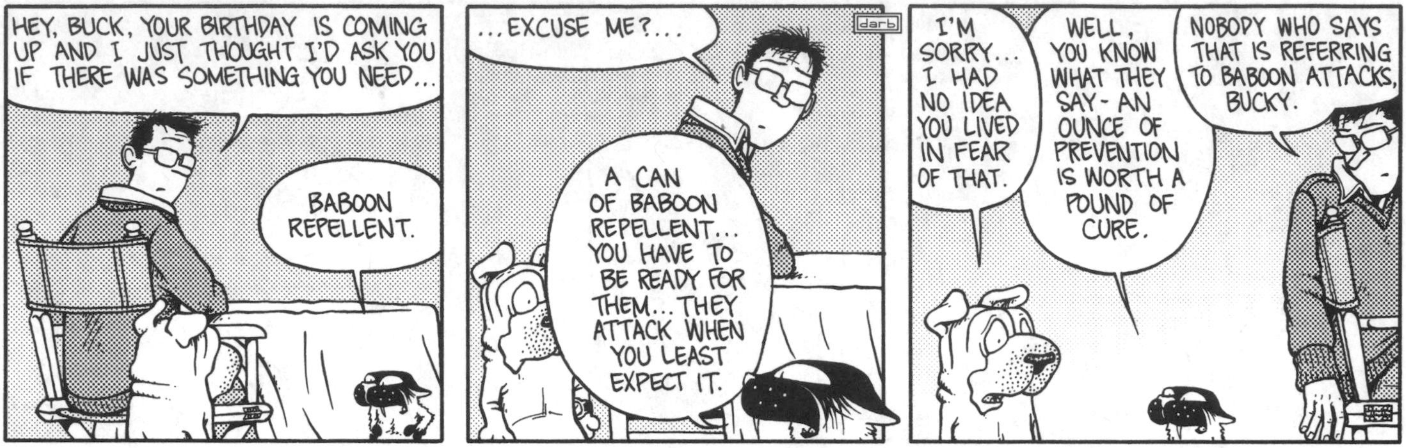
HEY, BUCK, YOUR BIRTHDAY IS COMING UP AND I JUST THOUGHT I'D ASK YOU IF THERE WAS SOMETHING YOU NEED...
BABOON REPELLENT.
...EXCUSE ME?...
A CAN OF BABOON REPELLENT... YOU HAVE TO BE READY FOR THEM... THEY ATTACK WHEN YOU LEAST EXPECT IT.
darb
I'M SORRY... I HAD NO IDEA YOU LIVED IN FEAR OF THAT.
WELL, YOU KNOW WHAT THEY SAY- AN OUNCE OF PREVENTION IS WORTH A POUND OF CURE.
NOBODY WHO SAYS THAT IS REFERRING TO BABOON ATTACKS, BUCKY.

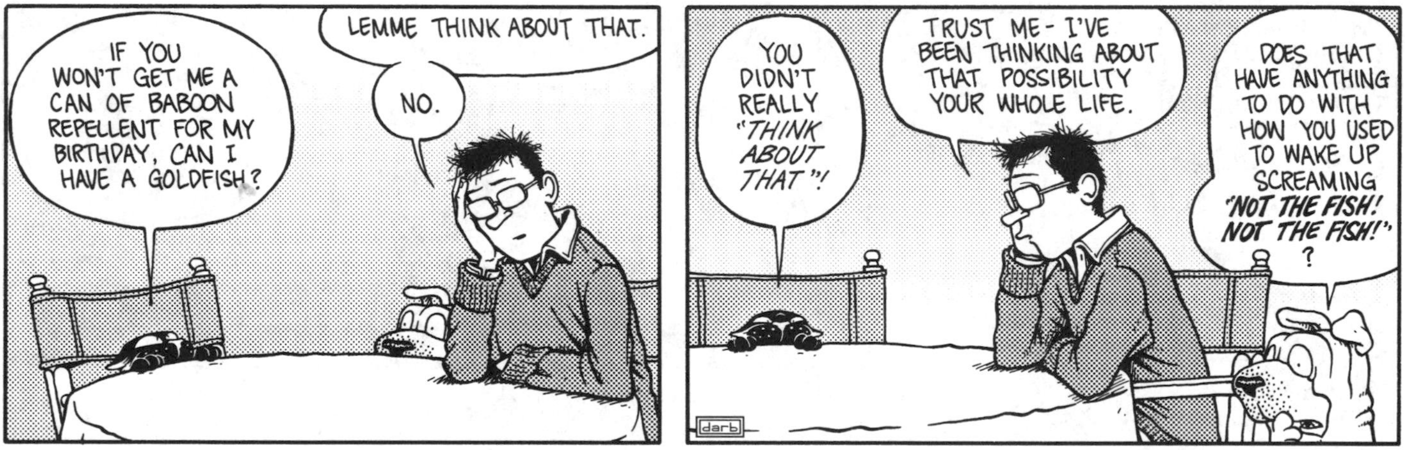
IF YOU WON'T GET ME A CAN OF BABOON REPELLENT FOR MY BIRTHDAY, CAN I HAVE A GOLDFISH?
LEMME THINK ABOUT THAT.
NO.
YOU DIDN'T REALLY "THINK ABOUT THAT"!
TRUST ME- I'VE BEEN THINKING ABOUT THAT POSSIBILITY YOUR WHOLE LIFE.
DOES THAT HAVE ANYTHING TO DO WITH HOW YOU USED TO WAKE UP SCREAMING "NOT THE FISH! NOT THE FISH!"?
darb

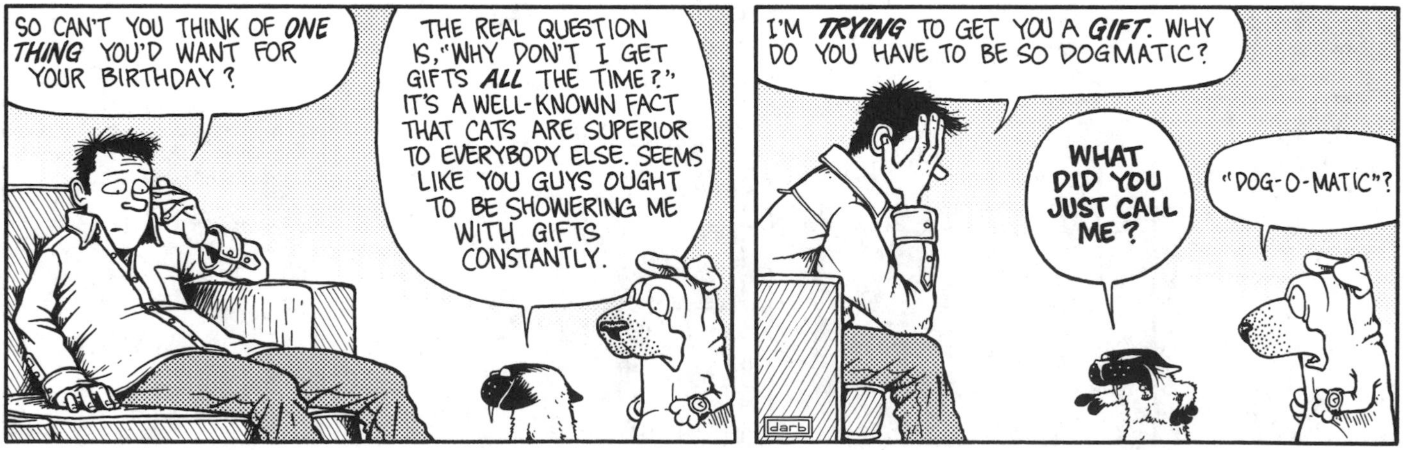
SO CAN'T YOU THINK OF ONE THING YOU'D WANT FOR YOUR BIRTHDAY?
THE REAL QUESTION IS, "WHY DON'T I GET GIFTS ALL THE TIME?" IT'S A WELL-KNOWN FACT THAT CATS ARE SUPERIOR TO EVERYBODY ELSE. SEEMS LIKE YOU GUYS OUGHT TO BE SHOWERING ME WITH GIFTS CONSTANTLY.
I'M TRYING TO GET YOU A GIFT. WHY DO YOU HAVE TO BE SO DOGMATIC?
WHAT DID YOU JUST CALL ME?
"DOG-O-MATIC"?
darb

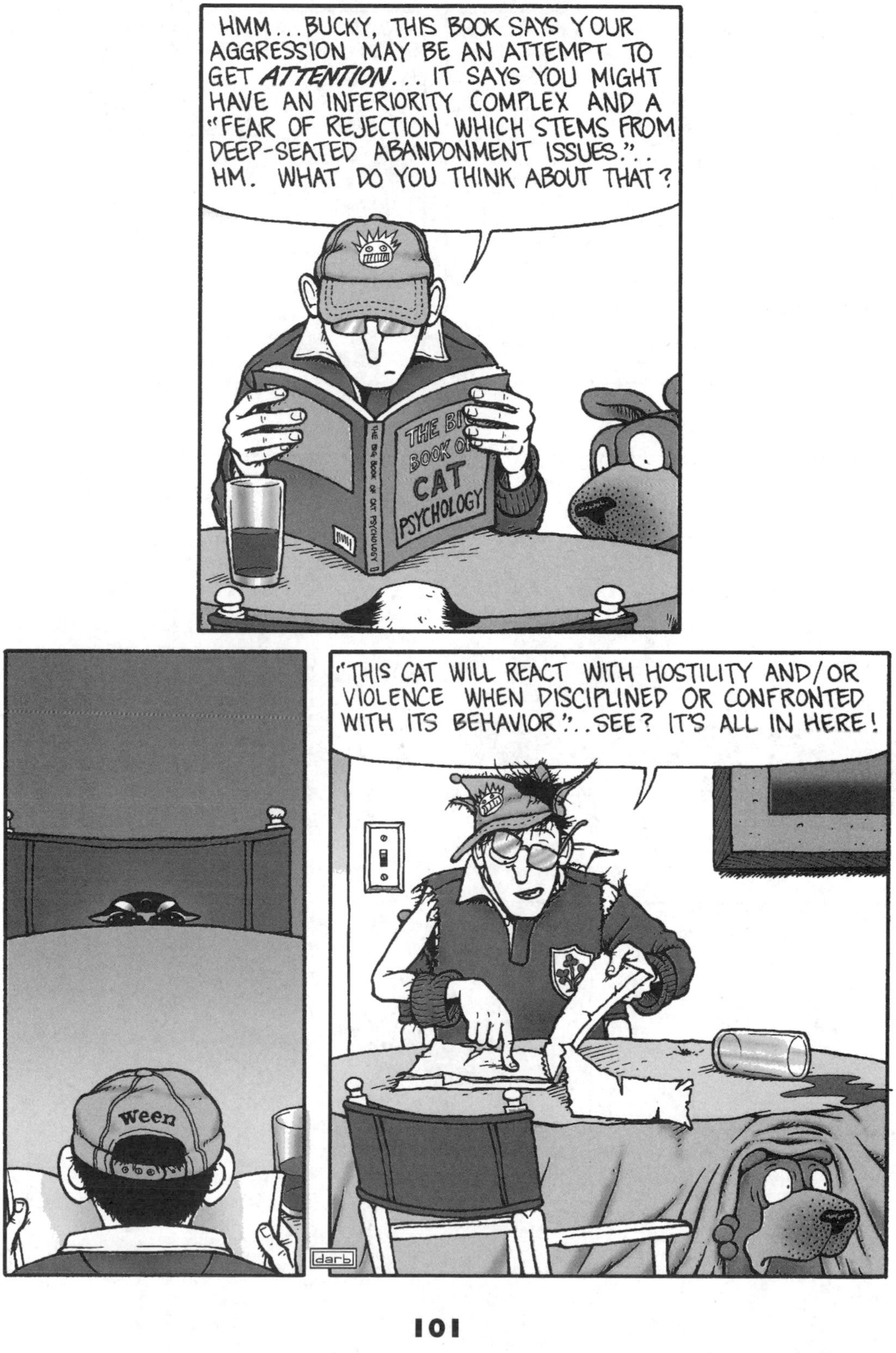
HMM... BUCKY, THIS BOOK SAYS YOUR AGGRESSION MAY BE AN ATTEMPT TO GET *ATTENTION*... IT SAYS YOU MIGHT HAVE AN INFERIORITY COMPLEX AND A "FEAR OF REJECTION WHICH STEMS FROM DEEP-SEATED ABANDONMENT ISSUES."... HM. WHAT DO YOU THINK ABOUT THAT?
THE BI BOOK OF CAT PSYCHOLOGY
THE BIG BOOK OF CAT PSYCHOLOGY
Ween
"THIS CAT WILL REACT WITH HOSTILITY AND/OR VIOLENCE WHEN DISCIPLINED OR CONFRONTED WITH ITS BEHAVIOR."..SEE? IT'S ALL IN HERE!
darb

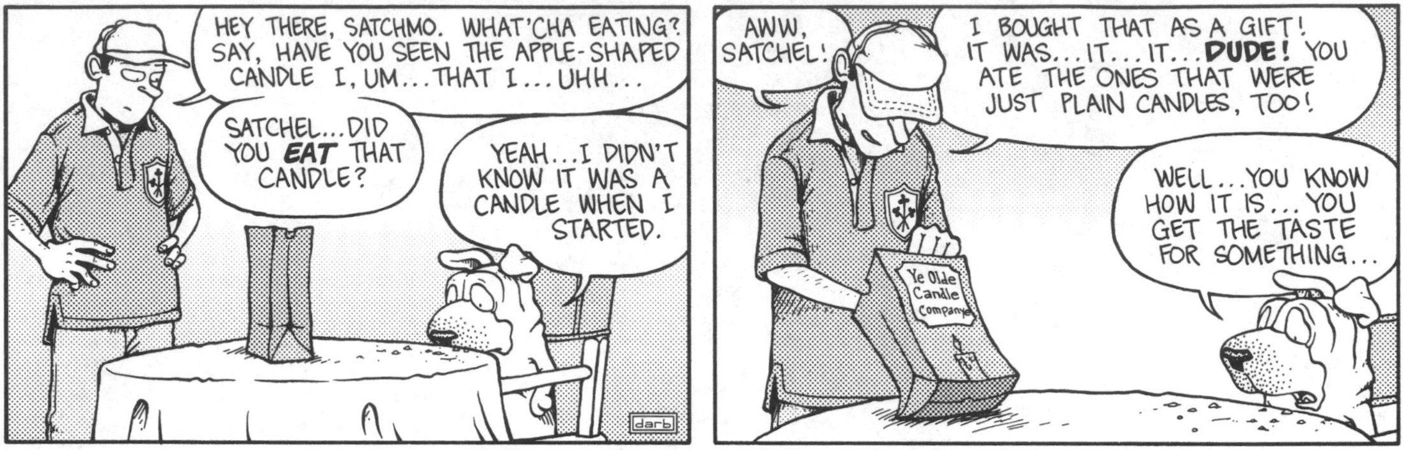
HEY THERE, SATCHMO. WHAT'CHA EATING? SAY, HAVE YOU SEEN THE APPLE-SHAPED CANDLE I, UM... THAT I... UHH...
SATCHEL... DID YOU *EAT* THAT CANDLE?
YEAH... I DIDN'T KNOW IT WAS A CANDLE WHEN I STARTED.
darb
AWW, SATCHEL!
I BOUGHT THAT AS A GIFT! IT WAS... IT... IT... **DUDE!** YOU ATE THE ONES THAT WERE JUST PLAIN CANDLES, TOO!
Ye Olde Candle Companye
WELL... YOU KNOW HOW IT IS... YOU GET THE TASTE FOR SOMETHING...

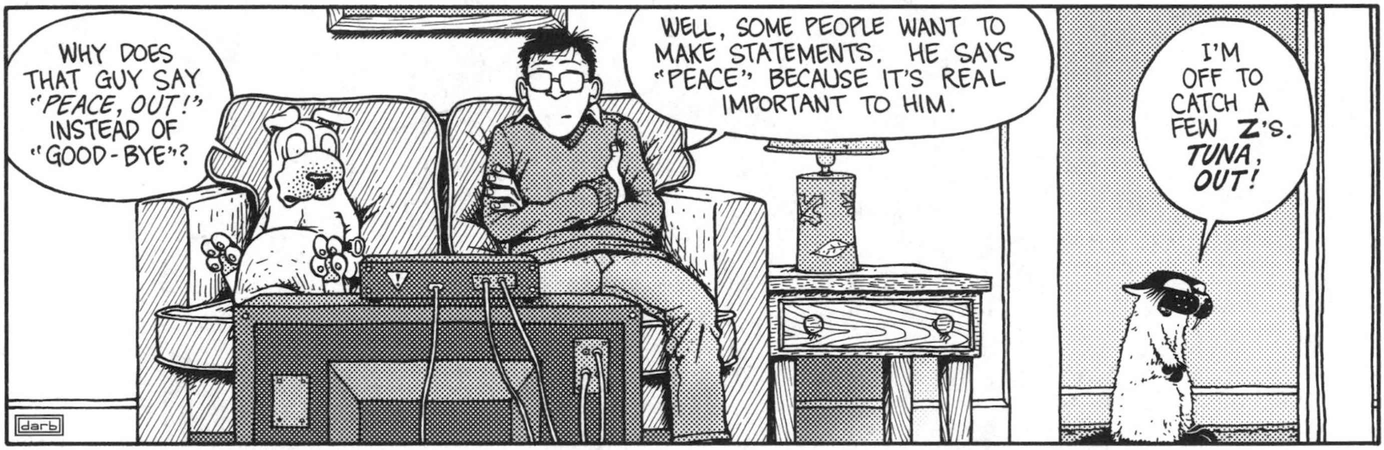
WHY DOES THAT GUY SAY "*PEACE, OUT!*" INSTEAD OF "GOOD-BYE"?
WELL, SOME PEOPLE WANT TO MAKE STATEMENTS. HE SAYS "PEACE" BECAUSE IT'S REAL IMPORTANT TO HIM.
I'M OFF TO CATCH A FEW **Z**'S. ***TUNA, OUT!***
darb

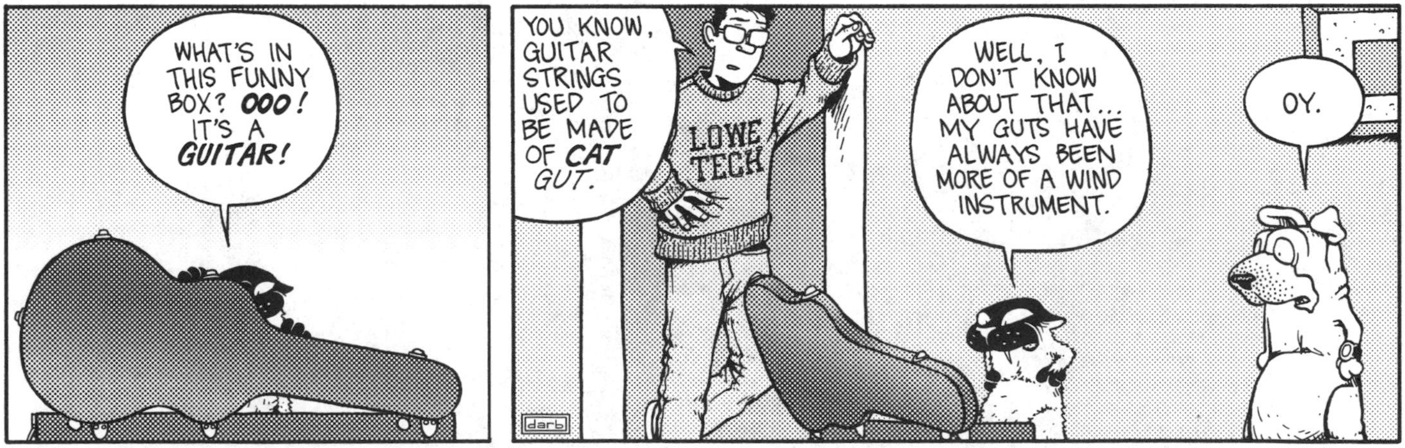
WHAT'S IN THIS FUNNY BOX? ***OOO!*** IT'S A ***GUITAR!***
YOU KNOW, GUITAR STRINGS USED TO BE MADE OF ***CAT*** *GUT*.
LOWE TECH
WELL, I DON'T KNOW ABOUT THAT... MY GUTS HAVE ALWAYS BEEN MORE OF A WIND INSTRUMENT.
OY.
darb

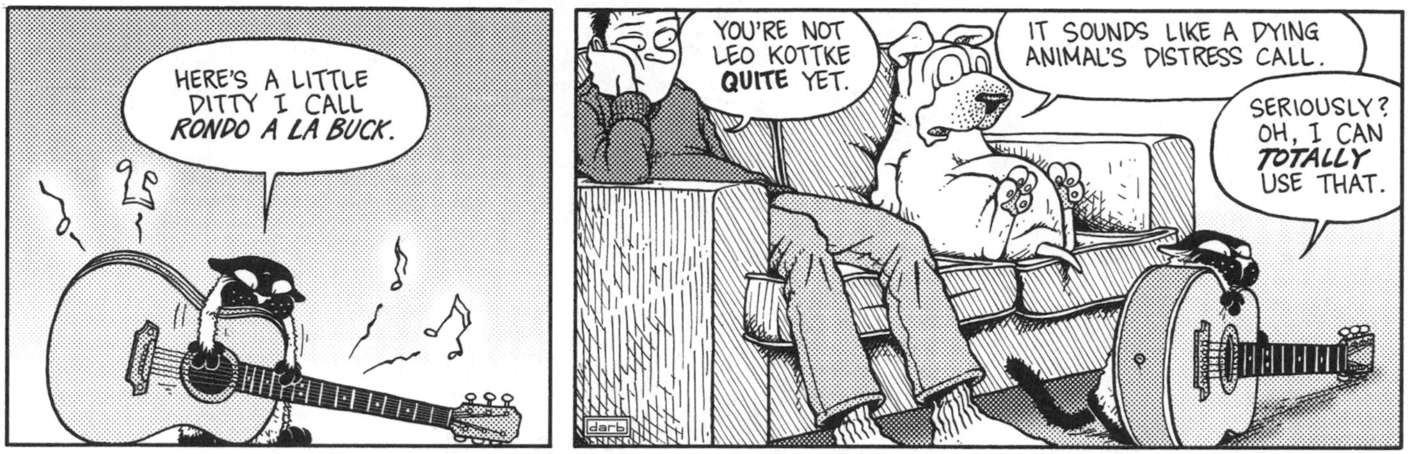
HERE'S A LITTLE DITTY I CALL ***RONDO A LA BUCK.***
YOU'RE NOT LEO KOTTKE **QUITE** YET.
IT SOUNDS LIKE A DYING ANIMAL'S DISTRESS CALL.
SERIOUSLY? OH, I CAN ***TOTALLY*** USE THAT.
darb

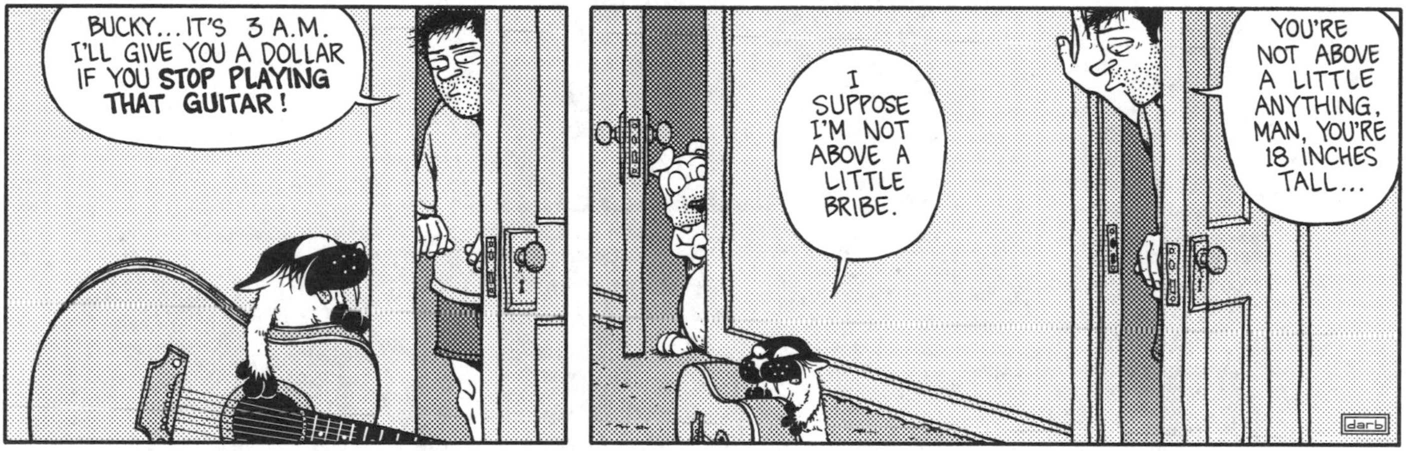
BUCKY... IT'S 3 A.M. I'LL GIVE YOU A DOLLAR IF YOU **STOP PLAYING THAT GUITAR**!
I SUPPOSE I'M NOT ABOVE A LITTLE BRIBE.
YOU'RE NOT ABOVE A LITTLE ANYTHING, MAN, YOU'RE 18 INCHES TALL...
darb

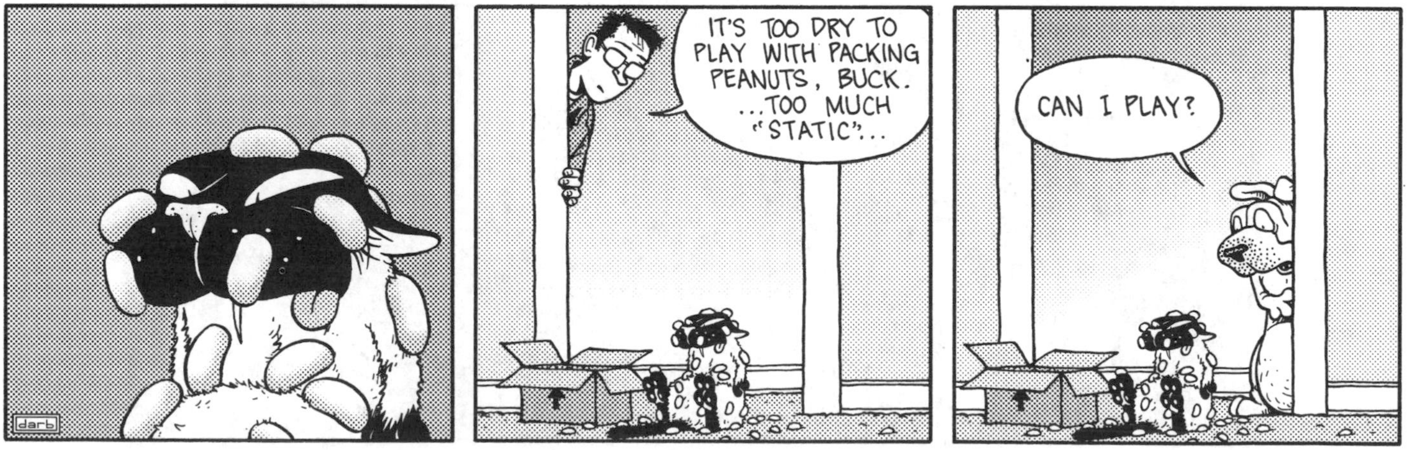
darb
IT'S TOO DRY TO PLAY WITH PACKING PEANUTS, BUCK. ...TOO MUCH "STATIC"...
CAN I PLAY?

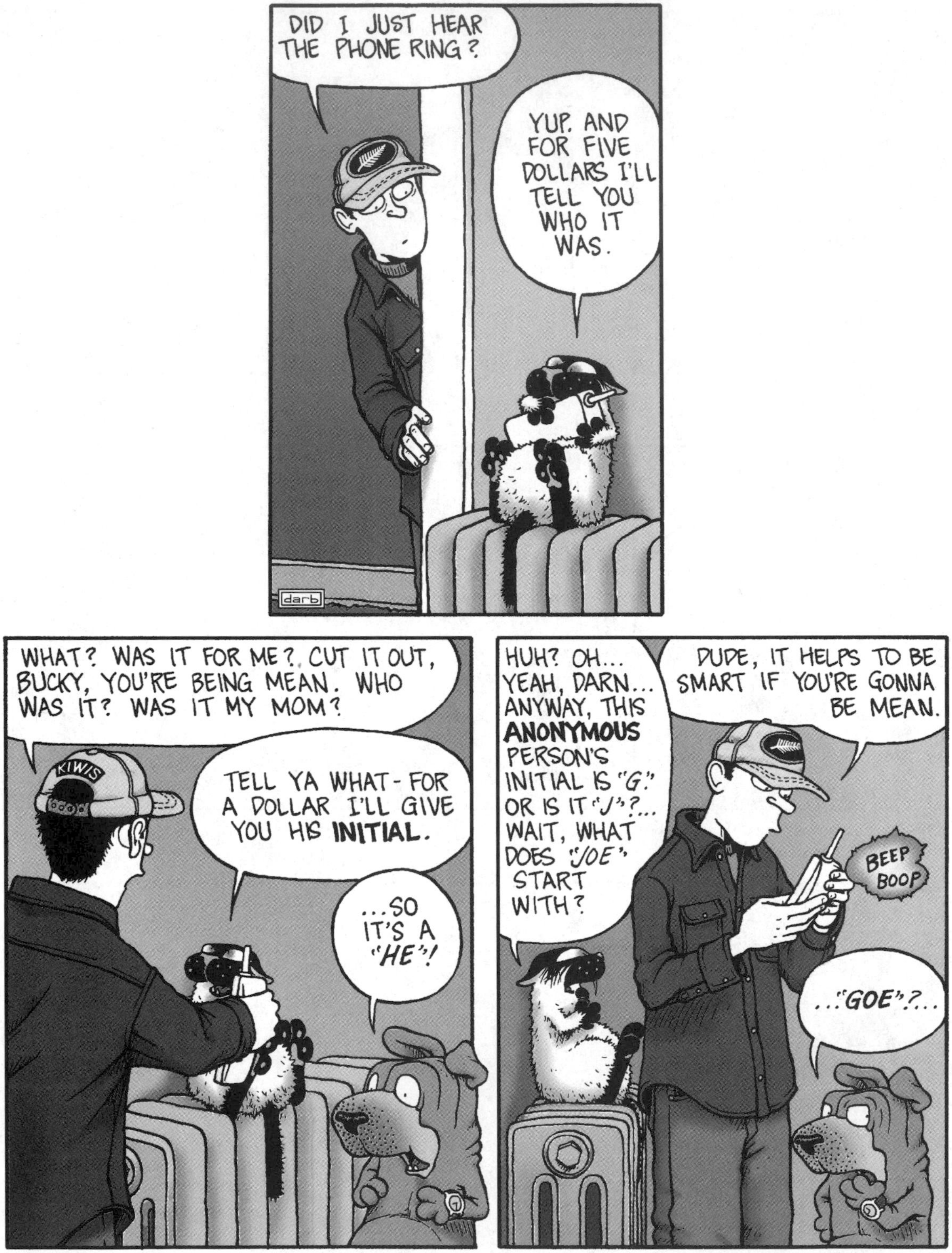
DID I JUST HEAR THE PHONE RING?
YUP. AND FOR FIVE DOLLARS I'LL TELL YOU WHO IT WAS.
darb
WHAT? WAS IT FOR ME? CUT IT OUT, BUCKY, YOU'RE BEING MEAN. WHO WAS IT? WAS IT MY MOM?
KIWIS
TELL YA WHAT- FOR A DOLLAR I'LL GIVE YOU HIS **INITIAL**.
...SO IT'S A *"HE"*!
HUH? OH... YEAH, DARN... ANYWAY, THIS **ANONYMOUS** PERSON'S INITIAL IS *"G."* OR IS IT *"J"*?... WAIT, WHAT DOES *"JOE"* START WITH?
DUDE, IT HELPS TO BE SMART IF YOU'RE GONNA BE MEAN.
BEEP BOOP
...*"GOE"*?...

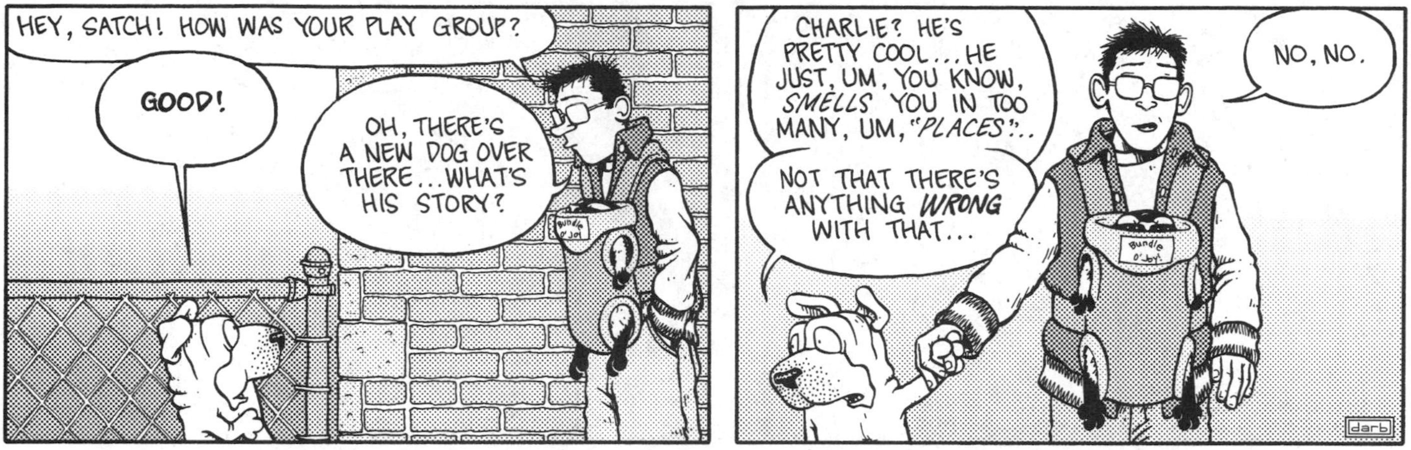
HEY, SATCH! HOW WAS YOUR PLAY GROUP?
GOOD!
OH, THERE'S A NEW DOG OVER THERE...WHAT'S HIS STORY?
CHARLIE? HE'S PRETTY COOL...HE JUST, UM, YOU KNOW, *SMELLS* YOU IN TOO MANY, UM, "*PLACES*"...
NOT THAT THERE'S ANYTHING ***WRONG*** WITH THAT...
NO, NO.
darb

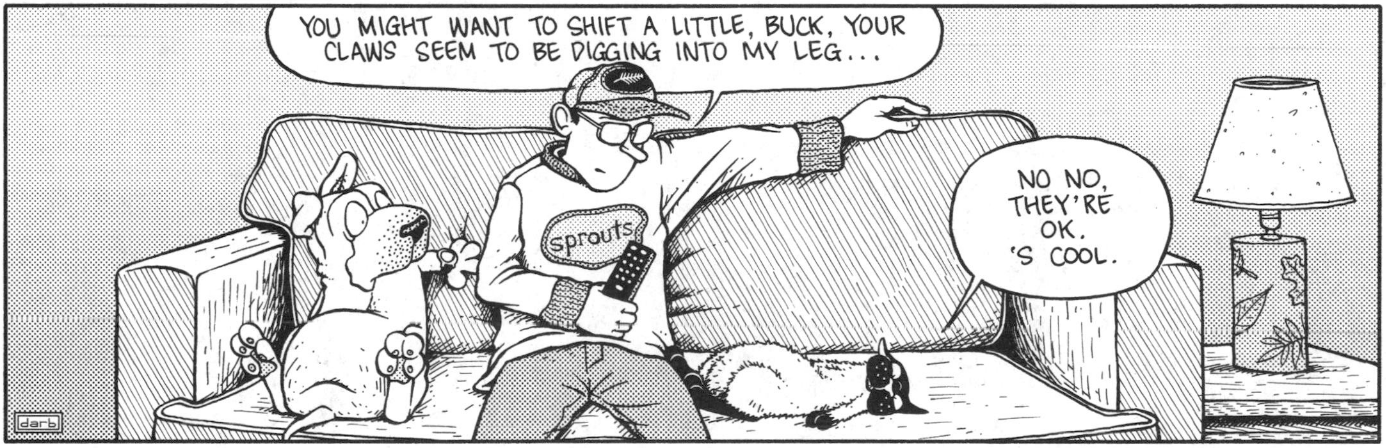
YOU MIGHT WANT TO SHIFT A LITTLE, BUCK, YOUR CLAWS SEEM TO BE DIGGING INTO MY LEG...
NO NO, THEY'RE OK. 'S COOL.
darb

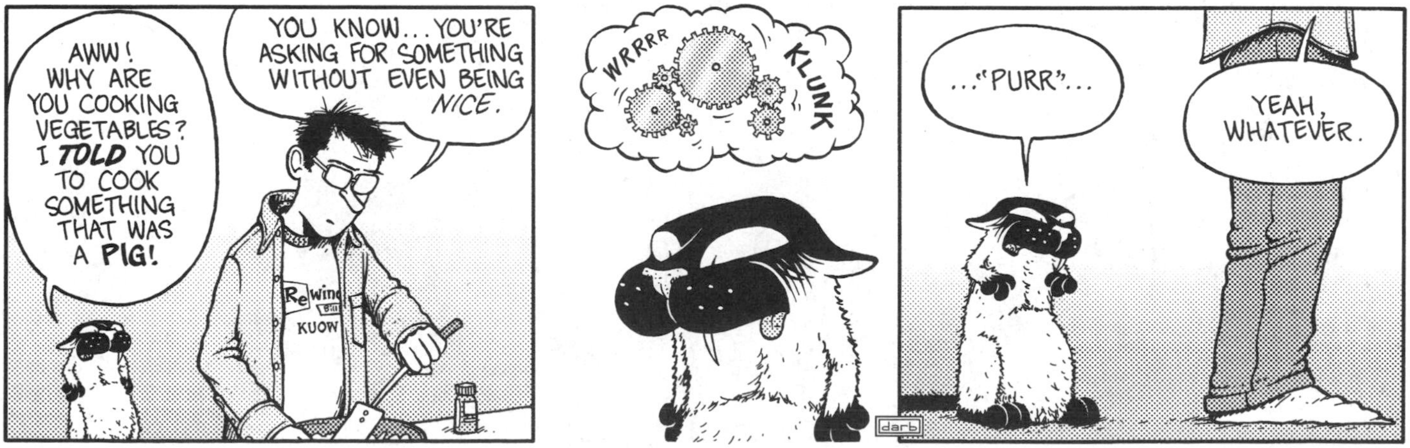
AWW! WHY ARE YOU COOKING VEGETABLES? I ***TOLD*** YOU TO COOK SOMETHING THAT WAS A **PIG**!
YOU KNOW...YOU'RE ASKING FOR SOMETHING WITHOUT EVEN BEING *NICE*.
WRRRR
KLUNK
darb
..."PURR"...
YEAH, WHATEVER.

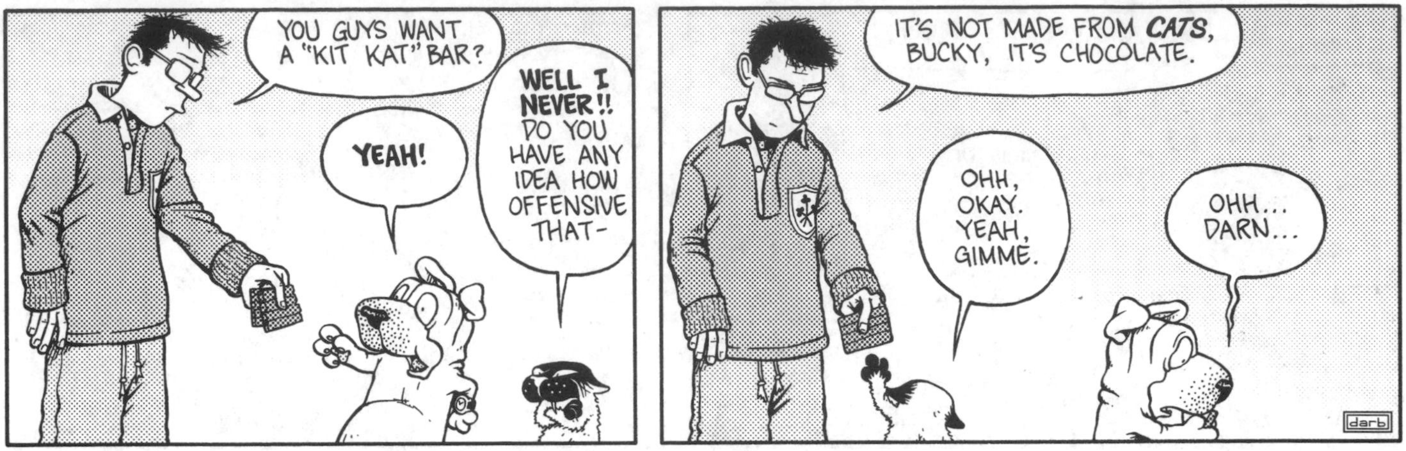

YOU GUYS WANT A "KIT KAT" BAR?
YEAH!
WELL I NEVER!! DO YOU HAVE ANY IDEA HOW OFFENSIVE THAT-
IT'S NOT MADE FROM CATS, BUCKY, IT'S CHOCOLATE.
OHH, OKAY. YEAH, GIMME.
OHH... DARN...
darb

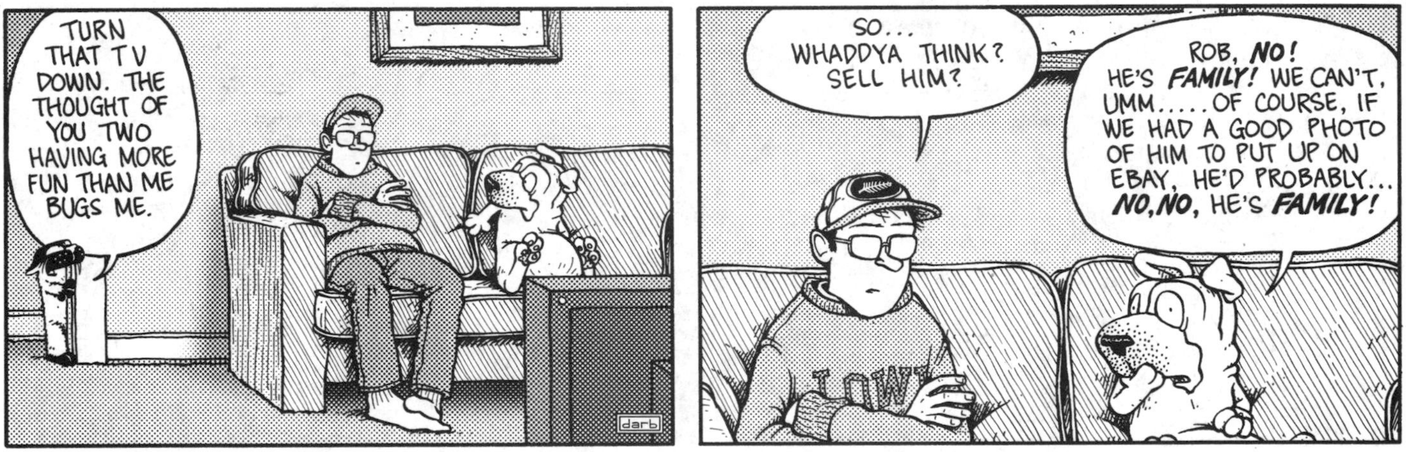

TURN THAT TV DOWN. THE THOUGHT OF YOU TWO HAVING MORE FUN THAN ME BUGS ME.
darb
SO... WHADDYA THINK? SELL HIM?
ROB, NO! HE'S FAMILY! WE CAN'T, UMM..... OF COURSE, IF WE HAD A GOOD PHOTO OF HIM TO PUT UP ON EBAY, HE'D PROBABLY... NO, NO, HE'S FAMILY!

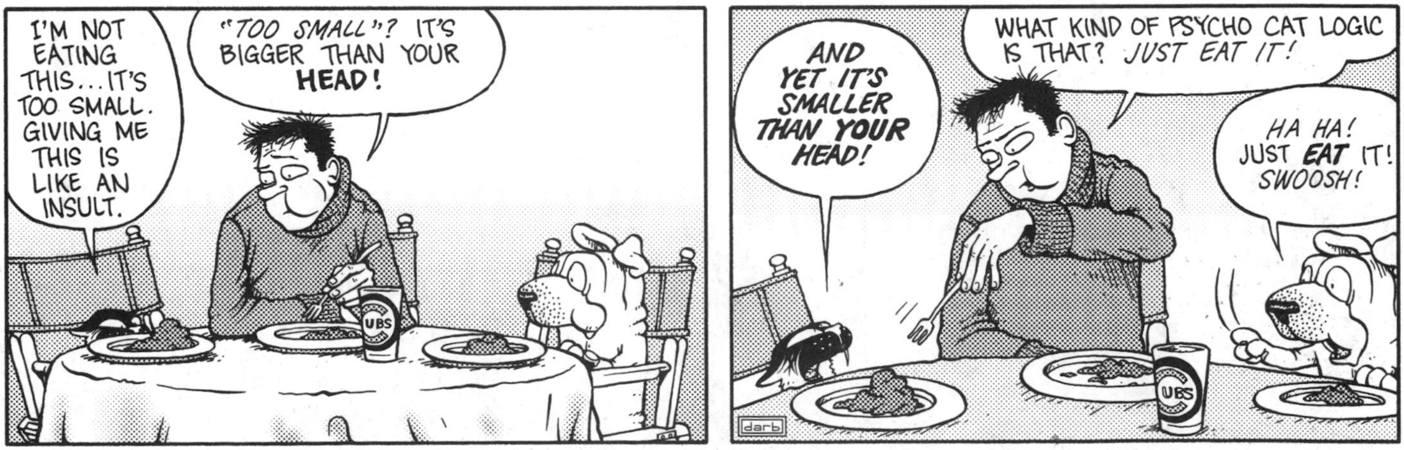

I'M NOT EATING THIS... IT'S TOO SMALL. GIVING ME THIS IS LIKE AN INSULT.
"TOO SMALL"? IT'S BIGGER THAN YOUR HEAD!
AND YET IT'S SMALLER THAN YOUR HEAD!
WHAT KIND OF PSYCHO CAT LOGIC IS THAT? JUST EAT IT!
HA HA! JUST EAT IT! SWOOSH!
darb

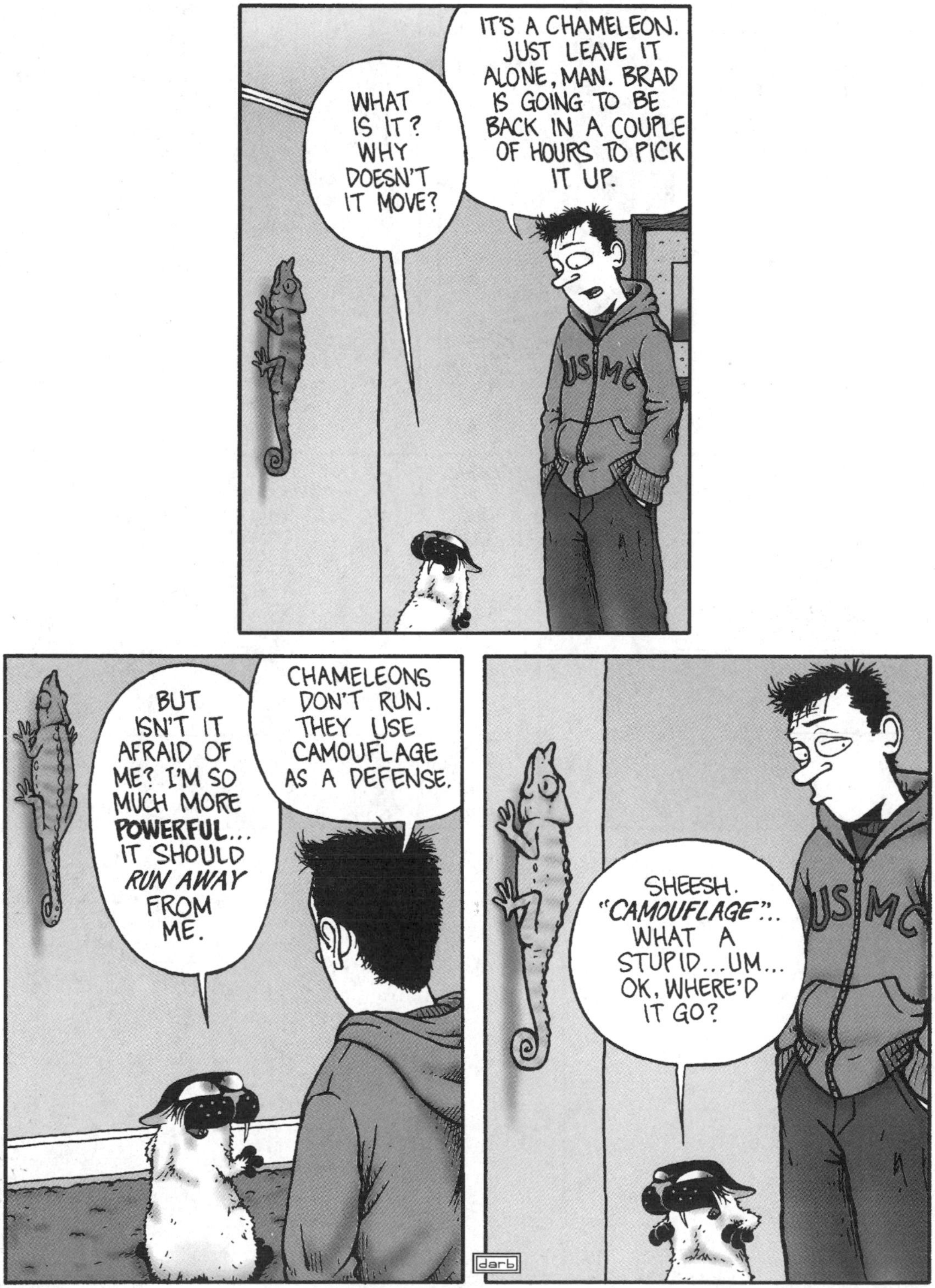
WHAT IS IT? WHY DOESN'T IT MOVE?
IT'S A CHAMELEON. JUST LEAVE IT ALONE, MAN. BRAD IS GOING TO BE BACK IN A COUPLE OF HOURS TO PICK IT UP.
BUT ISN'T IT AFRAID OF ME? I'M SO MUCH MORE **POWERFUL**... IT SHOULD *RUN AWAY* FROM ME.
CHAMELEONS DON'T RUN. THEY USE CAMOUFLAGE AS A DEFENSE.
SHEESH. "*CAMOUFLAGE*"... WHAT A STUPID...UM... OK, WHERE'D IT GO?
darb

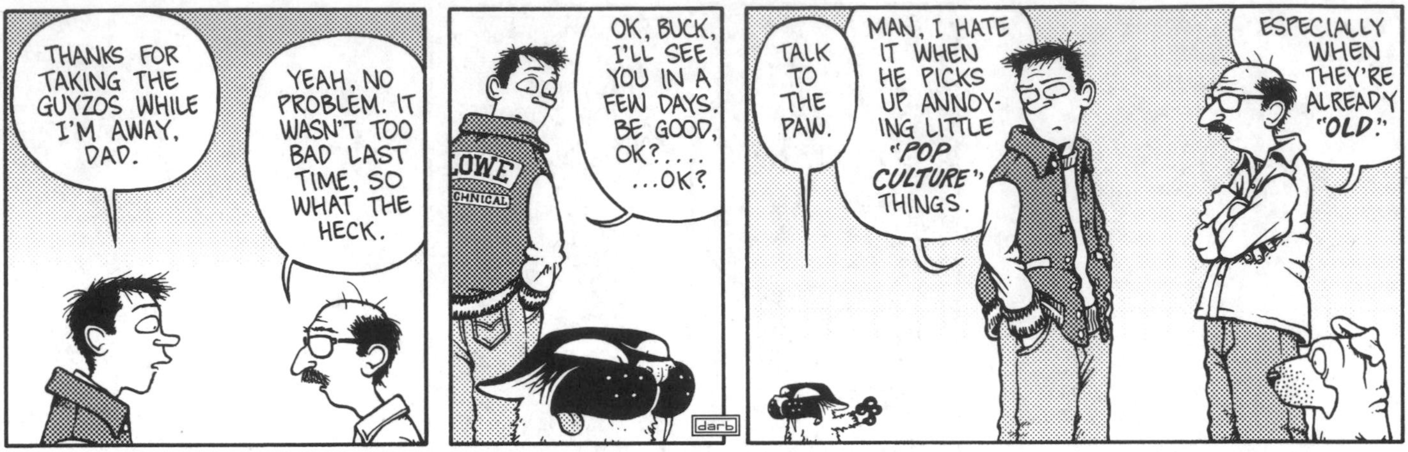
THANKS FOR TAKING THE GUYZOS WHILE I'M AWAY, DAD.
YEAH, NO PROBLEM. IT WASN'T TOO BAD LAST TIME, SO WHAT THE HECK.
OK, BUCK, I'LL SEE YOU IN A FEW DAYS. BE GOOD, OK?.... ...OK?
TALK TO THE PAW.
MAN, I HATE IT WHEN HE PICKS UP ANNOYING LITTLE "POP CULTURE" THINGS.
ESPECIALLY WHEN THEY'RE ALREADY "OLD."
darb

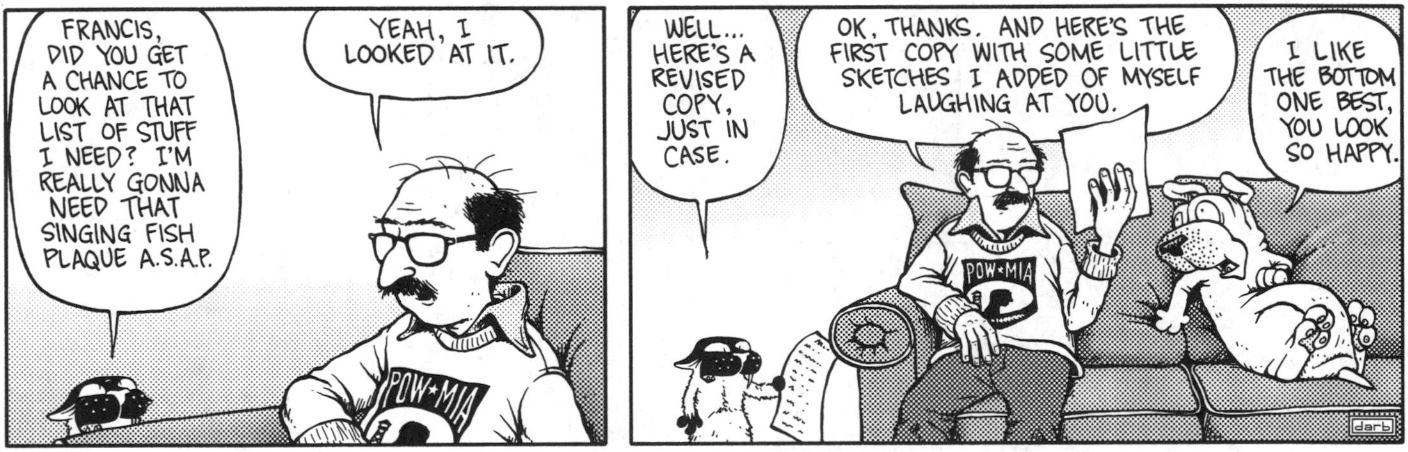
FRANCIS, DID YOU GET A CHANCE TO LOOK AT THAT LIST OF STUFF I NEED? I'M REALLY GONNA NEED THAT SINGING FISH PLAQUE A.S.A.P.
YEAH, I LOOKED AT IT.
WELL... HERE'S A REVISED COPY, JUST IN CASE.
OK, THANKS. AND HERE'S THE FIRST COPY WITH SOME LITTLE SKETCHES I ADDED OF MYSELF LAUGHING AT YOU.
I LIKE THE BOTTOM ONE BEST, YOU LOOK SO HAPPY.
POW★MIA
darb

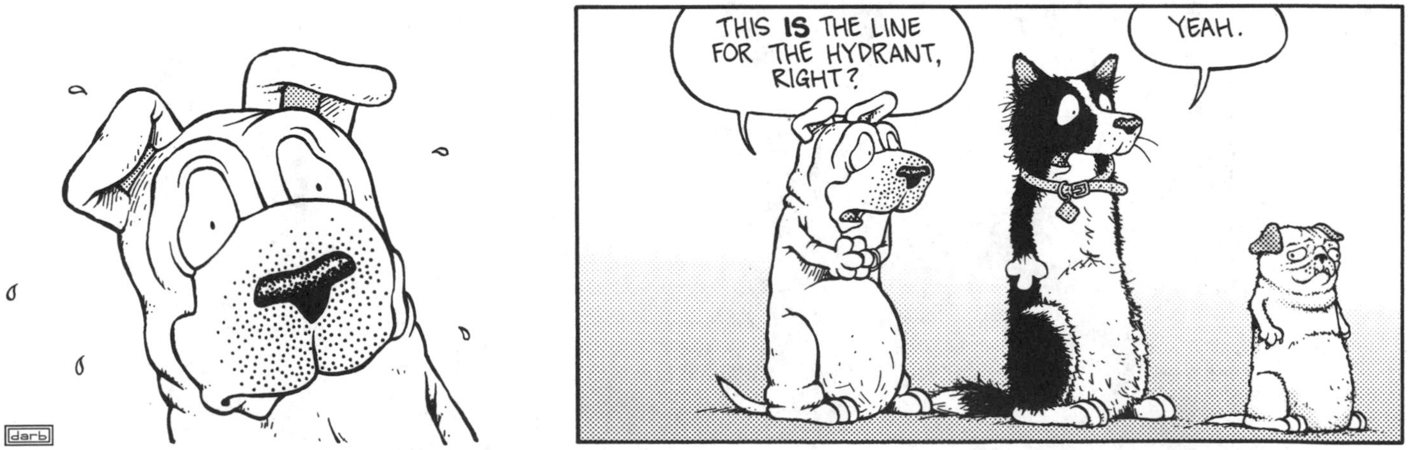
darb
THIS **IS** THE LINE FOR THE HYDRANT, RIGHT?
YEAH.

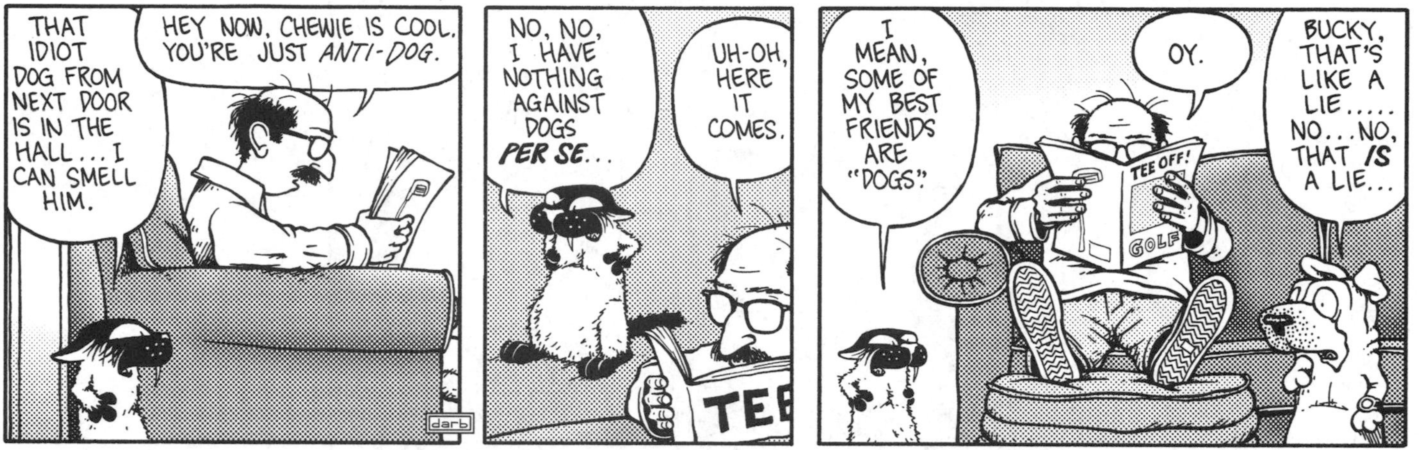
THAT IDIOT DOG FROM NEXT DOOR IS IN THE HALL... I CAN SMELL HIM.
HEY NOW, CHEWIE IS COOL. YOU'RE JUST *ANTI-DOG*.
NO, NO, I HAVE NOTHING AGAINST DOGS ***PER SE***...
UH-OH, HERE IT COMES.
TEE
I MEAN, SOME OF MY BEST FRIENDS ARE "DOGS."
OY.
TEE OFF!
GOLF
BUCKY, THAT'S LIKE A LIE..... NO...NO, THAT ***IS*** A LIE...
darb

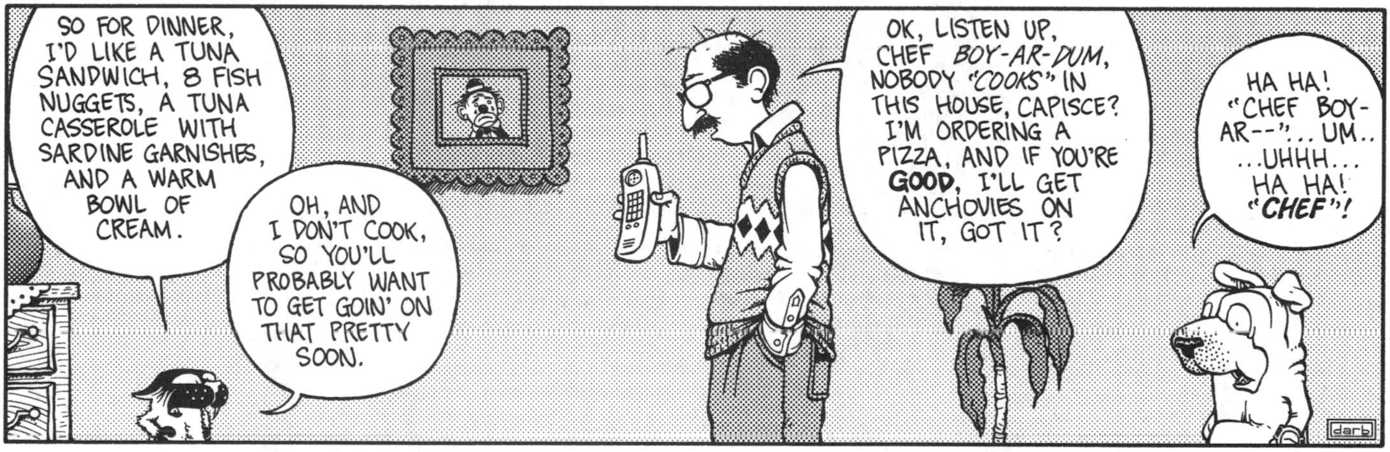
SO FOR DINNER, I'D LIKE A TUNA SANDWICH, 8 FISH NUGGETS, A TUNA CASSEROLE WITH SARDINE GARNISHES, AND A WARM BOWL OF CREAM.
OH, AND I DON'T COOK, SO YOU'LL PROBABLY WANT TO GET GOIN' ON THAT PRETTY SOON.
OK, LISTEN UP, CHEF *BOY-AR-DUM*, NOBODY *"COOKS"* IN THIS HOUSE, CAPISCE? I'M ORDERING A PIZZA, AND IF YOU'RE **GOOD**, I'LL GET ANCHOVIES ON IT, GOT IT?
HA HA! "CHEF BOY-AR--"... UM.. ...UHHH... HA HA! ***"CHEF"***!
darb

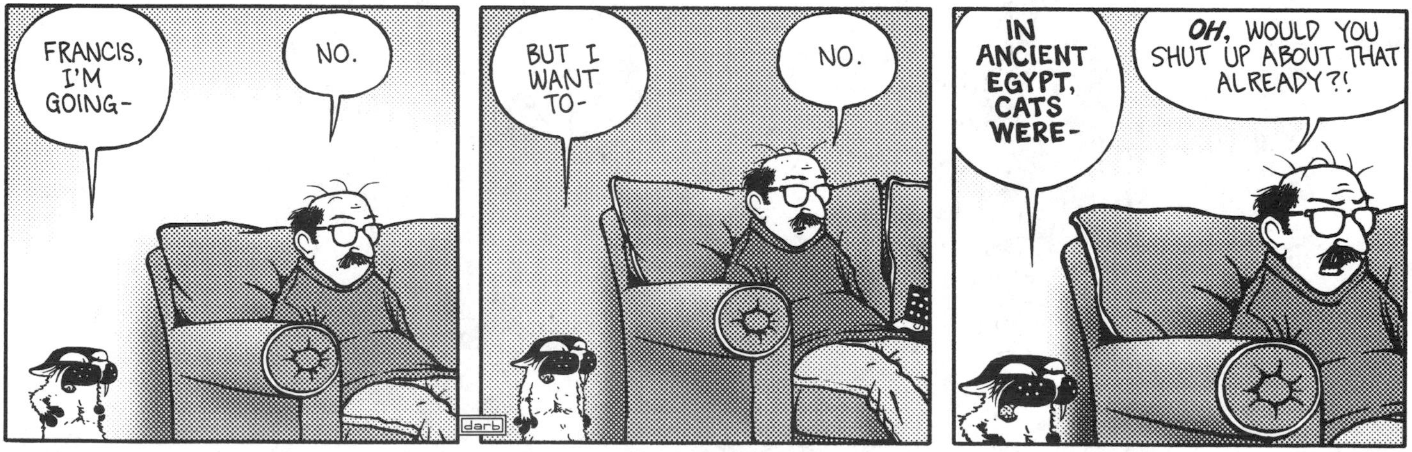
FRANCIS, I'M GOING-
NO.
BUT I WANT TO-
NO.
darb
IN ANCIENT EGYPT, CATS WERE-
OH, WOULD YOU SHUT UP ABOUT THAT ALREADY?!

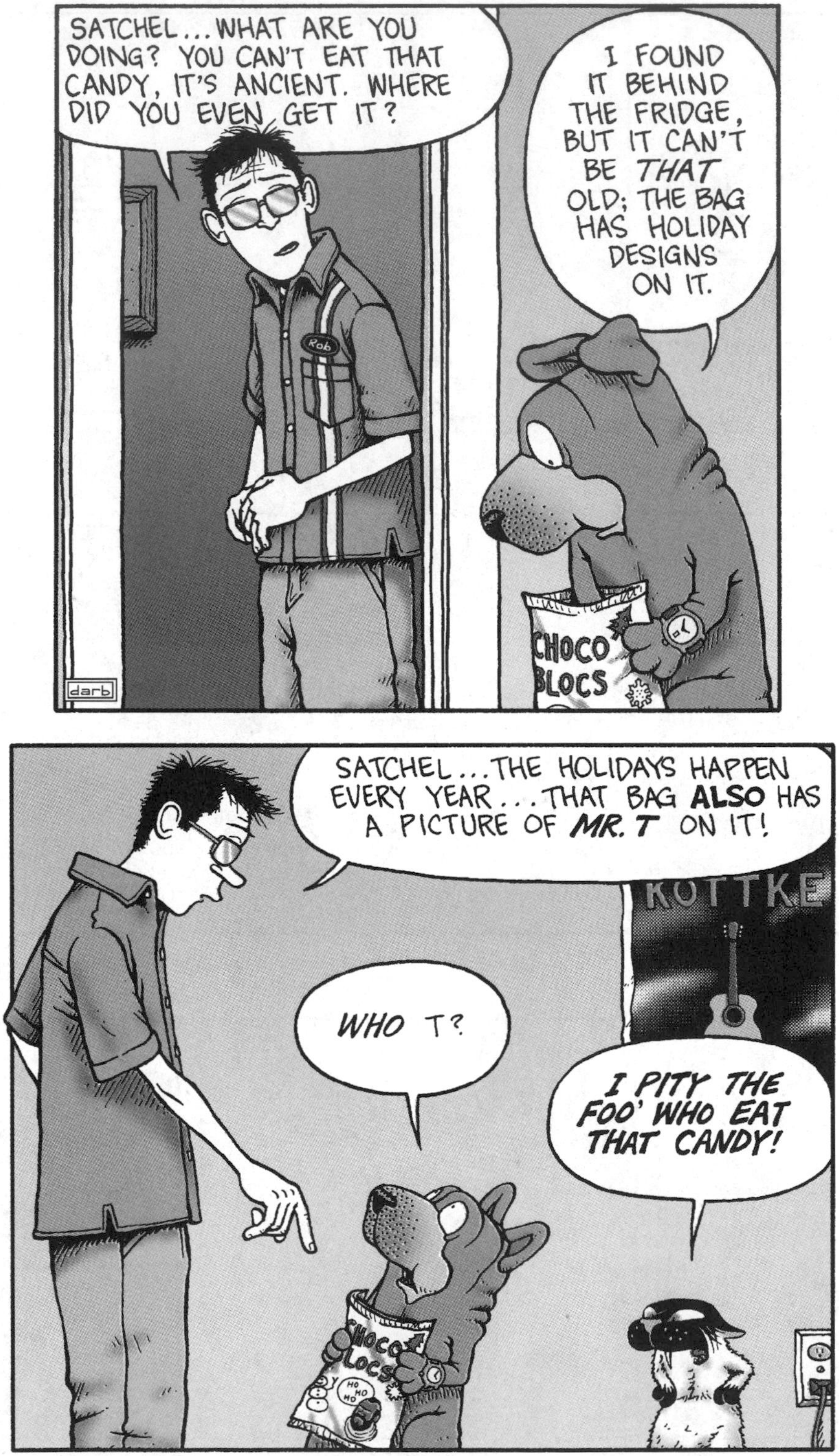
SATCHEL...WHAT ARE YOU DOING? YOU CAN'T EAT THAT CANDY, IT'S ANCIENT. WHERE DID YOU EVEN GET IT?
I FOUND IT BEHIND THE FRIDGE, BUT IT CAN'T BE *THAT* OLD; THE BAG HAS HOLIDAY DESIGNS ON IT.
Rob
CHOCO BLOCS
darb
SATCHEL...THE HOLIDAYS HAPPEN EVERY YEAR...THAT BAG **ALSO** HAS A PICTURE OF ***MR. T*** ON IT!
KOTTKE
WHO T?
I PITY THE FOO' WHO EAT THAT CANDY!
CHOCO BLOCS
HO HO HO

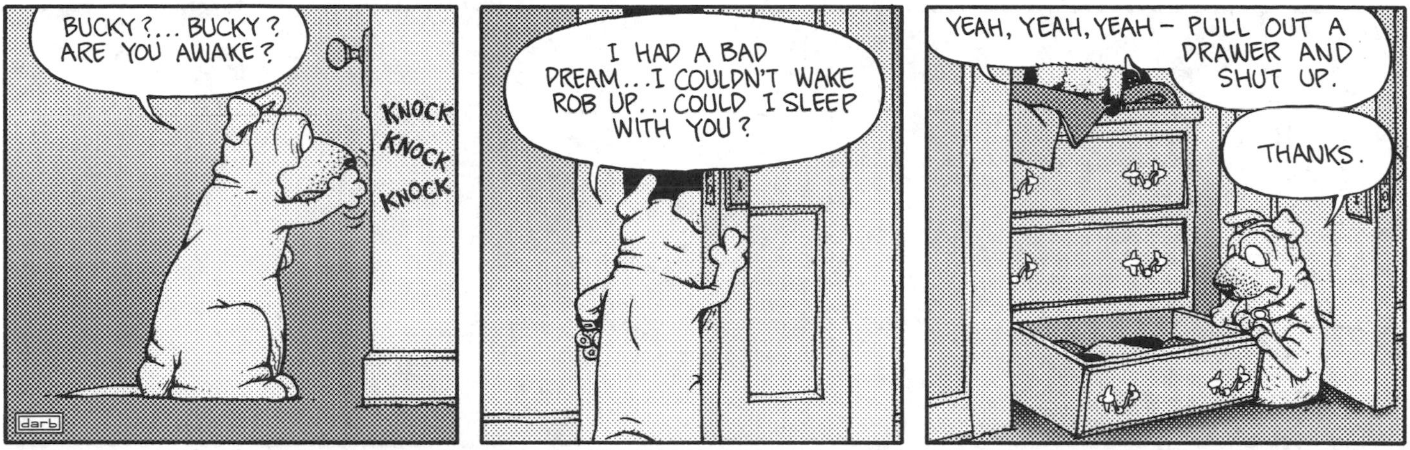
BUCKY?... BUCKY?
ARE YOU AWAKE?
KNOCK
KNOCK
KNOCK
I HAD A BAD DREAM... I COULDN'T WAKE ROB UP... COULD I SLEEP WITH YOU?
YEAH, YEAH, YEAH - PULL OUT A DRAWER AND SHUT UP.
THANKS.
darb

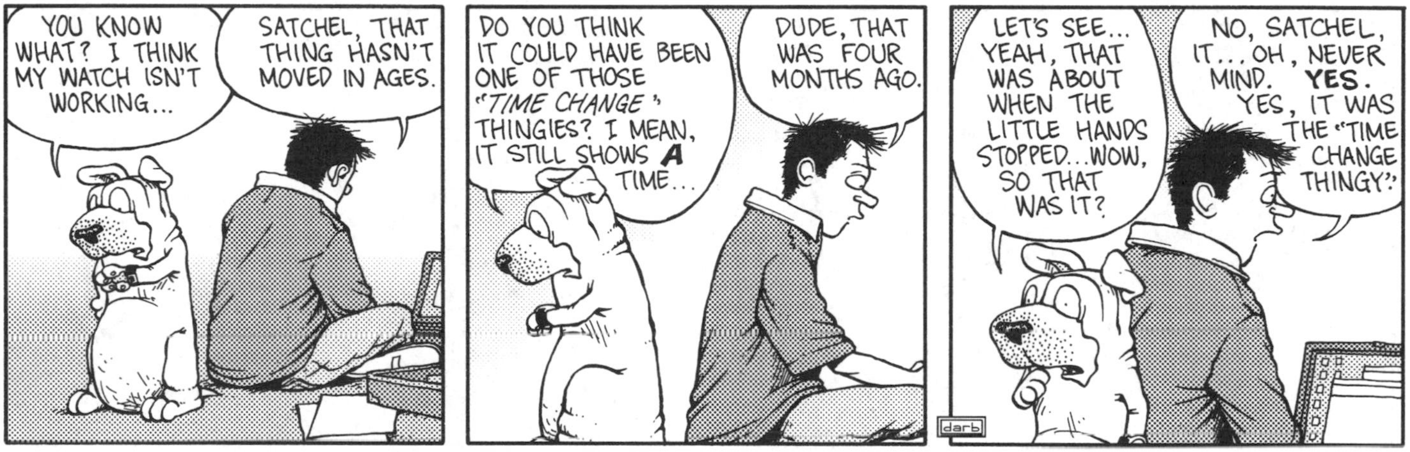
YOU KNOW WHAT? I THINK MY WATCH ISN'T WORKING...
SATCHEL, THAT THING HASN'T MOVED IN AGES.
DO YOU THINK IT COULD HAVE BEEN ONE OF THOSE "TIME CHANGE" THINGIES? I MEAN, IT STILL SHOWS A TIME...
DUDE, THAT WAS FOUR MONTHS AGO.
LET'S SEE... YEAH, THAT WAS ABOUT WHEN THE LITTLE HANDS STOPPED...WOW, SO THAT WAS IT?
NO, SATCHEL, IT... OH, NEVER MIND. YES. YES, IT WAS THE "TIME CHANGE THINGY."
darb

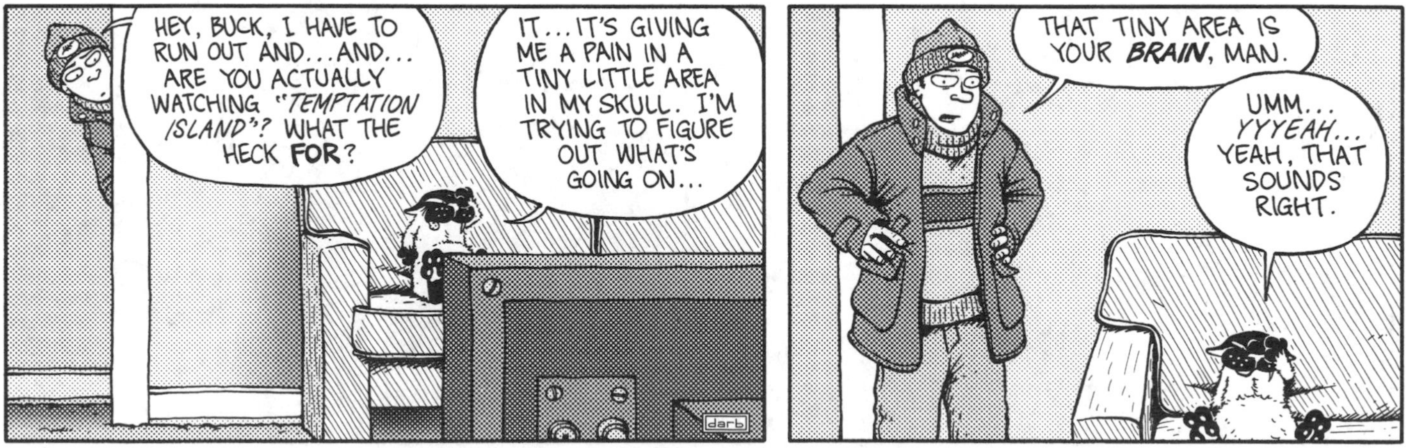
HEY, BUCK, I HAVE TO RUN OUT AND...AND... ARE YOU ACTUALLY WATCHING "TEMPTATION ISLAND"? WHAT THE HECK FOR?
IT... IT'S GIVING ME A PAIN IN A TINY LITTLE AREA IN MY SKULL. I'M TRYING TO FIGURE OUT WHAT'S GOING ON...
darb
THAT TINY AREA IS YOUR BRAIN, MAN.
UMM... YYYEAH... YEAH, THAT SOUNDS RIGHT.

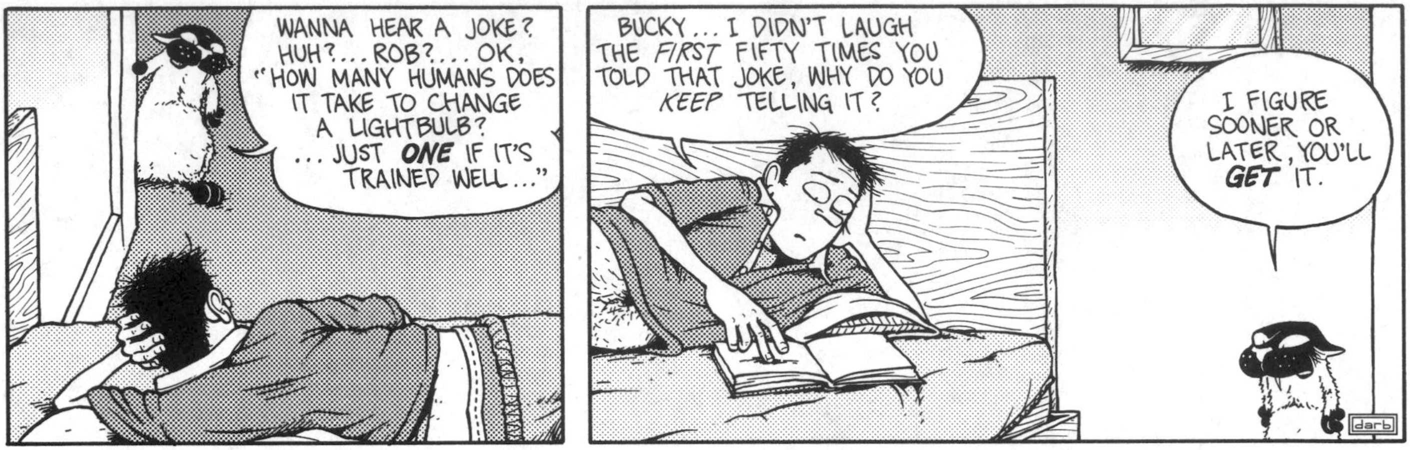
WANNA HEAR A JOKE? HUH?... ROB?... OK, "HOW MANY HUMANS DOES IT TAKE TO CHANGE A LIGHTBULB? ... JUST ONE IF IT'S TRAINED WELL..."
BUCKY... I DIDN'T LAUGH THE FIRST FIFTY TIMES YOU TOLD THAT JOKE, WHY DO YOU KEEP TELLING IT?
I FIGURE SOONER OR LATER, YOU'LL GET IT.
darb

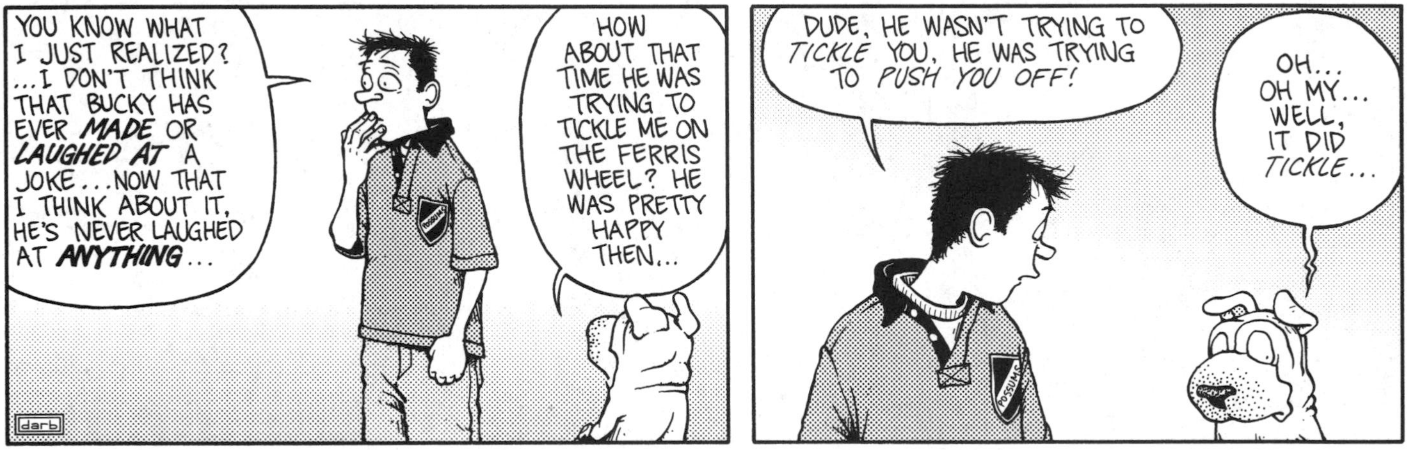
YOU KNOW WHAT I JUST REALIZED? ...I DON'T THINK THAT BUCKY HAS EVER MADE OR LAUGHED AT A JOKE... NOW THAT I THINK ABOUT IT, HE'S NEVER LAUGHED AT ANYTHING...
HOW ABOUT THAT TIME HE WAS TRYING TO TICKLE ME ON THE FERRIS WHEEL? HE WAS PRETTY HAPPY THEN...
darb
DUDE, HE WASN'T TRYING TO TICKLE YOU, HE WAS TRYING TO PUSH YOU OFF!
OH... OH MY... WELL, IT DID TICKLE...

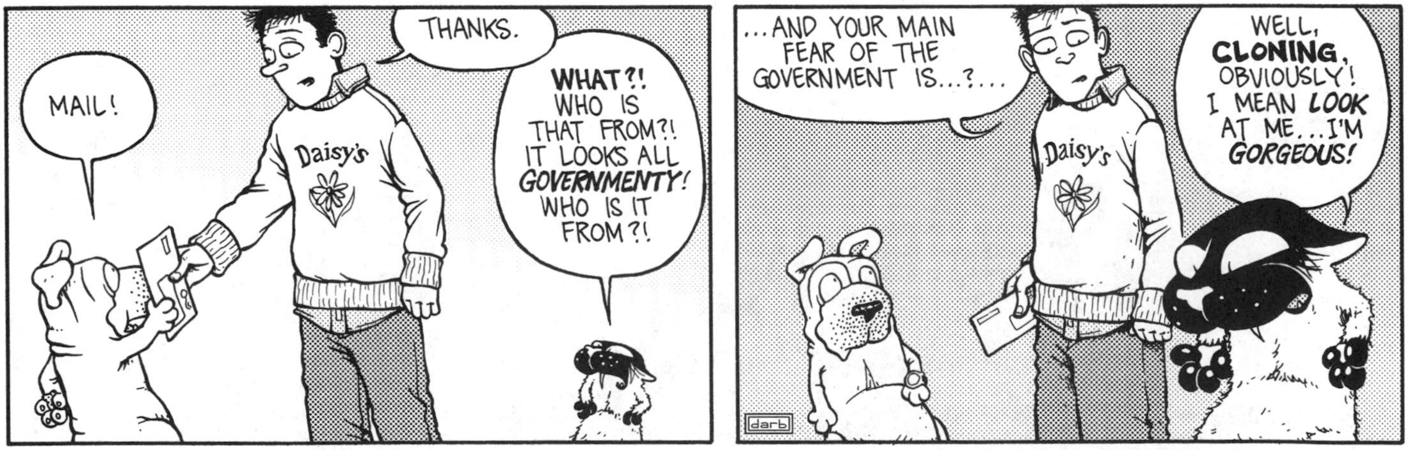
MAIL!
THANKS.
Daisy's
WHAT?! WHO IS THAT FROM?! IT LOOKS ALL GOVERNMENTY! WHO IS IT FROM?!
...AND YOUR MAIN FEAR OF THE GOVERNMENT IS...?...
Daisy's
WELL, CLONING, OBVIOUSLY! I MEAN LOOK AT ME... I'M GORGEOUS!
darb

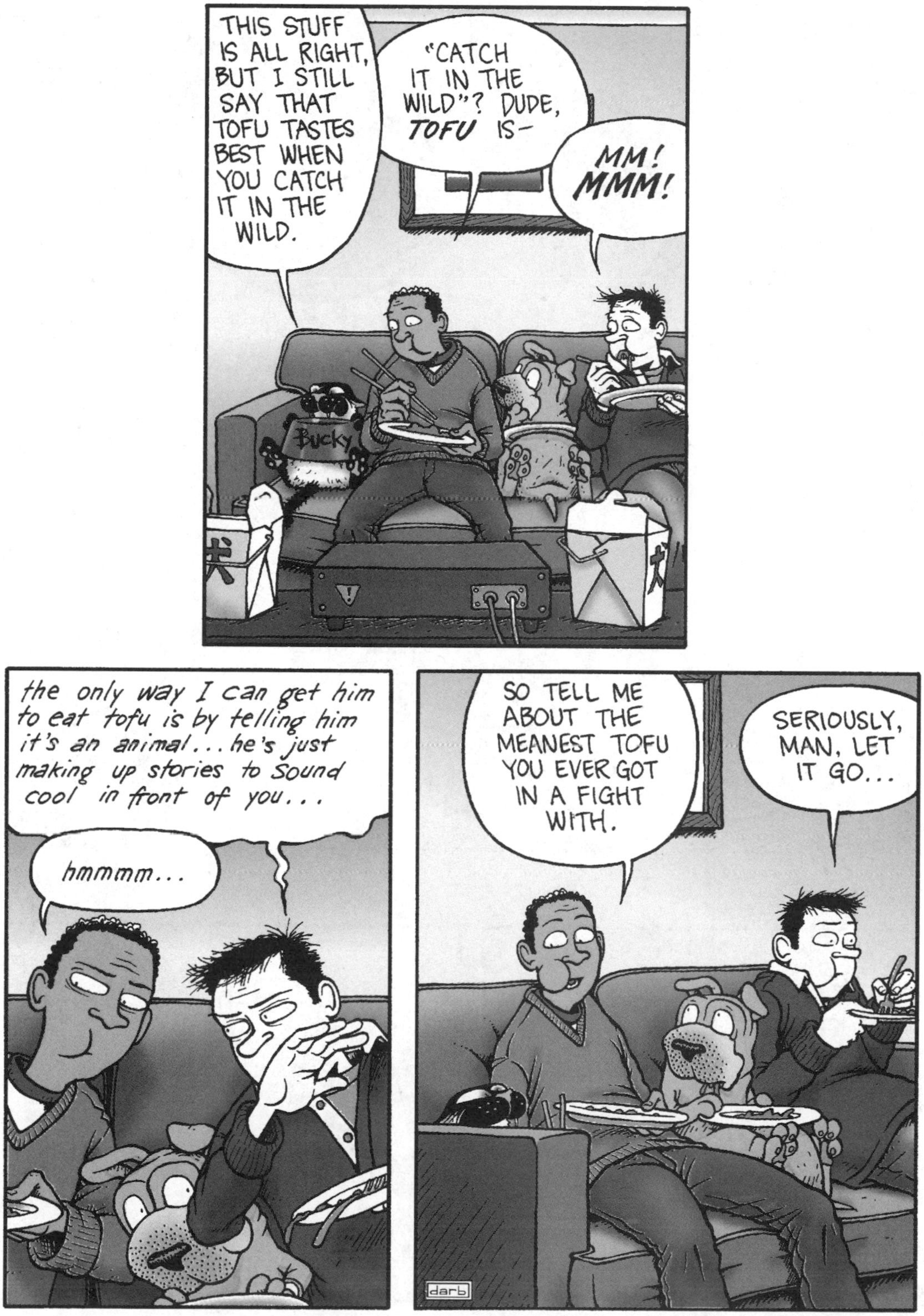
THIS STUFF IS ALL RIGHT, BUT I STILL SAY THAT TOFU TASTES BEST WHEN YOU CATCH IT IN THE WILD.
"CATCH IT IN THE WILD"? DUDE, TOFU IS–
MM! MMM!
Bucky
the only way I can get him to eat tofu is by telling him it's an animal... he's just making up stories to sound cool in front of you...
hmmmm...
SO TELL ME ABOUT THE MEANEST TOFU YOU EVER GOT IN A FIGHT WITH.
SERIOUSLY, MAN, LET IT GO...
darb

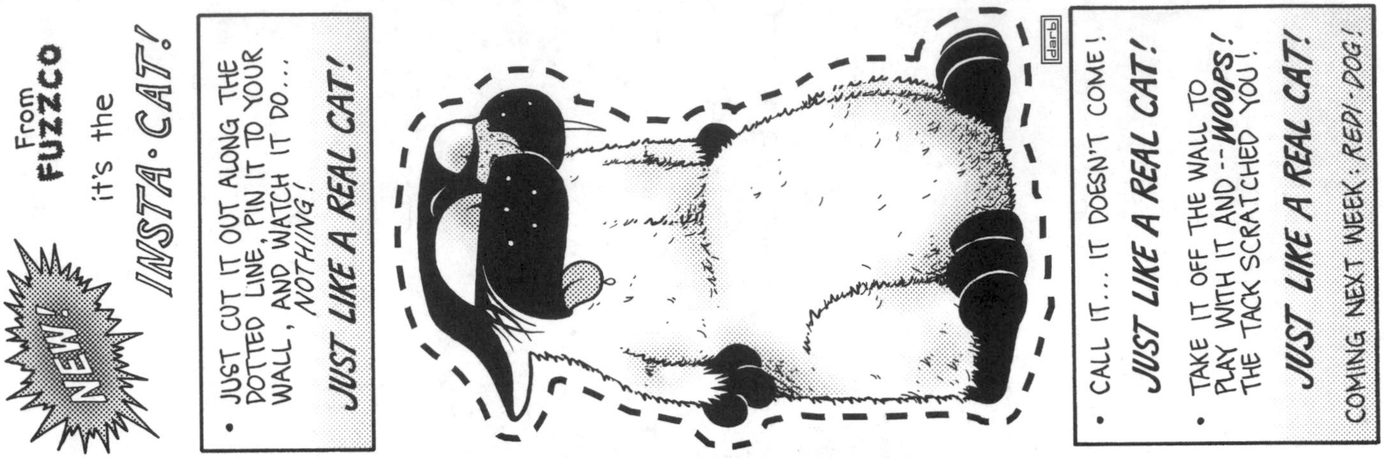
NEW!
From FUZZCO
it's the
INSTA-CAT!
• JUST CUT IT OUT ALONG THE DOTTED LINE, PIN IT TO YOUR WALL, AND WATCH IT DO.... NOTHING!
JUST LIKE A REAL CAT!
• CALL IT... IT DOESN'T COME!
JUST LIKE A REAL CAT!
• TAKE IT OFF THE WALL TO PLAY WITH IT AND -- WOOPS! THE TACK SCRATCHED YOU!
JUST LIKE A REAL CAT!
COMING NEXT WEEK: REDI-DOG!
darb

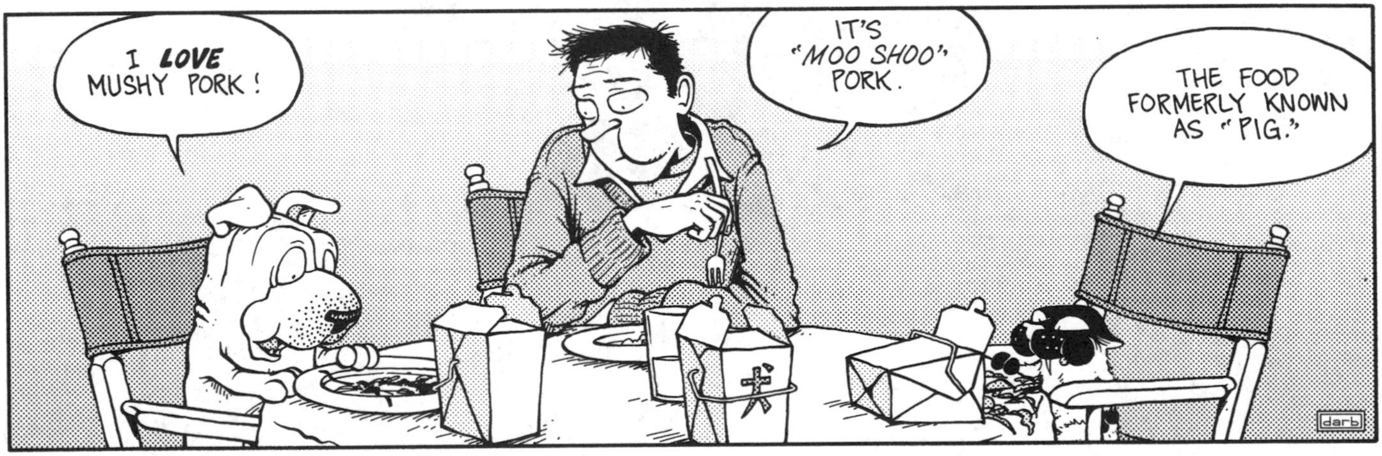
I LOVE MUSHY PORK!
IT'S "MOO SHOO" PORK.
THE FOOD FORMERLY KNOWN AS "PIG."
darb

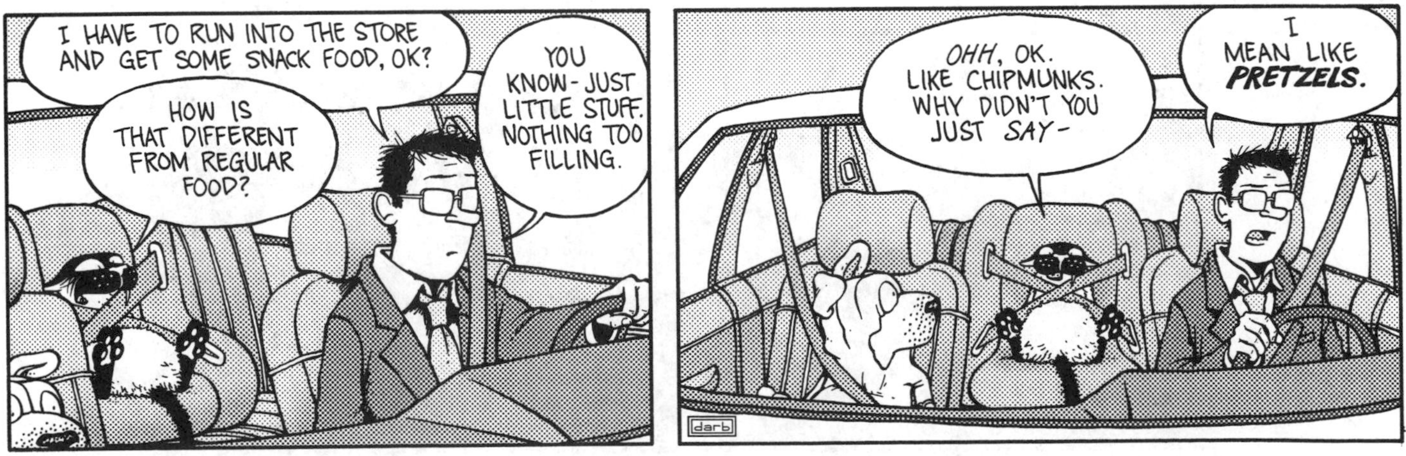
I HAVE TO RUN INTO THE STORE AND GET SOME SNACK FOOD, OK?
HOW IS THAT DIFFERENT FROM REGULAR FOOD?
YOU KNOW - JUST LITTLE STUFF. NOTHING TOO FILLING.
OHH, OK. LIKE CHIPMUNKS. WHY DIDN'T YOU JUST SAY-
I MEAN LIKE PRETZELS.
darb

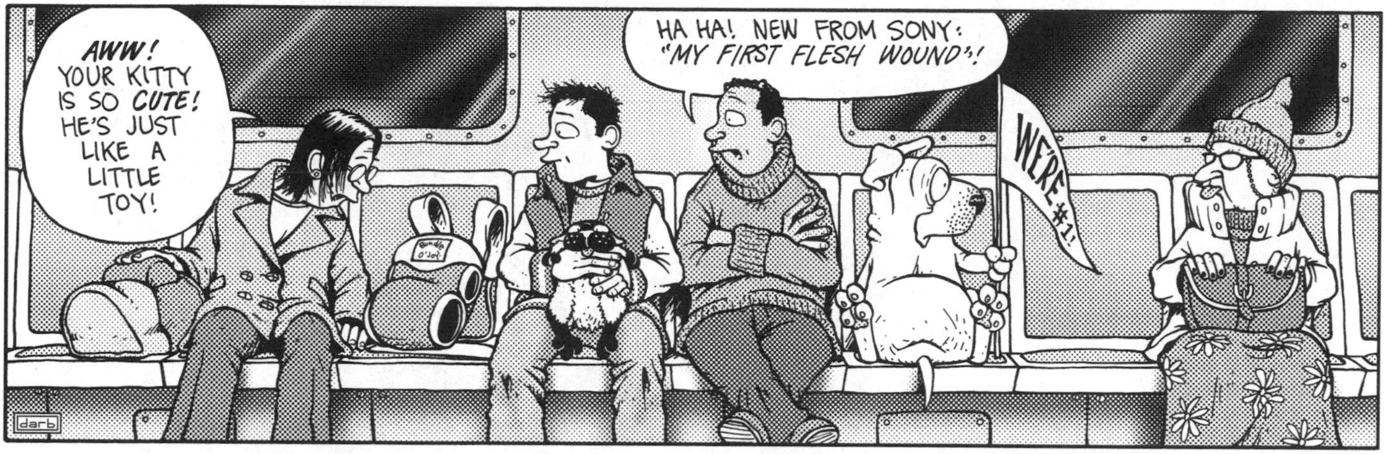
AWW! YOUR KITTY IS SO CUTE! HE'S JUST LIKE A LITTLE TOY!
HA HA! NEW FROM SONY: "MY FIRST FLESH WOUND"!
WE'RE #1!
darb

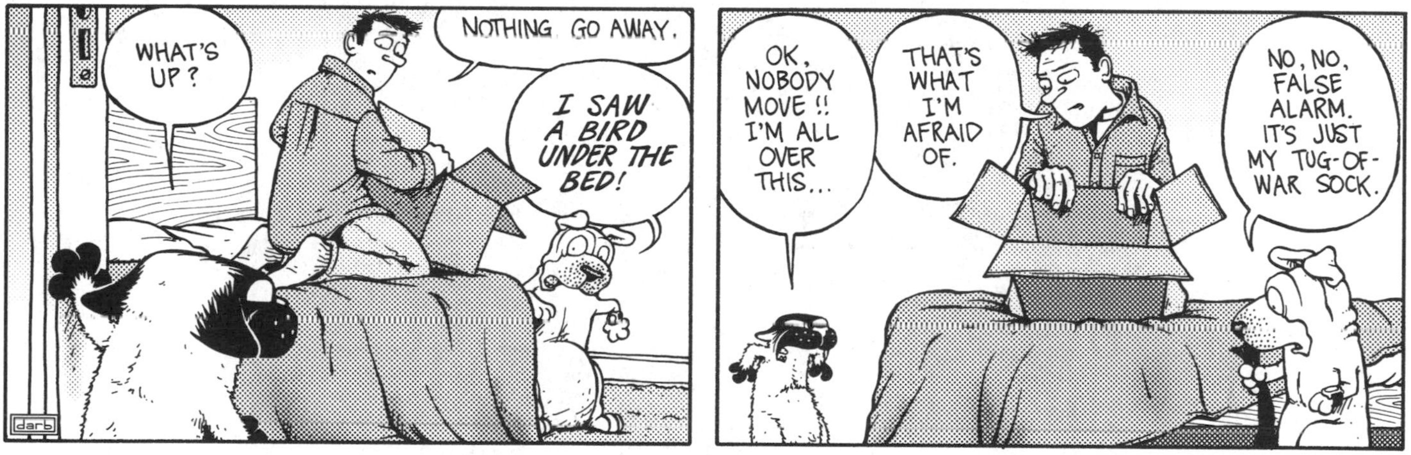
WHAT'S UP?
NOTHING. GO AWAY.
I SAW A BIRD UNDER THE BED!
darb
OK, NOBODY MOVE!! I'M ALL OVER THIS...
THAT'S WHAT I'M AFRAID OF.
NO, NO, FALSE ALARM. IT'S JUST MY TUG-OF-WAR SOCK.

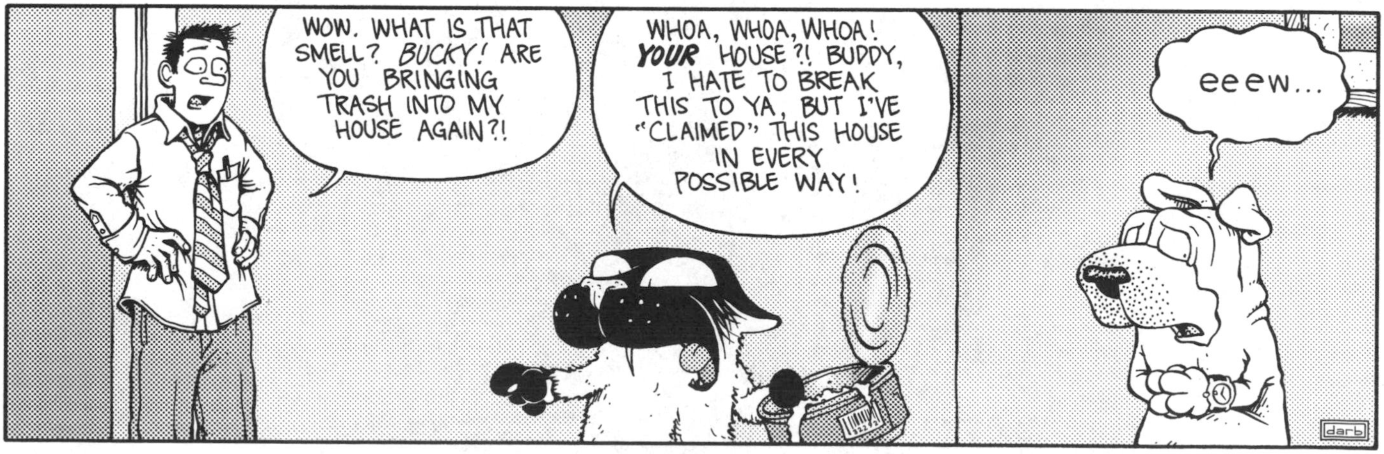
WOW. WHAT IS THAT SMELL? BUCKY! ARE YOU BRINGING TRASH INTO MY HOUSE AGAIN?!
WHOA, WHOA, WHOA! YOUR HOUSE?! BUDDY, I HATE TO BREAK THIS TO YA, BUT I'VE "CLAIMED" THIS HOUSE IN EVERY POSSIBLE WAY!
eeew...
darb

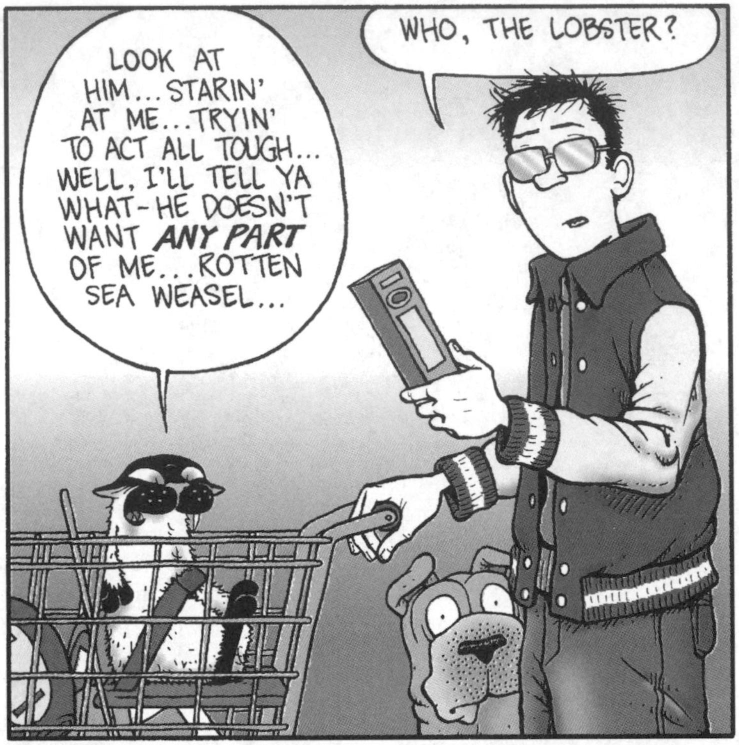
LOOK AT HIM... STARIN' AT ME...TRYIN' TO ACT ALL TOUGH... WELL, I'LL TELL YA WHAT- HE DOESN'T WANT **ANY PART** OF ME...ROTTEN SEA WEASEL...
WHO, THE LOBSTER?

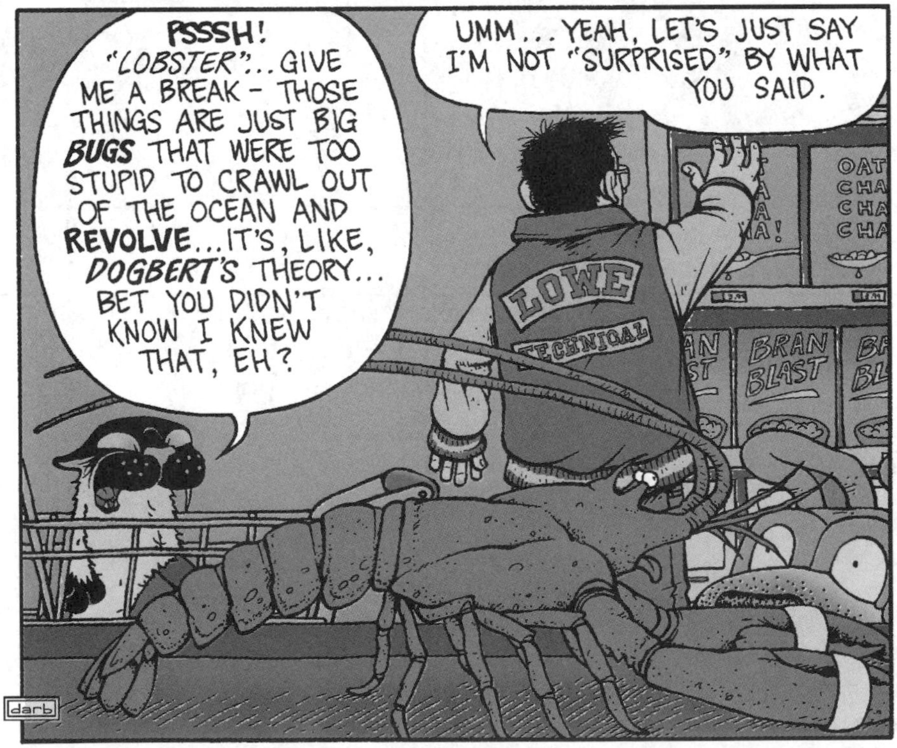
PSSSH! *"LOBSTER"*...GIVE ME A BREAK - THOSE THINGS ARE JUST BIG **BUGS** THAT WERE TOO STUPID TO CRAWL OUT OF THE OCEAN AND **REVOLVE**...IT'S, LIKE, ***DOGBERT'S*** THEORY... BET YOU DIDN'T KNOW I KNEW THAT, EH?
UMM... YEAH, LET'S JUST SAY I'M NOT "SURPRISED" BY WHAT YOU SAID.
LOWE
TECHNICAL
BRAN BLAST
darb

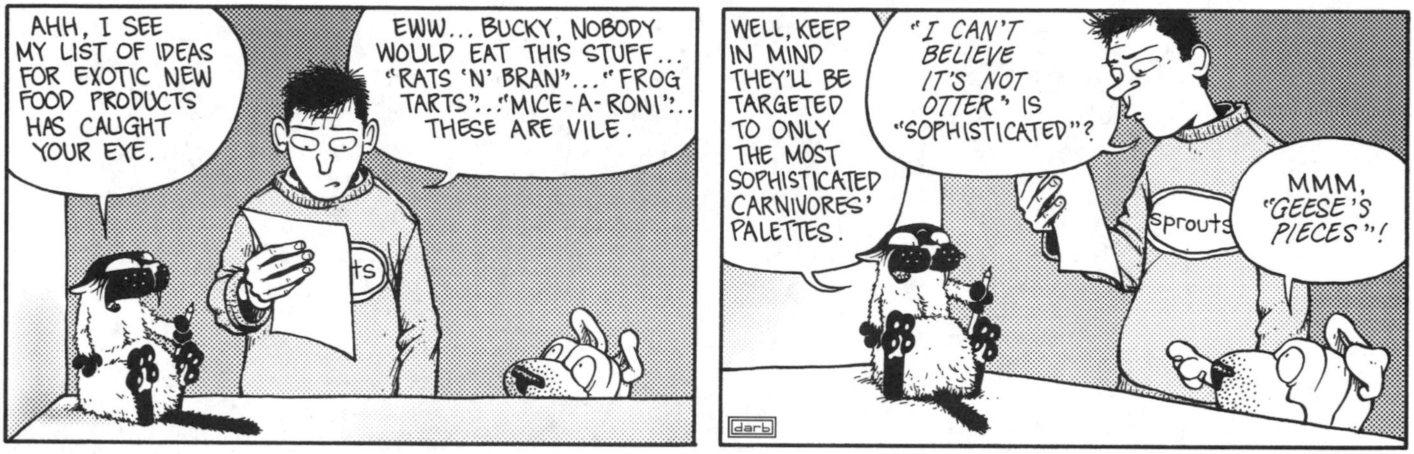
AHH, I SEE MY LIST OF IDEAS FOR EXOTIC NEW FOOD PRODUCTS HAS CAUGHT YOUR EYE.
EWW... BUCKY, NOBODY WOULD EAT THIS STUFF... "RATS 'N' BRAN"... "FROG TARTS"... "MICE-A-RONI"... THESE ARE VILE.
WELL, KEEP IN MIND THEY'LL BE TARGETED TO ONLY THE MOST SOPHISTICATED CARNIVORES' PALETTES.
"*I CAN'T BELIEVE IT'S NOT OTTER*" IS "SOPHISTICATED"?
sprouts
MMM, *"GEESE'S PIECES"*!
darb

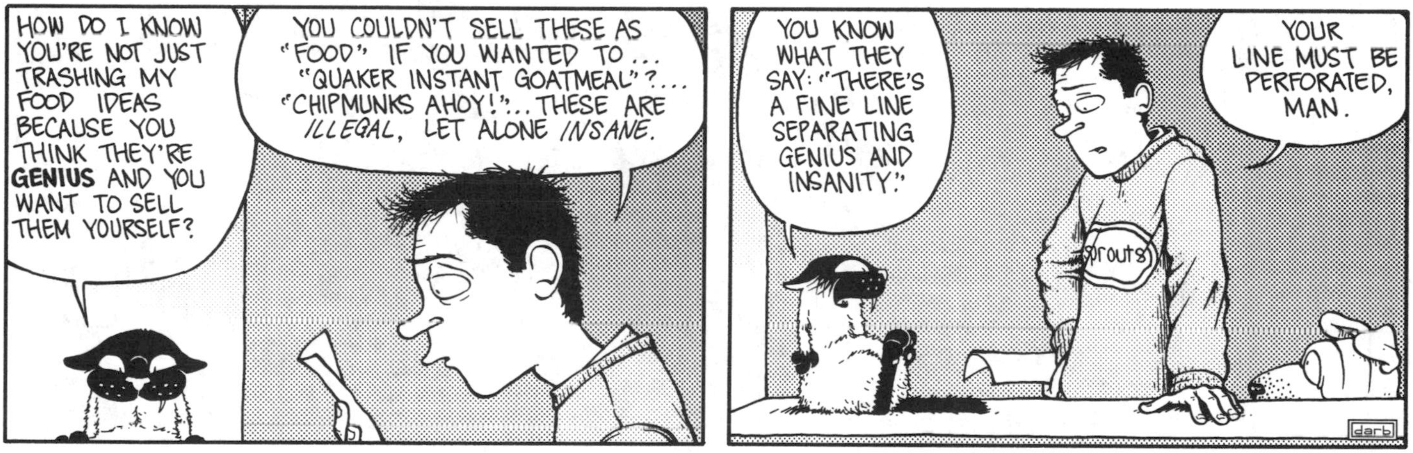
HOW DO I KNOW YOU'RE NOT JUST TRASHING MY FOOD IDEAS BECAUSE YOU THINK THEY'RE **GENIUS** AND YOU WANT TO SELL THEM YOURSELF?
YOU COULDN'T SELL THESE AS "FOOD" IF YOU WANTED TO... "QUAKER INSTANT GOATMEAL"?... "CHIPMUNKS AHOY!"... THESE ARE *ILLEGAL*, LET ALONE *INSANE*.
YOU KNOW WHAT THEY SAY: "THERE'S A FINE LINE SEPARATING GENIUS AND INSANITY."
sprouts
YOUR LINE MUST BE PERFORATED, MAN.
darb

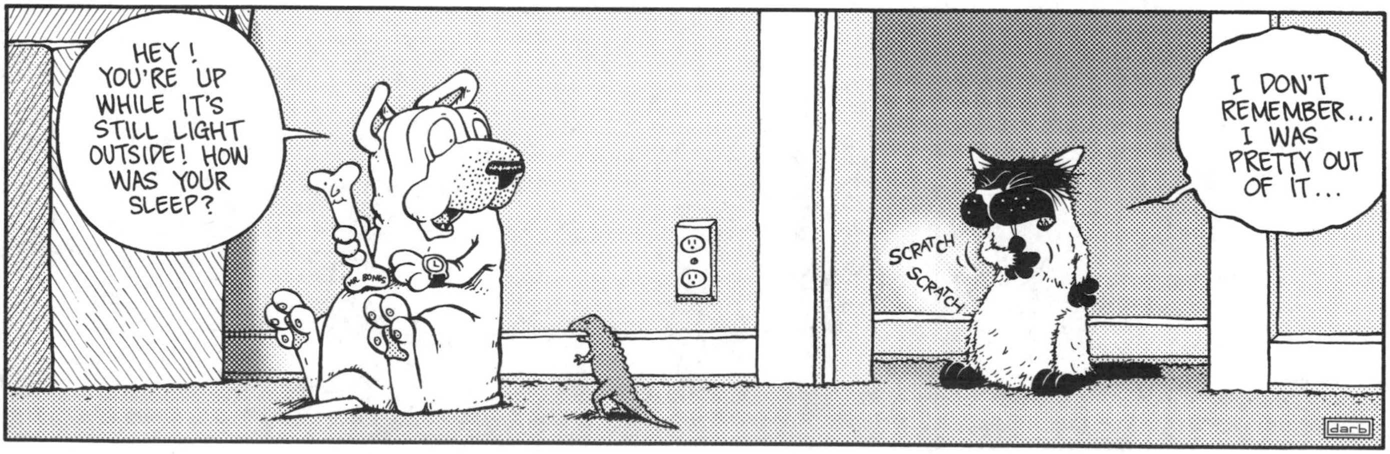
HEY! YOU'RE UP WHILE IT'S STILL LIGHT OUTSIDE! HOW WAS YOUR SLEEP?
SCRATCH
SCRATCH
I DON'T REMEMBER... I WAS PRETTY OUT OF IT...
darb

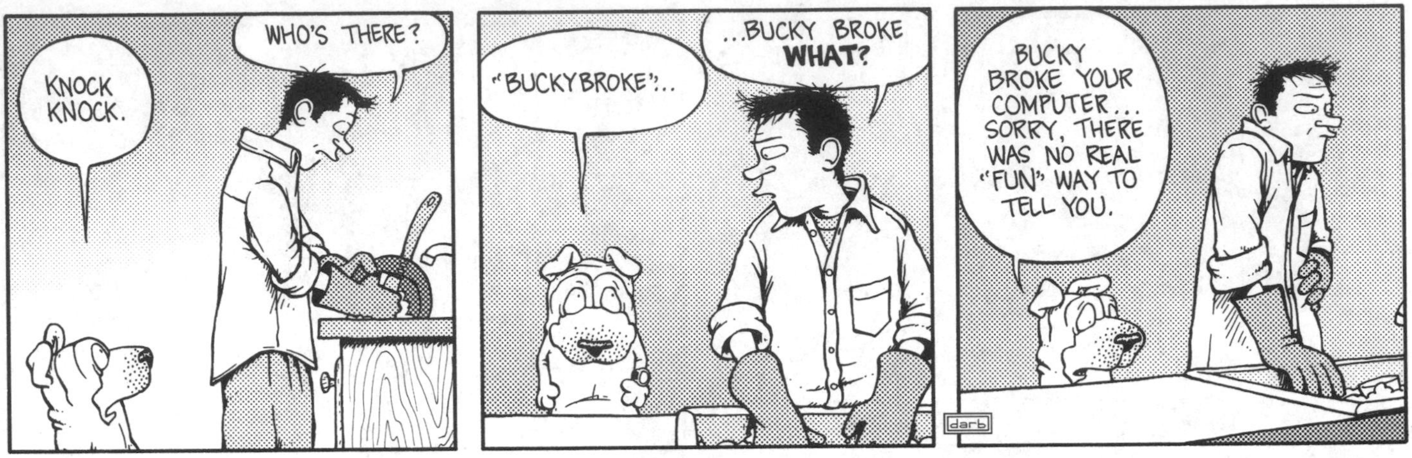
KNOCK KNOCK.
WHO'S THERE?
"BUCKYBROKE"...
...BUCKY BROKE **WHAT?**
BUCKY BROKE YOUR COMPUTER... SORRY, THERE WAS NO REAL "FUN" WAY TO TELL YOU.

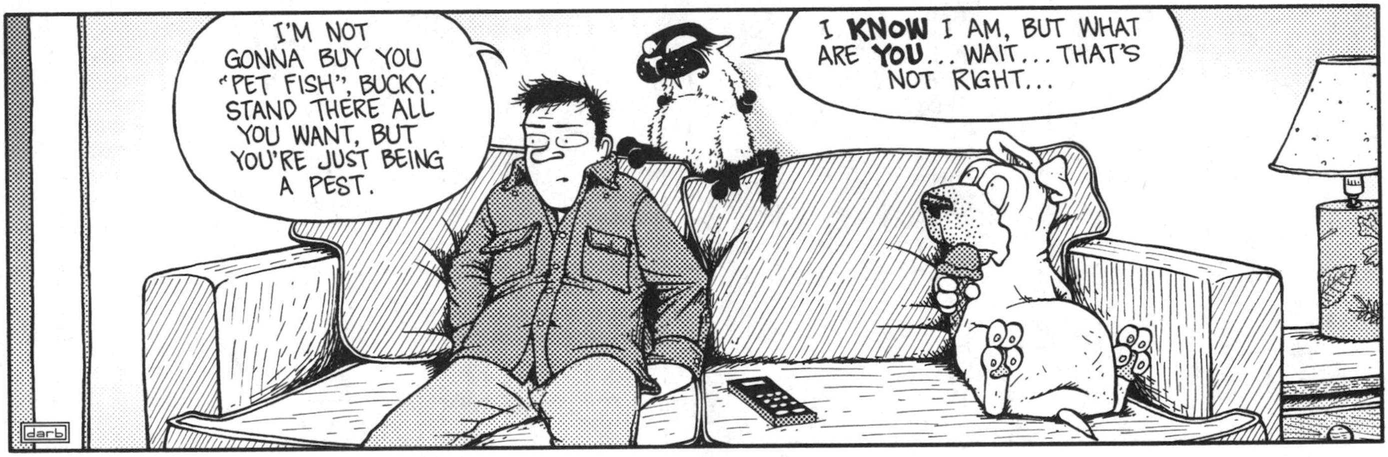
I'M NOT GONNA BUY YOU "PET FISH", BUCKY. STAND THERE ALL YOU WANT, BUT YOU'RE JUST BEING A PEST.
I **KNOW** I AM, BUT WHAT ARE **YOU**... WAIT... THAT'S NOT RIGHT...

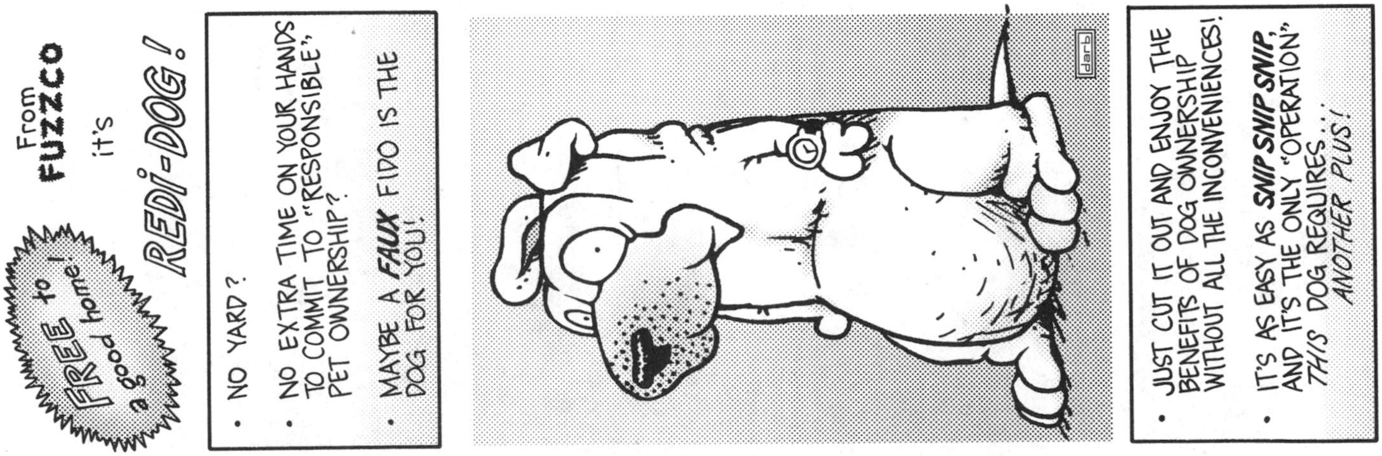
FREE to a good home!
From FUZZCO it's REDI-DOG!
• NO YARD?
• NO EXTRA TIME ON YOUR HANDS TO COMMIT TO "RESPONSIBLE" PET OWNERSHIP?
• MAYBE A *FAUX* FIDO IS THE DOG FOR YOU!
• JUST CUT IT OUT AND ENJOY THE BENEFITS OF DOG OWNERSHIP WITHOUT ALL THE INCONVENIENCES!
• IT'S AS EASY AS *SNIP SNIP SNIP*, AND IT'S THE ONLY "OPERATION" *THIS* DOG REQUIRES... *ANOTHER PLUS!*

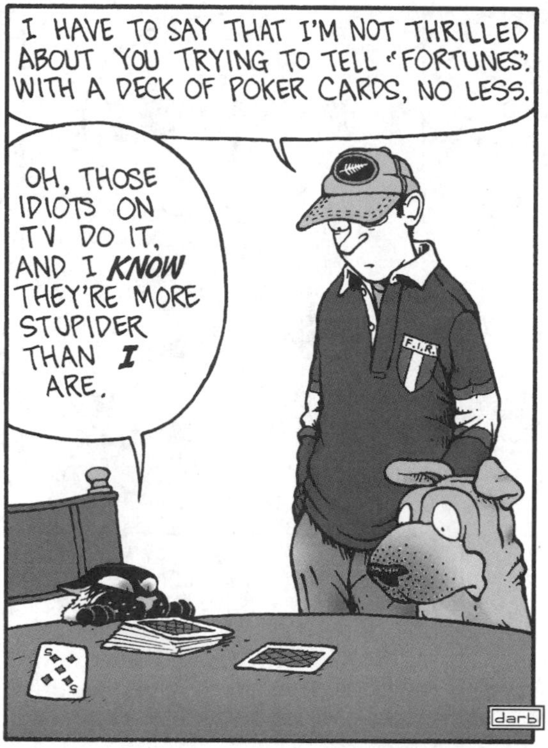
I HAVE TO SAY THAT I'M NOT THRILLED ABOUT YOU TRYING TO TELL "FORTUNES." WITH A DECK OF POKER CARDS, NO LESS.
OH, THOSE IDIOTS ON TV DO IT, AND I *KNOW* THEY'RE MORE STUPIDER THAN *I* ARE.
darb

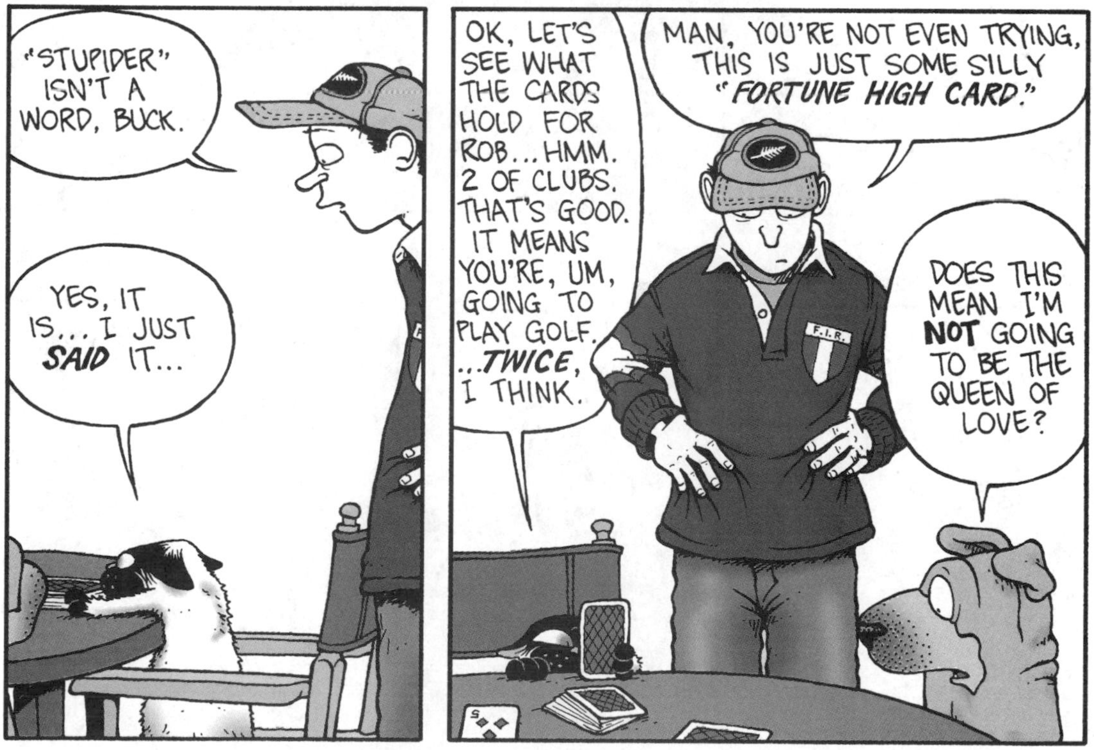
"STUPIDER" ISN'T A WORD, BUCK.
YES, IT IS... I JUST *SAID* IT...
OK, LET'S SEE WHAT THE CARDS HOLD FOR ROB... HMM. 2 OF CLUBS. THAT'S GOOD. IT MEANS YOU'RE, UM, GOING TO PLAY GOLF. ...*TWICE*, I THINK.
MAN, YOU'RE NOT EVEN TRYING. THIS IS JUST SOME SILLY *"FORTUNE HIGH CARD."*
DOES THIS MEAN I'M **NOT** GOING TO BE THE QUEEN OF LOVE?

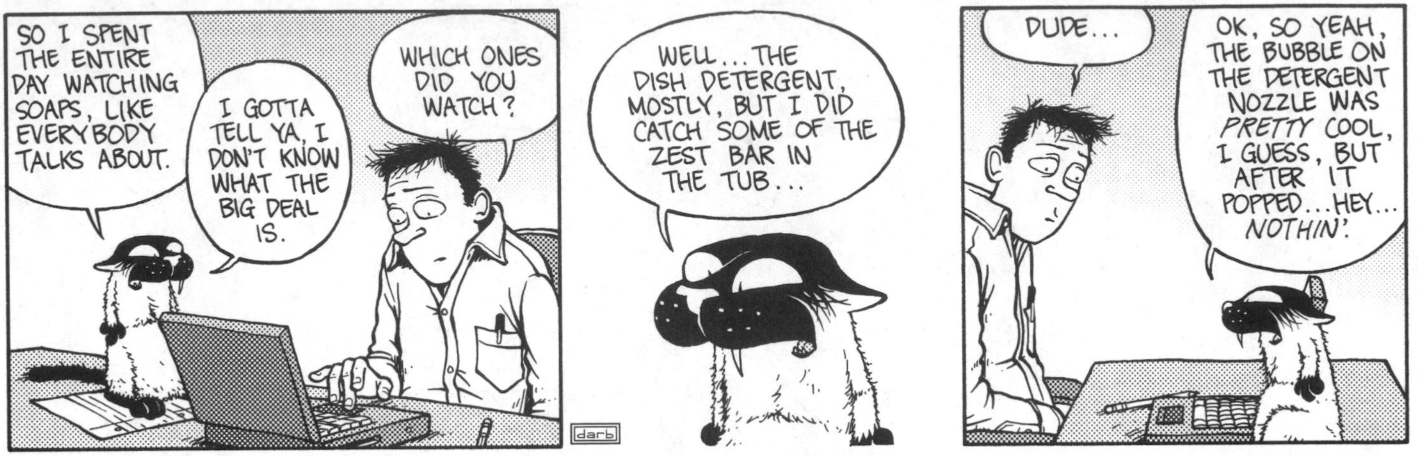
SO I SPENT THE ENTIRE DAY WATCHING SOAPS, LIKE EVERYBODY TALKS ABOUT.
I GOTTA TELL YA, I DON'T KNOW WHAT THE BIG DEAL IS.
WHICH ONES DID YOU WATCH?
WELL... THE DISH DETERGENT, MOSTLY, BUT I DID CATCH SOME OF THE ZEST BAR IN THE TUB...
DUDE...
OK, SO YEAH, THE BUBBLE ON THE DETERGENT NOZZLE WAS *PRETTY* COOL, I GUESS, BUT AFTER IT POPPED... HEY... *NOTHIN'*.
darb

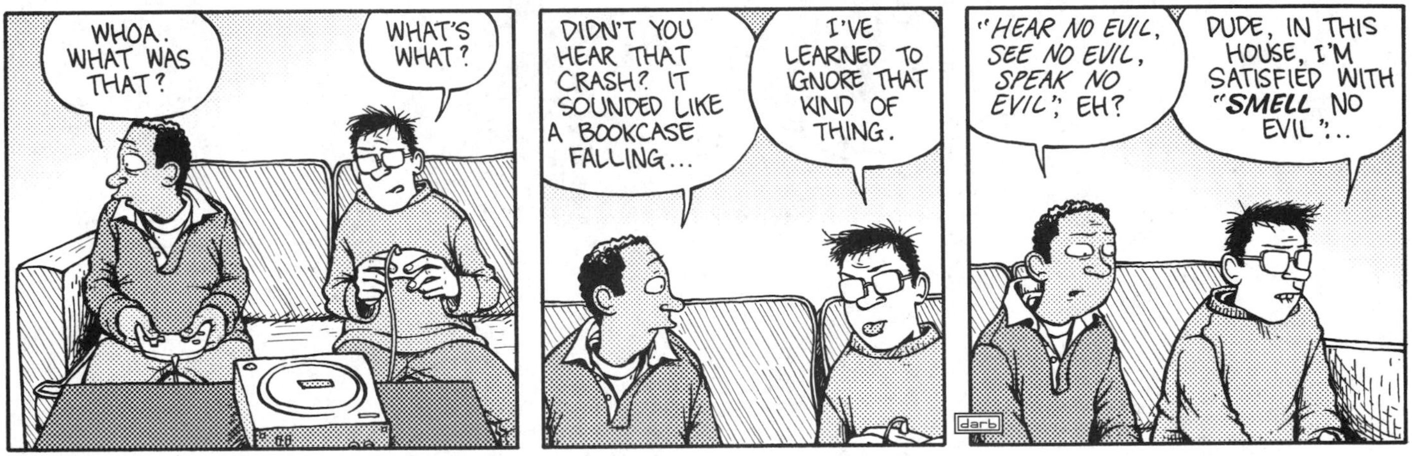
WHOA. WHAT WAS THAT?
WHAT'S WHAT?
DIDN'T YOU HEAR THAT CRASH? IT SOUNDED LIKE A BOOKCASE FALLING...
I'VE LEARNED TO IGNORE THAT KIND OF THING.
"*HEAR NO EVIL, SEE NO EVIL, SPEAK NO EVIL*," EH?
DUDE, IN THIS HOUSE, I'M SATISFIED WITH "***SMELL*** NO EVIL"...
darb

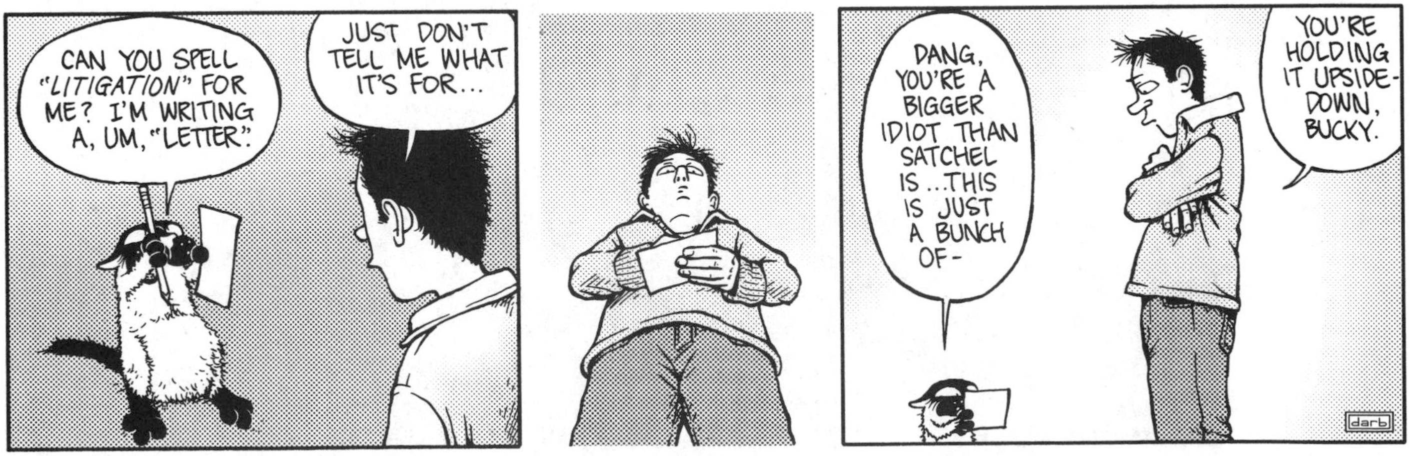
CAN YOU SPELL "*LITIGATION*" FOR ME? I'M WRITING A, UM, "LETTER".
JUST DON'T TELL ME WHAT IT'S FOR...
DANG, YOU'RE A BIGGER IDIOT THAN SATCHEL IS... THIS IS JUST A BUNCH OF-
YOU'RE HOLDING IT UPSIDE-DOWN, BUCKY.
darb

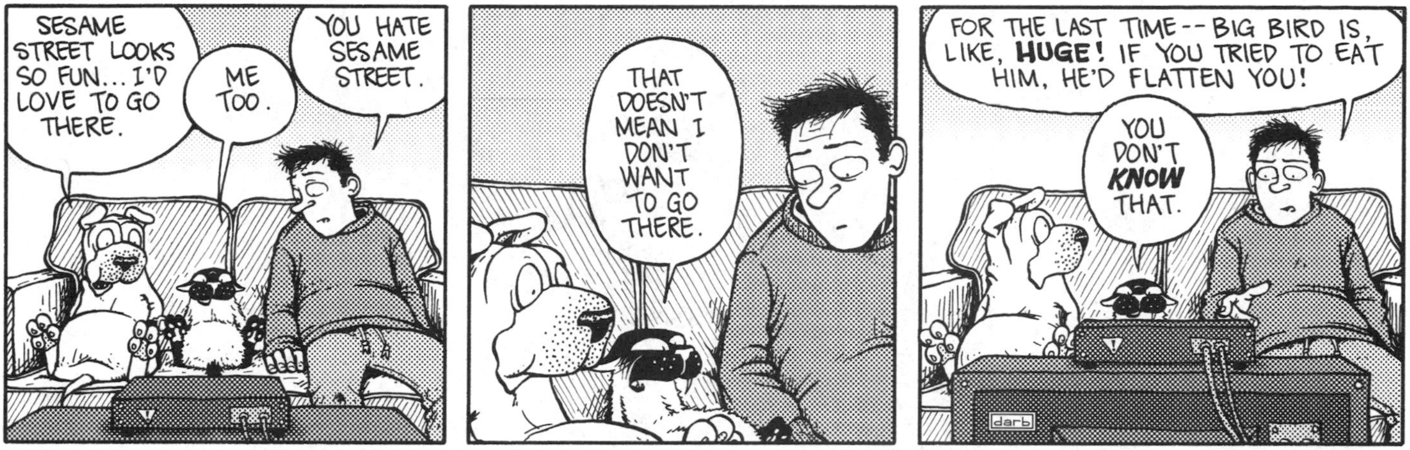
SESAME STREET LOOKS SO FUN... I'D LOVE TO GO THERE.
ME TOO.
YOU HATE SESAME STREET.
THAT DOESN'T MEAN I DON'T WANT TO GO THERE.
FOR THE LAST TIME--BIG BIRD IS, LIKE, **HUGE!** IF YOU TRIED TO EAT HIM, HE'D FLATTEN YOU!
YOU DON'T ***KNOW*** THAT.
darb

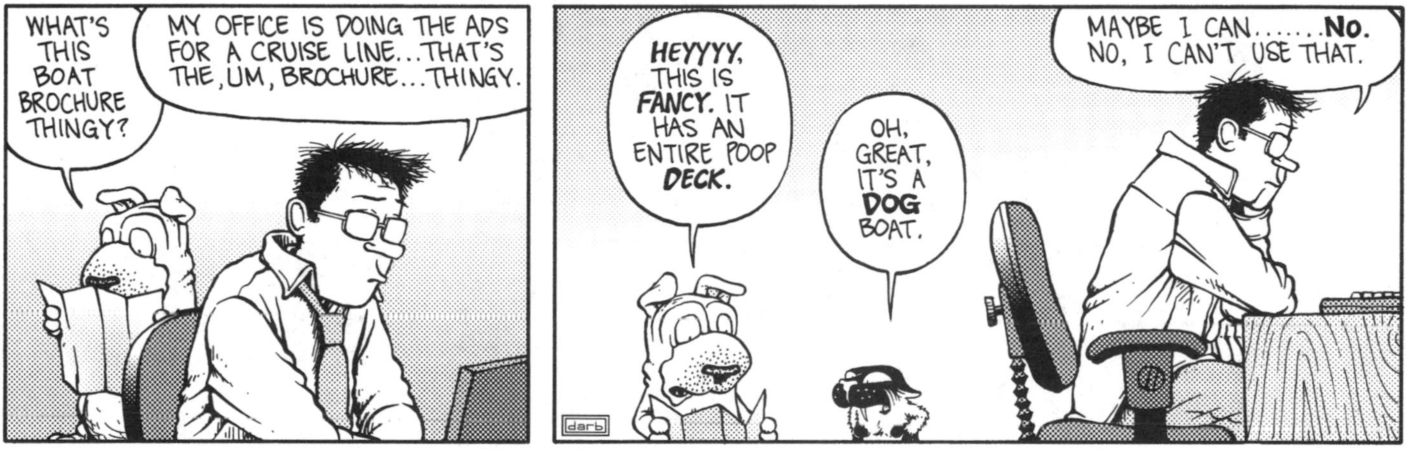
WHAT'S THIS BOAT BROCHURE THINGY?
MY OFFICE IS DOING THE ADS FOR A CRUISE LINE...THAT'S THE, UM, BROCHURE...THINGY.
HEYYYY. THIS IS ***FANCY.*** IT HAS AN ENTIRE POOP ***DECK.***
OH, GREAT, IT'S A **DOG** BOAT.
MAYBE I CAN.......**No.** NO, I CAN'T USE THAT.
darb

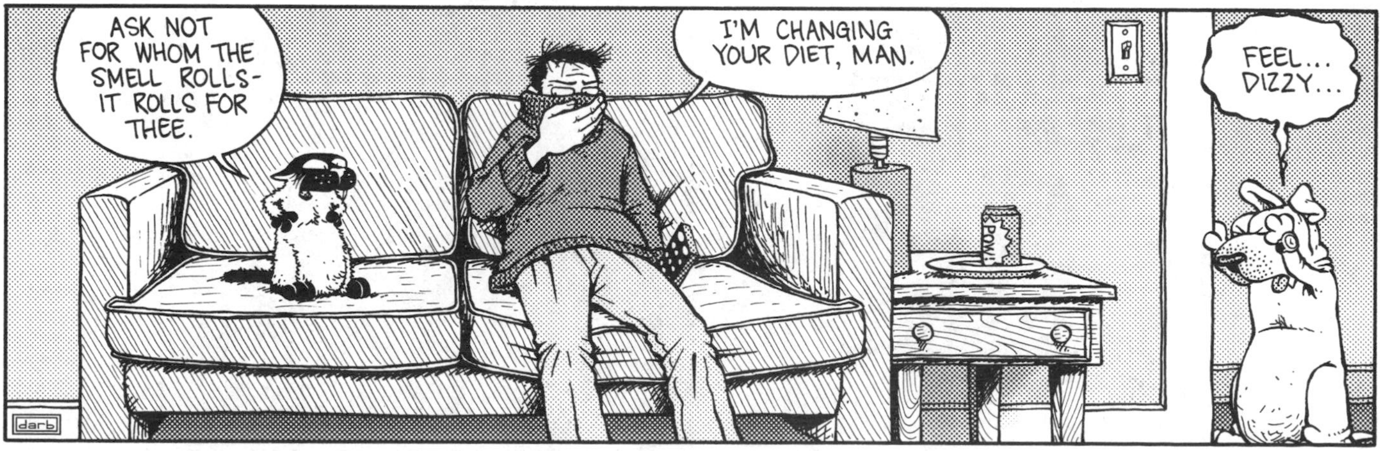
ASK NOT FOR WHOM THE SMELL ROLLS- IT ROLLS FOR THEE.
I'M CHANGING YOUR DIET, MAN.
FEEL... DIZZY...
POW!
darb

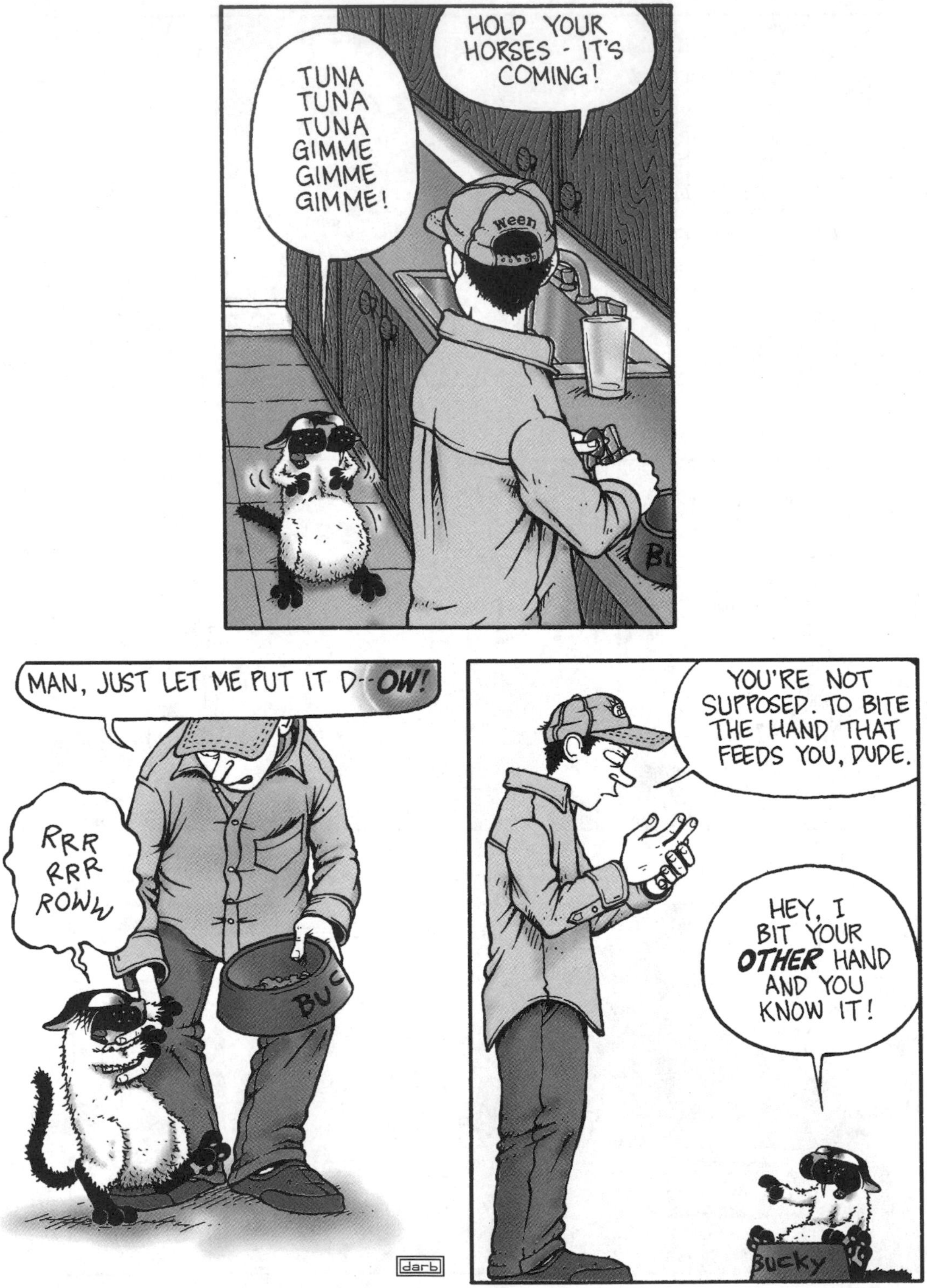
TUNA TUNA TUNA GIMME GIMME GIMME!
HOLD YOUR HORSES - IT'S COMING!
Ween
BU
MAN, JUST LET ME PUT IT D--OW!
RRR RRR ROWW
BUC
YOU'RE NOT SUPPOSED. TO BITE THE HAND THAT FEEDS YOU, DUDE.
HEY, I BIT YOUR OTHER HAND AND YOU KNOW IT!
BUCKY
darb

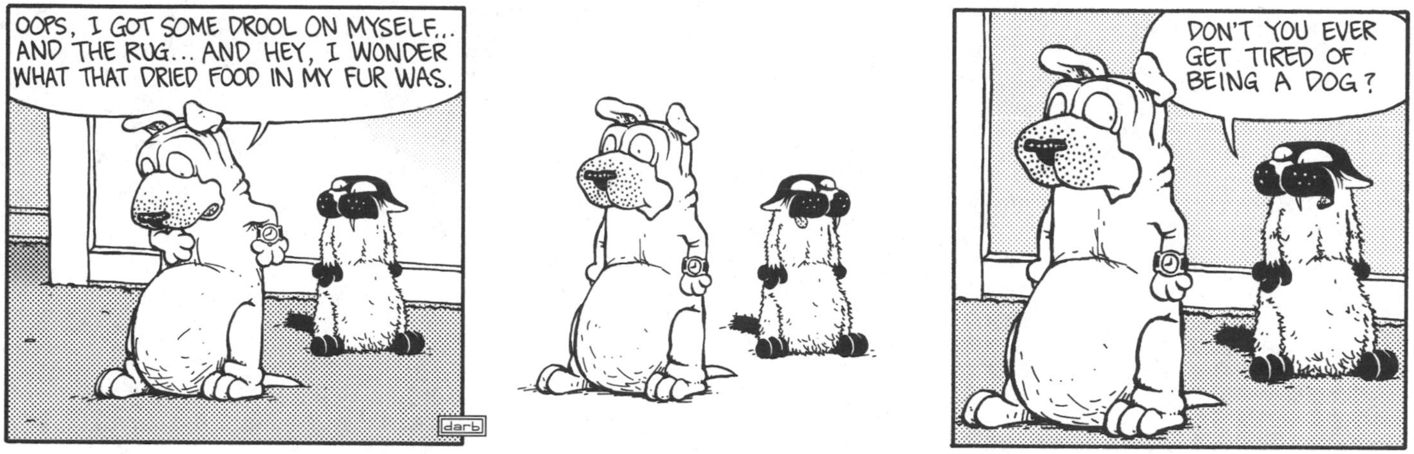
OOPS, I GOT SOME DROOL ON MYSELF... AND THE RUG... AND HEY, I WONDER WHAT THAT DRIED FOOD IN MY FUR WAS.
DON'T YOU EVER GET TIRED OF BEING A DOG?
darb

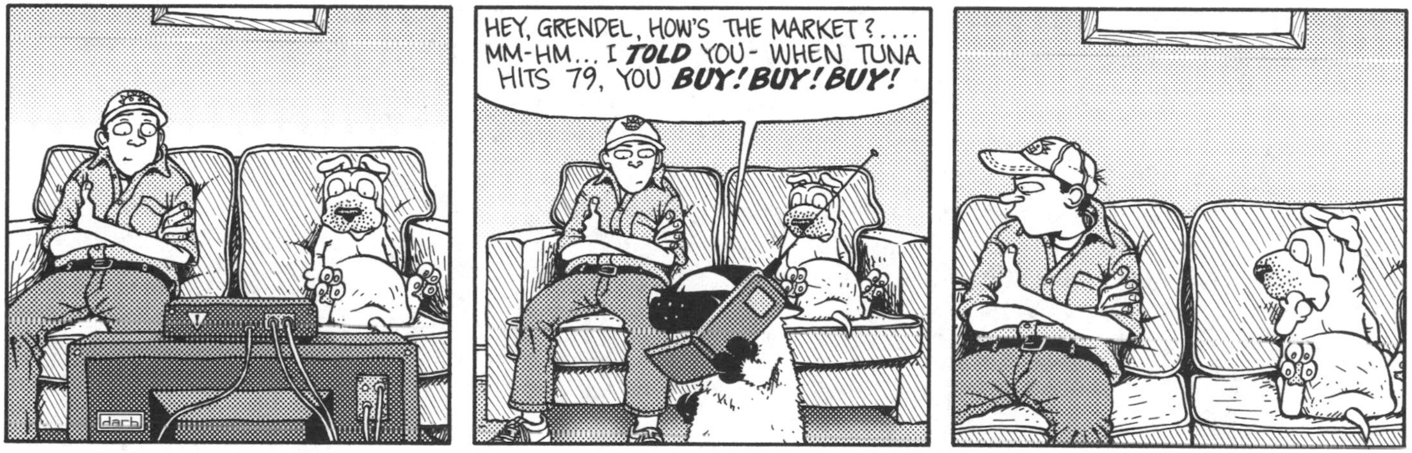
HEY, GRENDEL, HOW'S THE MARKET?.... MM-HM... I **TOLD** YOU- WHEN TUNA HITS 79, YOU **BUY! BUY! BUY!**
darb

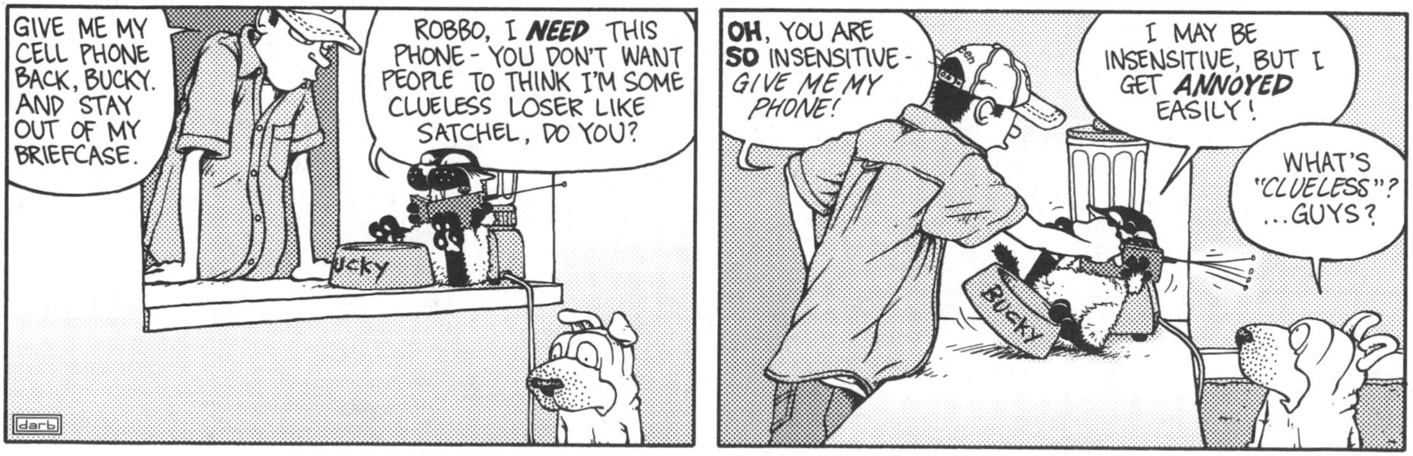
GIVE ME MY CELL PHONE BACK, BUCKY. AND STAY OUT OF MY BRIEFCASE.
ROBBO, I **NEED** THIS PHONE - YOU DON'T WANT PEOPLE TO THINK I'M SOME CLUELESS LOSER LIKE SATCHEL, DO YOU?
OH, YOU ARE **SO** INSENSITIVE - *GIVE ME MY PHONE!*
I MAY BE INSENSITIVE, BUT I GET **ANNOYED** EASILY!
WHAT'S *"CLUELESS"*? ...GUYS?
BUCKY
darb

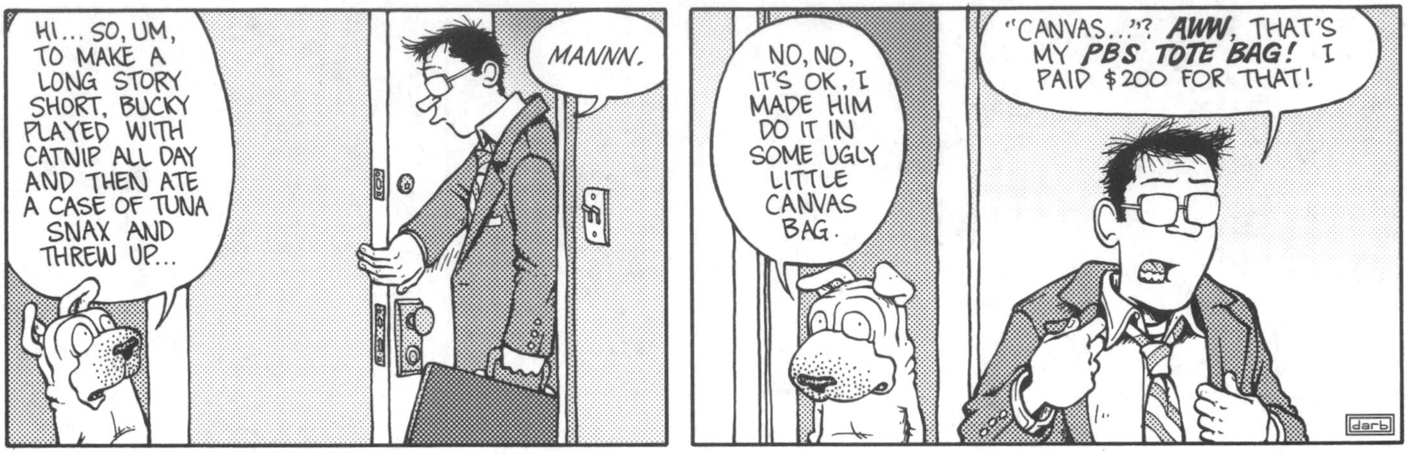
HI... SO, UM, TO MAKE A LONG STORY SHORT, BUCKY PLAYED WITH CATNIP ALL DAY AND THEN ATE A CASE OF TUNA SNAX AND THREW UP...
MANNN.
NO, NO, IT'S OK, I MADE HIM DO IT IN SOME UGLY LITTLE CANVAS BAG.
"CANVAS..."? AWW, THAT'S MY PBS TOTE BAG! I PAID $200 FOR THAT!
darb

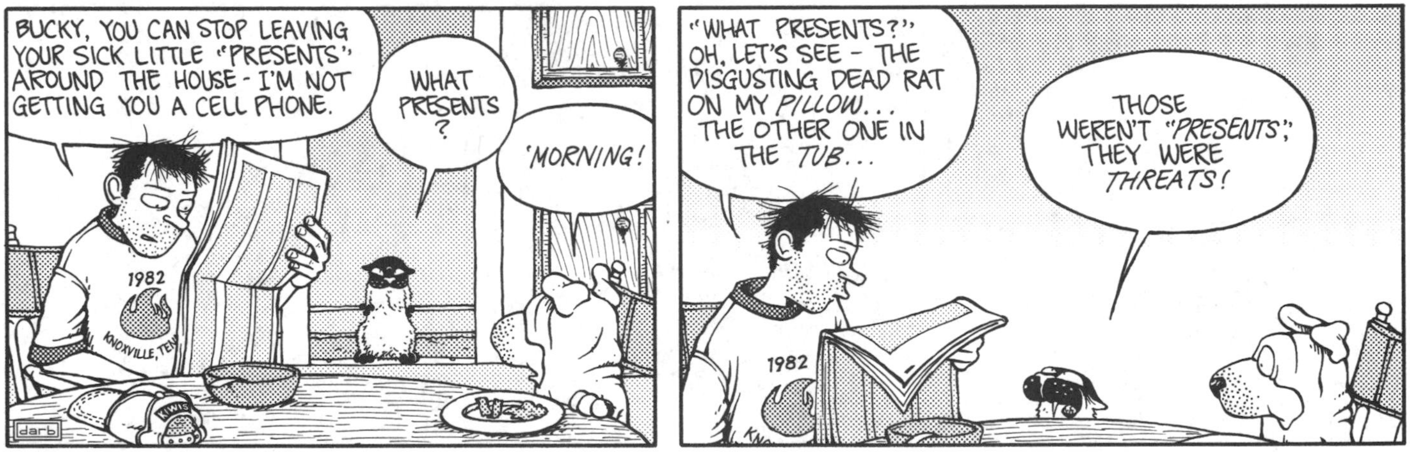
BUCKY, YOU CAN STOP LEAVING YOUR SICK LITTLE "PRESENTS" AROUND THE HOUSE - I'M NOT GETTING YOU A CELL PHONE.
WHAT PRESENTS ?
'MORNING!
1982 KNOXVILLE, TENN
darb
"WHAT PRESENTS?" OH, LET'S SEE - THE DISGUSTING DEAD RAT ON MY PILLOW... THE OTHER ONE IN THE TUB...
THOSE WEREN'T "PRESENTS," THEY WERE THREATS!
1982

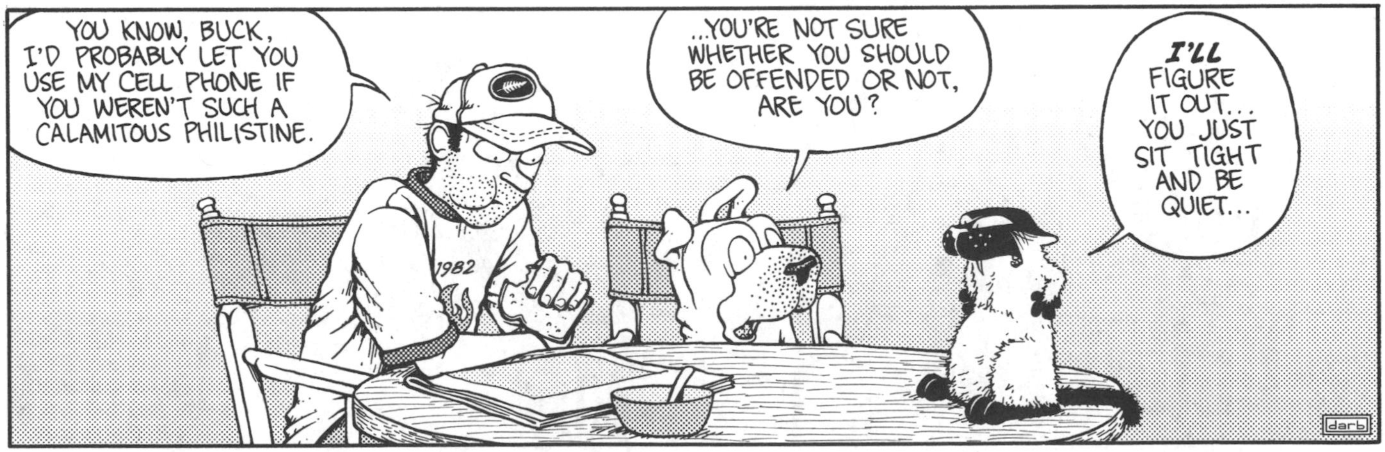
YOU KNOW, BUCK, I'D PROBABLY LET YOU USE MY CELL PHONE IF YOU WEREN'T SUCH A CALAMITOUS PHILISTINE.
...YOU'RE NOT SURE WHETHER YOU SHOULD BE OFFENDED OR NOT, ARE YOU?
I'LL FIGURE IT OUT... YOU JUST SIT TIGHT AND BE QUIET...
1982
darb

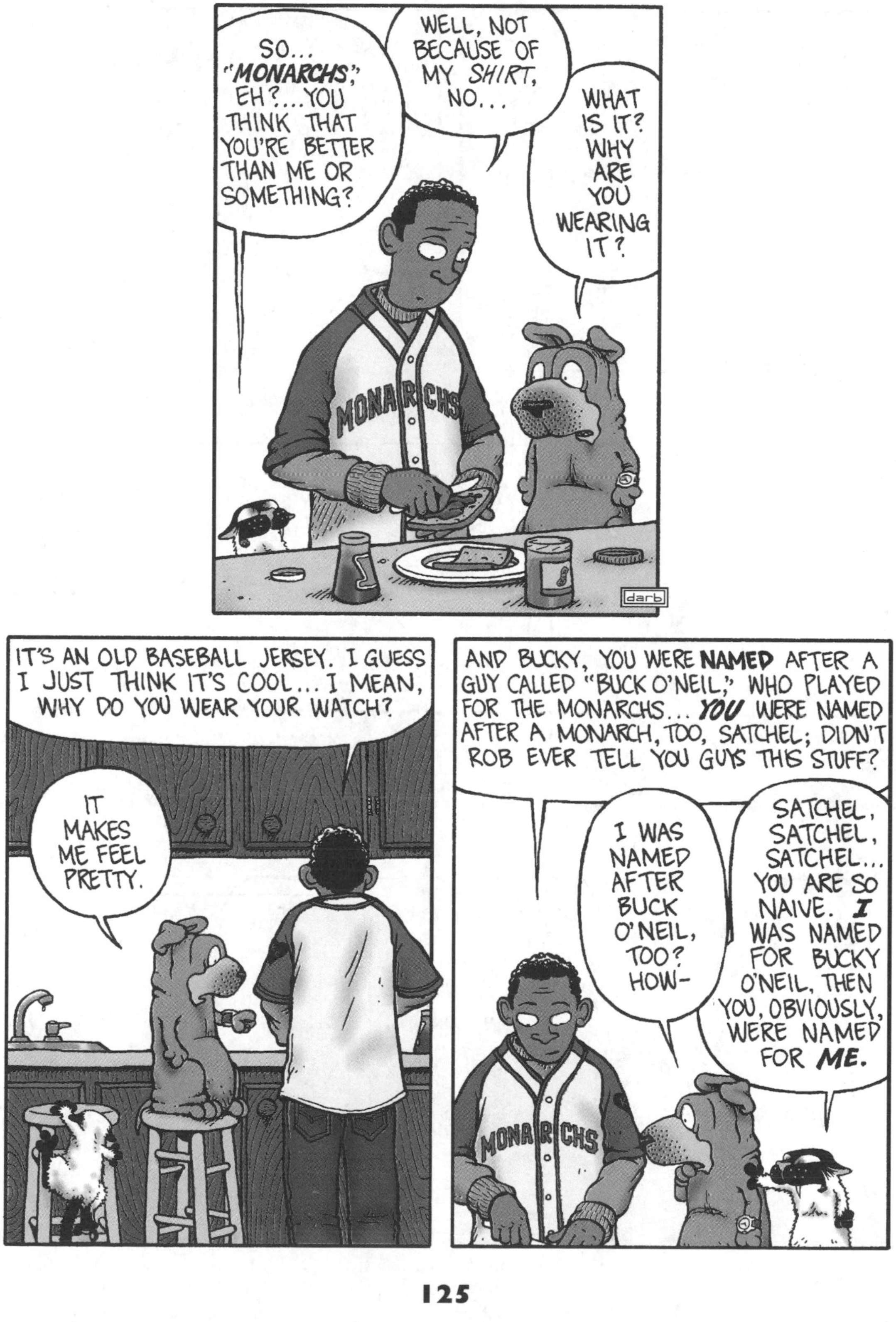
SO... "MONARCHS," EH?... YOU THINK THAT YOU'RE BETTER THAN ME OR SOMETHING?
WELL, NOT BECAUSE OF MY SHIRT, NO...
WHAT IS IT? WHY ARE YOU WEARING IT?
MONARCHS
darb
IT'S AN OLD BASEBALL JERSEY. I GUESS I JUST THINK IT'S COOL... I MEAN, WHY DO YOU WEAR YOUR WATCH?
IT MAKES ME FEEL PRETTY.
AND BUCKY, YOU WERE NAMED AFTER A GUY CALLED "BUCK O'NEIL," WHO PLAYED FOR THE MONARCHS... YOU WERE NAMED AFTER A MONARCH, TOO, SATCHEL; DIDN'T ROB EVER TELL YOU GUYS THIS STUFF?
I WAS NAMED AFTER BUCK O'NEIL, TOO? HOW-
SATCHEL, SATCHEL, SATCHEL... YOU ARE SO NAIVE. I WAS NAMED FOR BUCKY O'NEIL, THEN YOU, OBVIOUSLY, WERE NAMED FOR ME.
MONARCHS

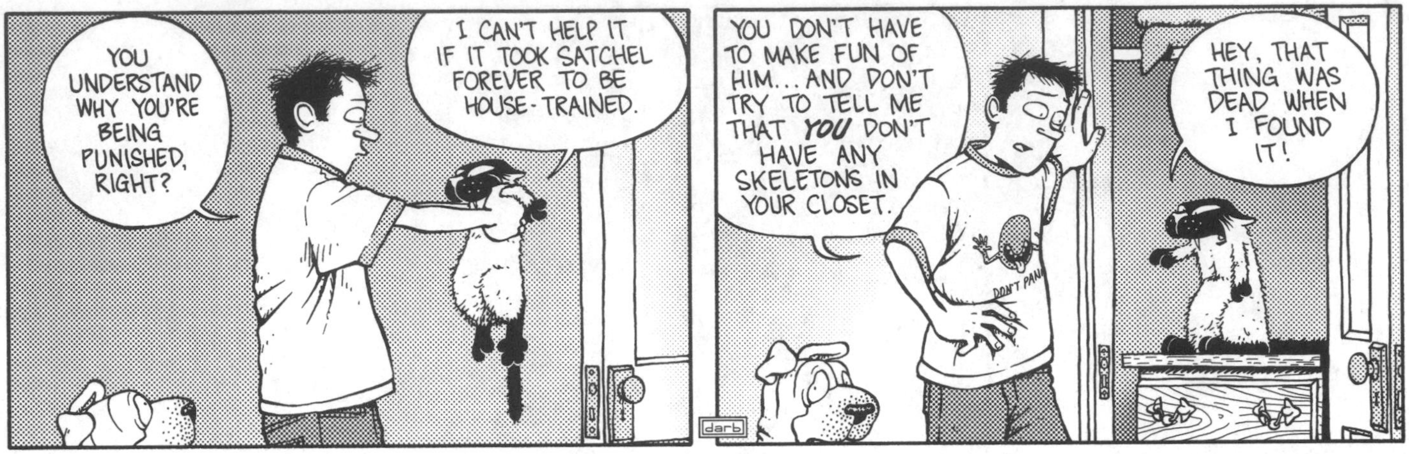
YOU UNDERSTAND WHY YOU'RE BEING PUNISHED, RIGHT?
I CAN'T HELP IT IF IT TOOK SATCHEL FOREVER TO BE HOUSE-TRAINED.
YOU DON'T HAVE TO MAKE FUN OF HIM... AND DON'T TRY TO TELL ME THAT ***YOU*** DON'T HAVE ANY SKELETONS IN YOUR CLOSET.
HEY, THAT THING WAS DEAD WHEN I FOUND IT!

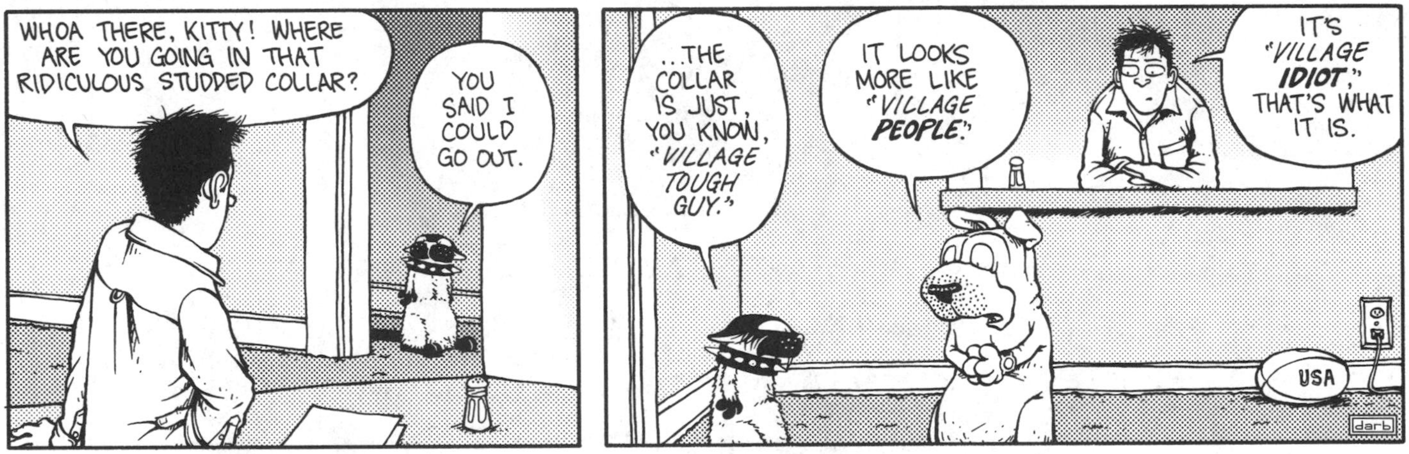
WHOA THERE, KITTY! WHERE ARE YOU GOING IN THAT RIDICULOUS STUDDED COLLAR?
YOU SAID I COULD GO OUT.
...THE COLLAR IS JUST, YOU KNOW, "*VILLAGE TOUGH GUY.*"
IT LOOKS MORE LIKE "*VILLAGE* ***PEOPLE***."
IT'S "*VILLAGE* ***IDIOT***," THAT'S WHAT IT IS.
USA

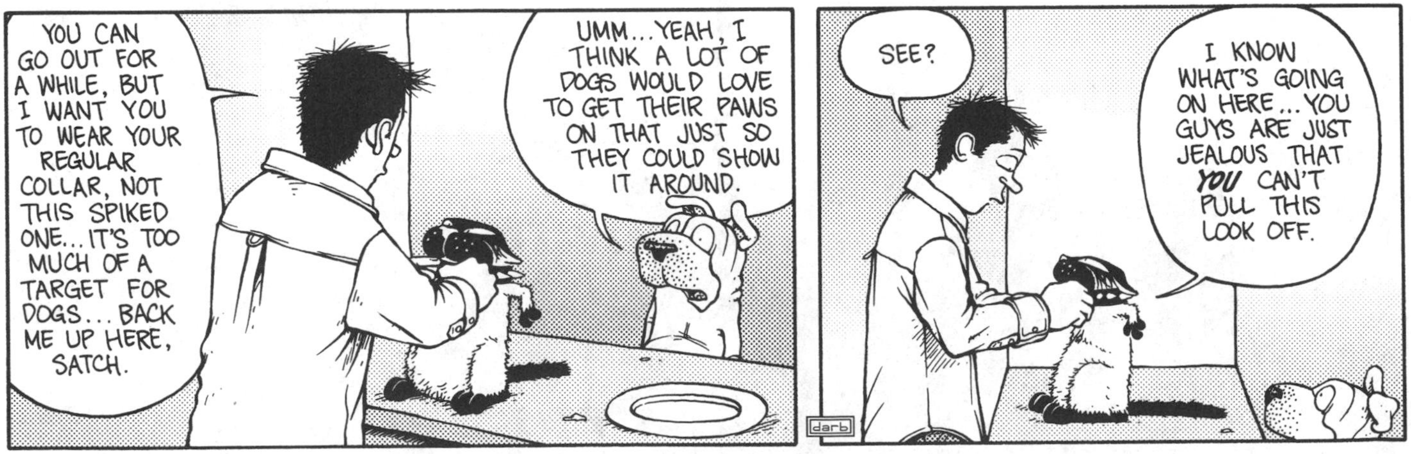
YOU CAN GO OUT FOR A WHILE, BUT I WANT YOU TO WEAR YOUR REGULAR COLLAR, NOT THIS SPIKED ONE... IT'S TOO MUCH OF A TARGET FOR DOGS... BACK ME UP HERE, SATCH.
UMM... YEAH, I THINK A LOT OF DOGS WOULD LOVE TO GET THEIR PAWS ON THAT JUST SO THEY COULD SHOW IT AROUND.
SEE?
I KNOW WHAT'S GOING ON HERE... YOU GUYS ARE JUST JEALOUS THAT ***YOU*** CAN'T PULL THIS LOOK OFF.

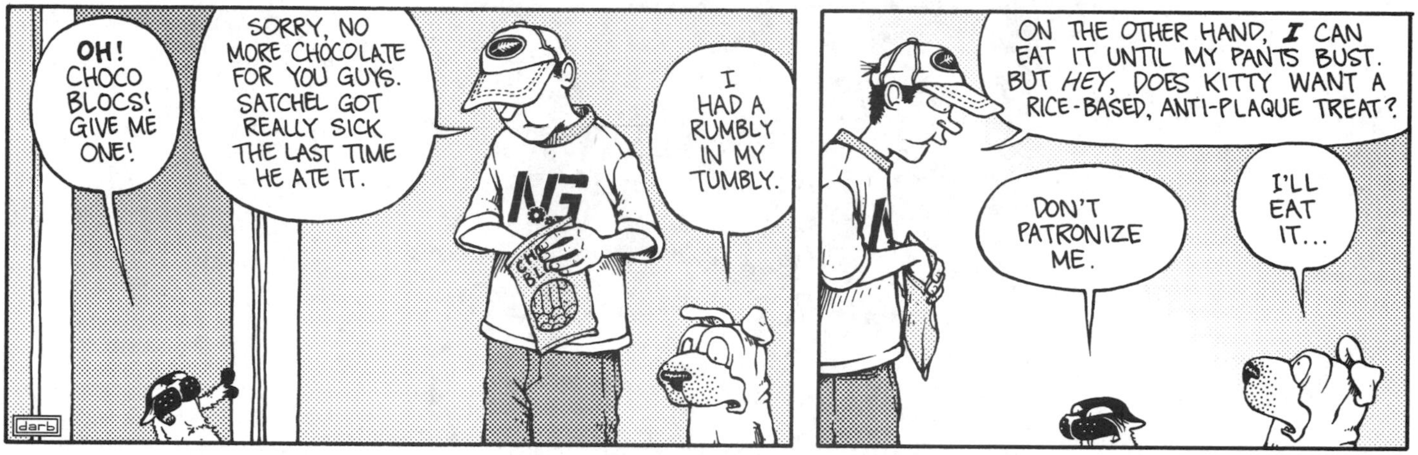
OH! CHOCO BLOCS! GIVE ME ONE!
SORRY, NO MORE CHOCOLATE FOR YOU GUYS. SATCHEL GOT REALLY SICK THE LAST TIME HE ATE IT.
I HAD A RUMBLY IN MY TUMBLY.
ON THE OTHER HAND, I CAN EAT IT UNTIL MY PANTS BUST. BUT HEY, DOES KITTY WANT A RICE-BASED, ANTI-PLAQUE TREAT?
DON'T PATRONIZE ME.
I'LL EAT IT...

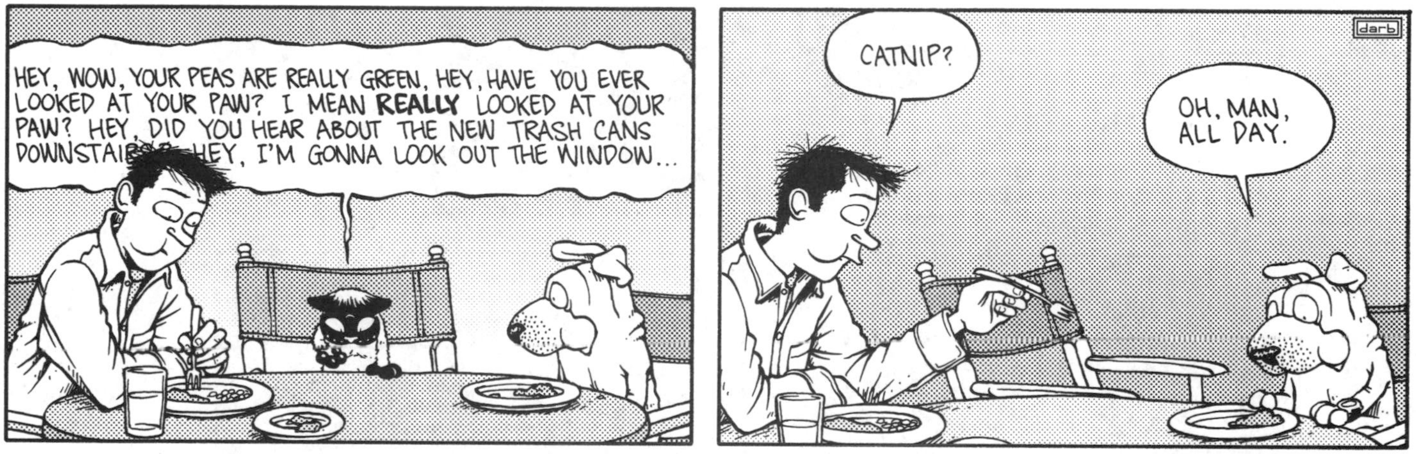
HEY, WOW, YOUR PEAS ARE REALLY GREEN. HEY, HAVE YOU EVER LOOKED AT YOUR PAW? I MEAN REALLY LOOKED AT YOUR PAW? HEY, DID YOU HEAR ABOUT THE NEW TRASH CANS DOWNSTAIRS? HEY, I'M GONNA LOOK OUT THE WINDOW...
CATNIP?
OH, MAN, ALL DAY.

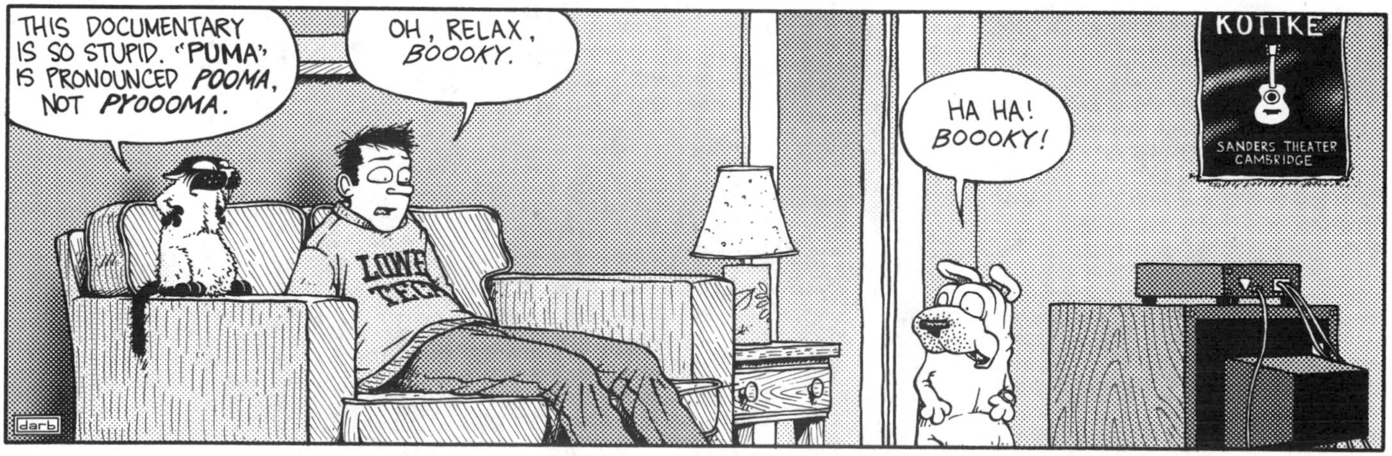
THIS DOCUMENTARY IS SO STUPID. "PUMA" IS PRONOUNCED POOMA, NOT PYOOOMA.
OH, RELAX, BOOOKY.
HA HA! BOOOKY!
KOTTKE
SANDERS THEATER CAMBRIDGE

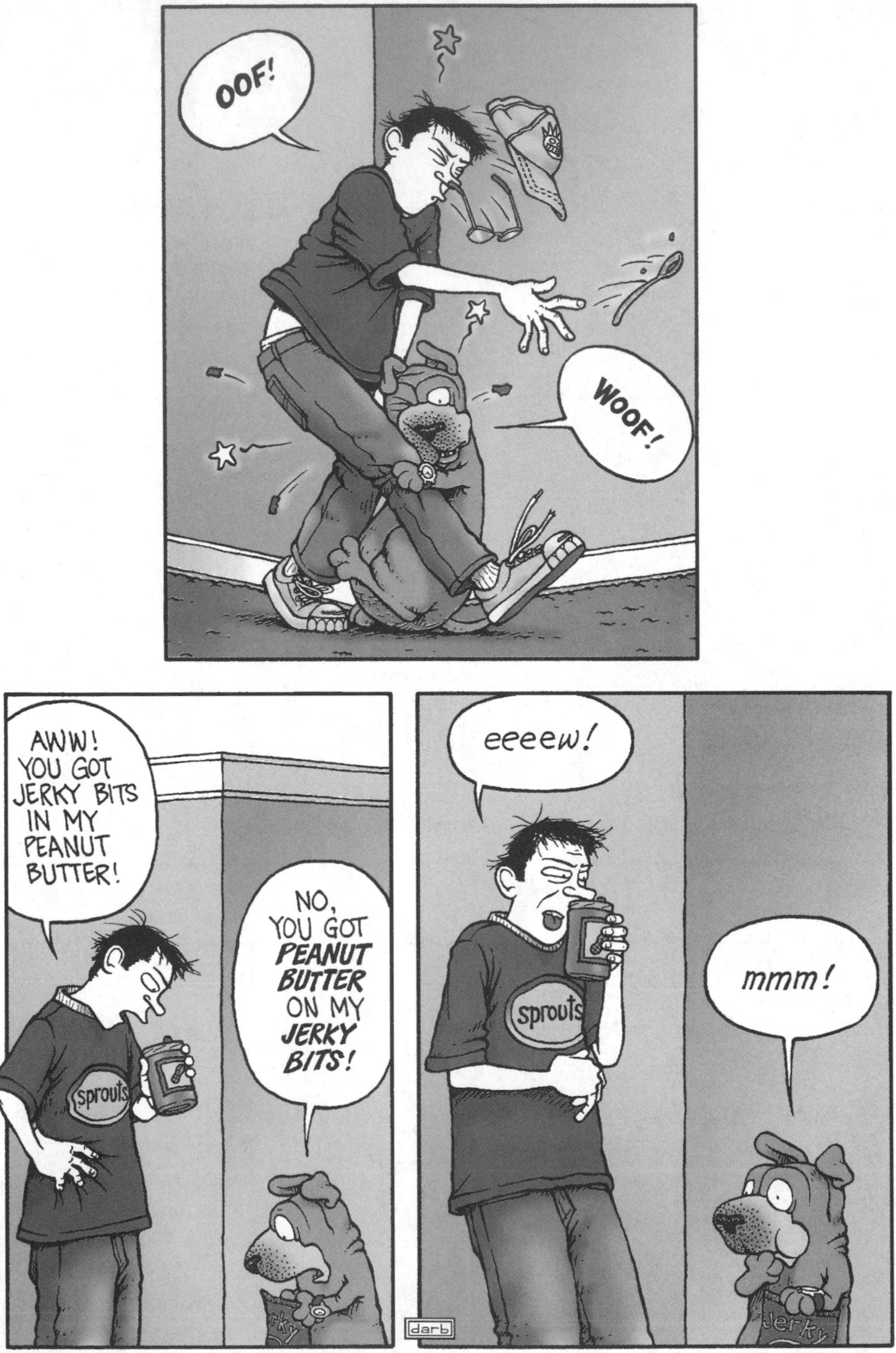
OOF!
WOOF!
AWW! YOU GOT JERKY BITS IN MY PEANUT BUTTER!
NO, YOU GOT PEANUT BUTTER ON MY JERKY BITS!
sprouts
darb
eeeew!
mmm!
sprouts
Jerky